p. 177

9

W9-AVS-545

LOSING OUR DEMOCRACY

HOW BUSH, THE FAR RIGHT AND BIG BUSINESS ARE BETRAYING AMERICANS FOR POWER AND PROFIT

Mark Green

SOURCEBOOKS, INC.
NAPERVILLE, ILLINOIS

Copyright © 2006 by New Democracy Project
Cover and internal design © 2006 by Sourcebooks, Inc.
Cover photos © Corbis
Sourcebooks and the colophon are registered trademarks of Sourcebooks, Inc.

All rights reserved. No part of this book may be reproduced in any form or by any electronic or mechanical means including information storage and retrieval systems—except in the case of brief quotations embodied in critical articles or reviews—without permission in writing from its publisher, Sourcebooks, Inc.

Published by Sourcebooks, Inc.
P.O. Box 4410, Naperville, Illinois 60567–4410
(630) 961–3900
Fax: (630) 961–2168
www.sourcebooks.com

Library of Congress Cataloging-in-Publication Data

Green, Mark J.
  Losing our democracy : how Bush, the far right and big business are
betraying Americans for power and profit
/ Mark
Green.
      p. cm.
  Includes bibliographical references and index.
  ISBN-13: 978-1-4022-0701-3
  ISBN-10: 1-4022-0701-8
  1. United States--Politics and government--2001- 2. Democracy--United
States. 3. Bush, George W. (George Walker), 1946---Political and social
views. 4. Bush, George W. (George Walker), 1946---Friends and
associates. 5. Big business--Political aspects--United States. 6.
Right-wing extremists--United States. 7. Conservatism--United States.
8. Authoritarianism--United States. 9. Political corruption--United
States. I. Title.

E902.G744 2006
973.931--dc22

2006012432

Printed and bound in the United States of America.
BVG 10 9 8 7 6 5 4 3 2 1

Also by Mark Green

Defend Yourself! How to Protect Your Health, Your Money, and Your Rights in 10 Key Areas of Your Life (2006)

What We Stand For: A Program for Progressive Patriotism (ed., 2004)

The Book on Bush: How George W. (Mis)Leads America
(with Eric Alterman, 2004)

Selling Out: How Big Corporate Money Buys Elections, Rams Through Legislation, and Betrays Our Democracy (2002)

Mark Green's Guide to Coping in New York City (2000)

The Consumer Bible (with Nancy Youman, 1998)

Changing America: Blueprints for the New Administration (ed., 1993)

America's Transition: Blueprints for the 1990s
(ed. with Mark Pinsky, 1989)

The Challenge of Hidden Profits: Reducing Corporate Bureaucracy and Waste (with John Berry, 1985)

Reagan's Reign of Error: The Instant Nostalgia Edition
(with Gail MacColl, 1987)

Who Runs Congress? (with Michael Waldman, 1984)

The Big Business Reader (ed. with Robert Massie Jr., 1980)

Winning Back America (1982)

Taming the Giant Corporation
(with Ralph Nader and Joel Seligman, 1976)

Verdicts on Lawyers (ed. with Ralph Nader, 1976)

The Other Government:
The Unseen Power of Washington Lawyers (1975)

Corporate Power in America (ed. with Ralph Nader, 1973)

The Monopoly Makers (ed., 1973)

The Closed Enterprise System (with Beverly C. Moore Jr. and Bruce Wasserstein, 1972)

With Justice for Some (ed. with Bruce Wasserstein, 1970)

Contents

INTRODUCTION

TOM PAINE OR ROBINSON CRUSOE?

"Two cheers for democracy, one because it admits variety and two because it permits criticism."
—E. M. FORSTER

"Democracy is like sex—it works best when you participate."
—Sign in a Store on E. 19th Street, Manhattan

Much has been written about Bush's war for democracy abroad, but how much have you read about his war *against* democracy at home?

Hidden in plain sight—and notwithstanding the president's passionate assertion that "freedom is God's gift to mankind"—Bush & Co. are engaged in the greatest assault ever against two centuries of American democratic practices and progress. True, Senator Joseph McCarthy was more personally menacing and unrestrained. But the Wisconsin demagogue did not control all three branches of government—and hold sway with much of the corporate, communications, and clerical communities, too. Also, McCarthy could not on his own say-so invade countries, suppress dissent, condone torture, and transfer trillions to his donors, all undermining democracy in the name of patriotism.

Bush can. And has. Hence this book.

It was a clear, mild day and the recently re-inaugurated president looked far more confident and comfortable than four years before. Bush's nearly three million vote margin may have been the smallest of any reelected incumbent in the past century, but it sure beat a 537 vote plurality in Florida. And he knew that his inaugural address could solve three problems at once: explain his invasion of a weapons of mass destruction-less Iraq, begin laying the groundwork for his legacy, and steal a major theme of Democrats from Wilson to Carter. "It is the policy of the United States to seek and support the growth of democratic movements and institutions in every nation and culture," he said convincingly to a crescendo of applause, "with the ultimate goal of ending tyranny in our time. The survival of liberty in our land increasingly depends on the success of liberty in other lands."

Ecstatic supporters compared it to Lincoln's and Kennedy's inaugural addresses. Commentators in near unison gave him high marks. The only problem—his "missionary Jeffersonianism," as one called it, was both fake and hypocritical. Rhetorical to the point of utopian, his words were essentially a *post hoc ergo propter hoc* attempt to put rouge on the pig of Iraq and to persuade scholars that his would be a heroic legacy.

Bush may well have been sincere in the narrow sense that he had persuaded himself he was on a mission from God. But was there any serious likelihood, based on the arc of history, that America could spread democracy by invading and occupying a Muslim country in a region torn by millennia of religious strife? Was there anything in his prior civilian or public life to indicate that he truly cared about democracy and freedom (other than freedom from regulated natural gas prices)? Had he *ever* given a speech as governor or president—outside of retroactive rationales for the invasion of Iraq—on what democracy is, why it is desirable, or how he'd advance it in America? Had he harnessed the epic civic energy released by the 9/11 catastrophe toward some great public goal, some advance of freedom and democracy either in America or in a (then) sympathetic world?

Actually, exactly the opposite is true. Presuming he can get away with almost anything if he says the opposite—e.g., his "Clear Skies" initiative, his "Leave No Child Behind" law, his declared preference for diplomacy to war in Iraq—George W. Bush has embraced democracy more as a prop than a policy. Any fair "democracy audit" would show America making a flawed start and steady, if interrupted, progress from 1789 to 2001—but then a ledger sheet of large withdrawals in 2001–2006. Just as his administration has created more debt in six years than all prior presidents in over two hundred years (except Reagan), Bush is in effect similarly blowing our democratic inheritance in the span of only one administration. And there's been only muted public outcry or exposure. It's time for an accounting.

What, exactly, is democracy? At the most basic level, it's self-governance—the philosophy that people themselves can arrive at more fair and intelligent judgments about what's best for them than elitists imposing edicts from above. From Thomas Paine's *Common Sense* (1789) to James Surowiecki's *The Wisdom of Crowds* (2004), pro-democracy advocates have argued that open, robust debate is more likely to expose or correct bad ideas, not to mention that citizens are more likely to accept adverse decisions if they at least had a chance to be heard. "Not every citizen expects to speak personally in the governing dialogue," wrote William Greider in his powerful 1994 book *Who Will Tell the People,* "but every citizen is entitled to feel authentically represented." Greider goes on to thoughtfully lay out several elementary principles: "Accountability of the governors to the governed. Equal protection of the law. A presumption of political equality among all citizens...The guarantee of timely access to public debate. A rough sense of honesty in communication between the government and the people." In other words, democracy is far more a general *process* than a particular *policy*—as in "due process of law"—because an open, honest, and accountable process will in turn produce the best solutions.

According to Sean Wilentz in his magisterial *The Rise of American Democracy,* the idea that "sovereignty rightly belongs to the mass of ordinary individuals and equal citizens" was a radical departure in Western thought in 1787. Not surprisingly, democratic principles often then went unmet. Senators were not popularly elected, nor indeed were presidents because of the convoluted Electoral College. Only the propertied class could vote, not poor working whites, blacks, or women. (Even John Adams, after the Revolutionary War, fretted over the idea that "every man who has not a farthing will demand an equal voice with any other.") Slavery was lawful but criticism of the government, according to the 1798 Alien and Sedition Act, was not.

Since then—especially with the Bill of Rights appending explicit civil rights and liberties to the original Constitution in a kind of legal do-over—democracy has proven its genius for self-correction. Women got the vote in the 1920s and blacks effectively one hundred years after the Civil War with the Voting Rights Act of 1965 (before passage, there were some 280 African American elected officials in the entire country; by 2006, there were 9,500). And reflecting popular will, the rise of the industrial economy saw a parallel increase in regulatory laws trying to make sure that food was clean, air was pure, working conditions safe, children not exploited, and labor-organizing protected.

By America's third century, democracy and capitalism were balancing and sustaining each other—capitalism producing wealth and democracy a) umpiring the rules of production, b) maintaining a justice system to resolve disputes and prosecute wrong-doers, and c) erecting a safety net for people who can't make it in the economic realm. If democracy without capitalism was socialism, a wag once wrote, capitalism without democracy was piracy.

But first the Reagan and now the Bush administrations had a decidedly different philosophy, namely that "government is not the solution, government is the problem" (Reagan) and the "goal is to cut government in half...down to the size where we can drown it in the bathtub" (conservative activist and insider Grover Norquist). Instead of democracy and capitalism being two different sides of the same coin called America, they saw it as a zero-sum game, so that if government grew, markets shrank. It was, in this view, a contest between "it takes a village" and "it takes an entrepreneur"—Hillary Clinton and Tom Paine vs. Ayn Rand and Robinson Crusoe.

Market libertarianism taps into a deep strain of antigovernment fervor in a country born from a tea party against the tyranny of a King George. But radical libertarians cannot understand how a democracy can *guarantee* markets, and enable them to function. In a helpful analogy, scholar William Galston explains that while each of us is free to choose our own car and route to destination, government must design the rules of the road—with licenses, signals, and yellow lines—so that our chosen cars don't smash into each other. Economists talk about "externalities"—when a cost of production like pollution is simply imposed on innocent people outside the buyer-seller relationship—and point to the "tragedy of the commons": i.e., if all are free to selfishly plant as they choose, then land will be depleted so there's no food for anyone.

The conservative case against democratic government—against collective action by majority rule—is grounded in two arguments: first, government bureaucracy is invariably inefficient (though oddly the same conservatives argue that government *can* be trusted to mete out the death penalty and invade other countries); and second, according to the *laissez faire* theory, market solutions are always preferable to government ones. While Bushites may question evolutionary Darwinism, they love Social Darwinism. But because of imperfect information, oligopoly power, corruption or deception, to name a few problems with free market theory, laissez *isn't* always fair. At the level of theory, the free market model is logical and appealing, until it smashes into realities such as the Depression, Love Canal, Enron, and Katrina—and then the public clamors for corrective regulation or services.

In the well-known dichotomy of political scientists, America is ideologically conservative yet operationally liberal. The real world benefits of the democracy model rather than the market model are pretty clear: thousands escape death every year because of government-mandated seatbelts and airbags; water pollution is cut by half due to Environmental Protection Agency standards; poverty among seniors is slashed by three-fourths due to Social Security; crib deaths are reduced by 90 percent because of Consumer Products Safety Commission rules; thousands of children do not start smoking because of restrictions on tobacco company ads and cigarette vending machines.

So when Bush & Co. announce they want to lead America into a new century, they appear to mean the nineteenth century, a gilded age when freedom meant child labor in factories and robber barons hand-picking senators. How did such a reactionary philosophy come to be so politically dominant in America today? If conservative Republicans are so anti-democratic, how did they get elected in a democracy? That's an important subject for other books and commentators, with Thomas Frank in *What's the Matter with Kansas?* being an excellent example. For our purposes, at least four phenomena have combined to elevate the anti-democracy crowd to current prominence.

First, there's some luck involved. Monica Lewinsky, butterfly ballots in Florida, and bin Laden's tape over the final weekend before the '04 election were all flukes that likely made decisive differences in close national elections in the past two election cycles.

Second, the serial manipulation of information—intelligence before the Iraq War being exhibit number one—has confused and misled millions of Americans accustomed to believing news put out by their president (see chapter 9 on "Information Manipulation").

Third, Republican conservatives have been nothing short of brilliant in marketing their brand. Memos by strategist Frank Luntz betray their view of voters as sheep—hence their brutal focus on being the party of flags and faith, which after 9/11 has proven a successful, if narrow, formula. This approach wins out in the world of products, too. Pepsi beats Coke in blind taste tests, yet of course Coke outsells Pepsi. Why? Superior branding. But while America can easily survive Coke outselling Pepsi, here's the unpalatable result of Republicans' better branding and rhetoric, according to Thomas Frank: "*Vote* to stop abortion; *receive* a rollback in capital gains taxes. *Vote* to make our country strong again; *receive* deindustrialization. *Vote* to screw those politically correct college professors; *receive* electricity deregulation. *Vote* to stand tall against terrorists; *receive* Social Security privatization."

Fourth, the disproportionate influence of corporate money in political campaigns has tilted elections to favor capital over labor. Because average voters pull levers but big donors pull strings, often public sentiment wants one thing while political elites, as noted, deliver something else. Greider tellingly describes this disconnect between the public and politicians when he cites a poll asking voters what they wanted a few days before the 1988 presidential election.

> Aside from what Bush and Dukakis are saying in their campaigns, what do you want the next president to pursue? The public responded with an unusual list of priorities: make sure wealthy and big corporations pay their fair share of taxes (important to 77 percent; unimportant to 5 percent); impose stricter environmental regulation on companies that produce toxic wastes (66 percent to 5 percent); help the poor and homeless find jobs and earn a decent living (66 percent to 5 percent). The list seems jarring because, as everyone knows, those were not the mobilizing issues of George Bush's campaign, nor did they reflect his own priorities.

Nor were they of George W. Bush's presidential campaigns of 2000 and 2004.

Around the world, with Communism and Fascism essentially vanquished, the number of democracies is on the rise because of the obvious virtues of majority rule and self-determination. Or because the price of tyranny is too high. In our country, of course, there are no soldiers shooting hundreds of unarmed protestors as in Uzbekistan; no arrests of the presidential challenger and his top supporters as in Belarus; no China ordering Google, Yahoo, and Microsoft to censor the keywords "Tiananmen Square Massacre"; no Putin announcing that henceforth governors will be appointed not elected. By those measures, America is surely democratic. But that aims far too low. For two centuries Americans have treated democracy, in Vaclav Havel's metaphor, as a horizon we always approach though never reach. So we've always been pushing to expand the franchise, engage more citizens, make elections fairer and government more transparent.

Until now. For while there is no Great Depression or 9/11 heralding the disaster, we are moving away from rather than toward the far horizon of a better democracy

+ when people of talent without wealth stop seeking public office because they can't compete with multimillionaires buying elections;
+ when 1 percent of Americans give more campaign contributions than the other 99 percent—and then, predictably, get 40 percent of all recent tax cuts;
+ when a consumer injured by an auto defect can't get access to any court for a class action suit;
+ when a state legislature dominated by one party enacts all bills on a party line vote without any hearings or debate or amendments;
+ when state legislatures draw lines that enable 100 percent of incumbents to win their "elections";
+ when millions of black voters—who as ex-cons have "paid their debt to society"—are disenfranchised in local and federal elections;
+ when an administration encourages torture and ignores eight hundred years of Common Law and Constitutional Law to incarcerate people without charges or access to lawyers;
+ when a president in "signing statements" claims the unilateral authority to ignore 750 duly enacted congressional laws that he disagrees with, in effect overturning the checks and balances and judicial review built into our constitutional system for some two hundred years;

- when a Congress overrides state law and judicial rulings to federalize an end-of-life decision for one brain-dead woman;
- when local school boards—preferring the Bible to the Constitution—seek to mandate the teaching of "intelligent design" in your fifteen-year-old daughter's biology class;
- when 45 percent of Americans elect 55 percent of the U.S. Senate (because of the "Connecticut Compromise" of 1787 giving large and small states two Senate seats) and then on party-line votes insist that 100 percent of judges be right-wing jurists;
- when corporate lobbyists who oppose an environmental bill obtain audiences with the members of Congress they contribute to, while local citizens supporting the bill get ignored both by members and by a local media all owned by Sinclair Broadcasting;
- and when the ratio of CEO to employee pay has gone from 40:1 in the 1960s to 431:1 today.

Losing Our Democracy pulls back the curtain of comfortable rhetoric about freedom and democracy abroad to show why we need a pro-democracy movement here at home. What is in effect a Democracy Audit in the following pages reveals a new authoritarianism in the executive, legislative, corporate, and religious spheres; a contempt for the rule of law and access to courts; a bare-knuckled willingness to suppress votes and bully the media and dissenters; and the Bush administration's persistent practice of distorting and hiding essential information.

But there is also the enduring asset of America, a place of so many different voices and views that it's hard to suppress the democratic spirit for very long. "There is too much common sense and independence in America," wrote Tom Paine in 1800, "to be long the dupe of any fiction, foreign or domestic."

Our democratic prospect requires civic energy and participation to expose problems, reduce corruption, and choose officials who have the values and the vision to advance justice. It's up to citizen patriots to reveal and reverse today's assault on democracy, as earlier generations occasionally had to do. Ralph Nader describes the process in his foreword to *Civics for Democracy:* "There was a steady, steadfast, and sturdy civic energy ranging from minorities of one to mass movements of Americans that have rescued their country from shame, error, cruelty, and decline."

{ 8 }

LEGISLATIVE TYRANNY I: A DEMOCRACY RUN BY LOBBYISTS

"The two of us have been immersed in Washington politics for thirty-six years. We have never seen the culture so sick or the legislative process so dysfunctional."
—NORMAN ORNSTEIN, Resident Scholar at the American Enterprise Institute, and THOMAS E. MANN, Senior Fellow at the Brookings Institution

The Congress of the world's greatest democracy is not a democracy, not even close. How did this happen?

In 1995, Republicans regained control of the House of Representatives after campaigning against what they called an entrenched, corrupt, free-spending Democratic majority. For years, they had been blistering the Democrats for their alleged ethical misdeeds, especially hammering at Speaker Jim Wright's self-enriching book deal and Ways and Means Committee Chairman Dan Rostenkowski's mail fraud. In retaking the House, they vowed to restore ethical standards to the body, limit power in the hands of baronial committee chairmen, and break the tyrannical stranglehold that the Democrats had held on the institution for forty years.

One of the architects of this effort was a young Republican from Sugar Land, Texas, who endorsed this vision of a reinvigorated democracy in the House but quietly had his own plan to seize power away from the Democrats. Representative Tom DeLay—diminutive though ferocious—sought to build a top-down hierarchy that consolidated power in the hands of a small cadre of Republican congressional leaders, lobbyists, and conservative activists.

Fast forward more than a decade later and it is clear that Tom DeLay's vision—no longer DeLay himself, but his vision—has come to fruition. Today's House is run by a small group of Republican leaders who control every facet of major legislation, even overruling the wishes of members of their own party on a regular basis. These leaders use a carrot-and-stick approach to maintaining control of their less senior colleagues, and they treat the minority party about the same way that West Point upperclassmen treat freshmen plebes. Democratic leaders Tom Foley in 1994 and Jim Wright in 1989 look like egalitarians compared to the dictatorial style of Hastert, Boehner, and DeLay, up until his resignation in 2006. Meanwhile, the Senate increasingly takes on the personality traits of the House as the upper chamber becomes a place where dissent is less frequent, mavericks are marginalized, the center is less influential, and party discipline is demanded as never before.

In both chambers, the actions of lawmakers are unrepresentative of the views of the American people. Round after round of tax cuts, the attempted privatization of Social Security, a Medicare prescription drug benefit favoring HMOs, cuts to social programs, and a go-it-alone war dominate national policy despite the public's opposition to each of these. A compliant Republican-controlled Congress abides by the wishes of its president: Senate Republicans back the administration's agenda 92 percent of the time and their House counterparts follow suit 84 percent of the time—both measurements vastly exceed the party's support for the legislative agenda of the last Republican president, George H. W. Bush. Meanwhile, W. is the first president in 176 years to serve a full term without vetoing a single piece of legislation. He really didn't have to since Congress had become the functioning West Wing of the White House.

A key element of the Republicans' recent dominance has been their tremendous success at gerrymandering congressional districts to match their voting strengths. Bucking precedent, Republicans didn't just limit their redistricting efforts to a post-census 2001. After additional victories in 2002, they sought to remap states again in order to net still more House seats. With a brassy disrespect for rules that only Donald Trump could admire, they successfully muscled the Texas legislature into a mid-census redrawing of district lines that yielded five new House seats for the party. One individual cropped up in nearly all of these efforts to consolidate power—in demanding party discipline, in inspiring extreme lobbying excesses, and in condoning gerrymandering—Tom DeLay.

DELAY AND ABRAMOFF: CORRUPTION SQUARED

Congress has been led by powerful, baronial leaders at regular intervals throughout American history. Commanding figures such as "Uncle Joe" Cannon, Sam Rayburn, and Lyndon Baines Johnson built ruthlessly efficient machines with which to pursue their personal and political agendas. These power brokers horse-traded and cajoled their colleagues in ways that the framers of the Constitution could not have imagined. But today's leadership in the House of Representatives is perhaps the most despotic and undemocratic regime to lead a chamber of Congress in a century, if not ever.

In the early twentieth century, Speaker Joseph G. Cannon, an Illinois Republican known as "Uncle Joe" to fellow members, controlled the legislative process by dictating which members of his party would serve on certain committees and employing his power as the House Rules Committee Chairman to determine the content of legislation. Despite serving in the latter part of the Progressive Era, Cannon obstructed many popular reforms which sought to rein in the power of corporations and industrialists.

Cannon was so powerful a figure that, in response to a request by a constituent for a copy of the House rules, one member of Congress imaginatively sent him a photograph of the House Speaker. The ranking Democrat on the House Rules Committee and the minority party's leader at the time, Representative John Sharp Williams of Mississippi, dourly described the committee meetings guided by Cannon: "I am invited to the séances, but I am never consulted about the spiritualistic appearances." Cannon was very comfortable thwarting the legislative goals of Democrats, but his downfall ultimately came when his tactics alienated a sizeable number of Republicans as well.

The Cannon era aside, for much of its more than two centuries of existence, Congress has been a clubby environment where elites often worked together crafting legislation by day and socializing by night. Legendary lawmakers such as mid-twentieth-century House Speaker

Sam Rayburn, a Democrat from Texas, cultivated an atmosphere where collegiality and seniority were the glue holding together a Congress of such disparate elements. Rayburn's House was one where he urged members in his famous aphorism, "to get along, go along." A young member—like Lyndon Johnson or Richard Bolling—would have little opportunity to be effective on the Hill without showing proper deference to their more senior partners. Working closely with members on both sides of the aisle, Rayburn often let his party's committee chairmen rule over their own fiefdoms, only calling in favors or putting down his foot on rare occasions.

Considered the most powerful Senate majority leader in history, Lyndon Johnson deftly ran the Senate from 1955–1960 by using his tremendous skills of persuasion and by earning enormous personal loyalty from other senators—then cashing it in the favor bank of politics when he needed a result. He often demonstrated a "chameleon-like quality," presenting himself as a good ol' boy when gathered with his southern counterparts or casting himself as a committed New Dealer when among his northern colleagues.

Yet perhaps no one built a more efficient machine for passing legislation, blocking the minority party, advancing party interests, winning elections, and undermining American democracy than did former majority leader Tom DeLay and his coterie of Republicans in the House of Representatives. After being elected to Congress in 1984, DeLay developed a corporate special interest factory that would alarm and astound the Founders.

Before he was stripped of his title because of an indictment in Texas and replaced by another general in the Republican army (Representative John Boehner of Ohio), DeLay's method of drafting legislation was to put Hill staffers in a room with Republican lobbyists writing language that explicitly benefited individual companies and entire industries. In turn, the beneficiaries of the legislation—the businesses, associations, and lobbying firms—were expected, even required, to make contributions to Republican candidates who supported their agenda. This enabled well-funded Republicans to then win elections handily, outspending their opponents by lavish amounts, and returning for another legislative session of advancing corporate interests. It is a near-perfect embodiment of the candid observation of Boies Penrose, a legendary three-hundred-pound Pennsylvania Republican senator at the turn of the last century, who once told a room of his corporate supporters: "I believe in a division of labor. You send us to Congress; we pass laws under which you make money...and out of your profits you further contribute to our campaign funds to send us back again to pass more laws to enable you to make more money."

To maintain their close connection to the Hill, many of the businesses and trade associations seeking help from Congress hire former DeLay staffers—at least twenty-nine of them were employed by lobbying firms in 2005—and those of other House Republicans to serve as lobbyists. These lobbyists not only woo their former bosses and colleagues for line items in various bills, but in recent years they've also added a new wrinkle to their duties—soliciting campaign contributions for the targets of their lobbying. Today's lobbyists host extravagant fundraisers and solicit bundles of contributions, ensuring that their allies on the Hill remain in power. Thus, the cycle of access and excess—with members and lobbyists so blurring their roles as to be indistinguishable—starts again.

How did "the people's chamber" end up under the thumb of a corporate cheerleader and shakedown artist?

After avoiding service in Vietnam and running a struggling extermination business for several years, Tom DeLay was originally drawn into the political arena by a battle with the Environmental Protection Agency over a banned pesticide called Mirex. DeLay depended on Mirex to destroy the nearly invincible fire ant, a bug which had migrated to the U.S. on steamships from South America. To exterminator DeLay's chagrin, the EPA had banned the pesticide because it is a toxin that does not break down in the environment and poses a significant threat to humans. The Mirex episode inspired DeLay's hatred of government regulation, a view which continued to guide his ideology. As an EPA official exclaimed upon hearing the story years later, "Christ, we could have lived with Mirex."

In 1984, DeLay swept into Congress on the coattails of President Reagan's landslide reelection victory over Walter Mondale. He made an early shrewd move by obtaining a position on the much-sought-after Committee on Committees, which he used to earn the loyalty of other Republicans by helping them secure positions on desirable committees.

He then compounded their loyalty by contributing directly to the campaigns of his fellow House members through his political action committee, Americans for a Republican Majority (ARMPAC), and by directing lobbyists to contribute to the campaign funds of these allies. All of this helped him win the 1995 majority whip race to become the third-ranking member of the House leadership.

Since becoming majority whip that year, DeLay steadfastly pushed his fellow Republicans ever further to the right. The causes of youth violence, argued the conservative Texan, were "daycare, the teaching of evolution, and working mothers who take birth control pills." When it came to paying the bill for Iraq by reducing corporate tax cuts, DeLay balked, saying, "Nothing is more important in the face of a war than cutting taxes."

DeLay had many weapons at his disposal to keep the party's moderates in step with his program, symbolized by the two braided-leather bullwhips he ostentatiously kept in his Capitol Hill office. Enforcing discipline meant using either stick or carrot, whatever worked. So New Jersey Republican Chris Smith was removed as chairman of the Veterans Affairs Committee after repeatedly criticizing party leaders for their deficit-spending habits; and Chris Shays of Connecticut was denied the chairmanship of the Government Reform Committee because of his ardent support of campaign finance reform. At the same time, as majority leader DeLay ran a savvy full-service operation for his Republican colleagues: if a member needed a plane to race off to yet another fundraiser, DeLay secured one. If a member was feeling particularly hungry during a late-night session of the House, DeLay's office was invariably stocked with Texas barbecue, Chinese takeout, or pizza to help keep up the troops' strength.

Ultimately, though, DeLay's rise as a politician was based on the influence of money in politics. He understood the simple calculus of the Beltway—corporations have legislative goals and available assets to advance those goals. Once DeLay's party gained the majority, he had the power to offer corporations what they wanted. In turn, corporations and their lobbyists have always had what politicians need to be effective and remain in power—tons of money and the perks of power.*

Guided by a blend of evangelical Christian theology and antigovernment ideology, Tom DeLay infused the legislative process with a sense of religious righteousness and fervor. He came to believe what he once told a restaurant manager who, citing federal government policy, had asked DeLay to put out his cigar. The congressman replied, "I am the federal government." That sense of moral and political superiority justified any sleazy or bullying tactic because, in DeLay's world of power, if the end doesn't justify the means, what does? So even though 68 percent of Americans opposed impeaching President Clinton, DeLay *demanded* that his GOP troops hang together to try to destroy Clinton—and they did. "It was DeLay who button-holed, buttoned up, and sometimes brutalized House members reluctant to join him on his quest," wrote Jacob S. Hacker and Paul Pierson in *Off Center*. "Perhaps most important, it was DeLay who blocked efforts to allow the House to vote on censure, which would certainly have passed. DeLay called his all-out struggle to force the ouster of Clinton, 'The Campaign.'"

But this ethic of anything-goes, pay-to-play, crush-the-opposition politics finally caught up with him. Indeed, DeLay would still be safely installed as House majority leader had his hubris and that of some of his political cronies not gotten the better of them. Delay's downfall stemmed from the fact that his arrogance undermined his carefully scripted game of shaking down corporations and lobbyists for money and browbeating other House members for votes. Consequently, he was admonished by the House ethics committee four times—and his money-juggling and associations with other odious characters made him the target of criminal inquiries.

It was the Texan's relationship with lobbyist Jack Abramoff, however, that best illustrated how the Republicans' quest for power had lost any ethical mooring. Abramoff was a walking *quid pro quo* who made a very prosperous living mixing fees, favors, and contributions based primarily on his access to such influential Republicans as DeLay. He established many of his contacts as a member of the College Republicans in the early

---

*As an example of this web of mutuality, even DeLay's critics were amazed when he flew back to Texas in a Phillip Morris private jet to be fingerprinted after his indictment. The in-your-face quality was the only surprising aspect of this flight. DeLay and Roy Blunt used private jets 140 times from January '01 to December '04, according to the *Washington Post*. A BellSouth spokesman candidly explained that the company approved requests from "people who are friendly to us"; he added, "They could be in a position to help or hinder legislative action that might be beneficial" or damaging to the firm.

1980s when he, Grover Norquist, and many other fixtures of today's Republican establishment began honing their Swift-Boat-style political tactics. Indeed, Abramoff and Norquist once implored their fellow college activists to memorize a speech from the movie *Patton,* but asked the young Republicans to replace references to Nazis with references to Democrats: "The Democrats are the enemy. Wade into them! Spill their blood! Shoot them in the belly!"

Abramoff got to the nation's capital in 1994, just in time for the Republican Party's resurgence. Working closely with DeLay, Abramoff initiated his system of taking members of Congress and their staff on corporate junkets around the world—Scotland being a favorite haunt—"comping" countless free dinners at a restaurant he owned, and earning astounding sums of money as a lobbyist. Members got free trips and campaign gifts and, in turn, helped Abramoff's clients, a classic of the give-to-get system that prosecutors proved amounted to bribery. Investigations of Abramoff by the Justice Department and the Senate Indian Affairs Committee have revealed that Abramoff billed the tribes for lobbying fees that were ten to twenty times higher than what other firms charged, all the while ridiculing his tribal clients as "morons" and "troglodytes"; prosecutors concluded that he bilked tribes out of some $80 million.

One revealing episode involving DeLay and Abramoff centered around the efforts of the duo to prevent the Commonwealth of the Northern Mariana Islands, a client of Abramoff's, from being subject to U.S. labor laws. The Commonwealth has been a territory of the United States since World War II. Its largest island, Saipan, became a major garment manufacturing center because, using its status as a U.S. territory, it is able to print "Made in the USA" labels on its products. At the same time, the island has operated under more permissive labor laws that allow companies to pay low wages and hire huge numbers of foreign workers.

In the late 1990s, the garment factories in the territory operated as a collection of sweatshops attracting thousands of foreign workers who paid sums as high as $7,000 for a chance to work in the Commonwealth. Once they arrived, some would earn as little as $3.05 per hour. Women who became pregnant while working at the garment factories were sometimes forced to have abortions in order to keep their jobs. At its peak in 1999, the Commonwealth's garment industry produced $1 billion worth of clothes.

DeLay had visited Saipan with his family and several aides on a junket sponsored by Abramoff during the winter of 1997–98. There he had proclaimed the Commonwealth "a shining example of a free-market success." While he and other Abramoff cronies enjoyed the islands' golf courses and resorts, the Department of the Interior saw something a bit different—a haven for labor and human rights abusers.

What happened next was described by then-Interior Secretary Bruce Babbitt as "a massive campaign of intimidation" against Interior workers who sought to rein in the abusive labor practices in the Northern Mariana Islands. The coalition of members of Congress and conservative activists working with Abramoff mounted an aggressive campaign to tout the economic policies of the Commonwealth and help it maintain its special labor status despite the abundant evidence of serious human rights abuses. Conservative think tanks and editorial writers served as an echo chamber commending the free-market practices of the Commonwealth, while House leaders threatened to de-fund the Interior Department's office carrying out the investigation. The effort succeeded. Saipan continues to operate under a radically different set of labor laws than any state in the U.S.

The ties between Abramoff and DeLay, however, went far deeper than just a few legislative favors here for a few free trips there. DeLay asked Abramoff—who he once referred to as "one of my closest and dearest friends"—to raise money for him in 2002, a request that prompted the lobbyist to solicit $200,000 for the then majority leader. A year before, DeLay had tried to help an Abramoff client arrange a meeting with Interior Secretary Gale Norton; the client, the Coushatta Indian tribe, ultimately secured a dinner meeting with the Interior Secretary but not until it donated $10,000 to a charity DeLay oversees and $50,000 to the Republican environmental group that sponsored the dinner.

DeLay's staff got so accustomed to dining for free at Abramoff's restaurant Signatures and sitting in his skybox to watch the NBA Wizards and NHL Capitals that one former staffer concluded that "Jack was sort of like a drug dealer. He'd give them [DeLay aides] a little taste and then get them hooked." And it was DeLay's own former press secretary and a former Abramoff business partner, Michael Scanlon, who pled guilty in late 2005 to defrauding the Indian tribes out of millions and then bribing members of Congress with gifts and contributions.

(The arrogance and flamboyance of the duo could be seen when Abramoff emailed Scanlon, "Fire-up the jet baby, we're going to El Paso!" after he had acquired a major tribe as a client. "I want all their money!!" replied Scanlon, to which the Capitol's leading influence-peddler responded, "Yowzah!")

Abramoff also maintained close ties with Speaker Hastert and the Bush White House. On a June evening in 2003, Hastert's Keep Our Majority political action committee raised over $20,000 at an Abramoff fund-raiser held at Signatures. Then a week later Speaker Hastert, no doubt coincidentally, sent a letter to the Secretary of the Interior asking her to deny a gambling license sought by a tribe competing with one of Abramoff's clients.

The influence-peddler also served as a "Pioneer" for the Bush-Cheney campaign in 2004, a title earned by raising $100,000 for the reelection effort. In 2000, Abramoff secured a spot on the Bush-Cheney Interior Department transition team which enabled him to befriend Deputy Interior Secretary J. Steven Griles, an official who the lobbyist sought assistance from and later offered a job. And White House procurement official David Safavian, the first figure indicted in the Justice Department's investigation of Abramoff, is also a close ally and former colleague. Safavian was charged with obstruction of justice related to favors he sought on behalf of Abramoff while serving inside the Bush administration.

Abramoff's connections with the White House were so extensive that, according to the disgraced lobbyist, he met with the president nearly a dozen times and was once invited to Bush's Crawford ranch. The White House, meanwhile, has denied that President Bush even knew who Abramoff was and refuses to release any communications between White House officials and the lobbyist nor photographs of them at several White House functions. But Abramoff remembers differently, saying of Bush that "he has one of the best memories of any politician I have ever met. Perhaps he has forgotten everything." But, Abramoff continued, "Almost any important Republican who...says they didn't know me is almost certainly lying."

Abramoff was seen as a cocky and charming rogue at the nexus of lobbyists and legislators until, walking out of court on January 3, 2006, in a black fedora and black trench coat redolent of *Dick Tracy* or the consigliere in the *The Godfather*, he pled guilty to fraud, tax evasion, and conspiracy to bribe public officials. Of the many members of Congress he dealt with, none has been tainted more extensively than DeLay. But the larger scandal has been how for years the congressman operated with little regard for the ethical implications of his actions. In the fall of 2005, DeLay's misdeeds were fully revealed to the public when a Texas district attorney indicted him for money-laundering. Forced to resign from his position as majority leader—and then to resign from Congress in mid-2006—DeLay blamed a "partisan vendetta" and called it "one of the weakest, most baseless indictments in American history."

The indictments of DeLay came about because of his involvement in the 2003 scheme to redistrict congressional seats in Texas. Because Texas state law makes it a felony for corporations to contribute money to state candidates, DeLay and the staff of Texans for a Republican Majority Political Action Committee (TRMPAC) had solicited campaign contributions from several companies for specific state candidates. These corporations then sent a $190,000 check to the Republican National Committee's state legislative campaign fund. In turn, the RNC forwarded the exact same amount of money to several handpicked state Republican candidates who could help Texas Republicans build a legislative majority large enough to approve a mid-census gerrymandering plan of their choice. The prosecutor deemed the state-to-federal-to-state transaction a ruse hiding the fact that Texas law was being violated.

DeLay was initially replaced as majority leader by his close protégée Majority Whip Roy Blunt, a politician who had successfully risen through the ranks following the DeLay model of lobbyist-congressman back-scratching. But when it came down to choosing a majority leader to guide the House Republicans through what is likely to be a very tough election year, rather than stick with a leader who came to power in the same bed with lobbyists the House Republicans chose someone who actually rents his bed (or at least his apartment) from a lobbyist.

It appears doubtful that DeLay's replacement, Ohio representative John Boehner, will present a new direction for House Republicans. In the mid-1990s, Boehner served as Newt Gingrich's liaison to the lobbying community and, in an episode that Boehner now says he regrets, once distributed checks from tobacco interests to members on the House floor. At the 1996, 2000, and 2004 Republican conventions, Boehner and aides ran what came to be called in the trade "Boehner parties"—huge soirees crammed with corporate lobbyists, interest groups, and fun-loving House members.

Meanwhile, Blunt remains safely installed as the majority whip, ensuring that K Street, the headquarters for many lobbyists, will have its way when it comes down to counting votes. If this is a new direction for the Republicans, then the old one must have been worse than was imagined. As *New York Times* columnist David Brooks wrote, "The real problem wasn't DeLay, it was DeLayism, the whole culture that merged K Street with the Hill, and held that raising money is the most important way to contribute to the team."

Unfortunately, that culture has not changed in any discernible way. For the problem, ultimately, is not so much DeLay or even DeLayism but what former Minnesota Democratic Congressman Tim Penny calls "partyology"—a loyalty to a political party that exceeds any commitment to beliefs or constituents. In recent years, for example, Republicans have abandoned long-standing party principles at a blistering pace. Since President Bush took office, the size of government has increased dramatically faster than under his predecessor. Only a few years after President Clinton proclaimed that "the era of big government is over" and with memories of a balanced budget amendment still flickering in the Washington air, pork-barrel spending by the Republican-led Congress has reached unprecedented levels.

Each year recently, there have been a growing number of "earmarks," spending in appropriations bills targeted toward individual projects in particular members' districts. The $286 billion transportation bill passed in August 2005 set a new record for such spending, designating $24 billion for 6,376 projects. While the earmark for years was a tool utilized by only the most powerful politicians, today it is a matter of course for politicians to lard up spending bills with pork. As former House Majority Leader Dick Armey admitted to a reporter prior to his retirement from Congress in 2002, "To the victors go the spoils."

So why do so many members put party above principle? The answer is power. "If you want to play in our revolution," DeLay announced at the height of his dominance, "you have to live by our rules." Consequently, nearly all House Republicans swallow their pride if not their beliefs and go meekly along with Hastert, Boehner, and Bush because such members would rather stay in the majority and keep their campaign contributions and White House cufflinks—and avoid a Republican primary from the right—than exercise their judgment as independently elected legislators.

DeLay's song is over, but the malady lingers on—and it won't stop tyrannizing Congress until voters retaliate by firing his choir and until the rules of the money game radically change.

THE EVIL OF ACCESS: MONEY AND MEMBERS

The evidence that money shouts in politics is mountainous: 94 percent of the time, the bigger-spending congressional candidate wins and 98 percent of House incumbents win. The average price of a House seat rose ten-fold from $87,000 in 1976 to $840,000 in 2000. Spending in the last New York and Pennsylvania gubernatorial elections, for example, tripled within one election cycle. It cost Ken Livingstone 80 cents a vote to win the London mayoralty in 2001, compared with Michael Bloomberg's $100 a vote in New York City that year.

As money metastasizes throughout our political process, its crippling impacts on our democracy should be evident to left and right alike:

✦ *Special Interests Get Special Access and Treatment.* While members publicly and indignantly deny that big contributions often come with strings attached, all privately concede the obvious mutual shakedown—or as one senator from a western state told the author, "Senators are human calculators who can weigh how much money every vote will cost them."

Two who violated the usual senatorial omertà gave depositions in the federal district court arguments on the McCain-Feingold law in 2002. "Who, after all, can seriously contend," said former senator Alan Simpson, "that a $100,000 donation does not alter the way one thinks about—and quite possibly votes on—an issue?" Former senator Zell Miller bluntly described the daily conversations from fundraising cubicles: "I'd remind the agribusinessman I was on the Agriculture Committee; I'd remind the banker I was on the Banking Committee.... Most large contributors understand only two things: what you can do for them and what you can do to them. I always left that room feeling like a cheap prostitute who'd had a busy day."

The access that money buys, of course, doesn't guarantee legislative success, but the lack of it probably guarantees failure.

After 9/11, for example, many legislators thought the argument for energy conservation and reduced dependence on Middle Eastern oil was obvious. So Senators John Kerry and John McCain were stunned when their effort to increase fuel-efficiency standards failed sixty-two to thirty-eight—with the average no vote getting $18,000 in donations from auto companies and the average yes vote only $6,000. One senator, insisting on anonymity, said: "That vote was one of the most politically cowardly things I ever saw in the Senate. We know how to be energy-efficient, and it starts with cars."

✦ *Fundraising Is a Time Thief.* Imagine if someone kidnapped all candidates for state and federal office for half of each day. The story would be even bigger than Jack Abramoff, and would surely lead to calls for tougher penalties against political kidnapping.

There is such a culprit. It's the current system of financing political campaigns, which pits each candidate in a spiraling "arms race," not merely to raise enough money but to raise far more than any rival. One Midwestern senator complained, "Senators used to be here Monday through Friday; now we're lucky to be in mid-Tuesday to Thursday, because Mondays and Fridays are for fundraisers. Also, members loathe voting on controversial issues, because it'll be used against you when you're raising money." So candidates start to feel like Bill Murray in *Groundhog Day,* trapped in a daily, stultifying repetition they can't escape. It's hard to overstate the physical and psychological stamina required in such an effort, and how little time and energy it leaves for all else.

✦ *The "Money Primary" Weeds Out Good Candidates.* Potential candidates know they have to succeed in not one but two elections: The first, in which contributors "vote" with their dollars, comes long before constituents have their say. And if you don't win round one financially, you might as well not bother with round two; after all, because incumbency attracts money and money entrenches incumbency, no challenger spending under $850,000 won a House seat in 2000. With odds like those, many talented women and men are "silent casualties" of the money wars, in the phrase of Judge Henry Friendly.

✦ *The "Pay to Play" System Especially Hurts Democratic Candidates and Values.* Most Republicans oppose new regulations and taxes out of authentic belief. So they regard the special-interest funding of public elections as a brilliant system. For them, principles and payments go hand in hand. Robert Reich, the labor secretary under Clinton, believes his party is losing its identity as the champion of the average family "because Democrats became dependent on the rich to finance their campaigns. It is difficult to represent the little fellow when the big fellow pays the tab."

This helps explain why polls show that so many Americans strongly favor higher minimum wages, quality daycare, publicly financed congressional campaigns, and stronger environmental protection, even at the cost of higher taxes—yet the political system can't produce any of these. The money system is a circuit breaker between popular will and public policy.

Put yourself in an honest legislator's shoes: What do you do when a big-business donor privately asks you, "So where do you stand on X?"—X being something that hugely helps or hurts his economic interests. You realize not only that your answer could immediately affect a large contribution but also that the cost of paying for X will fall on future taxpayers who are not listening on the phone. Or suppose you're already a government official. Once, as the New York City consumer affairs commissioner, the author was considering filing a legal action that could cost a Democratic businessman, whom I knew well, millions of dollars. I successfully sued, and he did lose millions, and he wouldn't speak to me for a decade. But this outcome did cross my mind as I weighed the decision to prosecute—given the current political money process, how could it not?

✦ *Wealth Buys Office.* As more and more multimillionaires run and win—the percentage of them in the Senate has risen to more than one-third, about the same proportion as it was before senators began being elected by popular vote in 1913—more and more experience-rich candidates are grilled by party leaders about how they can possibly run against experience-poor but wealthy candidates. And when a very wealthy candidate inundates TV, radio, and mailboxes with ads portraying him as a young Abe Lincoln and you as the Manchurian Candidate, the pressure to hustle special-interest money becomes even more intense.

As campaign reformer Ellen Miller describes it, "The problem [with] more and more wealthy people running and winning is that then tax policy, healthcare policy, and education policy are seen through the lenses of multimillionaires, people who don't need government services. They are a different class of people and from a different world than most Americans, who sit around the kitchen table calculating their finances."

Although issues like terrorism, healthcare, and pollution absorb far more public attention and concern, the scandal of strings-attached money should be paramount because it makes it harder to solve nearly all our other problems. How can we produce smart defense, environmental, and health policies if arms contractors, oil firms, and HMOs have such a hammerlock on the committees charged with considering reforms? The culprit is not corrupt candidates but a corrupt system that coerces good people to take tainted money.

Meanwhile, can the political process significantly reform not just the "soft-money" system—as it did with the McCain-Feingold law of 2002—but also the "hard-money" system of contributions directly to candidates?

The problem is 535 campaign finance experts in Congress don't want to change the rules that got them there and have kept them there; and there are hundreds of large interests who invest thousands and reap billions—a rate of return unrivaled since IBM and Microsoft went public—who like things as they are. So systemic reform may turn on the 2008 presidential election, and whether an aspirant runs on and then governs on campaign finance reform. Three proposals are feasible:

1. Public Financing. The rationale is simple: If, say, twenty special interests give a senator $100,000 each, they can own him or her; if instead a million taxpayers give $2 each in public funds, *we* own him or her. Isn't it preferable for elected officials to be responsive to all voters rather than to relatively few donors? "Democratically funded elections" could follow either the New York City or the Arizona models. Under the first, 4-to-1 matching grants are made for all gifts up to $250 from people who can vote for the candidate (so a $25 gift becomes $125); under the second, after a gubernatorial candidate crosses a certain threshold—raising four thousand contributions of at least $5—he or she receives all subsequent funding up to a specified ceiling from the public treasury, which could be raised by a "democracy charge" imposed on registered lobbyists, political consultants, and TV advertisers.

Public financing has worked in presidential campaigns and in New York City, Arizona, and Maine elections. It avoids First Amendment arguments, since it increases speech instead of limiting it, and majorities of 70 percent regularly support it. Two strategies can help win over even more voters and some legislators to democratically funded elections: because the current *private* system of financing costs tens of billions in corporate welfare, pollution, and lost productivity, any *public* financing system would be inexpensive by comparison. Also, the media and opposing candidates should constantly expose how bad policies—for example, privatization of Social Security and weaker fuel-efficiency standards—are linked to big contributions so voters understand the impact on their health and wallets.

2. *Spending Limits*. Because the financial "arms" race steals time and buys access, Congress and the Supreme Court should approve spending limits, which existed in the 1971 and 1974 federal campaign-finance laws until the 1976 *Buckley v. Valeo* decision threw them out. But isn't money protected by First Amendment speech, as Senator Mitch McConnell and columnist George Will prominently claim? No, money is property, as Justice John Paul Stevens concluded in a recent case, which is why the 1907 Tillman Act has banned corporate contributions for nearly a century. How does it advance First Amendment values to allow a few wealthy interests to spend millions of dollars more and drown out the voices and contributions of millions of average citizens?

3. *Free or Discounted TV*. Because the airwaves belong to the public under the 1934 Federal Communications Act, we provide broadcasters with federal licenses—for free—on the condition that they agree to serve "the public interest, convenience, and necessity." But they have not lived up to their end of the bargain, perhaps because broadcasters received $1 billion in revenue from political commercials in the 2000 elections. Reducing that revenue would mean cutting into profit margins that average between 30 and 50 percent.

Paul Taylor, executive director of the Alliance for Better Campaigns, a nonpartisan group that advocates free airtime, sums up the scam:

"Our government gives broadcasters free licenses to operate on the public airwaves.... During the campaign season, broadcasters turn around and sell access to these airwaves to candidates at inflated prices." He proposes that candidates who win their parties' nominations receive vouchers for electronic advertising in their general election campaigns. Candidates, particularly from urban areas, who don't find it cost-effective to advertise on television or radio, could trade their vouchers to their party in exchange for funds to pay for direct mail or other forms of communication. As historian Arthur Schlesinger Jr. writes, "America is almost alone among the Atlantic democracies in declining to provide political parties free prime time on television during elections." If it did so, it would "do much both to bring inordinate campaign costs under control and revitalize the political parties."

Only apologists for the status quo could believe it's okay for a powerful 0.1 percent of the population to make $1,000 contributions to dictate policy to the other 99.9 percent; for only the rich or the kept to win office; for candidates to spend half their time raising money so that the toll-takers known as broadcasters will allow public candidates to speak to the public over our publicly owned airwaves.

WASHINGTON LOBBYISTS AND TONY SOPRANO

In his 1988 classic *The Power Game,* Hedrick Smith described how Washington evolved from an insulated community of legislators, lobbyists, and journalists in the 1950s and 1960s into a sophisticated world of policymaking. By the mid-1980s, the number of lobbyists and corporate political action committees had climbed exponentially because, concluded Smith, of the business community's recognition of how much is to be gained or lost from decisions made by Congress.

The successes of organized labor and Ralph Nader during the 1960s and 1970s awakened the slumbering giant of corporate America. In a 1971 memo to his business clients, then lawyer (and later Supreme Court Justice) Lewis Powell explained why and how they had to counter-organize and beat Nader at the congressional game. "Business must learn the lesson, long ago learned by labor and other self-interest groups," Powell wrote. "This is the lesson that political power is necessary; that such power must be assiduously (sic) cultivated; and that when necessary, it must be used aggressively and with determination—

without embarrassment and without the reluctance which has been so characteristic of American business." As an influential segment of the political world, corporate America has not been reluctant to embrace what Powell suggested.

Today there are 34,000 lobbyists registered with Congress and their numbers continue to grow rapidly. A 2005 *Washington Post* article asserted that lobbying firms "can't hire people fast enough," signing up the best-connected Capitol Hill or Bush administration aides at starting salaries of about $300,000 per year. Lobbying, however, is no longer just a career choice for aging Capitol Hill staffers who want to cash in after years working on the government's pay scale. A 2005 Public Citizen report, *Congressional Revolving Doors: The Journey from Congress to K Street,* found that 43 percent of members of Congress who have left office since 1998 have become lobbyists.

Many, like former representative Bob Livingston—who was briefly slated to be Speaker Newt Gingrich's replacement—discovered enormous riches off the Hill. Immediately after abandoning his quest to become House speaker and resigning from Congress due to allegations he had been involved in an extramarital affair, Livingston opened a lobbying shop that brought in $4.8 million in only its second year. Public Citizen president Joan Claybrook argues that "members use it [their congressional careers] for job training and networking so they can leave office and cash in on the connections they forged as elected officials."

Washington now is dominated by such "supracitizens," in the neologism of author William Greider, describing the professional lobbyists who earn a living in Washington pulling the levers of power. These supracitizens also include think tank researchers backed by any number of corporate interests or public relations consultants who carefully frame an issue to advance their client's agenda. Often working in coalition with a vast network of groups to make their advocacy appear homegrown—hence the appellation "Astroturf" campaigns as contrasted with real grassroots campaigns—these supracitizens essentially create and then sell "democratic" expression to corporate clients. The crowning example of this faux democracy can be found in the massive and successful effort to block President Clinton's health care reform plan in 1993 and 1994. Those grassroots "Harry and Louise" ads were as authentic as Joan Rivers's face.

Since then, lobbying has become sophisticated to the point where lobbying firms are now involved in a range of activities including research, polling, advertising, and organizing interest groups—many of the facets of a political campaign. Some firms even specialize by focusing on a single political party, one chamber of Congress, a particular congressional committee, or a few influential lawmakers. Corporations will hire multiple firms simply because they each have access to specific members of Congress.

Indeed, an entire industry has sprung up around the Medicare law passed in October 2003. Drug companies, hospitals, insurance companies, and associations hired hundreds of lobbyists in Washington to monitor and influence the regulations issued by the federal government, knowing that billions of dollars were at stake. For example, drug companies now seek to have a new medication placed on the approved list of drugs covered under Medicare, or medical technology firms seek to obtain coverage for the use of new technologies such as PET scans. Remarkably, the health care industry exceeds the defense industry in lobbying expenditures, reaching a total of $325 million in 2004.

Although it might appear that at a certain point the multitude of influence-peddlers would start to cancel each other out, major pieces of legislation are becoming a conglomeration of corporate agendas. Consider the 2005 energy bill, a top priority of the Bush administration since taking office. Dr. Gal Luft, director of the Institute for the Analysis of Global Security, described the $11 billion bill as "the sum of all lobbies." It contained provisions offering billions in tax breaks to energy producers, relief to companies from paying federal oil and gas royalties, research grants to study how to extract hard-to-reach deposits, loan guarantees, and other financial aid to companies. The bill also granted new exemptions for energy companies from adhering to provisions in the Clean Water Act, the Safe Drinking Water Act, the National Environmental Policy Act, and repealed the Depression-era Public Utility Holding Company Act, clearing the way for a wave of consolidation among utility companies.

At a time of unprecedented dependence on foreign oil, the legislation failed to include any provisions to reduce oil consumption, encourage the increased use of renewable fuels, or increase auto fuel efficiency standards. (Only a one-third jump in gasoline prices in the spring of

2006 led President Bush to say that perhaps some of these tax goodies should be held up because of record industry profits—but of course no such repeal occurred.)

A look at the amount of money spent by energy companies on lobbying and campaign contributions reveals how this smorgasbord of industry-friendly legislation came to be enacted. According to the Center for Public Integrity, nearly 2,300 energy companies lobbied Congress between 1998 and 2004, earning their hired lobbyists $984 million. Since 1990, the oil and gas industry has contributed over $180 million to congressional candidates, nearly three-quarters of which has gone to Republicans. Republicans' share of industry contributions has increased every election cycle since gaining control of the House of Representatives in 1994. With billions in tax breaks, this bonanza for lobbyists and candidates' treasuries has clearly paid off for all parties involved, except unorganized consumers and taxpayers.

Ever resourceful corporations and their lobbying arms have also tried to exploit such "opportunities" as 9/11, the Iraq War, and Hurricane Katrina. In the days after the September 11 attacks, a steel industry beset with declining revenues and increased competition from abroad argued that it was a matter of national security that the steel industry continue to receive huge subsidies from the U.S. government and that steel imports be further restricted. In the aftermath of Hurricane Katrina's devastation, Washington lobbyist James Albertine told the *New York Times* that the federal government is "throwing money out [to respond to Hurricane Katrina], they are shoveling it out the door. I'm sure every lobbyist's phone in Washington is ringing off the hook from his clients. Sixty-two billion dollars is a lot of money—and it's only a down payment."

If exploiting 9/11 or Katrina fails, a more tried-and-true complement to lobbying is, again, contributing money. What used to be exceptional is now the norm: lobbyists give money to and host fund-raisers for the members they petition, a practice about as ethical as a defendant paying a judge's salary. According to the Center for Public Integrity, since 1998 lobbyists have served as the treasurers of the campaign committees or leadership PACs of seventy-nine members.

Representative Joe Barton, a Texas Republican who chairs the House Energy and Commerce Committee, has used his position to block legislation to secure chemical plants against terrorist attacks. Chemical plants are considered the nation's greatest terrorism vulnerability and have the potential to cause tremendous loss of life from an explosion involving as little as a single chlorine tank. Nonetheless, "Smokey Joe" Barton—a nickname he earned for his efforts to undermine clean air laws in his community—continues to obstruct passage of meaningful chemical plant security legislation, leaving more than one million Dallas-area residents who live near two chemical facilities at risk. There is one obvious reason Barton seeks to minimize regulation of chemical plants and other energy companies—he has received more than $1.8 million in campaign contributions from oil and gas concerns in addition to being a favorite of the chemical manufacturing industry which has given him over $180,000 since 1990.

With the Republicans controlling the House of Representatives for over a decade now—and the chairmanships of the committees that guide energy policy—energy companies have thrown in their lot with the GOP. In 1990, roughly 40 percent of the oil and gas industry's contributions went to Democrats. Fast forward to the 2003–2004 election cycle and you'll find that the industry gave only 20 percent of its contributions to Democratic candidates—a shift seen across entire sectors of the economy. In the 1991–1992 election cycle, the pharmaceutical industry gave 49 percent of its contributions to the then-majority Democrats; now that Republicans hold the majority, Democrats receive only 30 percent.

For decades, lobbying firms and corporations would work both sides of the aisle, hedging their bets for when administrations changed or when control of Congress switched parties. But since the 1994 Republican takeover of Congress, and accelerated by the election of President Bush in 2000, Republicans have used their majority status to break this tradition. They've established a seamless political machine that calls on lobbying firms to keep money flowing into Republican campaign coffers, provides jobs for Republican staffers and former members of Congress, which in exchange keeps the doors of Capitol Hill offices open to corporate special interests.

This effort, named the K Street Project after the Washington street where many lobbying firms are based, was an explicit plan to fill lobbying firms with loyal conservatives. At regular meetings while Congress was in session, Republican members of Congress, conservative activists, and

Republican lobbyists convened to discuss political strategy and job openings on K Street. Overseeing the meetings were Senator Rick Santorum of Pennsylvania and Abramoff's longtime friend, Grover Norquist.

The head of an organization called Americans for Tax Reform, Norquist has compiled a huge database containing the party affiliation, Hill experience, and political giving of each lobbyist in Washington, D.C. Anyone who has the slightest whiff of centrism or involvement with the Democratic Party is then blacklisted by the *ad hoc* group and, in some cases, prevented from securing employment within the lobbying industry. Following Senator Tom Daschle's reelection loss in 2004, for example, a Daschle staffer who believed that a job awaited him at a Washington lobbying firm found himself denied the position after months of discussions. Said a Senate aide with knowledge of the situation, "The implication was that [House Majority Leader Tom] DeLay had put the word out that Daschle staff should not be hired."

When lobbyists fail to adhere to the demands of the Republican leadership in Congress, revenge is exacted. After Jack Valenti, longtime head of the Motion Picture Association of America (MPAA) and a former LBJ adviser, announced he was retiring, a vigorous search for a successor took place. When the MPAA hired former Democratic Congressman and Clinton administration agriculture secretary Dan Glickman, Republicans were outraged at the gall of the association. The ubiquitous Norquist reacted by describing Glickman's hiring as a "studied insult [to Republicans]" and announced that "[Hollywood's] ability to work with the House and Senate is greatly reduced."

Several months later, as legislation containing $1 billion in tax credits for movie studios was being considered by a House-Senate conference committee, the benefits to Hollywood were stripped out of the bill. Some Republicans claimed that the move reflected a dissatisfaction with the content of movies and frustration with the industry's strong support for Democrats, but other members of the minority party in Congress claimed it was punishment for the hiring of Glickman.

It used to be that politicians would ask lobbyists for favors whether they were free golf outings, trips abroad, jobs, campaign contributions, or industry support for legislation. Now, politicians demand support for their initiatives, require lobbyists to host fundraisers for them, bully firms into hiring their staffers—all in all conducting business as would organized crime.

Author Elizabeth Drew describes the K Street Project as "a more thorough, ruthless, vindictive, and effective attack on Democratic lobbyists and other Democrats who represent businesses and other organizations than anything Washington has seen before." It is but one aspect of a Tony Soprano-style approach to policymaking that muscles members into doing whatever their dons want. Democrats toil away with their quixotic hopes of securing minuscule victories while Republicans enjoy a steady procession of legislative wins engineered by their corporate benefactors and their mob-like leaders. "That's a very nice district and incumbency you have there Rep. Smith," is the daily, unspoken premise. "Sure hope that nothing happens to it."

Yes, lobbying is legal and lobbying is necessary to educate members about issues they're not expert on. But given the grotesque one-sidedness of armies of professional soldiers facing a few community or public interest recruits—as well as the undeniable pay-to-play aspect—even conservatives who endlessly invoke "original intent" in the judicial context should appreciate how far removed we are from the democratic aspirations of our founding fathers and our original citizen legislators. Very little of the lobbying in the energy bill of 2005 brings to mind the idealized faction versus faction model posited by James Madison in *Federalist #51*.

II.

LEGISLATIVE TYRANNY II: A DEMOCRACY WITHOUT DEMOCRATS

"For my purposes, they're irrelevant."
—AMY STEINMANN, House Majority Whip Roy Blunt's
Director of Floor Operations, Describing House Democrats

*"When you look at the way the House of Representatives has
been run, it has been run like a plantation, and you know what
I'm talking about."*
—SENATOR HILLARY CLINTON, Martin Luther King Jr. Day Speech
in Harlem, January 2006

EXCLUDING HALF OF AMERICA

The most alarming consequence and cause of this new climate in Washington is that Democrats wield so little influence—notwithstanding the fact that they're, in one sense, the majority party. How can that be? The forty-four Democratic senators elected in 2000, 2002, and 2004 garnered 99.7 million votes during those three elections. Yet their fifty-five Republican counterparts, a stone's throw away from a filibuster-proof majority, received only 97.3 million votes over the same three elections. But the Senate is rigged in favor of small (often Republican) states since Wyoming and Utah (with populations of under a million) elect two senators, the same as California and New York (with thirty-seven million and nineteen million respectively). Similarly, although Al Gore won the popular vote in 2000, President Bush won a higher number of votes in forty-seven more congressional districts than his opponent did—and the presidency—due to the unusual math of the Electoral College.

The success of Republicans in winning elections, at least in the House, is in large part a function of skillful redistricting efforts. After their victories in the mid-1990s, the GOP held enough governorships and statehouses to add to an already strong advantage and leave a serious imprint on the post-census redistricting in 2001. They exploited their electoral advantage with such agility that, by the time the 2002 elections rolled around, the number of solidly Republican districts totaled over two hundred and the number of vulnerable Republican seats was under twenty. Looking at four states where the 2000 vote was split evenly between Bush and Gore—Florida, Pennsylvania, Ohio, and Michigan—Republicans held fifty-one of the seventy-seven House seats after the 2002 elections in those states due to redistricting.

One might think that this narrow electoral advantage would engender a collegial atmosphere in Washington whereby the majority party works closely with the minority, recognizing the tables could be turned at any time. This could not be further from the truth. Since gaining the majority in 1994, the Republicans, particularly in the House, have been ruthless in their treatment of the Democrats. No story illustrates the tyrannical behavior of the Republican leadership better than the passage of the 2003 Medicare prescription drug legislation.

On the night of the 2003 Medicare vote, with House Democrats almost unanimously opposed to the legislation, House Republicans engaged in a horse-trading circus that embarrassed the party, violated House precedent, and led to an ethics inquiry of then-majority leader DeLay. Desperately seeking enough ayes to pass the legislation, the vote was kept open for the longest period in history, three hours, well beyond the traditional fifteen-minute courtesy voting period. Whereas members typically are granted fifteen minutes to travel from wherever they are on the Capitol grounds to the House chamber to cast their vote on a piece of legislation, House Republican leaders spent three hours in the middle of the night coaxing and browbeating their colleagues to support the bill. When the majority Democrats had employed a similar tactic for thirty minutes in 1987 to win a vote, then-representative Dick Cheney described the maneuver as "the most heavy-handed, arrogant abuse of power in the ten years I've been here."

Indeed, Republican representative Nick Smith told a reporter the day after the vote that he was offered a reward of $100,000 in campaign contributions for his son Brad, a candidate running to succeed Smith upon his retirement, in exchange for his vote in support of the drug benefit. Smith later publicly recanted the charge, but a House ethics committee investigation determined that DeLay had, at a minimum, offered to endorse Smith's son in exchange for his vote in support of the Medicare benefit, either way a clear violation of House rules.

The Medicare vote is emblematic of a Washington in which the minority party, certainly in the House of Representatives, has virtually no power. It is a Washington where Democrats are excluded from drafting legislation, given little time to review bills before they are voted on, and basically prohibited from amending legislation once it comes to the floor. It's a Congress in which, as one Democratic staff member commented, "The Republicans believe nothing good can come from Democrats."

Making life difficult or miserable for the minority party is nothing new to Congress. During their forty years of congressional control from 1954 to 1994, Democrats indulged in their share of abuses of power. A 1993 report written by the Republican minority on the House Rules Committee complained bitterly about the tactics used by House Democrats, pleading for "the full and free airing of conflicting opinions through hearings, debates, and amendments for the purpose of developing and improving legislation deserving of the respect and support of the people."

But Democratic control was an Athenian democracy compared to how the Republicans have mechanized and perfected the tyranny of the majority. There's a difference between controlling legislation and monopolizing it.

In a 1993 floor speech, Florida Republican representative Lincoln Diaz-Balart described the "infamous closed rule"—a ground rule for a specific piece of legislation which limits debate and prohibits amendments from being considered—as "profoundly undemocratic." Yet Republicans have now gleefully embraced such undemocratic tactics— the use of closed rules has increased from only eighteen times in the 103rd Congress to twice that number during the 108th. Meanwhile, the number of open rules (which allow lengthy debate and numerous amendments) has fallen from roughly forty-nine in the 103rd Congress to twenty-eight during the last Congress.

House Republicans have also dramatically increased the number of bills and the amount of time dedicated to the suspension calendar, a waiting area for supposedly non-controversial bills such as those which name a post office after a popular local figure. Mondays, Tuesdays, and, increasingly, Wednesdays are now used to debate these mundane and unanimously supported bills in Congress. In reality, it is a cynical way to limit debate on the few controversial bills which come before the Congress. According to Massachusetts Democratic representative James McGovern, "The House has become a place where trivial issues are debated passionately and important issues not at all."

Republicans also monopolize legislation by using emergency meeting procedures and calling late-night meetings when members of Congress are unavailable or unprepared to set the rules for legislation, not to mention that reporters are less likely to be lurking in the halls of Congress. A rule established by the House Rules Committee at the start of the 108th Congress in January 2003, for example, required the committee to meet regularly at 10:30 on Tuesday mornings and at other times with forty-eight hours notice. However, an addition to the rule allowed the chair to call an emergency meeting "at any time on any measure or matter which the chair determines to be of an emergency nature." In the 108th Congress, more than 60 percent of the rules reported by the committee were approved as "emergency" measures. The odd hours at which the committee met—nearly 40 percent of rules were reported out of the committee after 8 p.m.—was a reason that one of the Republican members, Representative Deborah Pryce, chose to stop serving on the Rules Committee.

A worse example of the legislative "plantation" is the use of conference committees to dramatically alter a piece of legislation. President Reagan once said an apple and an orange could go into a conference committee and come out a pear. In today's Congress, that same apple and orange would come out as a giant subsidy to Halliburton or another company lining the campaign accounts of Republican congressional leaders. Conference committees are established when the House and Senate pass different versions of the same basic legislation. Party leaders then appoint conferees to iron out the differences.

Traditionally, those conferees merely negotiate over the disputed elements of the bill, but, increasingly, congressional Republicans are using the opportunity to add pork-barrel projects or provisions which will reward their corporate benefactors. Members of the minority party are occasionally pacified with a pork project of their own, but often Democrats are excluded altogether. In fact, they were completely blocked from participating in negotiations on the Medicare and energy bills during the 108th Congress. Massachusetts Democratic representative Ed Markey, a conferee appointed by the Democratic leadership, was left to ask lobbyists what provisions the energy bill contained.

Another weapon in the Republicans' arsenal is to speed up the legislative process to the point where members of both parties are given only a few hours to read a major piece of legislation—such as the October 2003 expansion of Medicare—before voting on it. This is how a provision authorizing congressional staffers to examine Americans' private tax returns was included in a 2004 appropriations bill. The provision was noticed too late to amend the legislation before the Senate approved it, but it was stripped from the $388 billion bill one month later.

Occasionally the disrespect shown to the minority provokes quarrels between the parties, even if they fall short of the infamous cane attacks, fistfights, and duels of the nineteenth century. At a July 18, 2003, House Ways and Means Committee hearing, the Republicans on the committee announced that they had dramatically altered a pension bill overnight without the input of Democrats. In reaction to the news, all committee Democrats but one adjourned to the nearby committee library to discuss their legislative strategy. While the Democrats caucused next door, Chairman Bill Thomas told his staff to bring the Democrats back into the room, instructing them to call the Capitol Police if necessary.

The Democrats had left one member of their caucus behind, California representative Fortney "Pete" Stark, to monitor the hearing. Stark had invoked a rule calling for Chairman Thomas to read the entire bill while Democrats met, but Thomas quickly approved the bill "without giving Stark a chance to object."

Representative Stark protested angrily and was told to "shut up" by Colorado Republican representative Scott McInnis. At that point, Stark challenged McInnis to a fight, calling him a "fruitcake" and a "wimp." Eventually the Capitol Police showed up at the committee library, but refused to usher the Democrats back into the hearing room. The following week Chairman Thomas issued a tearful apology on the House floor for summoning the Capitol Police.

In another example of House dissension, the chairman of the Judiciary Committee, Wisconsin's James Sensenbrenner, and other committee Republicans walked out of a June 10, 2005, hearing on the Patriot Act, leaving Democrats protesting with their microphones turned off. Sensenbrenner claimed that the testimony at the hearing by witnesses from groups including Amnesty International USA and the American Immigration Lawyers Association was irrelevant while other Republicans argued that the questions being raised by the groups were endangering the lives of Americans in uniform.

Perhaps the greatest affront to the Democrats in recent years occurred when the most junior member of Congress, Ohio Republican Jean Schmidt, attacked Representative John Murtha, a thirty-three-year House veteran and decorated Marine colonel who served in Vietnam, implying he was a coward for proposing a phased pullout of troops from Iraq earlier in the week. In a floor speech on November 18, 2005, Schmidt said, "A few minutes ago I received a call from Colonel Danny Bubp. He asked me to send Congress a message: stay the course. He also asked me to send Congressman Murtha a message: that cowards cut and run, Marines never do." (Enraged Democrats demanded that Schmidt retract her statement; within minutes she did.)

This contemptuous treatment of the minority party has profound implications for democracy. In the House, politics is no longer the art of compromise between the majority and minority parties, but is a process of collaboration between corporate interests and Republican leaders. The presidents of the U.S. Chamber of Commerce, American Petroleum Institute, and Business Roundtable—whom nobody elected—have more say and sway in Congress than minority leaders Nancy Pelosi and Harry Reid.

Speaker Dennis Hastert has established an informal policy of only bringing bills to the floor which are supported by a majority of the majority, something unheard of before but further depleting the arsenal of the House Democrats. In November 2004, Hastert scuttled an overhaul of the nation's intelligence community, despite the fact that the White House, the Senate, and a majority of House members, including Hastert himself, supported the legislation. Norman Ornstein of the American Enterprise Institute called this informal rule "a disastrous recipe" for addressing domestic issues.

Similarly, the increased use of omnibus legislation that allows multiple appropriations bills to be rolled into one piece of legislation enables members to tuck in many provisions which are rarely scrutinized. The November 2004 appropriations bill was sixteen hundred pages long, weighed fourteen pounds, and was passed under emergency procedures allowing little time for debate or scrutiny. In addition to the provision authorizing certain lawmakers and their staff members to review citizens' tax returns, the bill contained a subsidy for an environmentally friendly shopping mall in Shreveport, Louisiana, containing a Hooters Restaurant.

LITERAL "OVERSIGHT"

Just as the congressional leadership has abandoned the principles that guided it historically, it has also failed in its oversight function. After six years of seemingly endless investigations during the Clinton years, the current Congress has surrendered to "partyology" by refusing to investigate one serious issue after another since the Bush administration took office. The word "oversight" has now taken on an entirely different meaning than in past decades.

There have been no serious hearings into the extent the Bush administration downplayed terrorism pre-9/11 which could have allowed that successful attack (although there were several congressional inquiries into lapses pre-Pearl Harbor shortly after December 7, 1941). Despite repeated calls by Democrats and several unauthorized hearings by the Senate's Democratic Policy Committee, there has been no congressional study into allegations of war profiteering by military contractors in Iraq despite the fact that as much as $9 billion in U.S. spending remains unaccounted for. Additionally, no examination has occurred into how military resources authorized for Afghanistan were diverted for the war in Iraq, nor how deploying so many National Guard troops and reservists have compromised homeland security.

The prisoner abuse issue has garnered some grumbling, but no investigative hearings into a scandal that's probably done more to ruin America's reputation worldwide than any other sin of commission or omission in the past twenty years. "Even as American news media and European parliaments have produced report after report on the Central Intelligence Agency's handling of terror suspects," wrote Scott Shane in the *New York Times,* "the [Senate Intelligence] Committee has held no hearings on the topic and conducted no formal investigation." At the same time, Congress has refused to examine the role of White House officials in leaking the name of covert CIA operative Valerie Plame Wilson as a possible punishment for her husband's criticism of false White House statements claiming that Iraq had sought uranium from Niger. A Congress that spent years on "Travelgate" and Whitewater, yielding nothing, now spends no time exploring the buildup to a war that's killed over twenty-five hundred Americans, wounded tens of thousands of other servicemembers, and cost us more than it would take to provide universal health care.

On the domestic front, misleading assessments on the projected cost of the Medicare prescription drug benefit and veterans' benefits have been blocked from formal congressional investigation despite clear evidence that more accurate projections were hidden from lawmakers. Indeed, partyology has infected the oversight role of Congress to such a degree that Republican congressional leaders are unwilling to investigate *any* issue that might make anyone within the party look bad. One of the most glaring examples of this strategy can be found in the years of refusal of Kansas Republican senator Pat Roberts, chairman of the Intelligence Committee, to investigate the faulty intelligence-gathering in the lead-up to the Iraq war.

Democratic members of Congress began calling for an investigation once it became clear that no weapons of mass destruction were to be found in Iraq and as more details emerged indicating the possible manipulation of intelligence by the White House. In June 2004, the Senate Intelligence Committee issued a report criticizing the intelligence gathering and analysis of the CIA and other agencies. The report, however, failed to look at the way in which intelligence was handled and used in public statements by administration officials in justifying the war in Iraq. Republicans on the committee simply refused to include such information in the initial report. At the time, Senator Roberts stated that those questions would be examined following the 2004 presidential election so as to minimize the political implications. But with no such inquiry underway by late 2005, exasperated Democrats finally took matters into their own hands: on November 1, 2005, they invoked Senate Rule 21 to force the Senate into closed session. In dramatic fashion, the Democrats demanded that Roberts proceed with the second phase of the investigation. After significant and unflattering publicity, he reluctantly agreed.

Another instance of the Republican Party's tendency to cover up embarrassing news was on display in late 2005 when *Washington Post* reporter Dana Priest discovered that the CIA was detaining high-level al-Qaeda suspects in Eastern Europe so that they could not be visited by the Red Cross and other international monitors. They were hidden in a netherworld where torture and prisoner treatment standards barely exist. Rather than condemning the use of the secret prisons or at least investigating the propriety of them under U.S. law, Senate Majority Leader Bill Frist and Speaker Hastert initiated an inquiry into how news of the detention facilities was leaked to the press.

In a letter to the chairmen of the House and Senate intelligence committees, the leaders wrote: "We request that you immediately initiate a joint investigation into the possible release of classified information to the media alleging that the United States government may be detaining and interrogating terrorists at undisclosed locations abroad. As you know, if accurate, such an egregious disclosure could have long-term and far-reaching damaging and dangerous consequences, and will imperil our efforts to protect the American people and our homeland from terrorist attacks."

Congress was not always so subservient to an administration. Democratic senator Harry Truman held hearings into war profiteering by munitions firms *during* World War II—and FDR still (fatefully) chose him as a running mate in 1944. In 1965, the Democratic chairman of the Senate Foreign Relations Committee, William Fulbright, began well-publicized hearings into how a Democratic president was mishandling the war in Vietnam. Based on the past five years, the chance that the Republican Congress would hold the Bush administration responsible for any mistake or misconduct short of invading Canada or serial adultery is near zero.

Republican members of Congress acted slightly differently when they learned that President Bush had authorized a massive domestic surveillance program shortly after 9/11. Led by Pennsylvania senator Arlen Specter, a handful at least discussed the possibility of hearings regarding the program; however, what was remarkable was that the program had existed for four years—placing thousands of people in the United States under surveillance—and virtually no members of Congress were even aware of it. Unfortunately, once the hearings finally occurred, they were more designed to create a façade of congressional oversight rather than seriously examine an administration policy that nearly all objective observers agree is a clear overreach of executive authority. Attorney General Alberto Gonzales, the sole witness at the hearing, was not even required to be sworn in before testifying. Within days and under heavy pressure from the White House, Senate Republicans decided against holding a full-scale investigation of the wiretapping program.

CHANGING THE RULES

When congressional Republicans don't like the rules, they try to change them—as they did with the House ethics committee, judicial filibuster, mid-census legislative redistricting, Terri Schiavo, and the Medicare roll-call vote.

The Schiavo episode is recounted in detail subsequently in "Religious Tyranny." In sum, a Republican party that usually defers to "states' rights" thought it unfair that the decision of Terri Schiavo's husband to remove her feeding tube had been upheld after fourteen appeals in Florida courts and four refusals in the Supreme Court. So, overnight Congress passed and Bush signed a law allowing her parents to sue— unsuccessfully, it turned out—in federal court. When it comes to the ends justifying the means, Republicans are more radical than traditional.

Tom DeLay's first ethics admonishment came in May 1999 when the House ethics committee rebuked him for "badgering a lobbying organization over its hiring of a Democrat as its president." He had complained the prior year to the Electronic Industries Alliance and the Republican House leadership about rumors that the group was set to hire a former Democratic congressman from Oklahoma, Dave McCurdy, as its president. Responding to DeLay's complaint, House leaders postponed votes on two uncontroversial international trade bills that the Alliance wanted. McCurdy was ultimately hired as the group's president, but the episode reflected the climate of intimidation enveloping Washington.

Then, in October 2004, DeLay was again admonished by the ethics committee for three more rules violations. The first, as noted previously, was a result of his attempt to secure a fellow Republican's vote for a Medicare prescription drug benefit by offering political support to the retiring House member's son. DeLay received a second rebuke for creating a conflict of interest by raising money at a golf tournament sponsored by energy company Westar as the House considered legislation that would directly impact the company. A third admonishment was delivered because DeLay had used Department of Homeland Security resources to locate political rivals in Texas who had fled the state to block a vote on his redistricting plan to stack the Texas congressional delegation with more Republicans. To DeLay, apparently, the real terrorists were Democrats trying to thwart his power.

After picking up seats in both the House and Senate during the 2004 elections—besides, of course, retaining the presidency—congressional Republicans began to act like a permanent majority. Indeed, within days of winning another majority in the Congress, House Republicans were debating whether and how to shield their ethically troubled majority leader from losing his position of power. On November 17, 2004, House Republicans voted to change the existing rule that an indicted member had to step down from a leadership position to protect DeLay in case of a possible indictment stemming from the investigation into the fundraising efforts of TRMPAC. The rule change was hubris at its height, a clear sign that House Republicans had become the arrogant majority they had so despised a decade earlier.

The ensuing barrage of negative media embarrassed the party so badly that upon returning to Washington to start the 109th Congress, the majority in the House rescinded the new rule. But leaders taketh *and* giveth, because they then enacted a rule change that would prevent investigations from proceeding without the support of at least a majority of ethics committee members—and since the committee always maintains a five to five split by party, strict party loyalty here again would handcuff not bad members but the committee itself.

This rules change passed by a party-line vote of 220 to 195 and was drafted and developed without any consultation with the minority party. In recent history, House members of both parties had previously operated under something of a truce—sort of a gentlemen's agreement that investigations would not proceed unless there were serious acts of misconduct. In 1997, the House had adopted a rule that if no action is taken on a complaint within forty-five days, a preliminary investigation begins. The new rule meant that one party by itself could block the other from pursuing an investigation.

Apparently, many Republicans were dismayed not by ethics violations but by the ethics panel's chairman, Representative Joel Hefley of Colorado, who had presided over the three ethics rebukes of DeLay. In early 2005 Hefley was removed and replaced as chairman by DeLay ally Washington representative Richard "Doc" Hastings—and two new Republican members were added who had made contributions to DeLay's legal defense fund: the PAC of Texas representative Lamar Smith had given DeLay's account $10,000, while Oklahoma representative Tom Cole's PAC had contributed $5,000 to the fund. All in all, this was akin to Senator Hillary Clinton presiding at the impeachment trial of President Bill Clinton.

As details of committee activities leaked out, Democratic members refused to accept the rules adopted by the Republican majority and blocked the committee from performing its duties. At the same time, stories of Abramoff-sponsored junkets taken by DeLay and other members of Congress were grabbing newspaper headlines, but no investigation could proceed. Representative Barney Frank, a Massachusetts Democrat who had been reprimanded by the House in 1990 regarding a situation involving a prostitute living in his home, described the conditions under which the standoff took place on *Meet the Press* in April 2005: "I, fifteen years ago, had a problem because I behaved inappropriately. The ethics committee stepped in. Newt Gingrich had a problem. He was reprimanded; the ethics committee stepped in. The difference between us and Mr. DeLay is, I think, we changed our behavior. Mr. DeLay changed the ethics committee."

When eight of nine members agreed to take bribes from undercover Arab interests in the "Abscam" scandal of the late 1970s, the ethics committees met and doled out severe punishments. In 1996, when Speaker Newt Gingrich himself made false statements to the House ethics committee, he received a fine of $300,000 and a reprimand. By 2006 the committee had become an extinct volcano—despite the fact that evidence of ethics violations was appearing in the news media on a near-daily basis. Most notoriously, in late 2005 Representative Randy "Duke" Cunningham, a California Republican, ex-Vietnam pilot, and self-described superpatriot, resigned from Congress after pleading guilty to accepting $2.4 million in bribes from defense contractors. Cunningham had used the bribes to spend lavish amounts on a mansion, a Rolls Royce, a yacht called *Duke Stir*, and assorted antiques in return for helping his benefactors secure over $160 million in Pentagon contracts. When this loud, flag-waving bully—who had called Bill Clinton a traitor and compared John Kerry to Jane Fonda on the House floor—admitted his crimes, he burst into tears.

As the House was bickering over its ethics rules, the Senate was engaged in an epic battle of its own—a debate over whether to eliminate the judicial filibuster. The use of filibusters to block judicial nominees was an established but infrequently used weapon by senators that was brought into more frequent use by the Democrats once they fell into the minority after the 2002 elections. During the first term of President George W. Bush, filibusters were used to block 10 federal court nominees out of 216 who, Democrats argued, held radical views about environmental policy, property rights, abortion, and the role of government. One such nominee, California supreme court justice Janice Rogers Brown, had likened the Social Security program to an act of cannibalism by older people against their grandchildren. Another filibustered nominee, Texas supreme court justice Priscilla Owen, was blocked by Democrats because of her judicial activism in restricting reproductive rights for women. Attorney General Alberto Gonzales, when a colleague of Owen's on the Texas supreme court in 1998, described one Owen dissent in a case involving abortion and parental consent as "an unconscionable act of judicial activism."

While the filibuster of bills has an ancient heritage, the judicial filibuster was first used in 1968 when Senate Republicans opposed President Johnson's nomination of Abe Fortas for Chief Justice of the Supreme Court—and, partly as a result, Fortas's nomination was indeed withdrawn. During the Clinton administration, pocket filibusters—when senators could block a nominee from their home state who they didn't support simply by refusing to submit a blue slip with a nominee's name to the Judiciary Committee chairman—were the preferred method of blocking a president's nominees. That practice was discontinued in early 2001 after Republicans had used it to prevent over sixty of Clinton's judicial nominees from being considered and confirmed.

Around the same time the pocket filibuster was done away with, the Bush administration also ended a policy going back to the Eisenhower administration of having nominees screened by the American Bar Association. Taken together, Republicans seemed bent on converting their momentary majority in the Senate into conservative judicial dominance for decades.

Republicans claimed that the judicial filibuster was an abuse of the minority party's rights. Senator Frist had gone so far as to call judicial filibusters "nothing less than a formula for tyranny by the minority." Yet in 2000, Frist joined a group of Republican senators filibustering a Clinton nominee, Richard Paez, whose nomination had languished for four years. The senator who orchestrated the failed filibuster attempt, Republican Senator Bob Smith of New Hampshire, had done so because he believed that Paez was "out of the mainstream of thought."

During the Reagan administration, Senate Democrats and the Republican president maintained a relatively harmonious relationship in confirming judicial nominees. Then, administration officials would compile lists of prospective nominees and share them with the Democratic chairman of the Judiciary Committee who would make it clear which nominees would have trouble being confirmed and which ones would sail through easily. Just a handful out of the hundreds of Reagan nominees were removed from the confirmation process this way, but discarding that handful prior to any confirmation process spared the Senate, and the public, from ugly, partisan battles. "We did business that way [consulting with each other] for years, and it worked," said Delaware Democrat Joe Biden, a former Judiciary Committee chairman. "Now this crowd wants to shove everything down our throats. They don't pull back on anybody. So we escalated with the filibusters. And they escalate with the nuclear option."

After significantly enlarging their Senate majority in the 2004 election, Frist announced on the opening day of the new congressional session that he would no longer allow the Democrats to block judicial nominees using the filibuster. This effort, called the "nuclear option," would involve consulting the Senate's presiding officer, Vice President Dick Cheney, for a ruling on whether further debate on a judicial nominee is out of order. Vice President Cheney could then issue a rule limiting debate which would only need to be affirmed by a simple majority of senators, not the usual two-thirds required for a rule change. If the nuclear option were invoked, Senate Democrats warned that they would bring the Senate to a stalemate, using Senate rules to slow down the legislative process to a glacial pace.

Senator Frist and a well-organized group of conservative Christian activists tried to make the debate over judicial filibusters a proxy for the debate over the role of religious faith in politics and the judiciary. And despite the fact that different people had different interpretations of what the term "activist" meant, it soon came to be defined as liberal judges who endorse gay marriage, oppose including the words "under God" in the Pledge of Allegiance, and seek to prohibit prayer in public schools.

The Senate was beginning to morph into the House of Representatives. For an institution that has been forced to retain at least a superficial comity due to the minority party's rights, it seemed that the Senate was losing its tempering role in the American political system— the "senatorial saucer," as George Washington once described the body, was no longer cooling the hot coffee of the legislative process. Just as Frist was on the verge of invoking the nuclear option, a group of fourteen Republicans and Democrats announced they had reached a deal to avert the rule change by retaining the judicial filibuster in "extraordinary circumstances" and allowing three of the ten filibustered nominees, including Brown and Owen, to be confirmed. Although they were not enthusiastically supported by Democrats, the Roberts and Alito Supreme Court nominations failed to unify the Democrats enough to mount a judicial filibuster.

Republicans have also sought to exploit their advantages at the state level to advance the agenda of the party nationally, again at the expense of tradition and law. In Texas, the Republican majority in the state legislature undertook an unprecedented effort to reorganize the state's congressional districts only two years after a federal court had done so following the 2000 census. But when they won large majorities in the statehouse during the 2002 elections, based in part on the successful and possibly criminal fundraising of Tom DeLay and others involved in TRMPAC, the legislature's Republican majority began a redistricting process, again.

In a bizarre drama, Texas Democratic legislators fled first to Oklahoma and later to New Mexico during the 2003 legislative session to prevent the Republican majority from approving the redistricting plan. Attempting to deny the Republicans a quorum and the ability to force a vote on the mid-decade redistricting proposal, fifty-one House Democrats headed just across the state line to a hotel in Ardmore, Oklahoma, in May 2003. They had left Texas to elude state police who had been ordered by Republican leaders to bring all legislators to the state capitol. Had they returned to Texas, a redistricting plan expected to cost Democratic members of Congress at least five seats would have been scheduled for a vote.

As the Democrats were fleeing the state, DeLay contacted a Department of Homeland Security agency, the Air and Marine Interdiction and Coordination Center, in Riverside, California, for information on the whereabouts of Democratic legislator and former House Speaker Pete Laney. Eventually, the Democrats lost their resolve—after all, as elected officials, they couldn't stay outside of Texas forever—and the redistricting plan hatched by DeLay was signed into law by Republican governor Rick Perry.

This effort by Republicans to redraw lines mid-census (which also occurred in Colorado and Georgia) threatens to destabilize the American political system. Historically, the parties have known that once each decade there is an opportunity to gain an advantage over the opposing party. But what Texas did was to usher in an era of endless political muscling that could have dangerous repercussions. With Republicans taking advantage of any power available to them, what is to stop Democrats from doing the same? Indeed, the redistricting effort in Republican-dominated states has only slowed down because Republicans in other states, most notably House Speaker Dennis Hastert, have faced the threat of their own seats being redrawn. As Senator McCain had warned, Republican tactics have gotten so egregious that they had "better hope that the Democrats never regain the majority."

McCain's observation put the new congressional authoritarianism in a broader context reminiscent of a lesson from Robert Bolt's play *A Man for All Seasons*. In one scene, a callow and ambitious politician asks Sir Thomas More if he would give the devil the benefit of law. "Yes. What would you do, cut a great road through the law to get after the devil?" Replied the young pol, "I'd cut down every law in England to do that." To which More responded, "Oh? And when the last law was down and the devil turned round on you, where would you hide, the laws all being flat?"

A Teachable Moment?

In another fine example of political comity, Republicans in Congress have worked furiously but not very successfully arguing that the Abramoff scandal was a bipartisan one, largely because many of Abramoff's clients gave money to members of Congress from both parties. But this proved unconvincing because Indian tribes had previously given to Senate and House Democrats who had befriended Indian interests over the years, and *all* of Abramoff's own political fundraising was for Republicans, as expected, since he had been a lifelong Republican operative bragging about his access to Hastert, DeLay, and the Bush administration. This was as much a Democratic scandal as Watergate. Illinois Democratic senator Barack Obama noted, "Democrats are certainly not without sin," but the efforts of Abramoff, Scanlon, and the K Street Project "are Republican sins and Republican sins alone."

Still, if the culprits in today's "culture of corruption" are surely Republican, there is also an ongoing institutional corruption—i.e., the "pay to play" and revolving door systems described previously—that taints so many who run and serve. "The scandal is not what's illegal but what's legal," according to Michael Kinsley's rule of political scandal. So what this one sleazy Republican did (other than his outright fraudulent conduct toward his clients) was more customary than criminal, an extreme version of what occurs more quietly each day.

Given this broader context, will the DeLay-Abramoff scandals and developing congressional dictatorship catalyze into real institutional reform? With 88 percent of adults in a 2005 AP-Ipsos poll believing that political corruption is "very serious" or "somewhat serious," is this the kind of major teachable moment that produced the 1974 post-Watergate reforms (seniority, filibuster, and campaign financing)?

The loyal opposition hopes so and has an agenda. Over 120 House Democrats proposed a fourteen point overhaul of their rules at the start of the 2006 session. The proposal would ban lobbyist-sponsored travel; stop ex-legislators from lobbying on the House floor; require that all bills be available twenty-four hours before a vote; prohibit votes being held open longer than twenty minutes unless both parties' leaders or floor managers agree to it; and significantly increase penalties for violations. Over in the Senate, McCain joined with Senator Joe Lieberman of Connecticut in introducing a similar package, adding two more disclosures: retiring lawmakers and staff should reveal employment negotiations that could pose a conflict; and lobbyists should make sure that legislators pay the true cost of flying on corporate jets. A more significant institutional reform, proposed by Senators Susan Collins (R-ME) and Lieberman, would create an independent office to examine ethics abuses, professionally staffed and empowered to investigate and charge. But no significant leaders in either chamber were arguing for perhaps the most important reform, prohibiting lobbyists from bundling campaign funds from the members they lobby or serving as their finance chairs.

Even Majority Leader Frist felt the need to respond to the swelling scandals. "The leader expects a serious and credible lobby reform proposed for the Senate," said his chief of staff for him, "and the ideas proposed to date fit that bill to bring more transparency and accountability to the lobbying world." But when he then chose Rick Santorum, K Street's liaison to Senate Republicans, his expressed interest in reform didn't seem very "credible." And Speaker Hastert, presumably not intending to appear comical, proposed ethics training sessions to better allow "members on both sides of the aisle to understand the nuances of House rules." However, the issue is not nuances but ethics, not understanding but compliance.

Whether this is a teachable moment or a passing moment now depends on whether public pressure grows or ebbs—and whether members of Congress ever get to the point of fearing voters more than donors. As of May 2006 the prospects weren't good. Only modest reforms passed the Senate, involving more disclosure, further limits on gift-giving, and an extension of the waiting period from one to two years before a retiring member or staff could lobby Congress, while the House bottled up more significant reforms. Common Cause president Chellie Pingree complained about congressional amnesia a mere three months after Abramoff's sentencing. "We will be back to business, if not worse," she remarked. "Lobbyists could continue to organize fundraising events, go on trips with members of Congress, give gifts, and provide discounts on chartered jets."

On one hand, the shenanigans involving Abramoff and related contretemps are widely called one of the biggest congressional scandals ever—"the greatest congressional scandal in American history since Crédit Mobilier [of 1873]," writes author Sidney Blumenthal. But on the infamous other hand, the DeLay system of back-scratching donors and members has often ignored public opinion. Indeed, Hastert and Frist are still in charge and are still using the glue of partyology to hold together their tyranny of the majority.

III

RELIGIOUS TYRANNY: IS GOD REALLY A REPUBLICAN?

"Christian values should dominate our government. The test of those values is the Bible. Politicians who do not use the Bible to guide their public and private lives do not belong in office."
—BEVERLY LaHAYE, Concerned Women for America

One year before the 2006 elections, Ohio secretary of state and would-be governor Kenneth Blackwell stands before an astonishing rally at the state capitol building. It is led by a rising star in Religious Right circles, the Rev. Rod Parsley, who runs a megachurch and a handful of affiliated organizations. He is working to organize the state's "Patriot Pastors" to register four hundred thousand "values voters" before the 2006 election. Blackwell is a crowd favorite for his active support of an antigay constitutional amendment that won statewide on the 2004 ballot—and for his no-holds-barred use of his office to help ensure the reelection of George W. Bush as president.

In some ways, the scene has become so common that it's not surprising: Republican leader cozies up with the Religious Right to win votes. But Parsley is no sweet-talking Ralph Reed, carefully modulating his rhetoric for public consumption. "Shout it like you're going to carry the blood-stained banner of the cross of Christ the length and breadth of the Buckeye State!" he hollers to the boisterous crowd. "Sound an alarm. A Holy Ghost invasion is taking place. Lock and load...Let the reformation begin!" Parsley says of his plans for building power in Ohio, "It's an ambitious agenda. It's a bold agenda. But it's an agenda demanded by our times and commanded by our God....Man your battle stations, ready your weapons."

Parsley's theology, management style, and politics are about command and control. He and his family members sit at the helm of a series of interlocking organizations and ministries, none of which abide by the accountability guidelines of the Evangelical Council for Financial Accountability or of Ministry Watch. He controls a nearly $40 million annual budget, including school, Bible college, and television program broadcast on fourteen hundred stations around the world.

Parsely may call himself a "Christocrat" rather than a Republican, but he has moved deep into the Republican fold, with members of Congress, governors, and the White House ardently seeking his support. Parsley stood at Bill Frist's side at a press conference supporting the appeals court nomination of right-wing California supreme court justice Janice Rogers Brown, and was included on a Bush conference call with religious leaders shortly after John Roberts's nomination to the Supreme Court was announced.

For his part, Blackwell has 2006 elections and his run for the governorship on his mind. Speaking to more than three hundred pastors convened by the Ohio Restoration Project in August, he told the activists, "People think November 2004 was just an accident of history. They doubt your ability and your will and your commitment to your faith and your drive to stay engaged and sustain the battle." In case anyone missed the message, he adds, "We cannot sit back and let the public square be stripped naked of truth, of religion, and of God."

The partnership between Parsely, a white evangelical preacher and political activist, and Blackwell, an African American Republican politician, is in some ways an example of what's happening all over the country. The success of Religious Right leaders at mobilizing conservative evangelical Christian voters has helped right-wing politicians win office at all levels—including the White House—and with each success, elected officials move to embrace Religious Right leaders and keep their constituents happy and motivated to turn out for the next election. And these same religious and party leaders are working intensively to make inroads into the African American community through appeals to conservative pastors on issues like gay rights.

Those efforts are lubricated in some cases with piles of money in "faith-based" funding from the White House, which are bearing fruit with some high-profile African American church leaders who are joining team Bush on a range of issues. The host of a "Justice Sunday" rally on the eve of the confirmation hearings for Supreme Court Justice Samuel Alito, for example, was an African American pastor whose Philadelphia church had received $1 million in federal funds; he told reporters he didn't know much about Alito but agreed to host the event because he trusted President Bush.

Parsley also reflects the broadening of the Religious Right agenda well beyond the staples of antiabortion, antigay rights, and anti-separation-of-church-and-state politics. "I'm convinced the best thing government can do to help the poor is to get out of the way. If government reduced taxes, removed industrial restraints, eliminated wage controls, and abolished subsidies, tariff[s], and other constraints on free enterprise, the poor would be helped in a way that [Aid for Families with Dependent Children], Social Security, and unemployment insurance could never match." If that sounds more like Milton Friedman than Jesus of Nazareth, it's right at home in Religious Right circles.

The "reformation" Parsley is talking about—using religious language and people to build power for reactionary politicians and policies—has been under way for a long time. Its successes are clearly reflected in the dramatic shift to the right in the Republican Party over the past two and a half decades, the control of Congress House by politicians elected with the enthusiastic support of Religious Right leaders, and especially the presidency of George W. Bush. In the Bush administration, the Religious Right has definitively completed its march from the political fringe into the corridors of power. They have put two allies on the Supreme Court, with the prospect for radically redefining religious liberty in this country. Americans—and the rest of the world—will be living with the consequences of this paradigm shift for a long time to come.

If democracy presumes "a multiplicity of tongues" debating to arrive at sound policy, this group instead insists that their one catechism become law—or else. At a time when America is growing more religiously diverse, some Religious Right leaders are hardening their insistence that America is and was always meant to be a Christian nation, and are attacking anyone standing up for respectful pluralism as actually engaged in a war on Christianity.

RELIGION YES—THEOCRACY NO

Over four decades ago, presidential candidate John F. Kennedy, a Catholic, spoke eloquently about the place of religion in American public life, appealing to Americans' fairness with an explicit message about core constitutional principles. He traveled to Houston to address a group of Protestant ministers:

> I believe in an America where the separation of church and state is absolute; where no Catholic prelate would tell the president—should he be Catholic—how to act, and no Protestant minister would tell his parishioners for whom to vote; where no church or church school is granted any public funds or political preference, and where no man is denied public office merely because his religion differs from the president who might appoint him, or the people who might elect him.

In sharp contrast, during the 2004 campaign, presidential candidate John Kerry, a Catholic, was forced to choose carefully where to attend church because right-wing bishops threatened to deny him the Eucharist, turning Holy Communion into a weapon in the Right's holy war. But even that threat was not enough for President Bush, who during the 2004 campaign traveled to the Vatican and actually made a direct appeal for church officials to make U.S. bishops more supportive of his political agenda. In a meeting with Vatican secretary of state Cardinal Angelo Sodano, Bush "complained that the U.S. bishops were not being vocal enough in supporting Bush on social issues like gay marriage and abortion" and suggested that the Vatican "push the bishops." In fact, in a reflection of the increasingly strong alliance between right-wing Catholics and the Protestant Religious Right, conservative bishops subsequently joined conservative evangelical protestant leaders to preach that voting for Kerry— the first Catholic presidential candidate since Kennedy—would be a sin.

And while all presidents have invoked God in speeches and been believing men, George W. Bush appears to be religiously of a different magnitude. Imbedded in nearly all his formal talks are explicit or coded religious references. There are multiple reports of him saying privately that God both got him elected and wanted him to invade Iraq. Probably half his political base believe more in the Bible than the Constitution. And when he was asked at a March 2006 town-hall meeting in Cleveland whether he agreed with prophetic Christians who see the war in Iraq and the rise of terrorism as signs of the apocalypse, the head of America's secular government didn't say no. "Hmmm. The answer is I haven't really thought of it that way."

How did we get here?

Religion and religious people are an integral part of American history—and the debates about the proper relationship between church and state are literally older than our republic. The earliest English settlers, the Puritans, fled religious persecution in England but set up theocratic colonies that harassed and executed people they deemed heretics. The experience of state churches not only in Europe but also in the American colonies led to serious debates among our nation's founders about religious liberty. The result is that the first freedom in our Bill of Rights, mentioned in the First Amendment to the Constitution, is religious liberty: "Congress shall make no law respecting an establishment of religion, or prohibiting the free exercise thereof."

Protecting freedom of conscience means guaranteeing that people are free to worship and express their faith, and it means equally that the coercive power of the government should not be used to promote religious belief or take sides when it comes to matters of religion. Religious Right leaders ignore half of the First Amendment's approach to religious liberty, insisting with increasing ferocity that freedom of religious expression means freedom to use the power and resources of the government to promote their religious beliefs.

The modern Religious Right movement, as an explicitly political force, developed in the late 1970s, though the cultural conflicts and pressures had been building for far longer, in some ways since the 1859 publication of Darwin's *Origin of the Species,* in more dramatic ways since the middle of the twentieth century. Many conservative southern evangelicals were fully wedded to segregation, and justified it as a matter of faith; Jerry Falwell himself preached that the *Brown v. Board of Education* decision showed that the Supreme Court justices were not listening to God.

Conservative evangelicals were also furious about the Supreme Court's 1963 ruling in *Engel v. Vitale,* which declared unconstitutional the practice in New York state of requiring students to start the school day by reciting a prayer written by state officials. Of course, neither that ruling nor its successors "threw God out of the schools," as Religious Right leaders claim. Students are free to pray silently at any time, free to say grace over a lunch meal, and share their faith with friends. What the Supreme Court said in that and subsequent church-state rulings was that the government could not impose religion on students attending public school—could not, for example, require a group prayer based on religious liturgy before a basketball game. Later Supreme Court rulings have reiterated the constitutional principle of government neutrality toward religion.

Since the differences between reasonably accommodating religion and inappropriately promoting it are often close calls, there is a lot of gray area. This was exemplified in 2005 when the Supreme Court upheld the neutrality principle in overturning the display of the Ten Commandments in a Kentucky courthouse, but permitting a Ten Commandments monument (originally created as a publicity stunt for Cecil B. DeMille's movie epic) to remain on display outside the state judicial building in Texas because it had been there for so long and was part of a display of other historical markers.

But there's no gray area for the Religious Right, which wants to eliminate the underlying principle of government neutrality altogether. And they may be on their way to doing so, with the confirmation of Supreme Court Justice Samuel Alito to replace Sandra Day O'Connor, who had consistently upheld church-state separation as a bedrock of religious liberty.

Right-wing resentment against the Supreme Court escalated dramatically after the 1973 *Roe v. Wade* decision affirmed that women's right to privacy and personal liberty included the right to make decisions about abortion without undue interference by the state. Indeed, post-*Roe* legal and political organizing to restrict reproductive rights helped to overcome traditional differences between conservative evangelical Protestants and antiabortion Catholics.

The presidential campaign of Jimmy Carter, who spoke openly about his faith as a born-again Christian, energized many evangelicals, but they were bitterly disappointed when he failed to later support their conservative views. Carter recounts his bewilderment when in the summer of

1980 the newly elected president of the Southern Baptist Convention ended a White House courtesy visit by saying, "We are praying, Mr. President, that you will abandon secular humanism as your religion." The lifelong Baptist and Sunday school teacher was deemed by the fundamentalist leader to have abandoned his faith because he took some political stands that right-wing Baptist leaders disagreed with.

The exchange is emblematic of the basic conflict between the values of religious fundamentalism and the values of democracy. Fundamentalism, says Carter, is characterized by rigidity, domination, and exclusion. Since fundamentalists are the true believers, anyone who disagrees is ignorant or evil. They tend to view change, cooperation, negotiation, and other efforts to resolve differences—in other words, the tools of democracy—as signs of moral weakness.

It was during the Carter presidency that right-wing political strategists saw how religious conservatives, many of whom had stayed away from politics previously, could be exploited as a potentially powerful political force. It was then that Republican strategist Paul Weyrich and others made a visit to Virginia televangelist Jerry Falwell to recruit him into politics, and the Moral Majority was born.

The 1980 campaign of presidential candidate Ronald Reagan recognized and exploited this growing movement. In a watershed moment, Reagan appeared before a gathering of more than 2,500 conservative pastors and told them, "I know you can't endorse me, but I want you to know that I endorse you." The election of Reagan brought a heady insider status to people like Falwell, but also some grave disappointments for Religious Right leaders, including the nomination of Sandra Day O'Connor to the Supreme Court. She became a swing vote, disappointing and antagonizing Religious Right leaders with her support for reproductive choice and church-state separation.

Some Religious Right activists complained that Reagan had used them to win the election but was not especially interested in promoting their agenda—a sentiment that led televangelist Pat Robertson to run for president in 1988, acting, he said, on instructions from God himself. (After questioning Robertson on the CNN program *Crossfire* in that year, the author told him off-camera that he was running an interesting but marginal campaign. The reverend looked the author in the eye and said with real conviction, "But I *will* be president of the United States!")

While his presidential bid was a failure in the electoral sense, it left Robertson with a mailing list of more than a million donors across the nation who shared his vision of a Christian nation. After the campaign, Robertson hired young political operative Ralph Reed to turn that mailing list into a political movement. Together they built the Christian Coalition into a powerful grassroots organization that helped move the Republican Party, and the nation's political leadership, sharply to the right.

Robertson and Reed were clear about their goals. They set out in 1990 to take working control of the Republican Party over the next ten years. It was retail politics motivated by religious fervor. The Christian Coalition built political muscle by recruiting and training people to run for local party precinct offices, to serve on school boards, and enter the electoral farm league for higher office. At the time, Reed explicitly counseled stealth strategies, encouraging candidates to keep their goals hidden until after the election. "I want to be invisible," he declared. "I do guerrilla warfare. I paint my face and travel at night. You don't know it's over until you're in a body bag. You don't know until election night." It is, of course, a sign of the movement's growing political power that now the most extreme Religious Right candidates run openly and win election not only to local office but also to the U.S. House and Senate. (Reed himself is a candidate for lieutenant governor in Georgia.)

At the Christian Coalition, Reed made some major strategic shifts for the organization and the broader movement: he worried that the group would be marginalized within the GOP if it only focused on gays and abortion (though those have always been and still are the major issues for motivating people to give money and take action). So he moved the Religious Right to adopt the broad right-wing agenda. "Pro-family" would come to mean not only antigay, antiabortion, pro-censorship, and pro-government endorsed religion but would also mean tax cuts, opposition to public education, and hostility to government regulation of business. The far-right's ascension to power in the United States is largely due to this marriage of the pro-business corporate agenda with the social conservative agenda; although there are sometimes policy disputes between the two parts of the conservative coalition, they have far more often been allies in electing right-wing officeholders.

Reed also counseled Religious Right leaders to tone down their rhetoric and put a softer face forward, without moderating their political goals. While he could never convince his own boss, Pat Robertson, to follow that advice, it eventually became central to the strategy of George W. Bush, who ran for the 2000 GOP presidential nomination as a "compassionate conservative" and all-around nice guy.

In early jockeying for that election, many Religious Right leaders were lending their support to then-senator John Ashcroft, who withdrew to focus on maintaining his Senate seat. Bush, the overwhelming favorite of business and party leaders, quietly met with Robertson, Falwell, and other Religious Right leaders to win their support. Crucial to winning that support was his pledge to give them the kind of Supreme Court judges they wanted. And the Religious Right responded, publishing tens of millions of voter guides and mobilizing turnout through conservative churches.

After Bush strategist Karl Rove calculated that some four million Religious Right voters had sat out the 2000 elections, he focused with ferocious determination on keeping these voters motivated through a combination of policies, rhetoric, and fear-mongering. As Michele Kottle of *The New Republic* put it, "Karl Rove would rather risk an international holy war than a drop in Bush's support among Christian conservatives." A particularly toxic example of this strategy was mailings by the RNC during the 2002 elections claiming that liberals wanted to force people to give up their Bibles. By Bush's 2004 reelection bid, it all came together religiously and politically. The formidable Republican turnout machine focusing on conservative evangelical pastors and churches made a major contribution to victories for Bush and Senate candidates in a number of states, including the ultimately decisive Ohio race.

Some of the more overt politicking by churches and pastors—like Ohio's Rod Parsley—is drawing complaints to the Internal Revenue Service. The tax-exempt status churches enjoy under federal law and the tax deduction individuals can take for their contributions come with restrictions against electoral politics. The line between talking about issues (okay) and endorsing candidates (not) can be cleverly fudged. Religious Right groups and churches have often pushed the envelope, although their voter guides leave little doubt about their intentions. Endangered incumbent and Religious Right favorite Sen. Rick Santorum of Pennsylvania was featured on videotape, and essentially endorsed, by organizers of the Pennsylvania Pastors Network, which plans a 2006 get-out-the-vote effort run by a former Bush campaign aide. The IRS has said it will be taking a closer look at politicking by churches and other religious groups this year, but one of its most high-profile recent actions was not directed against the Religious Right, but was an investigation of a 2004 sermon by a pastor at liberal All Saints Episcopal Church in Pasadena, California, and a threat against the church's tax-exempt status.

WHO ARE THEY?

When we talk about the Religious Right, we're talking about a spectrum of groups, from Reconstructionists or Dominionists, who want to see their version of Old Testament law imposed on society, to political groups more concerned about electing enough right-wingers to public office to ensure that gay people are never treated equally under the law. And the lines that separate the fringe from the "mainstream" can be quite thin—U.S. Senator Tom Coburn, for example, who was elected with the energetic assistance of James Dobson, has said he would support the death penalty for doctors who perform abortions.

Here are just four of the key players who are not merely tolerated zealots but rather close confidants to Republican officials and leaders:

James Dobson is, according to *Time Magazine,* one of the "twenty-five most influential evangelicals in America." When it comes to politics, few can match Dobson's influence and reach. As the head of Focus on the Family, Dobson, a psychologist by profession, oversees a massive media empire which has enabled him to become a household name for millions who have come to know him through his books, videos, and radio programs providing parental and marital advice. Focus on the Family's eighty-one-acre headquarters in Colorado is so massive, in fact, that it has its own zip code.

Dobson uses his influence to promote a wide variety of right-wing political views, accusing the gay rights movement of seeking the "utter destruction of the family," urging parents to pull their children out of public schools, comparing federal court judges to Nazis, and even likening the U.S. Supreme Court to the Ku Klux Klan.

In recent years, Dobson has increasingly used his media empire and folk-hero status among conservative Christians to make himself a power broker in the Republican Party. He has threatened GOP leaders that he will urge his followers to abandon the party if its leaders do not push a right-wing social agenda more aggressively. He worked hard to try to defeat moderate conservative Sen. Arlen Specter, the long-time senator from Pennsylvania, campaigning in the GOP primary for Specter's right-wing challenger.

And since Democrat Ken Salazar won election to the U.S. Senate from Dobson's home state of Colorado in 2004, Dobson has essentially declared war on the freshman senator, launching a series of rhetorical attacks on Salazar and accusing him of religious bigotry.

Tony Perkins heads the Family Research Council, which was originally part of Dobson's empire and then spun off under the leadership of Gary Bauer before his own disastrous presidential bid. The FRC has become a central player in Washington politics—when it hosts its religious/political events, Perkins regularly shares the stage with leading members of the House of Representatives and the U.S. Senate.

Perkins is no stranger to the win-at-all-costs approach of the Religious Right movement these days. In 1996, he was the campaign manager for the Republican candidate running for the Senate from Louisiana. The campaign paid more than $80,000 to obtain the political mailing list controlled by former Ku Klux Klan Grand Wizard David Duke, and was eventually fined by the Federal Election Commission for attempting to hide the money it had paid to Duke. Perkins claimed to have nothing to do with the money changing hands, but his signature was on the document authorizing its approval.

Perkins and the FRC have worked closely with Dobson and Focus on the Family on a series of events designed to project the impression that "people of faith" are under attack from the federal courts. This supposed "persecution" has led Perkins to assert that "the court has become increasingly hostile to Christianity, and it poses a greater threat to representative government—more than anything, more than budget deficits, more than terrorist groups."

Dr. D. James Kennedy leads the ten thousand-member Coral Ridge Presbyterian Church in Fort Lauderdale, Florida, and heads Coral Ridge Ministries, the Center for Christian Statesmanship ("restoring a vision for Christian statesmanship among men and women in positions of influence and authority in government"), and the Center for Reclaiming America for Christ, which claims a five hundred thousand-member grassroots network. His Coral Ridge Hour televangelist show says that it is the third most widely-syndicated weekly Christian program, reaching "81 percent of the nation's television homes" on 550 stations, four cable networks, and the Armed Forces Network.

Kennedy has a firm belief that the United States was founded as a "Christian nation" but has fallen prey to "skepticism, atheism, Marxism, humanism, and secularism." He has been highly critical of church-state separation, calling it "diabolical," a "false doctrine," and "a lie" propagated by Thomas Jefferson. "How much more forcefully can I say it?" asks Kennedy. "The time has come, and it is long overdue, when Christians and conservatives and all men and women who believe in the birthright of freedom must rise up and reclaim America for Jesus Christ."

Kennedy's annual Reclaiming America for Christ conference regularly draws senior Republican officials. Among those who have appeared with Kennedy to accept his "Distinguished Christian Statesman Award" are John Ashcroft, Roy Moore, Dick Armey, Sam Brownback, Tom DeLay, and Marilyn Musgrave.

Bishop Harry R. Jackson Jr. leads the Hope Christian Church in the Washington suburb of Bowie, Maryland, and has emerged as a favorite black guest at religious-right events. In a *New York Times* article describing him as "part of a new breed of leaders who have warmed to the Republican stand on social values," Jackson said, "Historically when societies have gone off kilter, there has been rampant same-sex marriage." As Lou Sheldon of the Traditional Values Coalition explains of recruiting blacks into the right-wing movement, "We're looking for African American clergy members who have local authority, and we're getting them to hold a summit on marriage, just one issue."

In 2005, with Sheldon's support, Jackson launched the High-Impact Leadership Coalition, saying, "It is time for both righteousness and justice to reign in America and strong biblical principles must lead the way." Jackson has put forward a "Black Contract with America for Moral Values," featuring most prominently opposition to gay marriage and reproductive rights. Shortly before the 2004 election, he outlined a strategy against the "gay agenda": "Gays have been at the helm of a fourfold strategy for years, but the wisdom behind their spiritual, cultural, political, and generational tactics is clearly satanic."

One of the strategies these men employ is to create a fictionalized view of the Founders and their intentions. As noted, this includes

Thomas Jefferson, whose unorthodox religious beliefs even brought him condemnation from the fundamentalists of his day. But Jefferson's life and language do not neatly fit the Religious Right mold. One of the inscriptions on the Jefferson Memorial, taken from his Bill for Establishing Religious Freedom, says, "No man shall be compelled to frequent or support any religious worship or ministry or shall otherwise suffer on account of his religious opinions or belief, but all men shall be free to profess and by argument to maintain, their opinions in matters of religion."

Contrast that to the Bush White House, which is:

+ doling out billions of dollars to political friends through the "Faith Based Initiative";
+ diverting huge sums of family planning funds to religious "abstinence only" programs that replace comprehensive sex education with programs that deny potentially life-saving information about disease and pregnancy prevention;
+ pouring millions of dollars of federal funds into religious schools in the District of Columbia;
+ appointing federal judges who want to roll back precedents that protect public school students from religious coercion; and
+ trying to eliminate civil rights provisions that prevent federal funding for programs like Head Start from being used to support programs that discriminate in hiring on the basis of religion.

These actions seem to be motivated by a combination of the president's religious beliefs and Karl Rove's political calculations, which have built one victory after another by tending carefully to their Religious Right base. After Bush's 2004 victory, Religious Right leaders boldly announced Bush's debt to them and brandished it to their political ends. Noted the Southern Baptists' Richard Land, "As we say in Texas, he's going to dance with the one who brung him. We haven't come to this place to go home and not push our values and our beliefs." Even more bluntly, the president of the infamous Bob Jones University posted an open letter to Bush on the school's website: "In your reelection, God has graciously granted America—though she doesn't deserve it—a reprieve from the agenda of paganism. Put your agenda on the front burner and let it boil. You owe the liberals nothing. They despise you because they despise your Christ."

Early in 2005, members of the Arlington Group, an influential sort of coordinating council for the Religious Right, pushed Bush into publicly backing an antigay constitutional amendment by threatening to withhold support for his Social Security reform if he did not make their issues a higher priority. He obediently endorsed the federal marriage amendment, and now has no more loyal group of supporters.

The Religious Right's grip on the Republican Party nationally was affirmed in spring 2006 when Senator John McCain—long respected across the political spectrum for speaking his mind—agreed to give the commencement address at Jerry Falwell's Liberty University. During the 2000 presidential primaries, McCain had famously sparred with Robertson and Falwell, calling them "agents of intolerance," and was vehemently opposed by Religious Right groups. But McCain has apparently decided that he cannot win a Republican presidential nomination without the Religious Right's blessing. When McCain's kiss-and-make-up with Falwell drew groans of disappointment—Jon Stewart of Comedy Central's *Today Show* asked "Has the Straight Talk Express been rerouted through Bullshit Town?"—McCain said unconvincingly that Falwell was no longer an agent of intolerance. When Stewart asked on air if McCain was going to "crazy base world," McCain answered, "I'm afraid so." McCain's willingness to put at risk his strongest political asset—the public perception of him as an independent maverick—in order to pander to Falwell makes it clear that even his iconic status as a "maverick" war hero could not shield him from the Religious Right's power within the GOP.

THE IMPACT ON AMERICA

Until now, cornerstones of our constitutional democracy have been religious liberty, separation of church and state, and a bottom-up interaction between people and rulers. But with John Roberts and Samuel Alito joining the Supreme Court, and other vacancies possible during the Bush presidency, we could soon see an erosion of the constitutional principle of government neutrality toward religion, one of the few things that has kept the Religious Right in check. Then its impulse toward a kind of Religious McCarthyism—a top-down authoritarianism which squelches diversity and debate in favor of one God and one truth—becomes the new First Amendment.

While much of the daily assault on religious liberty and church-state separation happens well below the radar of the national media—at local school board meetings, in individual classrooms and courtrooms, in promises made behind closed doors—a lot of it is also being carried out in full view. Anyone who is concerned about the threat to democratic values posed by the increasing power of the fundamentalist right will not be able to say that they didn't see it coming.

Religious Right leaders, for example, are quick to denounce "big government" and support cuts in Medicare programs to pay for tax breaks for the wealthiest Americans. But they are more than willing to use the power of government to enforce their religious values and intrude into the most intimate personal areas of life, including who we love and how we live and die.

Their groups have worked hard and successfully in recent years to stop progress toward legal equality for gays and lesbians, and to actually begin rolling back advances that have been made in protecting the lives and families of gay Americans (see the section "Discrimination and Democracy" in chapter 8). Under the banner of "preserving" marriage, Religious Right organizations led ballot campaigns to deny marriage rights to gay and lesbian couples; but many of the constitutional amendments go much further to deny any legal recognition of non-married couples.

This agenda includes aggressive efforts to overturn *Roe v. Wade* de facto and de jure through passage of increasingly severe restrictions on choice and access (as in South Dakota) and by bullying and intimidating of doctors and health clinics. Legal journalist Dahlia Lithwick calls this the "theocratic heckler's veto."

This movement reflects what conservative writer Andrew Sullivan argues is an essential incompatibility between religious fundamentalism and democratic pluralism. Sullivan, who uses the word "Christianist" to describe those "who have used the Gospels to perpetuate their own aspirations for power, control, and oppression," writes:

> Could Opus Dei members refuse to prescribe contraceptive pills? Could scientologists refuse to prescribe antidepression medicines? Could a fundamentalist refuse Viagra to a gay man or a single woman? And so on. There was a time when religious faith was not so

extreme that it would not allow for a separate sphere for professional life—for dealing with people outside a particular tradition or faith. We once allowed for strong religious faith but also for a neutral but respectful public square. What fundamentalism does is demand the complete submission of all parts of life—professional, civic, political—to the demands of dogma. This is just the latest repercussion. It won't be the last.

Of course, the most visible display of the Religious Right's willingness to trammel democratic processes and butt into personal decisions was the wrenching case of Terri Schiavo. The family struggle that became a legal battle over the fate of this unfortunate woman had been going on for years. Most Americans, however, were only drawn into the debate in 2005 when the religious Far Right bullied Congress and the White House into a last-minute intervention to try to prevent the feeding tube from being withdrawn from a woman who had been in a persistent vegetative state for fifteen years. On one side was Terri's husband, Michael, who was seeking to remove the feeding tube that kept his wife alive, claiming this was Terri's expressed wish. On the other side were Terri's parents, who opposed Michael's efforts and who were increasingly aided by the Religious Right and the politicians who jump when those organizations make demands.

Terri Schiavo had inexplicably collapsed in 1990 as a young woman, and the resulting lack of oxygen to her brain caused catastrophic damage. It has been theorized that a chemical imbalance possibly related to an eating disorder could have been responsible, but no one really knows. After she had been kept alive by feeding tube for eight years, her husband Michael gave up hope of recovery and moved to have the tube removed. Many families face these excruciating decisions, and most come to a private and dignified close.

Michael had both the law and Terri's doctors on his side. But her parents launched a protracted legal and, eventually, political struggle to keep him from carrying out what he said were Terri's wishes. Florida legislators and Governor Jeb Bush repeatedly intervened, but Michael consistently won in court—about forty judges in six courts were involved in the case at one point or another always ruling in Michael's favor, and the U.S. Supreme Court declined to intervene six times. Then a Florida law that

Gov. Bush had used to order the feeding tube reinstated was overturned by the state supreme court, apparently clearing the legal obstacles for Michael to have it removed in mid-March 2005.

But the war between law and religion now grew even more contentious. While some Republicans hesitated to get involved where principles of federalism, judicial independence, and the sanctity of marriage applied—all supposedly bedrock conservative principles—armies of Religious Right activists were arguing that their beliefs took priority over Terri's and Michael's. Peggy Noonan then took to the pages of the *Wall Street Journal:* "The Republican Party controls the Senate, the House, and the White House. The Republicans are in charge. They have the power. If they can't save this woman's life, they will face a reckoning from a sizable portion of their own base. And they will of course deserve it."

The feeding tube was removed on the Friday before Palm Sunday, when most members of Congress had already left Washington for the Easter break. But Senate Majority Leader Frist and House Speaker Dennis Hastert were feeling the heat. Frist called the Senate back for a Saturday evening session that would allow House and Senate votes on Monday morning. He sought and obtained unanimous consent for a bill sponsored by Florida senator Mel Martinez to give Schiavo's parents standing in federal court to challenge the removal of her feeding tube—even though federal courts had already twice rejected, on jurisdictional grounds, efforts to move the case out of state courts. Florida legislators were also getting back into the act, with the state house passing the "Starvation and Dehydration of Persons with Disabilities Prevention Act."

During the jockeying, a memo accidentally given to a Democratic senator exposed the politics behind the principle. "This is an important moral issue and the pro-life base will be excited…This is a great political issue because Sen. Nelson of Florida has already refused to become a cosponsor and this is a tough issue for Democrats." The memo, it was eventually learned, was written by a legal counsel to Sen. Martinez, but before the staffer fessed up, some right-wing pundits were accusing Democrats of concocting the memo as a political dirty trick.

During the flurry of activity in Washington, Michael Schiavo had pleaded, "Come down, President Bush. Come talk to me. Meet my wife. Talk to my wife and see if you get an answer. Ask her to lift her arm to shake your hand. She won't do it." William Saletan, national correspondent for the online magazine *Slate*, described the absurdity of her self-proclaimed defenders' actions: "She couldn't speak, but Congress subpoenaed her testimony. She couldn't eat, but protestors brought her bread."

As governor of Texas, George W. Bush had signed a law allowing hospitals to save money by ending life support—even against a family's wishes—for poor patients. The law was actually used in the midst of the Schiavo debate when a Houston hospital removed the breathing tube from a six-month-old baby over the parents' wishes. Yet President Bush made a show of flying back to Washington, D.C., from Texas to sign the new bill, even though he could have done so from Texas. This was an example of the White House political strategy in motion—placate the base on an issue that they care passionately about, and hope that most Americans won't notice or care.

In the end, thanks to courageous judges, the high-profile interference failed. The federal courts quickly considered and dismissed the claims brought under the new law, saying that there was no reason to overturn the exhaustive examination and repeated rulings from the state courts. A judge similarly dismissed a House committee's subpoena for Terri. The U.S. Supreme Court also refused to intervene, and on March 31, 2005, Terri Schiavo was finally allowed to pass.

But the Religious Right and its political allies were not about to let her go peacefully. James Dobson called the Florida and federal judges who failed to intervene "guilty not only of judicial malfeasance—but of the cold-blooded, cold-hearted extermination of an innocent human life." At a conference convened in Washington by the Judeo-Christian Council for Constitutional Restoration shortly after her death, Dobson demanded the impeachment of Kennedy, O'Connor, Ginsberg, Souter, Breyer, and Stevens. Michael Schwartz, chief of staff to Sen. Tom Coburn, called the Schiavo case "an atrocious act of gang violence by judges" and demanded that they be impeached. "I hope they serve long sentences."

Another panel speaker demanding the impeachment of Justice Anthony Kennedy, Edwin Vieira, admiringly quoted Stalin, saying, "Stalin had a slogan and it worked very well for him whenever he ran into difficulty: 'No man, no problem.'" The *Washington Post*'s Dana Milbank suggested that Kennedy beef up his security detail, noting that the full Stalin quote is, "Death solves all problems: no man, no problem."

These threats come from people who have the ear of the White House, who form a political base that Bush feels obligated to satisfy or stroke. But the Schiavo situation turned out to be one where the Religious Right overreached. Not only did they lose in the courts, but they lost soundly in the court of public opinion. Polls showed that Americans overwhelmingly believed it was wrong for Congress and the president to get involved in this family's private struggle. Millions of Americans have faced or can imagine facing the same kind of difficult situation, and they didn't like the idea of a James Dobson trying to make the decision for them.

Former Republican member of Congress John Danforth, himself an Episcopal priest, wrote on the eve of Schiavo's death that "by a series of recent initiatives, Republicans have transformed our party into the political arm of conservative Christians....High-profile Republican efforts to prolong the life of Ms. Schiavo, including departures from Republican principles like approving congressional involvement in private decisions and empowering a federal court to overrule a state court, can rightfully be interpreted as yielding to the pressure of religious power blocs.... The problem is not with people or churches that are politically active. It is with a party that has gone so far in adopting a sectarian agenda that it has become the political extension of a religious movement." The party has "gone so far" because it is increasingly controlled by such intolerant, undemocratic religious McCarthyites. Kevin Phillips, author of *American Theocracy,* estimates that 15 to 20 percent of state Republican parties are controlled by the Religious Right. A *CBSNews/New York Times* poll in 2001 asked, "Which worries you more, politicians inattentive to religion or politicians too close to religion and its leaders?" Republicans emphasized "inattentive to religion" by 53 percent to 30 percent, while Democrats emphasized "too close to religion" by 59 percent to 27 percent.

According to Republican Party pollster Tony Fabrizio, "Every time I've stratified out the Republican Party, we've come up with roughly 45 to 50 percent of the party that falls into the category of being theocrats." As it stands, nearly half of the members of Congress are backed by the Religious Right, with 45 senators and 186 House representatives receiving 80 to 100 percent approval ratings from the most influential Christian-right advocacy groups.

THE EVOLUTION OF CREATIONISM

One of the contradictions about twenty-first-century America, where our daily lives depend in countless ways on scientific discovery and innovation, is that antiscientific religious fundamentalism has become a growing cultural and political force. So, in an era when the Hubble space telescope gives us breathtaking images of the birth and death of whole galaxies and insights into the formation of our own solar system billions of years ago, we also have rising on the outskirts of Cincinnati a $25 million Creation Museum dedicated to the belief that the earth was created in seven literal days just six thousand years ago, and that dinosaurs not only roamed the earth with man but also rode in Noah's Ark.

It might be tempting to dismiss the young-earthers as a fringe group with no real impact beyond its own tiny group of adherents. But one sign of their widening cultural influence is how some IMAX theaters, which often show science documentaries, are refusing to book features that even mention scientific theories which might offend religious fundamentalists' worldview. A dozen science centers with IMAX theaters turned down a 2003 documentary called "Volcanoes of the Deep Sea" because it included brief references to evolution. The Fort Worth Museum of Science and History initially decided not to book the documentary after showing it to a sample audience and getting negative comments from people who thought it was "blasphemous." (Fortunately, the museum reconsidered after a public outcry.) Because only a few dozen theaters show the large-format IMAX movies, even the refusal of a relative handful can have an impact on a film's revenues, which could make it harder for scientific documentaries to even get made.

In the 150 years since Darwin published his *Origin of the Species,* an overwhelming scientific consensus supporting the explanatory power of Darwin's theory has emerged. But for opponents, the theory of evolution reduces human beings' place in creation and leads to a host of ills. Typical is the comment by the Heart of Kansas Southern Baptists' Pat Bullock, who says "Same-sex marriage, abortion, are symptoms of the cause of rejecting a Supreme Being, taught through evolution."

The battle over the teaching of evolution in public schools has a long history. The defendant in the legendary 1925 *Scopes* trial, or "monkey trial," was a high school teacher who violated Tennessee's law against the teaching of evolution—Mississippi and Arkansas passed similar laws in the 1920s. Scopes was found guilty of a misdemeanor, but the high-profile trial, and the 1955 play and 1960 movie based on it, became sealed in the popular culture as a clash between science and religion.

Many scientists and religious people see no such conflict and have long reconciled faith with the quest to understand the universe. Brown University biology professor Dr. Kenneth Miller, for one, has written science textbooks as well as a book that critiques creationism and Intelligent Design and reconciles faith in God and faith in science. Dr. Robert Jones, the director of the Center for American Values in Public Life, says the creationists "are trying to get science to do something it's not designed to do—answer questions of ultimate meaning—or to get religion to do something it is not designed to do—answer questions about scientific mechanisms and processes."

Fundamentalists who think the teaching of evolution undermines faith have never given up their quest to get evolution out of science classrooms, or, more recently, to have it taught side-by-side with religious theories of creation. Until now, anyway, they have been stymied by the federal courts. For example, Tennessee was on the losing end of a 1973 federal court ruling that overturned a state law requiring that creationism be given equal time with evolution. The court said the law "advances a religious doctrine by requiring either the banishment of the theory of evolution from public school classrooms or the presentation of a religious viewpoint that rejects evolution in its entirety." And in 1987, the U.S. Supreme Court deemed unconstitutional a Louisiana law requiring schools to give fair and balanced treatment to creationism and evolution. In *Epperson v. Arkansas*, the Court said it wasn't permissible to tailor public school curricula to religious doctrine.

Creationism advocates immediately began to reposition themselves as advocates for scientific, not religious, critiques of evolution, repackaging creationism as "creation science" and later as "intelligent design." Advocates for intelligent design, or ID for short, have built think tanks and tout the presence of some PhD scientists to give them the appearance of credibility. They portray themselves as advocates for freedom of scientific inquiry battling an entrenched status quo. Their goal is to create the appearance that there is a robust scientific debate about the essentials of evolutionary theory, a debate being squashed by the scientific establishment. And mirroring the Religious Right's larger legal strategy to undermine church-state separation, they began to drape themselves in principles that appeal to Americans—fairness and free speech—and ask "only" that students be "taught the debate."

President Bush has publicly endorsed this strategy, saying that he hasn't made up his mind about evolution. He added that "both sides ought to be properly taught...so people can understand what the debate is about."

The screaming fallacy behind all of this is that there is no real debate within the scientific community. In oversimplified shorthand, intelligent design advocates claim that evolution cannot possibly explain some things, like the workings of an eye, or the complicated machinery of protein activities in cells. These systems, they say, require all the parts to be there to function, and so must have been created by an intelligent designer. This is not a new concept. Two hundred years ago, English clergyman William Paley said that if you found a watch in a field, you would know that someone had built it not that it had evolved.

This kind of example has some appeal to people without in-depth knowledge of the science—i.e., a vast majority of the public. But it has no serious following in scientific circles. *Newsweek*'s Jonathan Alter wrote in 2005 that "the most clever thing about intelligent design is that it doesn't sound like nonsense.... The scholarly articles are often well-written and provocative. But the science within these papers has been demolished over and over by other scientists."

A 2004 cover story in *National Geographic* focused on the "over-whelming evidence" for evolution. In 2002, the American Association for the Advancement of Science passed a resolution calling ID a "philo-sophical or theological concept" and said it should not be taught in science classes, a position shared by every reputable scientific organization. Indeed, there is practically no support for the "science" of intelligent design even among places where you might expect otherwise. Baylor University, a Baptist institution deep in the heart of Texas, bid goodbye to one of ID's prominent proponents, William Dembski, who set up a Center for Science and Technology at Southern Baptist Seminary in Louisville. The director of an institute on church-state studies at Baylor told a reporter, "I teach at the largest Baptist university in the world. I'm a religious person. And my basic perspective is intelligent design doesn't belong in science class."

Not to be deterred, ID's proponents, having failed in the scientific marketplace of ideas, are seeking what Alter calls the equivalent of a government bailout, "going around their scientific peers to Red State politicians trying to slip religious dogma into the classroom." And not just at the state level. Pennsylvania senator Rick Santorum almost snuck an amendment designed to discourage the teaching of evolution into President Bush's No Child Left Behind legislation; it actually passed the Senate before an outpouring of protest from the scientific community removed it from the final bill.

Unfortunately, their public relations campaigns, and the vocal support of Religious Right leaders and allied politicians, have had an effect on public opinion. About 45 percent of Americans believe humans were created in their present form ten thousand years ago, a statistic that shocks scientists and educators. And 60 percent support teaching evolution and creationism side by side.

One concrete way in which ID's political influence is being felt beyond the classroom is in the National Park Service, which since 2004 has stopped estimating the age of the Grand Canyon, and which stocks in its store at the Grand Canyon a book challenging the scientific consensus about the geology of the canyon in favor of a "young-Earth," great-flood interpretation.

Efforts to restrict the teaching of evolution or require some form of "equal time" pop up all over the country. One of the most recent high profile cases came out of central Pennsylvania. Lawyers at the Thomas More Law Center, funded by conservative Catholic Domino's Pizza billionaire Tom Monaghan, had been shopping for a school board willing to be a test case. They found one in Dover, Pennsylvania, where a number of school board members had a record of trying to get more religion into the schools. In 2004, with the promise of free legal representation by Thomas More, and over the advice of the board's own attorney, the board voted to require that a school administrator read a statement in classrooms questioning evolution and encouraging students to read *Of Pandas and People,* the main creationist/intelligent design textbook.

With the help of the ACLU and Americans United for Separation of Church and State, a group of parents took the board to court in what some considered the Scopes trial for the twenty-first century. At the trial, school board members tried to cover up the clear religious intent behind the new policy. But U.S. District Judge John E. Jones delivered a scathing rebuke to the board members in his ruling. "It is ironic that several of these individuals, who so staunchly and proudly touted their religious convictions in public, would time and again lie to cover their tracks and disguise the real purpose behind the ID Policy."

Judge Jones, described by an AP reporter as a Republican and a churchgoer, wrote that the trial yielded "overwhelming evidence" that ID "is a religious view, a mere re-labeling of creationism, and not a scientific theory." He said the policy was one of "breathtaking inanity" and that "[t]he students, parents, and teachers of the Dover Area School District deserved better than to be dragged into this legal maelstrom, with its resulting utter waste of monetary and personal resources."

Residents of Dover apparently agreed and were shocked by the $1 million legal bill suddenly foisted on their community. The school board's willingness to get in bed with the Religious Right—and put the town's education budget at risk—angered many of the voters in the overwhelmingly Christian community, and on Election Day 2005, a little over a month before Judge Jones's ruling, all eight school board members who initiated the policy were evicted by voters. Televangelist Pat Robertson was beside himself. Going on the air, he declared that Dover residents shouldn't even bother praying if a Katrina-like crisis came their way because they had snubbed God and so he wouldn't come to their aid.

Fortunately, scientists and advocates for the teaching of science are well organized and fighting back—and showing a sense of humor. In response to ID advocates' list of three hundred people with PhDs claiming there was a real debate about the "science" of ID, the National Center for Science Education produced a letter to the contrary (in memory of biologist Steven Jay Gould) that was quickly signed by more than five hundred scientists named Steven or Stephanie.

In addition to making clear that there is no real scientific "debate" to teach, scientific organizations are also exposing the religious purposes behind ID. They have published the "wedge strategy" memo by the Discovery Institute's Center for Renewal of Science and Culture, a major proponent of ID, which has as a principle goal the replacement of "materialistic explanations with the theistic understanding that nature and human beings are created by God." Percival Davis, professor of life science at Hillsborough Community College in Tampa, Florida, and a coauthor of ID textbook *Of Pandas and People,* said, "Of course my motives were religious. There's no question about it."

Fortunately, principled opposition to ID comes from across the political spectrum. Conservative columnist Charles Krauthammer has dismissed ID as a "tarted up version of creationism" and says, "To teach faith as science is to undermine the very idea of science, which is the acquisition of new knowledge through hypotheses, experimentation, and evidence.... To teach it as science is to discredit the welcome recent advances in permitting the public expression of religion. Faith can and should be proclaimed from every mountaintop and every city square. But it has no place in science class. To impose it on the teaching of evolution is not just to invite ridicule but to earn it."

Co-Opting the Courts

Several weeks before the November 2004 election, President (and presidential candidate) George W. Bush met with a group of major donors behind closed doors. Bush told the gathering that he would have one Supreme Court vacancy to fill shortly after his inauguration, and up to four during his second term. "Won't that be amazing? Can you imagine? Four appointments!" marveled one delighted donor.

The potential for a monumental shift on the Supreme Court under a second Bush term may have been news to that donor, but it was no surprise to Bush's backers in the Religious Right. As noted previously, the future of the Supreme Court, and Bush's praise for far-right Justices Antonin Scalia and Clarence Thomas, have been a primary motivation for the intense backing that Religious Right leaders gave Bush in both his presidential bids. They see the Supreme Court as the key to achieving all their major objectives, primarily overturning *Roe v. Wade,* bringing back state laws that criminalize gay people, and dismantling the separation of church and state.

If you don't listen to Religious Right radio or television programs, or follow the movement closely, you'd probably be surprised at the depth of anger and hostility directed toward the Supreme Court and the federal courts in general. Their broadcasts, publications, and emails bristle with denunciations of "judicial tyranny" and call for impeachment of Supreme Court justices and other judges. "Over the last forty years, liberals have won battle after battle in the war against Christianity—almost totally in the courts," says Rick Parsley's Center for Moral Clarity. "Beginning in 1962 with the ban on prayer in public schools to the removal of the Ten Commandments, liberals have used the court system and the judiciary tyranny they wage to circumvent the democratic process and further their political agenda. Because the judges of the Supreme Court are accountable to the law and not the people, they have no system of accountability…. As long as Christians sit idly by and allow black-robed radical judges to tear away at our moral foundation through their judicial activism, they will shape our culture as they see fit."

Pat Robertson has led prayer campaigns asking God to create vacancies on the Supreme Court, and has even said that revolution might be called for to free Americans from the tyranny of the courts. But the radical right doesn't need to resort to armed revolution. They're bringing about their constitutional revolution—actually a constitutional counterrevolution—by having elected a very conservative Senate and a president who shares their view of the Constitution, and who is about to cement that view for decades to come through his appointments to the Supreme Court.

Strangely enough, the most intense right-wing anger in recent years has been directed not at the court's moderate-to-liberal justices, but at the centrist conservatives Sandra Day O'Connor and Anthony Kennedy. Both were part of the majority in the 2003 *Lawrence v. Texas* decision, which overturned state sodomy laws. What underlies most of the anger is a fundamental divide over the meaning of religious liberty in America. This divide plays out daily in below-the-public-radar disputes in individual schools and in high-profile efforts by the White House to a) divert federal tax dollars into religious ministries, and b) to strip from federal law provisions that prevent federal dollars from funding programs that discriminate on the basis of religion.

A couple of stories make these divisions clear:

One day, Mississippi mother Lisa Herdahl stopped by her children's' school and heard prayers to Jesus over the school intercom. Herdahl, herself a Christian, instinctively knew that public school wasn't the place for that, and she tried to end the practice, first quietly and behind the scenes and, when that failed, with a lawsuit against the school district. Her neighbors in the conservative community of Ecru, Mississippi, quickly rallied against her and in defense of the school district. Herdahl's opponents said they were acting in the name of religious liberty. But of course Herdahl was not asking to restrict anyone's freedom to worship or express their faith or pass it on to their children but only that students attending public school not be required to participate in prayers that might or might not reflect their own or their family's faith. Herdahl stood up to widespread condemnation and abuse and won a 1996 federal court ruling ending the practice.

Florida parents Steven and Carol Rosenauer attended a school board meeting in 2003, at which their son was to receive an award. The parents were surprised that the meeting began with everyone being asked to stand for the Lord's prayer. The family, which is Jewish, tried quietly to have the practice changed. But when all efforts to reach a reasonable solution failed, they sued the school district with the help of People For the American Way Foundation. "It is very unfortunate that school board members have not recognized that simple respect for religious diversity and for families like ours could have ended this dispute long ago," Steven said. "My wife and I strongly object to the message that the board is sending to our children, and to other children in the community who don't share the board's religious beliefs, that they are somehow second-class citizens." The family's home and car were vandalized with red paint on Passover, and they were denounced by some religious leaders in their community.

A far more high-profile example is the case of Roy Moore, an Alabama judge who invited Christian clergy to lead prayers in his courtroom at the beginning of cases. After those practices were challenged, Moore built a huge following and won election as the chief judge on the state supreme court, where he installed a granite monument to the Ten Commandments in the state judicial center. When his efforts to use the power of his position to proselytize were challenged in court, Religious Right leaders and activists flocked to Montgomery and held rallies outside the courthouse. Moore was eventually removed from the bench for refusing to obey a federal court order to remove his monument and for placing himself above the law.

For his defiance, he has become a folk hero and may end up as governor, a troubling prospect for those who believe in religious liberty and in the rule of law. Moore's defenders said they were marching in the name of religious liberty. But removing the Ten Commandments from the courthouse was not in any way restricting the ability of individuals or pastors to preach, teach, and proselytize to their heart's content. It was about using the power of the government to take sides. Theirs.

They moved a lot closer to that goal when they helped elect and then re-elect George W. Bush to the presidency. The second time around, they didn't have to take him at his word when it came to the courts—he had already appointed some 210 powerful federal appeals and district court judges, many of whom shared the Religious Right's view of the Constitution. Among the judges that Bush nominated, and Religious Right leaders fought hard to confirm, were William Pryor, Janice Rogers Brown, Michael McConnell, Jeffrey Sutton, and Priscilla Owen.

As Bush had predicted to his donors in the fall of 2004, 2005 did in fact become a series of battles over the future of the Supreme Court. Even before Bush's re-inauguration, far-right leaders began getting ready for the inevitable Supreme Court nominations by demanding that Senate Republican leaders abolish the filibuster, a parliamentary rule that is at the heart of the Senate's design and function, because it allows senators to insist on extended debate and protects the rights of the minority party. It's a big part of what makes the Senate different from the House of Representatives, a central part of the checks and balances designed into our constitutional system of government.

As noted, Senate Democrats have used the judicial filibuster—which requires sixty votes to end debate rather than fifty to confirm a nomi-nee—to prevent confirmation of some of the worst of Bush's appeals court nominees. So right-wing groups demanded the end to the filibuster to clear the way for easy approval of even the most extreme nominee. Senate Majority Leader Bill Frist, with an eye to the 2008 elections and his desire to be the favorite of Religious Right leaders, promised to give it to them. But Frist didn't count on the fact that some of his col-leagues—even some quite conservative Republicans—would value two hundred years of Senate rules, principles, traditions, and roles, over the demands of today's Far Right.

Failing to end the judicial filibuster made the far Religious Right go ballistic with anger and threats. Dobson called it "a complete bailout and betrayal," adding that "I think a collision between right and wrong and good and evil is all wrapped up in the outcome of this particular issue."

Throughout more than a year of intense political back-and-forth about the Supreme Court—through the John Roberts, Harriet Miers, and Samuel Alito nominations—there were a few constants, one being Religious Right leaders' willingness to say and do anything necessary to winning a Supreme Court majority, including smearing opponents as enemies of Christianity. They had perfected this art during several of the appeals court nomination debates, running ads accusing Democratic senators of anti-Christian and anti-Catholic bigotry. The attacks got so perverse and extreme that C. Boyden Gray, a White House surrogate, organized ads accusing Catholics such as Ted Kennedy and Pat Leahy of being anti-Catholic because they opposed antichoice nominees.

Rick Scarborough, a Texas minister and leader of the Judeo-Christian Council for Constitution Restoration, explained why the O'Connor retirement was so important to the Religious Right: it gave Bush a "God-given opportunity to change the balance on the Supreme Court. On issue after issue—abortion, sodomy, public display of the Ten Commandments—O'Connor has sided with the court's liberal bloc. Time and time again, Justice O'Connor and her colleagues have used the Constitution as an excuse to force weird social experiments on the nation."

When President Bush was bullied by his own political allies into withdrawing Miers, replacing her with a Far-Right favorite, Samuel Alito, all was forgiven. Religious Right leaders rallied around Alito, praising Bush for what they said was fulfilling his campaign promise to give them a justice in the mold of Scalia and Thomas. On the separation of church and state, it is clear that Alito will move the court to the right and will undermine the principles that O'Connor steadfastly protected. It will be a while before we know if he is as radical as Clarence Thomas, who does not even believe that the First Amendment applies to the states, and that there is no constitutional problem, for example, with a state declaring itself to be officially a Christian state.

THE PERSECUTED MAJORITY: HOW CAN 10% REPRESS 90%?

At the peak of their political power—and while evangelical mega-churches are becoming the dominant institutions in fast-growing exurbia—Religious Right leaders still get significant mileage out of loudly claiming that Christians are a persecuted majority. The assertion that

Christianity is under attack in America—made every day to millions of FOX cable viewers and from thousands of pulpits—now gets an astonishing 60 percent agreement in polls. One of the latest examples is a 2005 book by Janet Folger called *The Criminalization of Christianity: Read This Book Before It Becomes Illegal!* A typical email to activists from the Family Research Council's Tony Perkins reads, "For years activist courts, aided by liberal interest groups like the ACLU, have been quietly working under the veil of the judiciary, like thieves in the night, to rob us of our Christian heritage and our religious freedoms. Many of these nominees to the all-important appellate court level are being blocked because they are people of faith and moral conviction."

In 2005 and early 2006, the Family Research Council organized a series of events under the rubric of "Justice Sunday." The format—a presentation in a large church, broadcast on Christian cable television and via satellite to congregations—was designed to reach and mobilize the conservative evangelical political base. The first Justice Sunday was promoted with the claim that the filibuster was being used to target people of faith, and with a flyer saying that it was unfair to force a young Christian to choose between his faith in Christ and public service.

The second Justice Sunday a few months later was designed to bolster the nomination of John Roberts, but focused on repeating the claim that the federal judiciary has been out to silence people of faith. Focus on the Family president Jim Daly said, "Although they try to intimidate us, Christians are not second-class citizens who need to keep their thoughts to themselves."

Another example of the persecuted Christians strategy was the incessant year-end drumbeating by FOX News commentators like Bill O'Reilly and Sean Hannity about a supposed "war on Christmas" in the United States—not to mention FOX talking head John Gibson's book *The War on Christmas: How the Liberal Plot to Ban the Sacred Christian Holiday Is Worse Than You Thought.* Of course this phony war is also an insult to Christians and other people of faith who face very real and brutal religious persecution in many parts of the world. Yet these religious demagogues go on to say, as Robert Knight of Concerned Women for America does, that stores using "happy holidays" is "an act of cultural cowardice and even an overt attack on Christmas and ultimately the Christian faith." (The Bush family's Christmas season mailing wishes all "happy holidays.")

In March 2006, Religious Right activists gathered in Washington, D.C., for a conference on the "War on Christians," where they were embraced by members of Congress, including Senator John Cornyn of Texas. The two-day conference focused on both the dire threat to the freedom of Christians in America and to their impending triumph over the forces of Satan (liberals, judges, and the like). At the event's banquet, author and activist Janet Folger's speech discussed how gays are well on their way to criminalizing Christianity in America (the theme of her recent book) and she warned people that if they exercise their "right to remain silent" in the face of that threat, they would soon be hearing those words on the way to a jail cell.

An extension of this reverse reality—that 90 percent are being persecuted—occurred at the Air Force Academy where cadets had to run a gauntlet of heavy-handed proselytizing from officers and conservative evangelical cadets. Cadets who chose not to attend religious services were harassed as "heathen." A report by Americans United for Separation of Church and state in April 2005 alleged "systematic and pervasive religious bias and intolerance at the highest levels of the Academy command structure." In June 2005, the superintendent of the Air Force Academy admitted that there was an atmosphere of religious intolerance and said it might take years to fix the deeply rooted culture.

Yet Religious Right leaders refuse to acknowledge the reality and instead claim that the investigation itself was an act of hostility toward the Christian majority. During House debate on an Armed Services Committee amendment designed to prevent coercive and abusive religious proselytizing, Indiana representative John Hostettler fulminated that "like a moth to a flame, Democrats can't help themselves when it comes to denigrating and demonizing Christians." He called the debate part of "the long war on Christianity in America."

PLURALISM IS PATRIOTISM

America's founders gave us the great gift of the First Amendment and its twin pillars of religious liberty—the free exercise clause and the establishment clause. It is the very separation of church and state that has allowed both religious freedom and religious practice to thrive in America like nowhere else, including evangelical Christianity, which by any measure is far stronger in the United States than in Europe. In addition, the Pluralism Project at Harvard University has documented the extraordinary growth of religious diversity in the United States. Project director Dr. Diana Eck says, "Chicago with its seventy mosques and a half a million Muslims is part of the Muslim World...Los Angeles, with its multitude of Buddhist communities spanning the whole of Asia, is the most complex Buddhist city in the world...Cities like Pittsburgh, Nashville, Atlanta, and Houston have splendid Hindu temples."

But rather than seeing that diversity as a reflection of the strength of our freedom, many Religious Right leaders see it as a threat. Our nation's founders wrote explicitly into the Constitution that "no religious Test shall ever be required as a Qualification to any Office or public Trust under the United States." Alexis de Tocqueville understood well the benefit and risk of this approach: when religious liberty was working, he wrote, it was easy to take for granted; but if one waits to see the results of its absence, it might be too late to recapture it.

But today's religious far (f)right show no such tolerance. Despite what the separation of church and state has done to promote the flourishing of religion in America, the Family Research Council compares Jefferson's "wall of separation" to the Berlin Wall, urging activists to "work to tear down this perilous wall and allow freedom to truly ring" lest the United States "follow the Soviet Union into the ash heap of history."

The Bush administration's active efforts to dismantle the wall include its campaign to divert vast sums of federal social service resources to faith-based groups—and to exempt those groups from civil rights protections against discrimination with federal funds. When Bush had a hard time pushing his plan through Congress, he implemented much of it through executive orders. And although administration officials say federal funds won't be used to proselytize, they eagerly tout drug-rehabilitation, job-training, and prison ministries that are built entirely around the need for participants to embrace fundamentalist Christian views.

Religious Right groups were delighted that Bush's 2007 budget earmarked $500 million for groups that would promote marriage. Even though the Department of Education came in for serious cuts in his budget proposal, Bush asked for a 16 percent increase—to $204 million—in programs to teach abstinence in high schools.

The kind of money we're talking about—billions spread throughout the federal government—is enough to win converts of its own.

Televangelist Pat Robertson once spoke out against Bush's plan, warning that government money might compromise the mission of religious groups. But he changed his tune after his Operation Blessing—which hires only Christians—got $500,000 in one of the first grants from the Bush administration's "Compassion Capital Fund." According to a 2006 news report, the group's annual revenue from government grants has jumped to $14.4 million.

Too many conservative Christian leaders are not satisfied with their enormous successes. They see behind harmless characters like Tinky Winky and SpongeBob SquarePants the frightening tentacles of the gay agenda. They don't want anything—neither the Constitution nor the Supreme Court—to stand in their way of building the "Christian nation" of their dreams, where government funds religious schools, where government officials use the power of their office to promote their religious beliefs, where respectful pluralism is denigrated as an attack on Christianity.

So millions of conservative evangelical Christians give Bush their political support because he is one of them—he speaks their language, does not shy away from talking about his faith, and is pushing policies that they like. But millions of other Christians have a hard time reconciling his policies with their understanding of the teachings of Jesus and the call of the Old Testament prophets for justice for the poor and the orphaned and the widowed. Amy Sullivan, a journalist and Christian, brilliantly dissected Bush's faith-based initiative in a *Washington Monthly* article. She pointed out that, for all Bush's talk of using the government to "mobilize the armies of compassion," when it came down to a choice between giving a huge tax break to the wealthiest Americans and changing tax rules to allow more Americans to deduct charitable contributions—a change that would have greatly helped small nonprofits—Bush chose rich over poor, something Jesus presumably wouldn't countenance.

Basically, Bush cannot and has not ever seriously challenged the approach of a constituency which is as profoundly anti-democracy as any group in America. Indeed, he hasn't challenged them because he *is* them. When Gary Bauer was asked who the head of the Religious Right in America was, he answered, "President Bush." President Bush, of course, frequently resorts to religious idioms in his remarks—and numerous reports since 1988, when he was his father's liaison to the

Religious Right, describe him telling ministers, journalists, and foreign leaders that God wanted him to run for president and that "God speaks through [him]."

One among the modern era's sharpest observers of American society, Bill Moyers, summarized it best: "One of the biggest changes in politics in my lifetime is that the delusional is no longer marginal. It has come in from the fringe, to sit in the seat of power in the Oval Office and in Congress. For the first time in our history, ideology and theology hold a monopoly of power in Washington. Theology asserts propositions that cannot be proven true; ideologues hold stoutly to a worldview despite being contradicted by what is generally accepted as reality. When ideology and theology couple, their offspring are not always bad but they are always blind. And there is the danger: voters and politicians alike, oblivious to the facts."

CORPORATE TYRANNY I: PUBLIC POWER IN PRIVATE HANDS

"It is to be regretted that the rich and powerful too often bend the acts of government to their selfish purpose...[But if government] would confine itself to equal protection, and, as Heaven does its rains, shower its favors alike on the high and the low, the rich and the poor, it would be an unqualified blessing."

—PRESIDENT ANDREW JACKSON

They can foreclose on our homes, decide whether we have life-saving surgery, hire or fire us, effectively shutter small towns, and decisively influence legislation. "They" are not official government, but rather the private governments called corporations.

Corporations reside uncomfortably in a democracy based on legal equality because a) they are nowhere in our Constitution since they barely existed in 1787 (so much for "original intent"), and b) they have become "more equal than others," in that self-contradictory axiom from *Animal Farm*. James Madison in *Federalist #51* may have assumed that factions would vie with other factions in the contest called democracy, but he could not appreciate how much influence big business would have in twenty-first century America. Today, Wal-Mart has more employees than Wyoming has people and annual revenues that equal the combined revenues of ten states. Bill Gates has one vote just as fifty million Americans each do, but his net worth exceeds that of this same fifty million.

Over the decades, however, constitutional democracy has decided that such mega-entities are the equivalent of your next-door neighbor or downtown barbershop, just a fictitious person with the privileges of a real human being (due process of law, free speech rights) but without all of the obligations (how does a corporation go to jail for criminal conduct?). In his 1971 book *Politics and Markets,* scholar Charles Lindblom described well the reality that large companies in America are elephants free to dance among the chickens:

> It has been a curious feature of democratic thought that it has not faced up to the private corporation as a peculiar organization in an ostensible democracy. Enormously large, rich in resources, the big corporations, we have seen, command more resources than do most government units. They can also, over a broad range, insist that government meet their demands, even if these demands run counter to those of citizens expressed through their polyarchal controls. Moreover, they do not disqualify themselves from playing the partisan role of a citizen—for the corporation is legally a person. And they exercise unusual veto powers...The large private corporation fits oddly into democratic theory and vision. Indeed, it does not fit.

To "fit" private governments with public power into democratic theory, we've developed a variety of mechanisms. Economic competition can inhibit their market power; state and federal regulation and legislation can limit their adverse impacts. True, businesses complain loudly and consistently about imposed obligations, from "excessive" corporate taxation to environmental, labor, consumer, antitrust, and securities "over-regulation." But the realities of oligopolies and lobbyists and PACs have given the large corporate enterprise a kind of off-the-books power to impose its will on democratic government—and also to keep labor under its thumb, to distribute wealth in grossly uneven fashion, indeed to evade the law itself. Sections on "Political Power: Business, as Usual," "Labor *Pains,*" "Corruption in the Boardroom," and "The

New Aristocracy of Wealth" describe this near-governmental authority in this and the next chapter.

POLITICAL POWER: BUSINESS, AS USUAL

With the rise of the trusts and big business in the late nineteenth century, America began to grapple with the anomaly of private interests being able to dominate markets and governments. In *Wealth Against Commonwealth,* Henry Demarest Lloyd in 1894 described how John D. Rockefeller's Standard Oil company "did everything to the Pennsylvania Legislature except refine it." That decade saw the first anti-big-business backlash, as the rise of the progressive movement at the turn of the century led to new regulatory approaches, such as the enactment of the Sherman and Clayton antitrust laws and the 1906 Food Safety law.

In two other notable periods, business found itself on the defensive politically. The Depression, of course, proved to the public that pure free enterprise could be very expensive. Nor did it help when widespread stock fraud was implicated in the collapse, as New York Stock Exchange president Richard Whitney—who had said "the Exchange is a perfect institution"—went to jail for securities theft. FDR's New Deal included a regulatory web of securities and later labor laws enacted over business's ardent objections. Then in the late 1960s-early 1970s, after Rachel Carson's *Silent Spring* and Ralph Nader's *Unsafe at Any Speed,* Congress again seemed to enact almost any consumer or environmental law proposed. This decade saw the creation of the auto safety agency, as well as the Environmental Protection Agency and the Occupational Safety and Health Administration, with the latter two being signed into law by Richard Nixon.

But with such notable exceptions, business-as-usual in Washington, D.C., and state capitals meant being pro-business. Robert A. Caro's *Master of the Senate,* for example, vividly describes how Texas oil and gas interests had a perfectly symbiotic relationship with Speaker Lyndon Johnson. They were the major source of jobs and contributions in the leader's home state—and he was only too happy to hand out tens of thousands of dollars of their cash in envelopes to grateful Democratic U.S. Senate candidates. They in turn showed their gratitude by supporting Johnson's agenda to help his oil and gas patrons, especially Brown & Root, a predecessor to what today is Halliburton. Here's Caro describing the Johnson way:

"On one occasion," [aide Bobby] Baker was to write, "I was asked to transmit five thousand dollars from Lyndon B. Johnson to Styles Bridges. As was the Washington practice, Johnson handed me the boodle in cash. 'Bobby,' he said, 'Styles Bridges is throwing an "appreciation dinner" for himself up in New Hampshire sometime next week. Fly up there and drop this in the kitty and be damn sure that Styles knows it comes from me.'" On another occasion, in 1957, Joe Kilgore relates, Texas's other senatorial seat to replace the retiring Price Daniel, and was running for the permanent seat in a special election.

"He [Johnson] called me to come over to his office," Kilgore says. "When I got there, he said, 'Come on, I'm meeting Bill Blakely down on the sidewalk.'" We left his office and went down in an elevator. While we were in the elevator, he [Johnson] said, 'Here, hold this,' and stuck something in my hand. I looked down and it was a big wad of money. When we got out of the elevator, we went into a closet—I think it was a janitorial closet. He told me to count the money. It was twenty thousand dollars. In one-hundred-dollar bills. I knew why he wanted me to count it. He wanted a witness. So that he could prove that he had given this money. He gave the money to Blakely saying, 'I just want you to know I'm on your side.'"

Chapter 1 described our current system of campaign finance which creates a presumption of reciprocity that is still anything but democratic. Two leading legislators explained psychologically and politically how it works. Senator Paul Douglas in the 1950s described business interests trying "by a series of favors to put the public official under such a feeling of personal obligation that the latter gradually loses his sense of mission to the public and comes to feel that his first loyalties are to his private benefactors. What happens is a gradual shifting of a man's loyalties from the community to those who have been doing him favors." And fifty years later, Rep. Barney Frank (D-MA) explained how "we are the only people in the world required by law to take large amounts of money from strangers and then act as if it had no effect on our behavior."

Beyond these ties that blind, corporate interests can politically purchase scientists or economists to manipulate data to make it seem, say, that toxic mercury and tax havens are just terrific for the average worker. If that doesn't work, they can send in the lobbyists. As earlier noted, the volume of registered lobbyists more than doubled from 2000–2005 to 34,000—or a quite astounding sixty-six lobbyists per member at any one time.

The sums most industries spend on lobbying are immense. According to the Center for Public Integrity, broadcast media firms spent $35.88 million in 2004 alone on lobbyists in Washington; telephone companies spent $71.97 million; cable and satellite TV corporations, $20.22 million; the drug industry during the same period spent $123 million to pay 1,291 lobbyists, 52 percent of them former government officials. Concludes author Sidney Blumenthal, "The results have been direct: the Food and Drug Administration has been reduced to a hollow shell, and Medicare can't negotiate lower drug costs with pharmaceutical companies. In the 2004 election cycle, the drug industry paid out $87 million in campaign contributions for federal officials, 69 percent of them flowing to Republicans." And since lobbyists now dispense not only selective information but also contributions, they can be pretty hard for a targeted representative or senator to resist.

Whereas almost all lobbying before the Bush era was confined to Capitol Hill, now one in five lobbyists approaches the White House directly. Consider the success story of Kirk Blalock, a former aide to Karl Rove, as deputy director of the Office of Public Liaison, where he coordinated political links to the business community. Then only one year out of the White House, he's become a senior partner in the lobbying firm of Fierce, Isakowitz, and Blalock, boasting thirty-three major clients, twenty-two for whom he lobbies his former colleagues in the White House.

"We've got a problem here," said Allen Cigler, a political scientist at the University of Kansas. "The growth of lobbying makes even worse than it is already the balance between those with resources and those without resources." Former Democratic senator John Breaux, a recently minted and high-charging K Street lobbyist, gallantly defended the honor of his ex-colleagues by explaining that a member would be more influenced by two thousand constituents than by a single lobbyist. In reply, columnist Michael Kinsley joked, "I guess if it's a lobbyist vs. nineteen hundred constituents, it's too bad for the constituents. That seems fair."

One way that corporate interests can go from mere influence to actual control is by getting appointed to make governmental decisions themselves. Just cut out the middleman. Before Vioxx and Celebrex were taken off the market by their manufacturers, an FDA panel had narrowly endorsed their continued sales. But there were nine members of the panel who had previously consulted for these drugs' manufacturers, and if they hadn't voted to approve their former employer's product, the FDA would have stopped sales of the dangerous Vioxx before Merck was forced to do so. Over at the Interior Department, former deputy secretary Steven Griles—who had been a lobbyist for a mining industry when appointed—has been accused of exploiting his position to assist convicted power broker Jack Abramoff.

Also, when the Justice Department was deciding what to do with a difficult tobacco litigation issue, it didn't hurt that the tobacco industry had the following friends around the table as key legal decisions were made:

–*Robert McCullen,* associate attorney general, was a partner in an Atlanta firm doing work for R.J. Reynolds;

–*Theodore Ullyot,* chief of staff, was a partner at Kirkland, Ellis, which had spent decades defending tobacco giant Brown & Williamson;

–*Raul Yones,* chief counsel to the attorney general, had represented Philip Morris and R.J. Reynolds in tobacco litigation;

–*Ralph Boyd,* assistant attorney general, had advised the industry at the Boston firm of Goodwin Proctor; and

–*Karl Rove,* over at the White House, had been a consultant in the 1990s to Philip Morris, doing polling and deciding which Texas candidates should receive tobacco contributions.

There's a final option if all these advantages—gobs of campaign money, data domination, armies of lobbyists, business appointees (so that the regula*ted* become the regula*tors*)—don't work to rig a decision. "If I get desperate enough," laughed coal industry lobbyist J. D. Williams to an audience of fellow lobbyists, "I can usually argue a case on the merits."

Now, in the first decade of the third century of our democratic experiment, nearly all the planets are in alignment for a business takeover of the public government because Bush conservatives control all of Washington's major oversight institutions. With 232 seats out of 435, Republicans have their largest House majority since 1949—and not since 1929 has the GOP held at least fifty-five Senate seats as well as the presidency. When Hewlett-Packard upped its lobbying budget in 2005 to save millions through reduced taxes on profits from its foreign subsidiaries, its director of government affairs admonished that "we're trying to take advantage of the fact that Republicans control the House, the Senate, and the White House. There is an opportunity here for the business community to make its case and be successful."

Consumer and tax policies are two areas where business has been pushing on the open door of our first MBA president, who doesn't appear to have ever initially opposed a corporate request in five years as president. Indeed, after W. refused to seek legislation that would reduce the risk of terrorist attacks on vulnerable chemical plants, but which the chemical industry had adamantly objected to, it became clearer what, notwithstanding his reams of rhetoric about 9/11, his real priorities were—he apparently loved business supporters even more than he loathed terrorists.

Consumer Policies

There are, of course, far more consumers than business executives, but while consumers are diffuse, unorganized, and interested in hundreds of products and services, business executives are usually well organized, well-off, and focused on one product, day after day and year after year. Not only can individual companies command the attention of politicians in areas where they have plants or facilities, but they are also members of national business organizations that amplify their influence. Consider six major trade groups in Washington: the Business Roundtable, the National Association of Manufacturers, the National Federation of Independent Business, the National Association of Wholesaler-Distributors, the National Restaurant Association, and the U.S. Chamber of Commerce. Altogether their constituents employ more than twenty-two million people and account for $5.2 trillion in goods and services. If this so-called Gang of Six were a country, it would be second only to the U.S. in GDP. Their ocean of lobbyists broke the weakened levees of power in Washington in the fifth year of George W. Bush's presidency and overwhelmed innocent consumers below sea-level who couldn't flee.

Take the class action and bankruptcy bills.

The theory of class actions is straightforward: if consumers are cheated in bulk, they should be able to sue in bulk against a dishonest company. So if there was negligence in manufacturing a car or a drug, it's more efficient and equitable for thousands of injured customers to file a joint lawsuit for damages based on similar facts than bring thousands of separate lawsuits clogging the courts.

Yet the 2005 "Consumer Fairness Act" turned this rationale on its head. It was drafted with a Catch-22 frame of mind that moved class actions from state courts to federal courts, where they were more likely to be so large as to be thrown out of court as "unmanageable," meaning that no court would in reality ever rule on the issue.

Jim VandeHei of the *Washington Post* described how numerous huge companies—including auto, gun, drug, and tobacco firms—hid behind a blandly named "Class Action Fairness Coalition" to enact the measure. Among the biggest players was Wal-Mart—the largest corporation in America and a big contributor to Bush and the GOP. Wal-Mart's $2.4 million PAC was the third largest in the country, giving 80 percent to Republicans; its officers gave Bush $30,000 in 2004. But this was only a small piece of a five-year, $168 million lobbying campaign led by the U.S. Chamber of Commerce to overhaul the civil liability system. The investment paid off brilliantly, as 229 of 230 House Republicans voted in early 2005 for the "reform."

Ditto the "Bankruptcy Reform" bill, which made it harder and more expensive for average Americans suffering financial distress to declare bankruptcy. In recent years, personal bankruptcy rates have grown to record highs in large part due to substantial medical bills and declining health insurance coverage, according to Elizabeth Warren, a bankruptcy expert at Harvard Law School and author of *The Two-Income Trap*. But stories of consumer misery were no match for the credit card industry, which made $30 billion in profits in 2004 and showered favored candidates with $7.8 million in contributions that year; in all, an estimated $100 million was spent plying the Congress over eight years.

Leading the way were four firms who were among the top twenty contributors to Bush's two presidential campaigns—MBNA, Credit Suisse First Boston, Bank of America Corporation, and Wachovia Corp— giving over $300,000 each.

One of the fortunate beneficiaries was Charles Grassly (R-IA), who blamed not joblessness or health care costs but "irresponsible consumerism" for record bankruptcies. His bill did nothing to stop large corporations seeking to escape pension liabilities by filing for bankruptcy and never mentioned how credit card companies lure the uncredit-worthy only to inflict quadruple interest penalties when one payment is missed. But the bill did make it far harder for ordinary consumers to seek traditional Chapter 7 protections if they were deemed "able" to pay debts out of future earnings and existing assets under a complex calculation of debt versus income. So United Airlines can get a fresh start, but not a family whose hospital bill for a stricken breadwinner sends them spiraling into a financial abyss.

Tax Policies

Taxes may be "the price we pay for civilization," according to Justice Oliver Wendell Holmes Jr., but corporations prefer that others pick up the tab. Their relentless lobbying to shift the tax burden from capital to labor has proven spectacularly successful. The percentage of federal revenues coming from corporate taxes has plummeted from 25 percent to 7 percent in thirty years. Today, the average line worker often pays only a slightly higher percentage of her income in taxes than the company she works for—and at times even more than the CEO who just left the firm with a $50 million golden parachute.

How do Bush and his business allies pull off "a form of looting," in the words of Nobel economist George Akerlof? Admitting to avarice won't do, so they simply repeat the theory that the economy will grow only if we cut taxes on the needy rich while we cut services to the undeserving poor. Never mind that there's little evidence to support this economic quackery and that slow growth under supply-siders like Reagan, Bush 41, and Bush 43 were only somewhat masked by massive deficits juicing the economy. "It is one of the world's most extraordinary social phenomena," wrote Lindblom thirty years ago, "that masses of voters vote very much like their elites. They demand very little for themselves."

Is it that they hope to *be* the elite? In a country where one survey showed that 19 percent of Americans sadly believed they were in the top 1 percent of income-earners, we're reminded that education must be the keystone of a progressive agenda.

Yet after Bush's four tax cuts reduced taxes on the wealthy some $1.5 trillion over ten years—even after those earning an average of a million dollars a year got a rebate from Washington totaling $89,000 each—Republicans weren't satisfied with lower rates on capital gains, dividends, and other "unearned income." They also wanted nothing less than the elimination of the "death tax." Of course, there is no "death tax"—99 percent of us die without paying anything in taxes—though there is an "estate tax" for the lucky 1 percent who leave behind more than $3 million in assets.

Still, Republicans complain about double taxation and inheritance tax rates of 50 percent to justify their lobbying to eliminate what they characterize as a perfect storm of death and taxes. Except that a) workers too are often "double-taxed" (with the same earnings subject to income taxes, sales taxes, not to mention road tolls), and b) the effective rate of estate taxes is 18 percent, not 50 percent, due to exemptions and charitable gifts, as well as a variety of other estate planning strategies.

The injustice of trying to eliminate what is in effect a "Dead Billionaire's Tax" is not lost on some thoughtful people of great means. The second wealthiest American, Warren Buffet, explained his opposition to the end of the estate tax in an op-ed entitled, "Billionaires Don't Need Another Tax Break":

> The taxes I pay to the federal government are roughly the same proportion of my income—about 30 percent—as that paid by the receptionist in our office. My case is not atypical—my earnings, like those of many rich people, are a mix of capital gains and ordinary income—nor is it affected by tax shelters (I've never used any). As it works out, I pay a somewhat higher rate for my combination of salary, investment, and capital gain income than our receptionist does. But she pays a far higher portion of her income in payroll taxes than I do.

She's not complaining: both of us know we were lucky to be born in America. But I was luckier in that I came wired at birth with a talent for capital allocation—a valuable ability to have had here during the past half-century. If the receptionist and I had both been born in, say, Bangladesh, the story would have been far different. There, the market value of our respective talents would not have varied greatly.

Now the Senate says that dividends should be tax-free to recipients. Suppose this measure goes through and the directors of Berkshire Hathaway (which does not now pay a dividend) therefore decide to pay $1 billion in dividends next year. Owning 31 percent of Berkshire, I would receive $310 million in additional income, owe not another dime in federal tax, and see my tax rate plunge to 3 percent.

And our receptionist? She'd still be paying about 30 percent, which means she would be contributing about ten times the proportion of her income that I would to such government pursuits as fighting terrorism, waging wars, and supporting the elderly. Let me repeat the point: Her overall federal tax rate would be ten times what my rate would be.

Buffet and William Gates Sr. represent a group of super-wealthy people who oppose eliminating the estate tax and dividend taxes because of its projected revenue loss of close to $1 trillion between 2012 and 2021, according to the Center on Budget and Policy Priorities. Remember President Bush's oft-repeated complaint about Social Security's imminent bankruptcy? One trillion would cover most of any shortfall over the next century. "Why should Congress be more concerned about protecting Paris Hilton's inheritance than grandma's Social Security check?" asked columnist E. J. Dionne. "How can a member of Congress even think about raising payroll taxes while throwing away so much other revenue?" They do, because of the power of partyology and a campaign finance system where legislatively interested donors expect and get a return on their political investments.

{ 95 }

So even after three prior huge regressive tax cuts, President Bush signed yet another tax break bill on October 22, 2004, only eleven days before the election. In a hypocrisy rivaling Speaker Newt Gingrich's attacks on President Clinton's sexual misconduct while romancing his own mistress, Bush signed the so-called "American Jobs Creation Act" at a morning rally in Wilkes-Barre, Pennsylvania. "The rich hire lawyers and accountants for a reason when it comes to taxes," the president told blue-collar workers roaring its approval. "That's to slip the bill, and stick you with it."

Of course, that was a pretty good description of exactly what he was doing to his credulous audience. Author Michael Scherer describes the "bill" in both its meanings:

> Though the law began as an effort to end a $5 billion-a-year corporate tax subsidy that had been declared illegal by the World Trade Organization, it had grown into a hydra-headed beast. The law's principal author, Ways and Means Committee chairman Bill Thomas (R-Calif.), jokingly referred to it as "Miss Piggy" on the House floor.
>
> Almost every industry in America received special favors. The tax cuts included half a billion for shipbuilders Northrop Grumman and General Dynamics, $100 million for NASCAR racetrack owners, and $9 million for arrow manufacturers. Importers of Chinese ceiling fans—like Home Depot—got a break, as did energy companies angling to build a natural gas pipeline in Alaska. About $231 million went to reduce the taxes of shopping-mall developers in the states of key House and Senate members. Four Texas companies received special dispensation to shelter their profits in the Caribbean. The law also cut taxes on railroads, coffee roasters, timber firms, and Hollywood studios. General Electric received tax benefits worth more than $1 billion over the next decade.

LABOR *PAINS*

Whatever its flaws, organized labor has an essential place at the table of democracy. Like any powerful organization, of course, it too can be unresponsive, self-perpetuating, even corrupt. But any fair-minded analysis would conclude that it has been an overwhelmingly beneficial institutional voice, in both the economic and political arenas.

When she was a child, Antonia Lopez Paz, a Mexican immigrant living in Tennessee, saw how her migrant vegetable-picking father was helped by the United Farm Workers. So when things got bad at the Koch Foods poultry plant, where she had a demanding on-your-feet-all-day job cutting wings, she knew what to do. "We need to convince people to join the union, that they shouldn't be afraid because the union is the only way to make things better and stop them from mistreating us."

Because the work was so continuous and hard, employees were told that they were not allowed to go to the bathroom during their shift. Lopez described the intense pain of not being able to relieve herself and how one time, when a woman requested permission to go, "the supervisor took off his hard hat and told her, 'You can go to the bathroom in this.'" Appalled about the poor treatment, "sometimes they wouldn't even let us leave to go home when we were sick," and the wretchedly low pay—the top wage was only $7.55 an hour, even for decade-long employees—Lopez finally filed a complaint in 2005. Her complaint helped spawn a wide-ranging grassroots effort to unionize poultry-plant workers in the burgeoning immigrant communities of southern and southeastern states, giving new life to labor in a region not known as a haven for workers' rights. "What I didn't like is they would yell at us and tell us we're good for nothing and we didn't know how to work." Well, Koch foods might think Lopez doesn't know how to work, but she seems to get the job done.

When workers organize, a real opportunity arises to clarify where and how labor's and capital's various interests intersect. Louis Brandeis thought that it is wise *not* to "assume that the interests of employer and employee are necessarily hostile—that what is good for one is necessarily bad for the other...While they have different interests, they are likely to prosper or suffer together." In other words, corporate capitalism need not be a zero sum game. Enabling workers to speak with one voice and negotiate with management in collective bargaining can boost productivity, profits, and pay. A 1982 New York Stock Exchange report showed that productivity would "increase an unheard of 20 percent in one year if employee ownership and involvement efforts were widespread." Economists Richard Freeman and James Medoff conclusively show in their far-reaching analysis, *What Do Unions Do?*, that by fostering a sense of job security and equity, labor unions result in higher perform-ance, dramatically lower turnover, and reduced training expenses.

Organized workers are often the only barrier between sheer corpo-rate exploitation and decent working conditions. Consider the recent story of the broad-based labor-community alliance, the Coalition of Immokalee Workers. It exposed how Taco Bell, one of the biggest restaurant corporations in America, was tolerating horrific conditions on the Florida plantations that grew its tomatoes. Through a combina-tion of boycotts, protests, and stockholder resolutions, low-income migrants, allied with labor organizers and national churches, managed to pressure Taco Bell into acknowledging and altering its predatory "performance pay." This pay had not only been stagnant since 1980 in spite of nearly *doubled* productivity, but workers performed under "near-slavery or indentured servitude conditions"—no holidays or sick days, working under the threat of violence, withheld pay, and squalid living arrangements—more akin to the late nineteenth century than the dawn of the twenty-first.

Maybe Taco Bell operated like this because Chambers of Commerce and CEOs assume that labor is merely a cost rather than an asset. But soci-ety must also pay when an antilabor company intensifies the poverty level in whatever county it operates, while increasing the burden on public assis-tance and stop-gap health providers. For instance, because so few of antiu-nion Wal-Mart's employees can even afford its cheapest insurance coverage on their galley-slave wages, they wind up in tax-payer funded emergency rooms or buying food with federally subsidized food stamps.

In the political realm, without labor's advocacy, we'd never have even the minimal minimum wage, let alone such luxuries as the two-day weekend, pension plans, or workplace-based health insurance. In private industry, three-fourths of union members have medical care benefits, compared with only half of nonunion workers. Indeed, most of our consumer, environmental, and health/safety laws were enacted with organized labor as an essential ally in broader coalitions. The equation is clear: no labor, no reforms.

But as unions disappear from the daily lives of more and more Americans—shrinking to 12 percent of the workforce from a high of over 30 percent fifty years ago—the playing fields of workplaces and legislatures tilt more and more toward wealth over work. Why the decline? Part of it has to do with the fact that fewer and fewer traditional businesses like Macy's or even the New York Metropolitan Transit Authority promote from within, choosing instead to contract out many previously unionized jobs. In the 1960s–70s, 12 percent of those who entered the labor force were stuck in low-wage work ten to fifteen years into their careers; in the 1980s–90s, this figure more than doubled to 28 percent. As Rodney Glenn, director of training for New York's Transport Workers Union Local 100, grimly puts it, "Entry-level no longer means entry-level. It means dead-end." Another part of this decline is more subtle. Elaine Bernard, director of Harvard Law School's Labor and Worklife Program, believes that many Americans now view unions as "a Contracts'R'Us operation that only services its existing members." And not always a very effective service at that, as the recent split in the AFL-CIO between Federation president John Sweeney and SEIU president Andy Stern graphically indicates.

Another obvious cause of labor's decline has been economic globalization, as plants and jobs move overseas where costs are lower, environmental laws fewer, and unions nonexistent. The economic consulting firm Economy.com estimates at least 1.3 million manufacturing jobs—a heavily organized sector—have relocated abroad since 1992, with most leaving after 2000, chiefly to Mexico and East Asia.

Labor's distress shows the natural consequence of broad economic trends like offshoring and outsourcing. Over the last few decades, large corporations and our own government have weakened the collective power of working people, speciously claiming that their attacks on labor are economically necessary to make America more competitive. Everyone remembers President Reagan's mass firing of striking air traffic controllers in 1982. But people tend to forget Reagan's concurrent massive de-funding of the National Labor Relations Board, a federal agency which is supposed to ensure that corporations and unions fight fair. By essentially disarming the major peacekeepers, Reagan set the stage for the lax NLRB of today—a partisan horror-house with a backlog of twenty-five thousand cases of unfair labor practices, each taking an average of 557 days to resolve. Since Bush's appointees have become a majority on the NLRB in 2001, more than twenty-five controversial cases have all been decided in favor of big business, including:

- ✦ increasing the difficulty of organizing temporary workers within an already unionized company;
- ✦ blocking union attempts to gather financial information from businesses during contract negotiations;
- ✦ making it easier for employers to engage in worker lock-outs during labor disputes;
- ✦ ruling against striking graduate students who wish to organize within their universities; and
- ✦ denying nonunion employees the right to have a coworker present when managers call them in for investigative or disciplinary meetings—a ruling that will affect 87 percent of American workers.

President George W. Bush is the first oilman and MBA to be president—and his NLRB perfectly mirrors his indifference or antipathy to organized labor. "They are pressing the outer limits of what could be a reasonable or legitimate interpretation of the balance between employer prerogatives and worker rights," says James A. Gross, a Cornell University professor and author of several books about the NLRB. Already reluctant to throw their objections into the NLRB's bottomless pit, potential whistleblowers now have little incentive to even file complaints in the first place.

President Clinton's attempts at reforming labor and workplace hazard laws, especially his new ergonomic regulations, were swiftly overturned in some of the earliest official acts of the Bush administration, which went on to exact its own loosening of the Occupational Safety and Health Administration's regulations begun by the Republican-led Congress in the mid-1990s. Within a few months, years of carefully crafted legislation decreasing workplace hazards was quietly shredded—despite having already been signed into law. Forget nagging anyone about the lousy job market when, with a deaf and dumb OSHA, those who still have jobs now risk life and limb to keep them.

Further undermining the democratic process within workplaces, according to a study by the U.S. Trade Deficit Review Commission, is the fact that "three quarters of employers facing a union drive hire management consultants and security firms to run antiunion campaigns and intimidate workers" the moment they catch wind of a campaign or strike, threatening to close plants and move them to China or Latin America unless all union activity ceases.

Illustrating this point perfectly are Titan International and its subsidiary, the Condere Corporation, manufacturers of wheel parts and assemblies with facilities in Iowa and Mississippi, which fired three hundred striking workers after threatening to replace workers, lower wages, move work, or close the plant because of the employees' involvement with the United Steelworkers of America. Labeled one of the "Ten Worst Corporations of 2000" by the watchdog group *Multinational Monitor*, Titan's complete contempt for workers' rights drew complaints from even the Republican dominated NLRB. Managers refused OSHA investigators entrance without a warrant, and the CEO laughed at the NLRB rebuke, adding, "I figure in five years they'll get [their lawsuit] to the first federal court. By that time, they'll all be enjoying retirement pay."

This attitude is not atypical. Labor laws in the United States make organizing workers here more on par with El Salvador than Canada—a country that looks like America economically, but has much higher union participation and few obstacles to organizing. The labor education research director at Cornell, Kate Bronfenbrenner, puts it clearly: "Workers have to go through hell to organize in this country." But the American government's and corporations' tag-team assault on unionization over the last fifty years signifies the slow surrender of government's umpire function between the two teams.

The original idea of the labor laws was to allow two interested parties to privately resolve their conflicts with government as neutral moderator. Now, business interests are pitching and, to steal Chief Justice John Roberts's metaphor, also calling balls and strikes. Nothing's foul when corporations get to play the offense and the defense, with labor always in the dugout. This fact is fine with the union-busters, who argue that organizing is just a fight over "property rights." Anyway, in this day and age of at-will employment—a clause that means you are free to be fired for whatever and whenever—these latter-day Pinkertons go so far as to claim that most workers don't even really want cumbersome, wasteful, money-hungry unions.

Which is simply not true. Ralph Nader answers the "right to work" canard: "Given the major benefits, not to mention other advantages of union membership, it is not surprising that, unobstructed and unintimidated, workers overwhelmingly choose to join unions. In the government employee sector, for example, where the employer generally does not contest unionization efforts and workers do not fear punishment, unions win approximately 85 percent of elections."

Even this is changing under Bush & Co. Using Hurricane Katrina as an excuse to call for more efficiency in rebuilding the devastated Gulf Coast, the current administration suspended previously untouchable, and "union-friendly," government contracting guidelines that stipulate payment of prevailing wages and require coherent affirmative action plans. Taking their cues, Republican governors of Missouri, Indiana, and Kentucky are also trying to weaken the unions of organized public sector employees, in part by revoking some collective bargaining rights and disingenuously blaming slashed state budgets and services on "union-blocked" government restructuring.

This is the New World Order, where labor retains rights in word but loses them in deed. Like the men and women of Titan International, workers who still manage to organize a strike are simply put on permanent leave—replaced without being actually fired, a condition allowing corporations to skirt the legal responsibilities of collective bargaining. The government actually protects this ruse in court, refusing to recognize the distinction between a legitimate "leave of absence" and a de facto firing. The hope is that the organizing employee inevitably quits out of frustration, and is denied even the benefit of collecting unemployment for his or her efforts.

These policies not only skate the line of legality, but often run right over it when corporate managers subject employees to hours of antiunion lectures, isolate union organizers, or just go ahead and fire those actively seeking equitable treatment. Adding to the chill is the fact that at least twenty thousand workers a year across the country are fired for trying to organize, despite this being protected action. Just toss these cases on top of the NLRB's mile-high pile. They'll get to it...some day. Now, when Wal-Mart breaks the law with its slash-and-burn antilabor tactics (famously once going so far as to shut down an entire regional Supercenter rather than allowing it to organize), they receive less than a slap on the wrist. The government falls in line and politely asks management to post apologies in the break room. That's it. No fines, no federal overseers, no government lawsuits, nothing to force a compliance with the letter *and* the spirit of the law.

That's because the workplace tilt towards those with the most cash is also felt in Congress. The dizzying expense of seeking office—spending by winners has increased ten-fold in twenty-five years as noted in the first chapter—means that hardly any elected representatives come from union or truly blue-collar backgrounds. Businessmen have Rolodexes of friends with money; nightshift managers do not. And once a candidate becomes a congressperson, he or she understands that incumbents benefit far, far more by cozying up to pro-business interest groups than labor PACs. The author recalls appearing on a *Firing Line* show in the 1990s that was based on this proposition from William F. Buckley Jr.: "Granted, labor has too much political power"—an assertion that fell to pieces when it was shown that corporate PACs outspent labor PACs by *seventeen to one.*

Corporate money swamps labor money not only in elections but also in lobbying. The AFL-CIO spent approximately $26.5 million on lobbying between 1998 and 2004, with only $4.3 million going out in 2004. But the total spent on lobbying in 2004 alone was near $2.14 *billion,* which means labor is being outspent by an astonishing ratio. Clearly, organized labor's ten decibel *micro*phone cannot compete with management's colossal *mega*phone. Yet if capital can have its say, then for democracy to work labor must also have a place at the table, especially because labor argues so consistently for public goods against private abuses. Democracy assumes a conversation, not a command. While capital does have special prerogative in the boardroom, this kind of pay-to-play government offends the First Amendment's bedrock notion that everyone's entitled to redress grievances and to have the ear of Congress—not just those who fund the campaigns of politicians who choose appointees who don't even believe in the labor laws they've sworn to uphold.

V

CORPORATE TYRANNY II: ETHICS AND PROFITS

"Where does income and wealth inequality start to impinge on civil and political rights and on America's long commitment to equality of economic opportunity? Where does it both reflect a failure of democracy and contribute to its weakening? There is a good argument to be made that we are already there."
—ECONOMICS JOURNALIST JEFF MADRICK,
in *The Fight Is for Democracy*

"We can have democracy in this country, or we can have great wealth concentrated in the hands of a few, but we can't have both."
—LOUIS BRANDEIS

CORRUPTION IN THE BOARDROOM

There's a built-in paradox in capitalism. Business leaders must be ambitious but not so greedy that they cut corners or break laws in pursuit of profits. British philosopher John Locke put the best face on this quandary in his timeless observation that "private vice makes public virtue"—and it's true that millions of individuals seeking rewards can produce a vibrant, prosperous economy. But sociologist Robert Merton was probably closer to the reality when he concluded that "a cardinal American virtue, 'ambition,' promotes a cardinal American vice, 'deviant behavior.'"

Which raises the relevant issue of—how much vice and at what cost?

Prevalence and Cost

Apologists for economic crime try to explain away its existence by noting that the public worries far more about street-crime than suite-crime. The *Wall Street Journal* editorialized that "it isn't very helpful to suggest that white collar crime is a more serious threat to the social order than predatory street crime, which inspires fear across the board." The fear part is surely true, for there's something about the massacred Clutter family that made *In Cold Blood* so riveting and frightening. In any comparison between being cheated online or held up with a pistol, losing some money seems like a good deal compared to the chance of losing your life.

Because there's no corpse or complaining victim when it comes to most corporate crime—it could take years to figure out that secretive price-fixing bloated the cost of constructing your home by 20 percent or that your daughter's illness traces to mercury released by a nearby plant—national crime statistics focus on seven measurable categories of physical crimes. But as Woody Guthrie sang, "Through this world I've rambled, I've met lots of funny men. Some rob you with a six-gun and some with a fountain pen."

Indeed, the accumulated economic costs of white-collar crime subtract exponentially more from our economic quality of life than violent crime—and that's no small thing, especially to a middle class straining not to slip into working poverty. Presumably the twenty-one thousand employees of Enron who saw their pensions disappear—or the thousands who suffered disease and death from Vioxx and Celebrex—would confirm the costs of so-called "non-violent" crime.

Business crime is as old and constant in America as business itself, from military suppliers overcharging the Union side in the Civil War, to the bid-rigging antitrust cases of the 1960s that ensnared such giants as GE and Westinghouse, and onto the wave of corporate bribery cases of the 1970s. More recently, spectacular crimes and crooks turned the business pages of American newspapers into veritable police crime blotters.

Since the marketplace is by definition an uncertain place, CEOs may come to believe that the only way to assure stability is to control market forces, which can mean conspiring with competitors or cooking the books. So when managers come under pressure from superiors to meet certain financial goals, they may choose illegality over failure. In his *Theory of Business Enterprise,* Thorstein Veblen wrote in 1904 that "honesty is the best policy" in a small-scale system of handicrafts and neighborhoods, where customers are attended to personally and frequently. But when industry is carried out on a large scale, "the discretionary head of an industrial enterprise is commonly removed from all personal contact with the body of customers for whom the industrial process under his control purveys goods and services."

Numerous surveys document that business fraud appears with disturbing frequency. Four-fifths of respondents to a 1961 survey of the *Harvard Business Review* thought some accepted practices in their industries were unethical. After the electrical machinery bid-rigging case that same year, one convicted executive remarked, "No one attending the gathering [of conspirators] was so stupid he didn't know the meetings were in violation of the law." To test that hypothesis, the author in 1970 sent a questionnaire to the presidents of *Fortune*'s top one thousand firms, asking, among other things, whether "many corporations price fix": 60 percent of the 110 respondents agreed.

A 1998 *Business Week* poll asked CFOs if other executives had requested that they misrepresent financial results; 55 percent said they were asked to cheat, and 12 percent admitted to having done so. A large survey of corporate employees by KPMG in 2000 found that half had observed violations of the law or company standards the year before (perhaps including KPMG executives themselves since eight former partners there were indicted in mid-2005 of tax fraud). And a 2003 analysis by the Ethics Resource Center reported that nearly a fourth of all employees had witnessed business misconduct the prior year.

But prevalence surveys and data alone cannot begin to convey the range and enormity of business crime. For example, it was both amusing and worrisome that when *Lessons from the Top: The Search for America's Best Business Leaders* was published in 1999, based on a "rigorous methodology aimed at identifying the very best business leaders in America," three featured leaders included Ken Lay of Enron, L. Dennis Kozlowski of Tyco, and Bernard Ebbers of WorldCom. If these corporate predators could be called the "best" leaders at one time, what does this say about all those not in the top tier?

Three case studies illuminate what's at stake by the impulse to profit at any price:

Merrill & Blodget

Henry Blodget was Merrill Lynch's rock star Internet analyst during the dot-com bubble. His prized opinions were disseminated on television shows, magazine articles, investor conferences, and trade papers. As *Forbes.com* noted, "Blodget...is a member of an elite group of Wall Street Internet pundits who have the power to decide which net-stock is worthy of investors' money. Their combined power, backed by each institution's sales force, can spark a massive Internet rally." They were the most embraced fortune tellers since the Oracle at Delphi.

With Blodget and others shining green lights on Internet stocks, small and large investors poured billions of dollars into them—investors who relied not only on the blue-chip reputations of major brokerages but also on the so-called "Chinese Wall" which requires brokerages to separate investment banking activity from public research departments; it supposedly shields research analysts from pressure to issue positive ratings with the intention of ingratiating themselves with CEOs in order to win deals worth millions in fees. So a firm's advice can be wrong, but it can't be compromised. Tiger Woods might miss a putt, but no one expects him to take a dive.

For years Wall Street's dirty secret was that the Chinese Wall had been scaled, tunneled under, and dismantled. "Everybody did it" was the mantra, and even after the Internet bubble popped no one expected regulators to do anything. Then Eliot Spitzer, attorney general of New York, dusted off the state's 1921 Martin Act and went after Merrill Lynch to explore whether Blodget's predictions weren't just irrational—but illegal.

Sifting through thousands of emails, he found that Blodget and Merrill Lynch *publicly* rated stocks as "accumulate" (Excite@home), "Top Ten Tech" (Internet Capital Group), "Favored 15 Tech" (Infospace.com), and "an attractive investment" ("Lifeminders"), while *privately* describing those same stocks respectively as a "piece of crap," a "disaster [with] no floor," a "piece of junk," and a "POS [piece of shit]."

Other emails exposed that these reports were issued to mollify investment bankers—and that management knew it. As one Merrill Lynch manager wrote, "We are off base on how we rate stocks and how much we bend backwards to accommodate banking." Analysts that didn't toe the line could find themselves fired.

Faced with this evidence, Merrill Lynch quickly settled with Spitzer for $100 million in penalties and agreed to reforms. Later, Spitzer and the SEC (which he shamed into acting) negotiated a $1.4 billion global settlement with several Wall Street brokerages. On December 21, 2005, a restitution fund began mailing 33,677 checks to investors who lost money because of tainted stock recommendations.

Marsh & McLennan

Marsh & McLennan, or "Marsh," is the world's largest insurance broker, helping clients find an insurance company willing to offer a specific insurance policy for the lowest price. Like all brokers, its legal duty is to the *client*. As Marsh touts, "[O]ur guiding principle is to consider our client's best interest in all placements...We are our clients' advocates, and we represent them in negotiations. We don't represent the [insurance companies]."

Acting on a tip, Spitzer discovered that Marsh secretly accepted payments from favored insurance companies as a reward for steering clients in their direction. Marsh's compensation was contingent on how much business it directed to a specific company, how much clients paid for the insurance, and whether Marsh got their clients to renew the policies.

The firm tried to hide the true nature of these payments by calling them "contingent commissions," "placement service agreements," or "market service agreements." But documents and emails showed the true nature of the schemes: bribes and kickbacks. One Marsh executive, for example, wrote, "We need to place our business in 2004 with those [insurance companies] that have superior financials, broad coverage, *and pay us the most*." Another noted that the "contingent commission payments determines who [we] are steering business to and who we are steering business from."

And Marsh's illegal activity often went beyond soliciting and receiving bribes. Sometimes Marsh solicited phony high-end "bids" from insurance companies during rigged auctions to trick clients into believing that Marsh used competitive bidding to select a company. The winner, of course, was preordained: the insurance company that gave Marsh the most money.

In 2003 Marsh grossed $800 million in "contingent payments" out of around $1.5 billion in revenue. In essence, Marsh was a criminal enterprise running an honest insurance brokerage on the side.

Who was victimized by this breach of trust? The direct victims were Marsh's clients, comprised mostly of large and small corporations, municipal governments, school districts, and individuals. (Once Marsh ripped off a South Carolina school district in two ways: by seeking contingent commission *and* rigging the bidding process.) *Business Week* called Marsh's activity "crimes against capitalism."

As a result of Spitzer's prosecution, Marsh's CEO resigned and the firm paid an $850 million settlement to compensate victims. It also eliminated contingent commissions and agreed to disclose all forms of compensation to their clients. Six insurance executives from three insurance companies pled guilty to criminal charges related to the scheme.

Enron

In 1935, FDR passed the Public Utilities Holding Company Act of 1935 (PUHCA), which busted up the conglomerates that controlled utilities in the 1920s, giving power companies local monopolies, guaranteeing them a reasonable profit, and requiring them to serve local communities. But as the Reagan era dawned, FDR's elegant structure came under attack from conservative think tanks and corporations which wanted to deregulate the nation's electricity markets. In the early 1990s, in Washington, D.C., Enron—a politically powerful gas trading company—and others argued that PUHCA should be repealed, allowing the nation's electricity business to be governed by market forces. Unable to accomplish that goal, they focused on deregulating state electricity markets, with California the grand prize.

The firm hired California lobbyists by the "bushelful" [sic] and "doled out tens of thousands of dollars in campaign contributions to politicians," according to the authors of *The Smartest Guys in the Room: The Amazing Rise and Scandalous Fall of Enron.* "Indicted [and later convicted] Enron titans Ken Lay and Jeff Skilling gave speeches touting deregulation's potential benefits to Californians." They promised efficient electricity markets, consumer choices, and lower prices.

California began deregulating its electricity markets in 1998 but by the spring of 2000 it was experiencing one of its worst energy crises since World War II. Wholesale energy prices skyrocketed while Californians suffered rolling blackouts—a condition usually associated with third world countries. While many factors contributed to the crisis, Enron's cheating ethic played a central role. Its traders had quickly learned how to "game" the electricity market that Enron had helped create. By employing schemes dubbed "Fat Boy," "Get Shorty," "Ricochet," and "Death Star," Enron's traders artificially restricted California's energy supply, raised electric prices, and sold power at those inflated prices.

The results: small businesses shutting down, students sent home from schools, and companies turning off air conditioners in one hundred degree heat.

How did California's crisis become Enron's gain? Subsequent investigations revealed how Enron employees helped create the shortages that produced rate increases of 40 percent. One recorded conversation revealed two Enron traders discussing the possibility of California recovering some of its losses from Enron. "So the rumor's true?" one asks. "[California's] takin' all the money back...you guys stole from those poor grandmothers?" "Yea, Grandma Millie," replies the other. "[T]he one who couldn't figure out how to fucking vote on the butterfly ballot.... [T]he one that Al Gore's fightin' for, you know?"

Another tape recorded the head of Enron's West Coast trading desk describing how a colleague "steals money from California to the tune of about a million." (Both later would plead guilty to illegally manipulating electricity markets.)

Indeed, the one thing investigators couldn't find among Enron's documents was a sense of shame. When a California wildfire temporarily made energy trades more lucrative, two traders described the "magical word of the day" as a "beautiful saying"—*burn, baby burn.*

What are the actual costs to our economy and our democracy of such business fraud?

✦ *The price of distrust.* How many consumers don't buy, how many stockholders don't invest, and how many businesses fail because widespread fraud undermines confidence in a system built largely on trust? Instead of "skill, foresight, and industry" determining market success, in the classic formulation of Judge Learned Hand, swindling and illegality do. "The pharmaceutical company which markets a new drug based on fraudulent test results," concluded criminologist Herbert Edelhertz, "undercuts its competitors who are still marketing the properly tested drugs, and may cause them to accept similar methods."

✦ *The price of price fixing.* As commentators as early as Adam Smith have observed, businessmen have paid lip service to free markets while trying to abolish them. One price-fixing solicitation was detected only because it was taped by Howard Putnam, president of Braniff Airlines. The following is a conversation he had on February 1, 1982, with Robert Crandall, then president of American Airlines, a conversation that led to a Justice Department investigation against Crandall.

PUTNAM: Do you have a suggestion for me?

CRANDALL: Yes, I have a suggestion for you. Raise your goddamn fares 20 percent. I'll raise mine the next morning.

PUTNAM: Robert, we...

CRANDALL: You'll make more money and I will, too.

PUTNAM: We can't talk about pricing.

CRANDALL: Oh, bullshit, Howard. We can talk about any goddamn thing we want to talk about.

Price fixing appears to be both extensive and expensive. A top law enforcement official at Justice told the author that he thought price fixing to be "prevalent," while another antitrust expert analyzed various empirical studies and concluded that, on average, price fixing "inflates prices by some 25 percent or more above the non-collusive or competitive level."

✦ *The price of pollution.* Based on pure-profit loss considerations, companies have a built-in incentive to pollute the surrounding environment: free waste disposal, to be sure, cuts production costs to the firm...but only because residents, workers, and other companies involuntarily pick up the tab in the form of more disease, higher health care premiums, increased mortality rates, decreased property values, higher repair costs, and stunted economic growth. These "externalities," as economists call them, are really a kind of transfer payment imposed by private managers on innocent bystanders. According to the EPA, proposals to strengthen the Clean Air Act protections alone would save between $51 billion and $112 billion each year in reduced medical care, sick days, and lost productivity.

✦ *The price of occupational hazards.* There is a long history of industrial workers often having to trade off health for wealth—injury for income. The good news is that since the creation of the

Occupational Safety and Health Administration (OSHA) in 1970, workplace injuries are down 15 percent and deaths 10 percent. The bad news is that each year, some six thousand workers are killed in workplace accidents (largely construction workers, steelworkers, electricians, loggers, and ditch diggers)—and 5 million are injured, with hospital treatment required for 3.3 million. The company running the Sago, West Virginia, coal mine had chronic violations and an injury rate triple the industry average before the explosion in January 2006 took the lives of twelve miners. OSHA's research arm (NIOSH), has estimated that exposure to deadly chemicals and other toxic materials in the workplace leads to 100,000 deaths annually and 390,000 new cases of occupational disease.

The economic toll of this human suffering? According to a 2003 report from Liberty Mutual, the county's largest workers' compensation insurance company, job-related injuries and illness cost nearly $50 billion annually. Yet during his first five years as president, Bush cut $4.9 million from 170 positions out of the Mine Safety Administration, even though there are only 2,240 federal and state OSHA inspectors to look at 8.7 million places of work. And the $550,000 fine against CBS for Janet Jackson's Super Bowl "wardrobe malfunction" dwarfed the $33,600 fine against the Sago coal mine for 276 violations in 2004 and 2005.

✦ *The price of product hazards.* In the 1920s, the president of General Motors confronted a classic dilemma between ethics and profits: should he put newly developed safety glass in Chevrolets? Eventually, Alfred Sloan Jr. rejected the safety glass because it might increase costs and thereby inhibit sales. "Accidents or no accidents," wrote Sloan to a Du Pont executive, whose firm made the glass, "my concern in this problem is a matter of profit and loss." A half century later in 1983, a federal grand jury indicted the Metropolitan Edison Company, the former operator of the Three Mile Island nuclear power plant, on charges of falsifying and concealing records about leaks at the plant before the accident that shut it down. Federal officials reported that such false reports could have contributed to the severity of the accident—one reactor's radioactive core partly melted when the plant's cooling system lost water.

As the Metropolitan Edison case indicates, the technology of harm has grown radically. It was one thing when a century ago the local blacksmith sold a customer a bum horseshoe: the buyer could soon spot the defect himself and the likely consequence was an unhappy horse. Today, even the most sophisticated consumers can't spot a hidden defect in machinery as complex as cars or reactors—and the potential for injury is not slight to one horse but severe to tens of thousands of people.

Very few businessmen deliberately set out to inflict harm. But occasionally their institutions can so overfocus on the sanctity of profit, the stupidity of "government overregulation," and the importance of being a "team player" that decent people make decisions at work that they would never make at home. The late John Z. De Lorean commented on this syndrome when he was senior vice president at GM:

> There wasn't a man in top GM management who had anything to do with Corvair who would purposely build a car that he knew would hurt or kill people.
>
> But, as part of a management team pushing for increased sales or profits, each gave his individual approval in a group of decisions which produced the car in the face of serious doubts that were raised about its safety, and then later sought to squelch information which might prove the car's deficiencies.

The total cost of all corporate abuse is of course nearly impossible to accurately gauge. But since antigovernment conservatives so often tally up the supposed cost of regulation, thereby highlighting only one side of the cost-benefit ledger, in fairness one should similarly guesstimate the other side.

So in 1986, the author gathered all the best empirical and scholarly studies about the cost of corporate "waste, fraud, and abuse" (to use the standard axiom). Waste included the inefficiencies built into "the corpocracy," i.e., the corporate bureaucracy. It *then* totaled $861.6 billion out of a $4 trillion economy. This number meant that some 20 percent of all spending bought nothing of value—which in today's $10 trillion economy, would mean $2 trillion of "waste, fraud, and abuse"—a number that would bother a George W. Bush or a Richard Cheney, if only they cared about consumers and democracy as much as they cared about corporations and capitalism.

Trends in Prosecution

Clearly, few among us would begin knocking over banks upon hearing that penalties for armed robbery had been halved or that budget cuts had reduced the number of police detectives. The reason is that bank robbery is *wrong*, regardless of the consequences of getting caught. But according to Justice Holmes's "bad man" theory of criminal law, criminal penalties exist to deter that small percentage of citizens tempted by unlawful gain.

This theory has special application to potential white-collar offenders. Most are sophisticated people who can make bottom line calculations about the profitability of illegality. Some businessmen may cross the ethical or legal line not merely because of organization pressure from superiors, but also because they think they can get away with it.

Historically, prosecuting prominent businesspeople has been difficult. Imagine prosecutors having to scale five high walls to apprehend a culprit protected in the castle:

✦ *Wall number one* is the difficulty of getting prohibitory laws enacted in the first place because corporations enjoy special influence in the legislative process. Their formidable political assets can dissuade compliant legislators from criminalizing or punishing economic abuses; for example, willfully producing and selling a defective car carries no criminal penalties, unlike violations of the Migratory Bird Act.

✦ *Wall number two* is the inadequate resources provided to enforce the law. In his 2004 book *The Cheating Culture,* David Callahan writes that "federal agencies like the SEC, the IRS, and the Justice Department have been starved of the resources needed to stop white-collar crime. Why not inflate earnings reports if the chances of being prosecuted are next to nil?"

✦ *Wall number three* is judges who usually have practiced corporate law and who do not like to sentence to jail the kind of clients they previously represented. When district court judge John Lord sentenced convicted school supply scammers in a 1960s antitrust case, he said, "All are God-fearing men, highly civic minded, who have spent lifetimes of sincere and honest dedication and service to their families, their churches, their country, and their communities...I could never send Mr. Kurtz to jail."

✦ *Wall number four* is fines that are tantamount to traffic tickets. Even should companies be caught, convicted, and fined, the deterrent value is minimal because the penalties are so small they are simply absorbed as the cost of doing business.

✦ *Wall number five* is that even when a company is punished, responsible executives aren't. Juries engage in a logical impossibility: they convict the company, yet exonerate the only executives capable of having committed the prohibited acts. When culprits are called pillars of the community and appear to be only a link in a corporate chain of misconduct, the ardor of jurors for retributive justice cools.

Add all this up, and the percentage of culpable executives who actually get caught, tried, and punished is tiny. Writes law professor and criminologist Christopher Stone, "The arrow of whatever law [the executive] has broken is obligingly deflected to the corporation itself, and passed through it to the shareholders, and perhaps, the consumers and creditors...The people who call the shots do not have to bear the full risks."

Just as Troy fell and the Maginot Line was outflanked, so too can law enforcers occasionally overcome these barricades to find and punish suspects within the protected fortress. So while there's been political and prosecutorial quiet on the white-collar crime front over the decades, more recently there's been a significant shift due to a wave of publicized corruption—most prominently the Enron scandal and convictions of Ken Lay and Jeff Skilling—that angered the public and prodded officials to respond.

The results have been mixed. Let's consider presidential, prosecutorial, and congressional responses.

President Bush, and top advisor Karl Rove, quickly saw the political peril when Enron—his largest patron in Texas and whose CEO he called "Kenny Boy"—came to embody corporate America. To stay ahead of the crescendoing scandals, Bush went to Wall Street for a speech on July 9, 2002, to prominently attack corporate criminality. Rhetorically, it was as if Ralph Nader had won the 2000 election. "We will use the full weight of the law to expose and root out corruption," he told the one thousand corporate leaders at the cavernous Regent Wall Street Hotel. "My administration will do everything in our power to end the days of cooking the books, shading the truth, and breaking our laws...For corporate leaders found guilty of fraud and theft, there will be no more easy money, just hard time."

Yet the speech was panned by a broad range of commentators. Missing were basics like protections for whistleblowers, limitation of offshore tax havens, restrictions on bidding for procurement contracts by misbehaving companies, rules on expensing of stock options, and many other specifics. The *Financial Times* noted that the reform bill in the House that Bush preferred "is backed by the accounting firms (and would leave regulation in the industry's hands), instead of the Senate bill, which would increase government oversight." According to *Newsday*, executives emerged from the Regent Hotel "grinning like they'd just been handed fat new stock-option deals...The executives Bush came to pillory, they swore they loved the speech. And why not? Savvy Wall Streeters realized what any half-intelligent person would. This was for the cameras."

The president also told his audience, "I urge board members to check the quality of their company's financial statements; to ask tough questions about accounting methods; to demand that audit firms are not beholden to the CEO; and to make sure the compensation for senior executives squares with reality and commonsense." But urging board members to behave like board members is not exactly FDR creating an SEC to stop stock fraud or JFK jawboning down steel prices in 1962. When it comes to the profit motive, suggesting voluntary virtue is a throwback to the era before Upton Sinclair disclosed the sickening conditions in food processing plants in his 1906 classic *The Jungle*.

The day after his speech the Dow dropped 282 points, the largest one-day fall since the September 2001 terrorist attacks.

No, W.'s heart is in the boardroom, not the courtroom. His indifference to the existence or costs of business illegality—if you Google "Bush" and "business fraud," not much comes up in his presidency other than his Wall Street speech—could perhaps be traced to his sensitivity over having probably committed it. The best evidence (summarized on pages 70–73 of the author's previous *The Book on Bush*) indicates that he engaged in insider trading by dumping Harken Energy stock in the early 1990s just before its value plummeted on bad news he had learned about as a board member.

President Bush can surely give a speech in front of a huge banner with the words "Corporate Responsibility" printed over and over in bold letters. But he won't readily prosecute corporate crooks because he won't staff or fund key agencies to do so.

Take the SEC.

It was a long decline from its dynamic inception in 1934—the first commission chairs were Joseph Kennedy and William O. Douglas—to

President Bush's appointment of attorney Harvey Pitt as chairman in 2001.

A longtime lawyer for the accounting industry, Pitt spearheaded its fights against the proposed reforms of his predecessor, Chairman Arthur Levitt. To his later regret, Levitt backed down after taking a beating in Congress from the Pitt-led accounting lobby and from members of Congress from both parties. In 2000, when Levitt proposed a rule prohibiting accounting firms from offering both auditing and consulting services to their clients—precisely what got Arthur Anderson and Merrill Lynch in trouble—forty-six senators and representatives wrote letters of opposition to Levitt. In the ten years prior, these same forty-six legislators received $39 million in contributions from the industry. In his recent book *Take On the Street,* Levitt describes Pitt's position on auditor independence: "[E]ach firm would customize its specific standards, and each auditor would determine whether he was in compliance." Levitt and others thought "self-regulation by the accounting profession is a bad joke."

None of this meant that Pitt would necessarily run the SEC as a tool of the accounting industry, which the commission is supposed to regulate. When FDR appointed Kennedy, the former Wall Street insider, JFK's father confounded critics by turning his insider knowledge to good use in regulating the industry from which he came. But Pitt, rather than start his new job linking himself to FDR's crusades against corporate fraud, instead called to mind the less auspicious presidency of former President George Bush by promising a "kinder, gentler place for accountants." "Mr. Pitt's apologetic tone is troubling," worried the *Washington Post.* "Given that the Levitt reforms were moderate, and that it was the auditors who mounted an unkind and distinctly ungentle campaign to bury them…It risks creating an impression that the new rules will not be implemented as vigorously as they should be."

Even after the demise of Enron, much of the media remained unimpressed with the way Pitt remained so close to his old clients. According to *Newsweek,* "The problem is not that Pitt represented the accounting industry and corporate defendants as a lawyer (and thus has recently had to recuse himself twenty-nine times from pending SEC cases)…The problem, as crusading New York attorney general Eliot Spitzer says, is that Pitt has 'internalized the values of his clients.' He came in talking about a 'kinder, gentler' SEC, and held cozy meetings with the folks he should be regulating aggressively."

At the level of appointments, Bush tacked in two directions. When Pitt eventually had to resign due to a series of gaffes during the run of scandals, the president chose William Donaldson, seventy-two, the former chairman of the New York Stock Exchange and a close social friend of the Bush family. Donaldson surprised many, perhaps including his president, by often joining with the commission's two Democrats to support serious reforms. One finally approved the so-called expensing of stock options; another required the registration of hedge funds.

But when a pro-reform commissioner resigned and Donaldson saw himself on the losing end of future three to two votes, he abruptly resigned in 2005. Bush quickly chose as his replacement, Rep. Christopher Cox, who ironically had led the congressional charge against expensing stock options alongside Harvey Pitt years earlier. His top contributors were the securities and accounting industries—and on the House floor he had called securities law "a legal torture chamber." He had also been the lead sponsor of the 1995 law making shareholder lawsuits far more difficult, thereby coaxing the Enrons and WorldComs to push the envelope of illegality. Appointing a laissez faire Republican to run the SEC after Donaldson was, as one former commissioner told *The American Prospect,* "the worst thing to happen in the SEC's seventy year history." But prosecutorially, the story was different. Initially because of Eliot Spitzer—who as New York State attorney general was not under Bush's thumb and whose prosecutions showed up a laggard SEC—prosecutors were able to successfully pursue the worst offenders. A record number of serious indictments, convictions, and sentences ensued, as the accompanying chart indicates:

The New York Times, Tuesday, September 20, 2005

Sentencing Roundup The sentences L. Dennis Kozlowski and Mark H. Swartz received yesterday in New York State court are comparable in length to the terms given to other high-profile executives in the last four years.

CASE ■ CONVICTED ◆ PLEADED GUILTY

Name	Company	Position	Case	Years
Bernard J. Ebbers	WorldCom	Chief executive	■ Masterminding an $11 billion accounting fraud	25
L. Dennis Kozlowski	Tyco	Chief executive	■ Looting the company and deceiving investors	8.3-25
Mark H. Swartz	Tyco	Chief financial officer	■ Looting the company and deceiving investors	8.3-25
Jamie Olis	Dynegy	Midlevel executive	■ Falsifying the company's books to hide a $300 million loan	24
Timothy J. Rigas	Adelphia	Chief financial officer	■ Looting the company and lying to investors	20
Martin R. Frankel		Financier	◆ Looting insurance companies and raceteering	16.7
John J. Rigas	Adelphia	Chief financial officer	■ Looting the company and lying to investors and regulators	15
Reed Slatkin		Money manager	◆ Stealing hundreds of millions from investors	14
Alan B. Bond	Albriond Capital	Money manager	◆ Stealing from investors and taking kickbacks from brokers	12.5
Franklin C. Brown	Rite Aid	Vice chairman	■ Played a leading role in accounting scandal	10
Andrew S. Fastow	Enron	Chief financial officer	◆ Inflating the company's value and defrauding the company	10
E. Kirk Shelton	CUC International	Vice chairman	■ Conspiracy and fraud to inflate the company's value	10
Robert E Brennan	First Jersey Securities	Founder	■ Money laundering and bankruptcy fraud	9.2
Martin L. Grass	Rite Aid	Chief executive	■ Accounting scandal that inflated the value of the company	8
John M. Rusnak	Allfirst Financial	Currency trader	◆ Hiding $691 million in trading losses over five years	7.5
Samuel D. Waksal	ImClone Systems	Founder, chief executive	◆ Securities fraud and perjury	7
Scott D. Sullivan	WorldCom	Chief financial officer	◆ Leading role in $11 billion accounting fraud	5
Ben F. Gilsan Jr.	Enron	Treasurer	◆ Manipulating the company's financial statements	5

Last, the political process responded with the Sarbanes-Oxley law. Bush's Wall Street speech had initially cooled the fever for reform—so that on June 10, the *New York Times* reported that the congressional push for change was "all but dead." Yet only one month later—when the other shoe of WorldCom and Ebbers dropped—the Senate passed the Sarbanes-Oxley law ninety-seven to zero and Bush signed it in a Rose Garden ceremony.

To avoid conflicts of interest and phony accounting, the law had several significant provisions: it created an accounting oversight board, prohibited audit firms from doing non-audit consulting work for clients, banned corporate loans to company executives, mandated that top executives personally certify company accounts, and created new whistleblower protections for anyone providing lawful information about suspected fraud. Section 404, the most controversial part of the bill, required that managers assess their companies' internal financial controls and have outside accountants audit those controls annually. Violators faced stiff criminal penalties.

Views of the act varied greatly. Many businesses complained about the cost of compliance, as *The Economist* leadingly asked "A Price Worth Paying?"—answering in effect "no" by relying on one business school study pegging the cost at $1.4 trillion. Responding to such wild hyperbole, Rep. Michael Oxley (R-OH), coauthor of the law, said, "How can you measure the value of knowing that company books are sounder than before?" Indeed, some two thousand companies have had to issue financial restatements, and untold others presumably have not cooked their books because of a greater likelihood of getting caught.

But when it came to significantly advancing shareholder democracy, the law flinched. A proposal by Donaldson and pension fund activists, for example, for directors to stay on only if a majority of shareholders voted "yes" was never seriously considered by the Congress. New York State comptroller Alan Hevesi, a leader of this movement and the lead plaintiff in the WorldCom civil litigation, said, "We've had some success in corporate governance reform [but] in other areas—such as giving a greater voice to shareholders to elect independent directors and curbing excessive executive compensation—we haven't been as successful. I worry about whether the necessary reforms have really been institutionalized."

THE NEW ARISTOCRACY OF WEALTH

Because democracy is more a process than a result, there's no obviously ideal average income, desirable net worth, or appropriate ratio of top pay to bottom pay. But if tens of millions of workers do not enjoy a rough equality of *opportunity* (not of *income,* but *opportunity*)—or if the ratio of CEO to line-worker went from 40:1 in 1960s to, say, 4000:1 in 2020—is it still a democracy? That it's hard to draw a line along this "slippery slope" doesn't mean we shouldn't. Abraham Lincoln put it well when he said that America should be a place where all would have "an open field and a fair chance [for their] industry, enterprise, and intelligence." But at what point does a gross mal-distribution of income and wealth so stretch the social contract that it snaps—that a democracy becomes a kleptocracy or a plutocracy? Or does the governing philosophy of democracy simply have to accept any scale of wealth produced by the economics of capitalism?

This has hardly been a newsworthy or political topic for obvious reasons: what candidate wants to bite the hand that funds him—and what journalist wants to take on the owners of her paper or station? Republicans, for their part, have come up with various defenses and arguments to protect their financial base from criticism over excessive pay and perks. It's envy. It's class warfare. It's the market. It's globalization.

Actually, this is a taboo topic not because enormous wealth disparities are inevitable—capitalism seemed to work fine when CEOs earned $1 million a year in the 1960s and 1970s, not $10 million to $20 million today—but because those who excessively profit from growing inequality want to maintain their power and wealth.

The taboo was recently broken by, ironically, some maverick billionaires such as Warren Buffet, Ted Turner, and George Soros, who cautioned that a concentration of wealth can create a new aristocracy which stifles growth because too much capital is controlled by heirs rather than innovators. Then in 2004, it was that socialist, Alan Greenspan—as Federal Reserve chairman he was not in hock to corporate donors for his position and pay—who revealed in his usual indirect way what politicians wouldn't. "For the democratic society," he told Congress in testimony about growing income disparity, "that is not a very desirable thing to allow to happen."

Here's the "not very desirable thing": America is going through a new Gilded Age based on the same philosophy of Social Darwinism that prevailed in the 1890s and 1920s. Not since that corrupt era have corporate elites earned so much and been so unapologetic, even shameless.

First, consider the astronomical and growing rewards to top CEOs, which bring to mind Oscar Wilde's observation that, "nothing succeeds like excess." *Crain's New York Business* produced a chart in mid-2005 called the "Fortunate 100" with the following total annual pay for the top four: Mel Karmazin at Sirius Satellite Radio, $151 million; Lew Frankfort at Coach Inc., $101 million; Sumner Redstone at Viacom, $62 million; and Mario J. Gabelli at Gabelli Asset Management, $55 million. That's *annually.* Then there is CEO Lee Raymond of ExxonMobil, whose pay package of $368 million in 2005 meant that he earned more in an *hour* than the minimum-wage worker earned in a *year.*

The saga of Morgan Stanley spoke volumes about corporate pay in America in the twenty-first century. After a bruising battle at the CEO level, Philip Purcell left and was succeeded by John Mack. For his failures at the troubled investment firm, Purcell walked "the platinum plank" with a $113.7 million good-bye package to ease his pain—not to mention that his protégé Stephen Crawford, only three months on the job and with no prior experience of running a business division at the bank, was awarded $32 million to leave. (Rewarding failure is not at all uncommon in corporate suites. More than three hundred executives among Standard & Poor's five hundred companies have contracts that obligate the firm to pay at least the equivalent of a year or more of salary and benefits if they leave—for most, even if they quit.)

When these stunning "golden parachutes" sparked a furor among stockholders and staff, John Mack reconsidered his own deal of a $25 million guaranteed annual salary; he proposed instead a supposed "merit pay" standard that would pay him no less than the average pay package given the CEOs at Goldman Sachs, Lehman Brothers, Merrill Lynch, and Bear Stearns. "Pay for performance" is a positive trend in corporate America because it links rewards to results. On the other hand, it's just another version of "capitalism without risk" to be guaranteed what your competitors are receiving because compensation consultants play up to the CEOs who hire them by arguing that none of them should earn much less than the others. This was called "the epitome of what is wrong with America today," by bestselling author Tom Friedman. "We are now playing defense. A top CEO wants to be paid not based on his performance, but based on the average of his four main rivals! That is like Lance Armstrong saying he will race only if he is guaranteed to come in first or second, no matter what his cycling times are on each leg of the Tour de France."

The signs of our new aristocracy of wealth are everywhere around us. It's the $100 million Kenneth Lay earned the year Enron went bust. It's when Jack Welch's retirement package—beyond a $120 million pay-out—specifically includes Red Sox tickets, country club memberships, free use of a corporate jet, and a Manhattan apartment for life—along with flowers, wine, and laundry service. It's David Brooks, CEO of bulletproof vest manufacturer DHB Industries, who earned $525,000 in the pre-Iraq year of 2001, but $70 million in 2004 because of contracts to provide vests to soldiers in Iraq—and who, according to the *Daily News,* hosted a $10 million party for his teenage daughter and her friends at Rockefeller Center, replete with Aerosmith, the Eagles, and rapper 50 Cent.

It's workers at the bankrupted Delphi parts division of GM watching its new CEO, Robert Miller, seek a wage reduction from $27 to $10 an hour, while receiving a signing bonus of $3 million. In a similar "restructuring," it's when United Airlines agrees to a deal to emerge from bankruptcy that severely cuts employees pay but awards ten million shares—or eight percent of company assets—to four hundred executives. It's *Forbes* magazine's four hundred richest Americans being six times richer in 2005 on average than the four hundred richest in 1985, notwithstanding an intervening market crash. It's the top 10 percent earning 30 percent of all income from the 1940s to the 1970s, but 40 percent now. It's a Cornell Study finding that corporate assets used to pay the top five executives doubled from 5 to 10 percent between 1993 and 2003.

And it's the showy wealth described in a *New York Times* series on new money encountering old money in Nantucket:

> Nina Chandler Murray, an eighty-five-year-old relative of the Poor family from Standard & Poor's...was

appalled at a recent dinner party when a woman leaned over to her and said, 'My husband paid $250,000 to join the golf club.'...So finally the question comes up: 'How do you get over to the island?' and she says, 'We come by plane.' And he says, 'A G-IV.' And so the wind comes out of the guys sails. 'The old money guy has a twin-prop airplane that is pretty incredible. Now he is talking to a guy who is half his age who has a transcontinental jet. That is then end of the conversation.'*

It's admittedly hard to devise reforms that actually stop the more recent grotesque excesses. Beyond various pay-for-performance guidelines, Rep. Barney Frank (D-MA) has proposed a bill to allow shareholders to vote on "change of control" compensation schemes and to force firms to return monies if it later had to restate earnings. But even Frank admits that "it is the shareholders' money [and] if they want to pay for Jack Welch's newspaper, they have that right."

If such riches were truly linked to performance—like the huge but earned rewards given to such pioneers as Edwin Land, Frederick Smith, or Pierre Omidyar for creating the Polaroid Company, FedEx, and eBay, respectively—that would be one thing. Or *if* it were a truly free market that rewarded such people rather than boards and compensation consultants they chose, that too could be theoretically justified.** Or *if* not a handful but many people earned significant sums—or at least had a real opportunity to earn a decent living—then very large incomes would not undermine the system of democracy. To be angry at super-skilled people who earned a fortune in a fair system *would* be envy.

But who believes that's the case today? When the top economic

---

*New SEC Chair Christopher Cox in early 2006 usefully proposed greater disclosure of the actual total value of all pay, perks, and options for a company's five highest paid executives. But mere disclosure is like trying to lasso a comet. As the compensation guru Graef Crystal notes, existing disclosures largely enable compensation consultants to tell boards to raise compensation by pointing to anyone earning more than their top guys.

**Elaborating on Crystal's point above, Warren Buffet wrote in the 2005 annual report of his company, Berkshire Hathaway, "A mediocre-or-worse CEO—aided by his handpicked VP of human relations and a consultant from the ever-accommodating firm of Ratchet, Ratchet & Bingo—all too often receives gobs of money from an ill-designed compensation arrangement."

echelon changes the rules to shift income and wealth to them, why is it called "class warfare" when the other 95 percent points this out? The problem is not so much the riches of an aberrational few but a growing income gap that relegates millions to no-exit and low-pay work.

In the 1960s, as noted, the average Fortune 500 CEO earned $1 million annually while his line-worker earned $25,000, or a 40:1 ratio. By 2004, it had ballooned to a 431:1 ratio—if the minimum wage had comparably grown, it would have been an ample $23.03 an hour, not the measly $5.15. Also in the 1960s, corporate CEOs made forty times more than an average public school teacher; now its 264 times as much. Between 1980 and 2002, the share of income earned by the top 0.1 percent of taxpayers more than doubled while the share of income earned by the other 90 percent declined.

According to the Century Foundation, the mean income of the top 5 percent of households over the last twenty years grew four times as fast as the mean income of the bottom 80 percent. Indeed, just the *increase* in mean income of the top 5 percent ($115,416) was three times larger than the income *level* of the bottom 80 percent of all households. The report also showed new wealth is now far more skewed: while the top 5 percent of *income* earners have five and a half times the income of the remaining 95 percent, when it comes to *wealth* the top 5 percent have twenty-three times more than everyone else put together. Again, the *increase* alone of $5.15 million per household of the top 1 percent was forty times the *level* of wealth of the bottom 90 percent. The U.S. now has the society most concentrated by wealth and income of any of the Western nations surveyed.

Compounding this income problem for blue-collar workers are crises in healthcare and pensions. Because of weakening labor markets, companies now often negotiate give-backs and co-pays, further eroding real incomes. In 1987, employers provided care for 70 percent of America's working age population; by 2003 that number had fallen to 63 percent, according to the Employee Benefits Research Institute in Washington, D.C., a decline which translates into eighteen million people who have to try to make their own private arrangements.

Our growing economy is somehow producing shrinking retirement benefits. We are experiencing a new phenomenon of companies escaping their pension obligations by declaring bankruptcy. Compounding this loss to employees, profitable firms of the rank of IBM, Verizon,

Lockheed Martin, and Motorola are abandoning traditional corporate-funded pension plans for 401(k)s based on employee contributions and subject to the whims of financial markets. Economist Gene Sperling describes the gathering storm: while more than half of all Americans now own stocks, typically in small holdings, "nearly half of Americans have no savings for retirement. Some 92 percent of the working poor...lack even an employer-provided retirement account. And a disturbing 86 percent of part-time workers and 83 percent of employees working in small firms have no 401(k)-type account. In other words, most American workers remain dependent on Social Security, meager savings, and the equity accumulated in their house for retirement, if they can even afford to retire."

While the bulk of President Bush's public remarks obviously focus on taxes and terrorism, there was actually a day—June 22, 2005, to be exact—when he tried to show empathy for workers. "I know some workers are concerned about jobs going overseas," Bush told a labor audience. "I know some are concerned about gaining the skills necessary to compete in the global economy that we live in. I know that families are worried about health care and retirement, and I know moms and dads are worried about their children finding good jobs." Notice the rhetorical device of saying he "knows" these things but not proposing policies to actually *do* something about them.

The Bush administration's incessant focus on transferring assets from workers to the already wealthy ignores the reality of what the widening income and wealth gaps are doing to the lives of the lower middle class/working poor. Recent books such as Barbara Ehrenreich's *Nickel and Dimed,* David Shipler's *The Working Poor,* and Tamara Draut's *Strapped* describe how millions of Americans are on a treadmill that they can't get off of and can't keep up with—how they "spend everything and save nothing." Or as the politicized hip-hop artist Kanye West has sung about his time as a Gap clerk, "You can't shine on $6.55."

Imagine problems that cascade one into the other creating a chain reaction of despair. Here's Shipler's version: "A run-down apartment can exacerbate a child's asthma, which leads to a call for an ambulance, which generates a medical bill that cannot be paid, which ruins a credit record, which hikes the interest on an auto loan, which forces the purchase of an unreliable used car, which jeopardizes a mother's punctuality at work, which limits her promotions and earning capacity, which confines her to poor housing." And now appreciate that she cannot easily afford to file for bankruptcy to wipe her slate clean because Bush and credit card companies forced a Bankruptcy "Reform" Law through Congress that essentially transferred yet more funds from debtors to creditors. Safety nets that took generations for government and business to weave are being slowly snipped or eliminated altogether.

The dramatic rise in income for the wealthy and backsliding for workers has come about by what could be called "intelligent design"—i.e., not merely the "unseen hand" of a pitiless market, but also the willful policies of Republican political leaders. Nearly every proposal or law in the era of Bush 43—from cutting job training programs, eroding the minimum wage, weakening unions, reversing ergonomic standards, reducing overtime pay—contribute to the trend, as the section on "Labor *Pains*" described previously.

The chief culprit, however, has been fiscal policy. When Bush entered office in 2001, the percentage of federal revenues from corporate taxes was at its lowest point in fifty years and the earnings of the top 1 percent had grown from 14 percent of all income in 1990 to 21 percent by 2000, in part because of the stock market boom of the 1990s. Nonetheless, Bush set out to further reduce taxes on corporations and high-end individuals—and succeeded beyond Ronald Reagan's wildest dreams; recall that "Dutch" felt the need to raise taxes significantly in 1982 when deficits grew too mountainous, a step hard to imagine for today's Texan.

The results: those making $100,000 to $200,000 will pay 5 to 9 percentage points more of their income in federal taxes than those earning over a million dollars annually, assuming the Bush tax cuts are made permanent. After real incomes generally rose year after year in 1940s to 1970s, in 2001–2005 under Bush 43 average real income has fallen for five years in a row, the first such sustained decline on record. The median (after inflation) income of $44,389 in 2004 was the lowest since 1997. "It looks like the gains from the recovery haven't really filtered down," concluded Phillip L. Swagel, a resident scholar at the conservative American Enterprise Institute in Washington, D.C. "The gains have gone to owners of capital and not to workers."

In his monumental 2002 work, *Wealth and Democracy,* Kevin Phillips spoke of a "plutocracy [due to] the ability of wealth to reach beyond its own realm of money to control politics and money as well." Phillips detected and lamented the irony that "in just a little over two centuries the United States went from being a society born of revolution and touched by egalitarianism to being the country with the industrial world's biggest fortunes and its largest rich-poor gap."

A DEMOCRATIC BACKLASH TO CRONY CAPITALISM?

Oddly, the rise of corporate political influence and the new aristocracy of wealth is happening with little public debate. The disappearance of Natalee Holloway in Aruba probably received ten times more cumulative attention that month than the disappearing after-tax incomes of most Americans did in the prior decade. But George Bush is redistributing income and wealth far beyond the dreams of George McGovern, except the flow of funds is now up not down.

An unrepentant Bush, not satisfied with four tax cuts shifting more than $1.5 trillion from labor to capital, now seeks the elimination of the estate tax. By doing so he unconsciously mimics the response trade-unionist Samuel Gompers gave when asked a century ago what labor wanted— "More!" he famously answered. As Bush & Co. seek "more" for their own, and wealth and power are held in fewer and fewer hands, at what point do the majority of workers wake up and protest that they will not tolerate such a split-level economy, will not quietly endure their impoverishment? So far, the only serious backlash has been seventeen states and several cities—like Florida and New York City—where labor and grassroots organizations have forced living wages to be enacted so that local employees of firms with public contracts pay over the meager federal minimum wage, now worth less in real terms than at any time since 1955.

Exactly what is the answer to this question—if America is obviously far wealthier over the past thirty years, why are wages stagnant? How long will Republican leaders continue to get away with cutting taxes for Ken Lay and cutting programs and incomes for blue-collar workers?

One would again have to go back to the turn of the nineteenth century to decipher what's happening today at the nexus between democracy and capitalism. For generations America has been comprised of two brains with different spheres—a left-sphere of democracy based on the values of participation, transparency, and rights, and a right-sphere of capitalism based on competition and production. But in a hostile, if quiet, takeover, the right brain is now subsuming the left and the balance of spheres has tilted.

Whatever the trappings and disguises—no matter how often Republican leaders invoke flag, faith, the "ownership society," or the "war on terrorism"—the one enduring value and goal of Republican public policy is this: what business wants, business gets.

Corporations don't just lobby the Bush government—they've *become* the Bush government. Although the president's clique constantly refers back to America's First Republican, the ethic in Lincoln's Gettysburg Address of a government "of, by, and for the people" has been supplanted by America, Inc. So W. and his allies happily accept their campaign contributions, enact their bills, cut their taxes, eliminate regulations and lawsuits aimed at them, undermine their unions, drill in wilderness areas, increase the number of lucrative no-bid contracts, appoint their executives to high positions—and then privatize, deregulate, or shrink government.

This has been called "crony capitalism." Instead of a system combining free speech and free markets, crony capitalism perverts both democracy and capitalism. Here's the way a rigged system of corporate government works. Once in control of the executive branch, a Republican administration installs cronies like Christopher Cox, Philip Cooney, and Michael Brown—and scores of lesser knowns—to offices where they can both alter policy to suit their former paymasters and/or direct contracts to them. Corporate donors provide large donations to keep Republican majorities in both chambers of Congress, which will then cut taxes to the rich during periods of growth ("it's your money") *or* periods of no growth ("supply-side economics").

Washington has become a city where the veneer of government masks a giant redistribution machine. In this new world, hundreds of billions of dollars and numerous decisions are wrenched out of public hands and given over to major business leaders to benefit a small economic elite. "Their wish-list," concluded Ralph Nader, "has become the Capital City's to-do list." Consider this stunningly revealing March 18–22, 2001, email exchange between Joseph Kelliher, the energy secretary's top assistant, and Dana Contratto, a natural gas lobbyist: Kelliher solicitously asked, "If you were king or Il Duce, what would you include in a national energy policy, especially with respect to natural gas issues?"

The excesses of the late 1800s trusts and go-go 1920s did produce civic, cultural, and then political backlashes that in turn led to the original antitrust laws and then regulated capitalism of the 1930s. Already there are tremors of a growing backlash. Commentators attribute the anomaly of decent economic growth in 2005-2006 with sharply declining consumer confidence (only 29 percent rate the economy "good" or "excellent") to the cavernous income gap between the economic elite and the other 90 percent. David Callahan in *The Cheating Culture* speculates whether the democratic process will again checkmate corporate abuse:

> Americans love the free market; but again and again they have risen in revolt when market forces became too powerful.... Many of the conditions that have catalyzed such backlashes in the past are now present: growing public concerns about unchecked private power; high-profile scandals that underscore the corrupt role that corporations play in American politics; and mounting unease with the social and cultural consequences of extreme competition and materialism. It is worth adding that every past popular revolt against laissez-faire excesses has come on the heels of a Republican presidency in which the White House was widely seen as too cozy with big business.

VOTER SUPPRESSION: AFTER FLORIDA AND OHIO

"Give us the ballot. Give us the ballot!"
—Address at the Prayer Pilgrimage for Freedom, Delivered before the
Lincoln Memorial, DR. MARTIN LUTHER KING JR.,
1957, Washington, D.C.

THE LEADER OF THE DEMOCRATIC WORLD?

Since the end of World War II, the United States has seen itself as the leader of the free world, the "shining city on the hill," when it comes to embodying democratic values and virtues. Under the Bush administration, the decibel level about promoting democracy abroad has become almost deafening. Whether discussing Iraq, Russia, China, or Africa, the president holds America up as the model of democratic institutions that other countries should emulate. Based on all this, one might think that the health of our democratic processes, particularly our election processes, would exceed that of all other nations—or at least, of most other nations. But a brief set of comparisons shows how misplaced our patriotic hubris is.

Although the United States is the oldest democracy in the world with over two centuries of practical experience in administering elections, voter turnout remains dismally low. Since 1945 it has averaged 48.3 percent of eligible adults in presidential years, which places us only 139 out of 172 countries. If "democracy poverty" were defined as those countries performing in the bottom 20 percent of participation, then the U.S. would be a candidate for massive international charity. While some of the countries with high voter turnout are "usual suspects"—technologically, economically, and politically advanced nations, like New Zealand (86.2 percent), Austria (85.1 percent), and Belgium (84.9 percent)—some of the highest performing states include those still categorized as third world, like Cambodia (90.5 percent), Somalia (87.1 percent), and Mongolia (82.3 percent). The level of participation does not seem to depend on a country's length of existence as a democracy or on economic wealth.

Overall, the U.S. is a statistical drag even for the North American region, which averages 60 percent voter turnout. Our closest neighbors, Canada and Mexico, achieved 68.4 percent and 48.1 percent since 1945, respectively. But before we boast about the .2 percent difference between the U.S. and Mexico (48.3 vs. 48.1), it is worth noting that over time Mexico's voter turnout has been going up while America's has been sliding down. Western Europe has the highest average turnout (77 percent) followed by Eastern Europe (68 percent) and Asia (62 percent).

While one key gauge of a successful democracy is full exercise of the franchise, another is the political system's reflection of the population as a whole. Are the elected representatives people who broadly represent the population? Rarely is representational inequality more pronounced than in the United States. In 2002, the members of the United States Congress were 14 percent women, 7 percent African American, 3 percent Hispanic, and 1 percent Asian American. Yet the nation's population is over 50 percent women, 12.5 percent Hispanic, 12.3 percent African American, and 3.6 percent Asian American. Some countries have achieved near gender parity in their national parliaments, including Rwanda (48.8 percent) and Sweden (45.3 percent).

Another useful area for international comparison is in the quality and technological competence of election administration. Here again, to steal Winston Churchill's line, we "have much to be modest about." There are many other countries where the integrity of elections far outshine the crazy quilt of state, county, and municipal regulations and administration we rely on here.

Brazil, for example, is a leader when it comes to new and important election administration processes. In 1994, when the dot-com movement was just getting underway in the U.S., Brazil was experimenting with Direct Recording Electronic voting machines (DREs), then a new e-voting technology. By 2000, Brazil had expanded electronic voting across the country to roughly 117 million eligible voters. One-hundred percent of municipal elections were conducted on electronic voting machines, which were designed to function much like a personal computer with a custom keyboard with six keys: begin, yes, no, blank vote, void ballot, and end. In 2002 voter turnout was an impressive 79.5 percent. And the people in Rio don't have to say of their neighbors, "Well, that's Sao Paulo, they have their own way of doing things."

Not only are their elections technologically advanced, but the Brazilian government is responsive as well. Reacting to a political scandal involving President Luiz Inácio Lula da Silva in 2005 that soured public trust in the government, public officials approved legislation requiring that electronic voting devices be made voter verifiable. By the addition of an extra printer to the DRE voting machines already in use, voters were able to see their choices printed on a slip of paper, behind a transparent window. When confirmed, the vote slip is inserted into a sealed bag retained by election officials—a paper record that can later be used in an audit of the electronic tally or for a possible recount.

How fairly, in addition to how competently, elections are administered is another vital measure of a democracy. Prior to the November 2004 election, Jimmy Carter was asked if he would consider sending his international election-monitoring team to monitor the United States elections. "We wouldn't think of it," the former president told a radio interviewer. "The American political system wouldn't measure up to any sort of international standards."

The voters' confidence in elections is contingent on their perception that the process is uncorrupted by partisan influence. That's why most elections in democracies are administered by a nonpartisan or bipartisan electoral commission which oversees the entire election process. Canada's system of election administration is often held up as exemplary, most recently by the Carter-Baker Commission on Federal Election Reform. In Canada, the chief electoral officer (CEO) is appointed by the House of Commons and is expected to serve until the age of sixty-five. The CEO can be dismissed by the governor general, but only with the consent of both the House of Commons and the Senate. He/she is not answerable to any cabinet member, and supervises a team of election administrators in charge of ensuring compliance and enforcement of Canada's Elections Act.

Voter registration policies also play a large role in voter turn out. If the process is cumbersome, restrictive, or confusing, fewer eligible voters will register and fewer will turn out during an election. In many countries the state takes the initiative, automatically registering new voters. In some countries election officials go door-to-door canvassing neighborhoods to find new voters, while in others state agencies and institutions locate and transmit data on qualified new voters to the proper election officials. Indeed, almost every European country prefers state-initiated (or universal) registration to voter-initiated systems like America's. At least twenty other countries, such as France, Australia, and Brazil, require voters to register or else face a fine. By contrast, most states in the U.S. impose pre-registration deadlines between twenty-eight and thirty-one days from the election.

A widespread belief that every citizen has a civic duty to participate in the political process also has a profound effect on voter turnout. Australia's election law broadly states that "it shall be the duty of every elector to vote at each election." Compulsory voting has its origins in Belgium in 1892, and has been implemented in diverse countries around the world—from Fiji to Switzerland, Singapore to Uruguay.

People in these countries favor their mandatory voting systems, citing political equality as a primary reason. Non-voters in Australia who fail to show up at the polls are sent a penalty notice by an election official advising them to pay a penalty of $20 Australian ($15 U.S.) for the first notice and $50 Australian ($40 U.S.) for the second notice. While this rule may sound odd or big-brotherish in America, it's not that different than sitting on a jury, paying taxes, or wearing a seat belt, which are not voluntary but legally required.

Looking closer to home, we don't need a passport to observe that other democracies, including several even in our own backyards, are achieving far greater levels of participation than the United States. Puerto Rico averages an impressive voter turnout of 81.7 percent of eligible adults, while 2.4 out of 2.5 million Puerto Ricans are registered voters. A direct path between civic engagement and quality of life is made obvious there through comprehensive voter education and the fact that nearly every election has been high stakes. They are only held once every four years, but it is an occasion when seats for all 1,020 elected officials are up for grabs—one governor, one resident commissioner, 27 senators, 51 representatives, 78 mayors, and 862 municipal assembly people. So much is at stake on Election Day that it is a public holiday. So in addition to the ninety thousand poll workers who count each and every ballot by hand, the whole nation pauses from one workday to watch, too.

Anna, a self-aware and politically conscious native of Puerto Rico, spoke about her voting experience there. "It's easy," she said to an interviewer. "In your third or fourth year of high school, depending on the year of the election, the Election Commission goes to your high school, signs you up, and gives you a license to vote. It's a really easy process and people are familiar with it. People treat it as a national duty."

A DEFICIT OF DEMOCRACY: ELECTION WOES

In our democracy, there are three major obstacles to achieving full electoral participation. The first are outright attempts at discouraging and suppressing the vote—a practice that didn't die with the Voting Rights Act in 1965. The second is a flawed administration which keeps people off the rolls or turns them away from the polls. Third are the long-term, structural roadblocks that prevent people from joining the process, either by erecting formal procedural barriers to participation or by discouraging people from voting. Together, they paint a picture that is different from the one President Bush holds up to the world.

Partisan Intimidation

While the "one person one vote" principle of the Supreme Court's 1962 case of *Baker v. Carr* may be settled constitutional law—indeed axiomatic—in fact a very large number of people engaged in American elections don't really believe in that landmark decision at all. Even though the Supreme Court unequivocally ruled that "a citizen's right to a vote free of arbitrary impairment by state action has been judicially recognized as a right secured by the Constitution," for them the question of the health of our democracy is a distant second to electoral success. So real efforts have been put into keeping turnout low and reliable—a battle between bases. As Michigan Republican state representative John Pappageorge said in a revealing moment in 2004, "If we do not suppress the Detroit vote, we're going to have a tough time in this election cycle."

Some of the examples belong in *Ripley's Believe It or Not*. In a number of places during the 2004 presidential election, unnamed or deceptively named groups distributed materials designed to frighten or confuse people out of voting. Efforts were particularly targeted at students and communities of color—groups more likely to vote Democratic. Students at Dartmouth College in New Hampshire received flyers telling out-of-state students that they would lose their financial aid if they registered or voted in the state. Students who thought they were signing a petition for a state referendum or petitions in Texas and Florida unknowingly had their political party changed to Republican and their address changed. An address change prompts a polling place change, meaning that students would arrive at an incorrect polling place.

Among the most cynical efforts at voter suppression played upon the apprehension that exists among many poor or minority families of running afoul of the law or of administrative rules. A sign in Cuyahoga County, Ohio, said that people couldn't vote if they hadn't paid their utility bills. Here's another from Ohio:

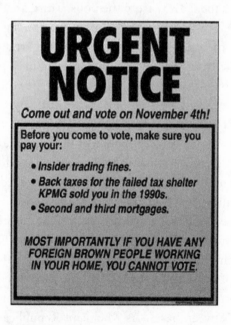

In Allegheny County, Pennsylvania, a flyer announced that to avoid overcrowding from an unexpectedly high turnout Republicans should vote on Tuesday (Election Day) and Democrats on Wednesday:

McCandless Township
Allegheny County, PA

-Attention voters-

Due to the immense voter turnout that is expected on Tuesday, November 2 the state of Pennsylvania has requested an extended voting period.

Voters will be able to vote on both November 2 and November 3. In an attempt to limit voter conflict Allegheny County is requesting that the following actions be made.

Party	Voting date
Republican	November 2
Democrat	November 3

Thank you for cooperating with us in this endeavor to create a peaceful voting environment. We are sorry for any inconveniences that these changes may cause.

Your local representative,

Anne Ryan

[signature]

In the event of an emergency, voting stations may not be opened. Stations are opened or closed on an as-needed basis. In an emergency, please stay tuned to local media or call the Emergency Operations Center at (813) 272-6900 to confirm which voting stations are open.

Other attempts deploy implied threats. In Wisconsin, flyers made to look like a statement issued by the "Milwaukee Black Voters League" were distributed under the benign title of "Some Warnings for Election Time." It said:

MILWAUKEE BLACK VOTERS LEAGUE

SOME WARNINGS FOR ELECTION TIME

IF YOU'VE ALREADY VOTED IN ANY ELECTION THIS YEAR YOU CAN'T VOTE IN THE PRESIDENTIAL ELECTION.

IF YOU'VE EVER BEEN FOUND GUILTY OF ANYTHING, EVEN A TRAFFIC VIOLATION YOU CAN'T VOTE IN THE PRESIDENTIAL ELECTION.

IF ANYBODY IN YOUR FAMILY HAS EVER BEEN FOUND GUILTY OF ANYTHING YOU CAN'T VOTE IN THE PRESIDENTIAL ELECTION.

THE TIME TO REGISTER FOR VOTING HAS EXPIRED. IF YOU HAVEN'T REGISTERED YOU CAN'T ANYMORE.

IF YOU VIOLATE ANY OF THESE LAWS YOU CAN GET TEN YEARS IN PRISON AND YOUR CHILDREN WILL GET TAKEN AWAY FROM YOU.

A phony advisory written on Lake County, Ohio, Board of Elections stationery targeting newly registered voters said that if they had been registered by the NAACP, America Coming Together, or the John Kerry for President Campaign, then their registrations would not count and that the voter registration deadline had passed:

LAKE COUNTY BOARD OF ELECTIONS
105 Main Street PO Box 490, Painesville, Ohio 44077-0490

URGENT ADVISORY

October 22, 2004

Dear Newly Registered Voter,

The voter registration deadline passed on October 4, 2004 and we registered a record number of new voters. The demand on our office has been great and we appreciate your cooperation. Unfortunately independent efforts by the NAACP, America Coming Together, John Kerry for President and the Capri Cafaro for Congress campaigns have been illegally registering people to vote and apply for absentee ballots. This is a terrible occurrence that will undermine the process of democracy. If you have been registered by any of these entities then you may run the risk of being illegally registered to vote. Please be advised that if you were registered in this capacity that you will not be able to vote until the next election. We apologize for these problems and we will pursue these entities to the fullest extent. Please notify the Lake County Sheriff's office if you have any questions.

In another incident, a flyer was distributed in Jefferson County, Alabama, that simply gave the wrong date for voting: "Attention: Jefferson County!!!!! See you at the Poles [sic] November 4th, 2004."

Then there is the use of sheer intimidation tactics on Election Day itself. In the 2003 Philadelphia mayoral election, an enormous fleet of three hundred black cars spent Election Day cruising African American neighborhoods. The cars bore insignias or decals resembling those on vehicles of federal agencies and were driven by men designed to mimic law enforcement agents. They would ask prospective voters to show identification in an effort to intimidate people from going to the polls.

In a less crude but just as transparent a way, Republican Party operatives have attempted to take advantage of "election challenger" laws in some states, like New Jersey, Michigan, Ohio, and Wisconsin. The goal was to turn people away from the polls and also create turmoil in order to lower turnout among voters who couldn't wait or didn't want to deal with the unpleasantness. On Election Day, Michigan Republicans filed a lawsuit accusing Detroit City Clerk Jackie Currie of wrongfully expelling some poll challengers from precincts. Later that day a judge barred the city from throwing out poll challengers without citing violations, effectively ruling that the rights of poll challengers be upheld over the rights of voters.

In another incident, the Wisconsin Republican Party asked that an additional 5,619 people challenged in Milwaukee be removed from voting lists. The Milwaukee board of elections refused to discard the registrations, but did comply with a request to require these voters to show identification at the polls after the GOP produced a list of thirty-seven thousand "questionable" addresses just minutes before the deadline for challenging voters was set to expire.

Voter suppression through "election challengers" was particularly galling in Ohio, the make-or-break contest in the Bush-Kerry race. After Republican mail-checks on all new Ohio voters turned up a list of thirty-five thousand voters whose mail was returned, they proposed to hold hearings on each person to determine his/her eligibility. The controversy resulted in two lawsuits filed in October that challenged the constitutionality of a 1953 Ohio law regarding poll challengers.

The first lawsuit was brought by Marian and Donald Spencer, two longtime civil rights activists in Cincinnati, who took up the issue because "these challengers were a manifestation of old Jim Crow laws" designed to "intimidate African Americans at the polls." Indeed, a sociologist from the University of Cincinnati found that 77 percent of African American voters would be challenged by partisan operatives while only 25 percent of white voters would be challenged. A similar lawsuit was filed in Akron by the Summit County Democrats. Federal judges ruled in favor of both plaintiffs, arguing that the challengers would discriminate against black voters in Hamilton County and that poll workers should determine voter eligibility, not challengers, in Akron.

These decisions sparked a countermovement to reinstate election challengers as necessary to ensure the purity of the election. On the very morning of election day, November 2, a three-judge panel ruled 2–1 to issue an emergency stay to the federal judges' decisions, which effectively allowed poll challengers to monitor the election process and to act on any alleged instance of voter fraud. In the opinion of the court, Circuit Judge John M. Rogers concluded that the concerns of long lines and voter intimidation posed by poll challengers certainly warranted some attention, but not enough to count as a "severe burden upon the right to vote that requires that the statutory authority for the procedure be declared unconstitutional." Circuit Judge James L. Ryan, in his concurring opinion, said that the grievances brought to the court were "wholly speculative, conjectural, and hypothetical." At the end of the day, the challengers didn't even appear, but the controversy and fear of their presence no doubt discouraged some voters from coming to the polls, as was the intent.

Suppressing and discouraging the vote by partisan operatives is bad enough. But unquestionably worse is when election officials sworn to uphold democracy are themselves the ones attempting to suppress it.

The most notorious example of this, of course, was Katherine Harris, former secretary of state of Florida, who is now attempting to parlay her disgraceful conduct during the 2000 election into a U.S. Senate seat. It is by now well documented that Harris, while serving simultaneously as the state's chief election official and the cochair of the Bush campaign in Florida, initiated an unprecedented purge of felons from the voter rolls. She used four million dollars of public funds and a Republican-connected company to prevent people from voting even when their rights had been restored in their home states, and even when the "match" between voter and felon was a dismal 80 percent. Despite the fact that the company itself, ChoicePoint, warned Harris of the "likelihood of a significant number of false positives and made recommendations to reduce those numbers," she barreled on ahead to make sure that Bush carried Florida, which he did only because of the purging from the roles of 57,700 people, and the legal debarment of over 800,000 potential voters, largely minority.

What is less well known is that Florida tried to do the same thing all over again in 2004. Secretary of State Glenda Hood conducted a second felon-purge of the state's voter list, and then refused to make public the list of forty-eight thousand potential felon voters. Alerted by what happened in 2000, U.S. Senator Bill Nelson and several media groups, including CNN, went to court and demanded the names be made public. When a court required disclosure of the names it turned out that huge numbers of African Americans were on the list, but only sixty-one Hispanics were. The list wrongly included twenty-one hundred former felons who had served their time, received clemency, and reacquired the right to vote. The state then abandoned use of the list. Not because it was the right thing to do, but only because they were caught.

Back to Ohio, where Secretary of State Kenneth Blackwell—a black Republican—is attempting, Harris-like, to parlay his own 2004 misconduct into a 2006 gubernatorial win. Blackwell undertook a number of blatantly partisan activities designed to keep turnout low. The first was a brazen and unsuccessful effort to refuse to allow people to register by saying he would only accept voter registrations if they were brought to the election offices on a particular kind of 80-pound card stock. Issued less than one month before Ohio's voter registration deadline, the directive would have invalidated all registration forms downloaded from the Internet, printed in the *Cleveland Plain Dealer*, and all those copied by organizations seeking to register voters. In fact, voter registration forms obtained at Blackwell's office itself were printed on 60-pound paper. Blackwell retracted the decision in September 2004 only after, once again, the scandal was exposed by advocates and the media.

The other effort to suppress the vote was to selectively interpret provisions of the 2004 Help America Vote Act (HAVA). For example, HAVA required that voter registration forms contain a box for people to check if they were citizens. But there is already a swearing or attestation statement on the card where an applicant states that they are a citizen. Even though people may have signed the statement attesting they are citizens, Blackwell ruled that they could not register if they had not *also* checked the box. In Florida, more opportunities to reject voter registration cards on the basis of a checked box arose with the inclusion of three boxes—one each for U.S. citizenship, felony status, and mental capacity—and also a space to include an identification number. An estimated ten thousand registrations were dismissed, and people were not allowed to vote by Florida's secretary of state Glenda Hood for failure to check off all boxes and to include a personal identification number. Yet in New Mexico and Iowa, the secretaries ruled that checking the box was duplicative and unnecessary.

Then Blackwell made a critical decision on provisional ballots about what to do if people went to the wrong polling place when they cast their provisional ballots. Although HAVA had mandated provisional ballots, it was unclear whether votes would be valid for those offices common to the two polling places, or if they would be rejected entirely. Blackwell used his discretion to reject them entirely, again unnecessarily disenfranchising many eligible voters. A federal judge issued a statement blaming the failure to issue clear, provisional voting guidelines on Blackwell: "The primary cause of the exigency is the defendant's failure to have issued Directive 2004–33 relating to provisional voting for nearly twenty-three months after HAVA's enactment...Blackwell has never explained why he waited so long to do anything to bring Ohio's provisional election procedures into line with federal law."

Procedural Failures

Not all voter suppression is as deliberate as that of Blackwell or Harris. Poorly trained poll workers, malfunctioning machinery, inadequately funded election processes, and other failures of administration also frustrate democracy at its point of impact—the voting booth.

One big problem is that the workforce overseeing our elections is simply inadequate. Because elections only take place a few times a year, the administrative mechanism involves a few professionals in each town or county and then a large corps of one-day-a-year people who staff the polling booths themselves. More than 1.2 million workers are required to conduct a U.S. presidential election. The National Conference of State Legislatures reports that the average workday for an election is fourteen to sixteen hours; yet most states do not allow "shift changes" and the average pay is only $6 per hour. A week before the November 2004 election, the federal Elections Assistance Commission (EAC) announced that the country was short about five hundred thousand poll workers. In addition, the New York Times reported that there was an acute shortage especially in urban areas, where the EAC and local election boards were having trouble finding poll workers who could speak more than one language.

Because of the irregular nature of the employment and low pay, poll workers are often elderly and retired people, unfamiliar in many cases with new technologies and usually selected because of political loyalty to one party or another. The training is often woefully inadequate. In a few places, municipal or county employees are allowed to take days off to work in the polls, while in others high school students are encouraged as an act of civic engagement. But by and large, this workforce is underpaid, under-trained, and ill-equipped for the challenges that they face.

Flawed Lists

Many voters are also discouraged and excluded from voting because of the poor quality of lists of eligible voters. Historically, voters have only been allowed to vote if their names are on such lists kept by the election administrators and distributed to workers at the polling places the morning of an election. Anyone who uses a credit card knows that the computer systems employed to maintain consumer spending records are pretty technologically advanced, but no one checks to see if one of their charges was inadvertently left off the monthly statement. Insurance companies, state highway patrols, and police departments can instantly access vast amounts of centralized data. Yet no such system can be found in the voting arena.

Before the Help America Vote Act mandated standardized voter registration databases, the management of voting lists, too, was a nightmare of irregular, localized, and uncoordinated procedures. In most states, lists have been kept by individual counties, and in a number of states by individual town election officials. In 2002, eight states maintained no voter records at all at the state level. In almost all of the states, still, lists are not cross-checked with each other, nor do they include names of people who have died or moved, and often do not even have the names of people who *have* registered.

How can this happen? In many cases, it's as simple as clerical error at the election office, failing to enter cards received or mis-entering them. Also, the people collecting voter registrations may not turn them in, either by error, as in the case of many motor vehicle agencies, or because, as was the case in Arizona in 2004, the firm collecting the forms didn't like the party choices of the new registrants! In any event, large numbers of eligible voters came to the polls in 2000, only to be told to go home. In many cases, busy phone lines and arguments with election staff resulted in the same non-voting outcome.

To respond to this problem, HAVA set out a requirement that every state and U.S. territory must have a database that is "a single, uniform, official, centralized, interactive computerized statewide voter registration list, defined, maintained, and administered at the state level that contains the name and registration information of every legally registered voter in the state and assigns a unique identifier to each legally registered voter in the state." States are now trying to comply with this mandate. But the process of switching from locally kept lists to statewide lists, and from old computer systems to newer, web-based systems, is technologically and politically complicated.

HAVA also created the concept of "provisional ballots" to be used when voters thought they should be allowed to vote but were not on the list. Provisional ballots would ensure that no registered voter would be turned away from the polls because of inaccurate lists. But the regulations about how provisional ballots should be implemented were very unclear in the law, creating a great deal of confusion over provisional ballots once they were cast.

In a 2004 national survey, Demos, a leading voting rights organization, found evidence of states that ignored both the spirit and letter of HAVA's provisional ballot requirement. In a report entitled "Placebo Ballots," the group described how election officials across the nation had instituted a confusing patchwork of provisional ballot rules that resulted in differing standards about how they should be offered or counted. The result was that registered voters in over half these states were given a ballot in 2004 with no promise that their vote would count. Demos found that "thirty-one states rejected provisional ballots cast in the wrong precinct—even when voters are selecting candidates for statewide offices like governor or U.S. senator, where the polling place error is immaterial."

Long Lines

If the visual image of the 2000 election was the "hanging chad," the residual image of the 2004 election consisted of long lines, sometimes appallingly so, especially in low-income communities of color and especially in Ohio. At Kenyon College, in Gambier, Ohio, students waited as long as nine hours before being able to vote. When the Democratic Party asked a judge to keep the polls open longer to deal with the line issue, he refused. Many polling places in the inner-city neighborhoods of Ohio had fewer voting machines in the 2004 election than in the

2000 election. Nearly half of the 146 wards in Ohio's Franklin County had fewer machines than four years ago, despite predictions before the election that Ohio's voter turnout would be much greater than in 2000. Yet these problems magically did not crop up in surrounding suburban counties.

A former chairman of the Cuyahoga County Board of Elections testified that, since the 1988 elections, the state had "reduced the number of precincts and the number of voting places, they've reduced the number of voting poll workers in each precinct. We had ten thousand that we used to use every election. It went down to six thousand. And they also reduced the voting machines."

Professor Jamie Galbraith of the University of Texas tells the following story:

"The real scandal of this election became clear to me at 6:30 p.m. on Election Day, as I drove a young African American voter, a charming business student, seven months pregnant, to her polling place at the Finland Elementary School in south Columbus, Ohio. We arrived in a squalling rain, to find voters lined up outside for about a hundred yards. Later the line moved indoors; we were told that the wait had averaged two hours for the entire day. By the time the doors closed at 7:30 p.m., it was considerably longer.

"Why such a line? Yes, turnout was a factor. But the real problem was a grotesque shortage of voting machines. Finland Elementary serves three precincts: Ward 37, A, B, and C. The election officer at the door told me that the smallest of these precincts had some four hundred registered voters, the middle-sized one had more than eight hundred, and the largest, 'thousands.' Voters were being limited to five minutes to finish their ballot, and because of its length and complexity most were using the full time.

"Each precinct had two functioning voting machines. The largest precinct was supposed to have three machines. One was broken at the opening, and later replaced with another machine that also did not function. It's not hard to do the math. Five minutes per voter means twelve voters per machine per hour. Ohio polls were open for thirteen hours, for a maximum throughput of 156 voters per machine, or 312 voters per precinct. That's barely enough for a 75 percent turnout in the smallest precinct of the three. For the larger precincts, it was a joke—on the voters.

"The miracle was the mood of the voters. They arrived in all their all-American splendor: work-clothes and sweatsuits, ponchos and umbrellas, baby packs and walkers, with almost infinite patience and good humor. In forty minutes I waited at the door, a half dozen voters left without voting. Only half a dozen—but multiply that over thirteen hours, and over the thousands of precincts, and you have the difference in this election. As I wrote this, waiting in the car at 8 p.m. and a half hour after the polls officially closed, perhaps three hundred more were still waiting inside the school. Most of them would stay there until they could vote. My young friend would tough it out."

Was this the result of deliberate misallocation of voting machines by election officials seeking to discourage people? A report by Michigan congressman John Conyers Jr., cataloging incidents of pervasive voting irregularities in Ohio, included specific mention of "wide discrepancy between the availability of voting machines in more minority, Democratic, and urban areas as compared to more Republican, suburban, and exurban areas." And Blackwell's previous partisan unfairness made his administration very vulnerable to the charge of willful suppression.

Machine Madness

So the election workforce is rickety, the lists inadequate, and machines often poorly allocated. But none of these issues have come close to getting the level of debate and acrimony that the voting machines themselves have generated. At first, if there was one thing people could agree on, it was that new machinery was essential to the modernization of the election process in the country. Punch cards were at the heart of thousands of miscounted votes in Florida in 2000, especially among elderly voters. The lever machines used in a number of states were invented in the 1890s, and have ceased to be manufactured, with old machines being cannibalized for parts for the remaining machines. New York City's lever machines are over fifty years old. It's not surprising then that machine shortages and failures are commonplace. When HAVA was passed in 2004, the bulk of the $3.9 billion dollars appropriated was expected to be spent on the purchase of new, computerized machinery.

But the need for new and effective machinery collided with the privatized, amateur, and decentralized nature of our election system with Katrina-force winds. Books, let alone a chapter, could be written about the controversies that have exploded around the transition to new voting technologies. Shortly after the 2000 election, when it became clear that there was about to be a major investment in the procurement of new machinery, machine companies of various kinds sprang into action. Electronic voting machine makers, whose products had gained only a little acceptance before 2000, partly because of their cost, began to lobby heavily for the acceptance of direct recording electronic machines or DREs. The other major technology for voting machines, optical scanning machines (pencils and bubbles), also began to make the case that they were the sensible alternative to punch cards and lever machines.

Local and county administrators proved no match for the sophisticated sales and lobbying techniques deployed by the machine companies. There were no federal standards for the machines, and no federal agency with any authority to set these standards or mediate disagreements. The certification process for new machines was a ramshackle system in which three private laboratories, all located in Alabama, certified machines according to standards set by the National Association of State Election Directors, an informal association of election directors from the states. Meanwhile, the companies insisted that their source codes were trade secrets and could not be revealed to election authorities. Secretaries of state, the chief election officials of states, had to make complicated decisions quickly and without adequate information about the machines they were being pressured to purchase. It was only a matter of time before controversy and distrust erupted.

The DREs had an initial advantage, especially when HAVA in October 2002 required that each polling place have one machine accessible to handicapped voters by the 2006 election. By contrast, the optical scanning machines, though cheaper, operated on the technology adopted in the 1950s by standardized testing agencies, with the pencil and paper electronically scored. They seemed more old-hat than the wave of the future.

Skeptics—led initially by Bev Harris, author of *Black Box Voting*, and including a good number of computer experts—claimed also that the electronic machines were inherently untrustworthy, subject to outside hacking and corporate programming manipulation. We have "not even sought the counsel of the very people who understand this type of accounting: Accountants, bookkeepers, and auditors!" Harris observed.

They argued and lobbied for a "VVPT," a voter-verifiable paper trail, like the Brazilian system. Harris warned, "any computerized voting system that requires us to trust a few computer scientists and some corporate executives constitutes a flawed public policy...The real problem is that we've created a voting system controlled by someone else." The "electoral photo finish" has highlighted this problem. The integrity of the democratic process will depend on a voter-verifiable paper trail system of the kind optical scanners provide that can easily reproduce the results of an election—how else to ensure that an election outcome really represents the people's mandate?

This controversy became inflamed by comments from Wally O'Dell, the president of Diebold, an Ohio-based company and manufacturer of most electronic voting machines, when he said that he would "do everything possible to deliver" the state of Ohio to George Bush in 2004. The controversy widened when a Diebold insider dubbed "Dieb-throat" charged that O'Dell had tried to "evade meeting legal requirements or implementing appropriate security measures and had put corporate interests ahead of the interests of voters." Among the many problems categorized by Bev Harris was the example of a computer program titled "rob-georgia.zip," which was left on an unsecured server and downloaded over the Internet by Diebold technicians before they loaded the unauthorized software onto Georgia voting machines.

Several states that were initially ready to purchase the DREs pulled back from them, preferring to wait until the paper trail issue could be resolved or a new technology solution found. In several states, the process stopped and reversed course midstream when pre-testing of machines revealed major malfunctions. Then in March of 2006, Maryland's House of Delegates voted 137–0 to drop its Diebold machines and switch to more reliable (and unhackable) paper ballots.

The problems of finding the right machinery are now largely unsolved. The discredited punch cards of Florida in 2000 are still in use in 11 percent of the voting precincts around the country, while lever machines continue to be used in 11.6 percent of voting precincts, despite tremendous difficulties in getting replacement parts and despite their lack of accessibility for people who are blind or disabled. Overall, seventeen states reported to the National Association of Secretaries of State that they will miss the January 1, 2006, deadline to comply with Help

America Vote Act's provision to replace punch card voting systems. Of those states, four have blamed slow state legislatures and seven stated the bidding process was the cause.

Gradually, however, progress is starting to be made as more states are requiring voter-verified paper trails and electronic features that guarantee the disabled will be able to cast a ballot. The federal government, through the Election Assistance Commission, is due to take over the testing and certification mechanism for new machines. But a perfected system, with voters able to have confidence that machines will work and that they are free from hacking and manipulation, is still far away.

LONG-TERM STRUCTURAL FAILURES

Making It Hard for People to Register and Vote

The attention of the nation has focused on the failures of election administration since the Florida fiasco of 2000. In fact, there remains a long, daunting, and persistent set of barriers that have restricted full participation in our democracy. In terms of numbers of people affected, these structural problems are undoubtedly a greater deterrent to voting than either the partisan efforts to intimidate voters or the stark flaws in election administration.

Perhaps the most egregious problem is the legal disenfranchisement of almost five million citizens because they were convicted of a felony, a policy that began largely in former slave states in the late nineteenth century. There are millions more who are effectively disenfranchised due to confusion over how incarceration affects their voting rights and whether, when, and how these rights can be restored following release, as seen recently in Florida. This issue is far more than an individual criminal justice issue—it is a racially discriminatory exclusion that stains the fabric of democracy.

Sasha Abramsky, a senior fellow at Demos, gives two examples of the lifelong impact of felony disenfranchisement on pair of young men: "Twenty-five years ago, a young African American man from Dothan, Alabama, got drunk and wandered into a stranger's house. Frightened, the woman called the police and the teenager was arrested. He was told that he faced several years in prison for breaking and entering; instead, the judge listened to testimonials about the eighteen-year-old's character from the local boys' club and other organizations, and decided to put him on probation. Over the past quarter century, the man has remained crime-free and has become a model citizen. He has been a volunteer for decades with the Boys' Club, a mentor to local teenagers—yet, because of his one felony conviction, he still cannot vote." A Vietnam War veteran told Abramsky, "I was [arrested] on the 1965 voting rights march from Selma. I was fifteen years old. At eighteen, I was in Vietnam fighting for my country. And now? Unemployed and they won't allow me to vote."

In the summer of 1999, twenty-five-year-old Jamaica S. was convicted of a low-level felony that came about as a result of a crime committed by her boyfriend. This conviction permanently prohibited her from voting in Tennessee unless she is able to either convince the governor to pardon her, or persuade the district court that she was worthy of having her rights restored—two difficult tasks for an ex-felon in a tough-on-crime southern state.

In an interview, Jamaica laments, "It seems when you're convicted of a felony, the scarlet letter is there. You take it everywhere with you...I've told myself that I don't deserve it [the vote]. That I do make bad decisions. Why should I make decisions for anyone when I can't take care of myself? But it's been five years, and I realize my point of view is very important. I feel like not a whole person in many ways. It makes me feel like there's a caste system and I've become one of the untouchables. It's unbelievable it could happen in America. It's ironic they go overseas and seek to promote democracy in other countries—force it on other countries—but in America they deny the right to vote to so many people. It's the hypocrisy of our democracy. They assume anyone who's been in trouble is not intelligent and probably don't care about their right to vote."

Florida House Speaker Tom Feeney, a Republican and opponent of restoring the vote to felons, said in a 2001 interview, "at some point you have to ask yourself whether or not an electorate that is increasingly less likely to be literate, whether expansion of the franchise to just everyone who has two arms and two legs, is the best way to govern a democracy for the future. It's less important to me that I have the right to vote than the people that do are upholding the integrity and legitimacy of the society and culture."

As Feeney's comments unintentionally reveal, felony disenfranchisement laws have their roots in the Jim Crow laws in the South and the resistance to ethnic immigrant city-dwellers in the North. Florida's disenfranchisement law, for instance, was first enacted in 1868. In many states, the laws were designed to include felonies more often committed by newly freed slaves. In 1906, Carter Glass, a delegate to the Virginia Constitutional Convention, said of the felony disenfranchisement statute: "This plan will eliminate the darkey as a political factor in this state in less than five years."

Because there are no federal standards, felony disenfranchisement laws vary dramatically from state to state. In some states an individual convicted of a first-time nonviolent offense, such as a writing of a bad check, may be permanently disenfranchised. In numerous other states, individuals regain the right to vote upon completion of their sentences. In four states—Kentucky, Virginia, Florida, and Alabama—once you have been convicted, your voting rights are lost permanently. In Florida alone, almost eight hundred thousand people are barred from voting (which is a lot more than the 537-vote margin of the 2000 general election vote there), including 25 percent of the African American men in the state. In Alabama, 31 percent of African American men cannot vote for this reason alone.

Another major barrier to full electoral participation is the arbitrary determination of advance deadlines for voter registration. In a majority of states, the deadline by which a person must register to vote is about twenty-eight days before an election. Again, these deadlines have roots in the early part of the twentieth century, when political elites attempted to make it difficult for unwelcome newcomers to enter the body politic.

Justified more recently by the need for understaffed election administrators to get the voting lists ready for Election Day, this rule is perfectly designed to shut down registrations just when interest in the election process peaks. It particularly affects young people, including college students who are going to a new city when registration deadlines take effect; people who move more frequently; new citizens; and lower-income people generally. There are six states that have Election Day Registration (EDR), and the difference in turnout in these states is remarkable: in the 2004 election, states with EDR had a turnout rate of 14 percentage points higher than in states where people had to register in advance.

Joe Courtney, a Democratic candidate for Congress in Connecticut in 2002 who lost to a Republican incumbent, expressed frustration that on Election Day many people, particularly young people, came up to him and said they wanted to vote for him but couldn't because they had missed the deadline for registering. "We say we want young people to participate; why do we make it this hard for them to enter the process?"

Another registration failure is the massive non-implementation of the public assistance provision of the National Voter Registration Act, known as the "Motor Voter" law. Passed in 1993, the incorrectly nicknamed law requires states to allow people to register when they are applying for a drivers' license or by mail; it also requires the public assistance agencies of the state to offer people the right to register to vote when they apply or recertify for services or when they inform the agency of a change of address. Ten years after the law went into effect, the driver's license provision and the mail-in provision have been broadly implemented, but the public assistance requirement has been very largely ignored. Recent investigations by Demos and Project Vote have shown that in most states compliance has been inadequate, and that the percentages of people registered at the agencies have been very low. If it were consistently implemented, it would create literally millions of opportunities each year for people to become registered and join the election process.

Beyond making it cumbersome to register, our election process has also made it pretty inconvenient to vote. Going back to the agricultural origins of the nation, we have an Election Day on a working Tuesday in November. Ambassador Andrew Young has formed a group with the simple name, "Why Tuesday?" Rather than make Election Day a holiday or hold it on a weekend, we have a created a situation in which people who work, and certainly people with children or elderly parents or other responsibilities in addition to working, have a serious challenge in voting within the specified period. In addition, in most states balloting by mail (interestingly called "absentee balloting") is restricted to people with certain kinds of excuses, such as ill health or absence from the state. Banks have decided that it is important to allow people to bank at the hours that are convenient for them by instituting ATMs and online banking. Stores are open twenty-four hours to meet people's schedule. But our democracy operates on eighteenth-century farmers' hours.

Uncompetitive Elections

Americans have increasingly stressful and busy lives, with both parents of a family working most of the time, or a single head of a household working double time. It is not a hard leap for people to say, "I just don't have time for this" when it comes to the political process.

As previously discussed, fewer and fewer congressional elections are even competitive, which makes it that much more likely that a potential voter will decide it doesn't matter. In the November 2004 election, of the 410 House incumbents facing reelection, all but 5 were reelected; and all 26 senators facing re-election were re-elected.

Why so little competition? One reason is the redistricting process. By carefully redrawing their districts, state officials and legislators are picking their constituents when it's supposed to be the other way around. With sophisticated computer and demographic tools at their disposal, legislative redistricting committees draw lines carefully, often in a bipartisan manner, to protect incumbents of both parties and narrow the range of contested elections. So instead of voters calling the shots, mapmakers do. In California in 2004, not a single one of the 153 legislative and congressional seats changed hands. In Massachusetts in 2004, over one third of candidates for legislative races had no opponent whatsoever. The Council for Excellence in Government and the Campaign Legal Center jointly reported that "the 2002 and 2004 congressional elections saw fewer competitive seats than ever (perhaps 35 of 435), and a higher percentage of incumbents winning re-election (97.7 percent) and winning by greater margins (90.6 percent with 55 percent or more of the vote)." Since residential patterns are becoming more and more segregated politically as well, it doesn't take much to eliminate competition in the vast majority of races.

America's winner-take-all system adds to the alienation. Because of it, a candidate with 51 percent of the vote gets 100 percent of the victory, and the losing candidate and his supporters get zero percent, even if he got 49 percent of the vote. So unless a race is genuinely competitive, there is little incentive for a voter to go out and help the favored candidate because it won't make any difference in the outcome. Some argue that proportional representation would be a system that far more closely reflects voters' preferences. If a "list" of candidates were nominated for a slate of positions, the result would be a mix of representatives that approximated the percentages of the votes cast for each of the candidates. Nearly thirty countries have integrated some form of proportional representation into their election system, including Germany, Hungary, the United Kingdom, Israel, and Nicaragua. Many places in America originally had variants of proportional representation, but they have mostly been replaced by these winner-take-all systems.

The problems of the winner-take-all system are readily apparent in the Electoral College's role in presidential races. The division of the country into so-called red states and blue states, many of which are considered fundamentally un-winnable or un-losable for one major party or the other, narrows the number of states where campaigning for a presidential campaign makes sense. This can have the dual impact of over-killing the "battleground states" and creating apathy in the solidly one-party states because a candidate will never campaign there or learn about those voters' issues. This short-shrifts debate on all kinds of important topics, and it also depresses the vote for "down-ticket" elections in states that are solidly Democratic or Republican.

Winner-take-all campaigns also allow a candidate to win with a plurality of votes but far short of a majority. In a four-way race, 26 percent of the voters could be enough for a candidate to be elected. To prevent this outcome, a number of jurisdictions have instituted runoffs in elections with more than two candidates. But the problem with these races is that the runoff, often conducted weeks or even over a month later, usually attract only a fraction of the number of votes cast in the original election. So candidates can win with an even smaller number of votes.

One solution is Instant Runoff Voting (IRV). In IRV, candidates are ranked by voters in order of preference. If no one receives over 50 percent, the last vote-getter is dropped off, and the votes are redistributed—electronically and instantaneously—to voters' second choices. This way, a majority of people will always elect the winner on election night, since the process is continued until someone gets a 50 percent majority.

Stridently negative campaigns also have a large role in keeping people from the polls. In many races, by the time the candidates get finished making chopped liver of each other, voters may be forgiven for thinking that neither of the candidates are worth voting for. The truth is that candidates don't need to get a large percentage of voters to cast a vote in order to win; they just need to get one more vote than their opponent. While the comparing and contrasting of views and candidates can make a race exciting, barrages of personal attacks and name-calling hardly inspires ordinary citizens to participate in the process. Consider the

New Jersey gubernatorial mudslinging contest last year, when the estranged former wife of Senator John Corzine was employed in an "attack ad." In other ads, one candidate's face morphs into that of a hated figure. Even corporate America has not gone down the road of negative campaigning against competitors' products. At least not yet.

Finally, the campaign finance system cannot help but tilt the conversation and even the mindset of candidates toward the needs of the wealthy and away from the poor, toward special interest and away from common good. Increasingly, self-financing candidates with multi-million dollar checkbooks are sought after by parties who have elevated money over merit in their choice of candidates, as chapter 2 covers in greater length.

A "Fraud"ulent Excuse

Conservatives understand that the way in which the electorate is enlarged or kept small can affect outcomes, both electoral and legislative. So they make the specious charge that we need many of these hurdles to voting because elections are being subjected to massive voter fraud

With hardly a shred of evidence, John Fund of the *Wall Street Journal* has also claimed that elections are being stolen and that the process is far too voter-friendly and must be further restricted. Prior to the election of 2004, John Fund wrote:

> Five thousand to eight thousand fraudulent voter-registration forms had recently come in—courtesy, election officials believed, of the Public Interest Research Group, a liberal advocacy outfit...Project Vote, another left-wing advocacy group, had filed scores of applications with phony addresses and other questionable items...Why is such activity proliferating? It flows from the success of Democratic lawmakers in pushing aside clear, orderly, and rigorous voting procedures in favor of elastic and "inclusive" election rules that invite manipulation.

Republicans in Washington state claimed that voter fraud put Christine Gregoire into the governor's office, but no serious evidence was ever produced, and the courts dismissed the challenges to her election. In

Wisconsin, a cadre of Republican legislators have loudly cried fraud, but, just recently, U.S. Attorney Steven Biskupic, a Bush-appointee charged with leading a year-long investigation into claims of voter fraud, revealed that there was no "massive conspiracy to alter the election in Milwaukee" and only spotty evidence of individual voter fraud.

Arguments about preventing voter fraud have become a fig leaf for a draconian system of requiring identification from voters. This proposal was unveiled at the federal level by the Carter-Baker Commission, which was the successor to the Carter-Ford Commission, cochaired by Jimmy Carter and James Baker. Baker, based on his partisan and successful experience in Florida in 2000, outmaneuvered the commission and hijacked its high-minded purposes with a call for using the "REAL ID Card" as the basis for identifying voters at the polling places. The commission's recommendation for a REAL ID Card seemed to innocently extend the standard state-issued ID card to include a simple check on voter eligibility. The REAL ID Card would require a state-issued ID card to be "adapted for voting purposes to indicate whether the individual is a U.S. citizen."

But it's one thing to require multiple proofs of identification in order to operate a motor vehicle, and another to require voters to visit the DMV every time they move or switch political affiliation just to make sure they can exercise the right to vote in the next election. It's also not reasonable to expect groups that generally do not drive (elderly, disabled, and low-income) or are more likely to move (students, low-income communities, and incarcerated individuals) to smoothly adjust to such a complex rule. In fact, one of the most bizarre non-findings in the Carter-Baker commission report was that "despite a lack of evidence, fraud does exist."

Georgia is a fascinating story in itself. The voter identification bill there was conjured up, again, without any evidence or allegation of voter fraud whatsoever. Secretary of State Cathy Cox strongly opposed the bill, arguing it was unnecessary. When proponents of the measure were pressed about the lack of evidence or allegations, they had to pull up a case from years before that involved absentee vote buying schemes in Dodge County, a case that would not even have been prevented by requiring photo ID at the polls. Nevertheless, with Republicans in full control of the legislature for the first time since Reconstruction, they flexed their muscles fully and passed the ID bill, even though a large number of legislators walked out of the chamber in protest.

Because Georgia is covered under Section 5 of the Voting Rights Act, however, any major changes in its election processes must be "precleared" before they go into effect. Although the Bush Justice Department did preclear this law, it was immediately challenged by many of Georgia's black lawmakers. Democratic Representative Bob Holmes of Atlanta, Georgia, said, "This is something that will depress the voter turnout, particularly among the poor, elderly, and rural, and a segment of the African American community." U.S. District Judge Harold Murphy enjoined enforcement of the law, stating that in his judgment a strong prima facie case existed that the law was in violation of the Voting Rights Act because the requirement that a voter have a driver's license or a $20 state-issued card was tantamount to a forbidden poll tax. Shortly afterwards, the bill was revised to provide "free" photo IDs to voters, but only to individuals who have the time and money to obtain four proofs of identification. The bill still passed in Georgia's Senate.

After the court decision came down, some internal Justice Department documents were leaked to the *Washington Post* showing that the career lawyers for the Voting Rights division had strongly recommended opposing the law, but were overruled by the political appointees in the department, which permitted the state of Georgia to go ahead. Moreover, the leaked memo revealed that the bill's primary sponsor, Georgia House representative Sue Burmeister, had said that if African Americans were "not paid to vote, they don't go to the polls," and therefore the photo ID bill would not affect African Americans anyway.

We can expect the mantra of voter fraud to be repeated often and vehemently in coming elections. But a Demos study in 2003, *Securing the Vote,* still the most serious effort to assess voter fraud, had as its central conclusion that "available evidence suggests that the incidence of election fraud is minimal across the fifty U.S. states, and rarely affects election outcomes" and that "efforts to make it easier to register and vote are compatible with the prevention of election fraud."

BRINGING VOTERS BACK INTO ELECTIONS

The problems in creating a democracy that is vibrant and inclusive are obviously numerous. But there is real reason for a new optimism, both at the federal level and especially the state level.

Activity at the Federal Level

"Four months after the presidential contest ended with calls for fundamental changes to the electoral system," lamented columnist David
Broder, "almost no remedial laws have been enacted and the sense
among election administrators is that the opportunity for significant
improvements may have been lost." But five years later, the level of continuing change at the federal and state levels is remarkable, as is the
sense that even larger changes are coming.

First of all, after months of gridlock and charge/countercharge, the
federal Help America Vote Act was passed in October of 2001. Contrary
to early expectations, it has indeed put a substantial amount of federal
money into the project of changing and modernizing the administration
of elections in this country. The law authorized $3.9 billion to be spent
over three years, with financing available not only for new voting
machines but also for upgrading the voting lists, professionalizing poll
worker training, and for a variety of voter education and civic engagement projects. It also set significant timelines for improvements at the
state level, including computerized voting lists in each state by January of
2006, the outlawing of punch card voting systems, and the requirement
that every polling place have at least one machine designed to be usable
by handicapped people. In addition, HAVA created the Election
Assistance Commission (EAC), a new federal commission (deliberately
not called an "authority") to help establish national standards and promote best practices throughout the sphere of election administration. And
while this commission was given very little enforcement power, it did
receive significant resources and a strong research agenda, as well as the
ability to set guidelines and standards in a variety of areas.

The implementation of HAVA and the commission did indeed get off
to a slow and bumpy start. To begin with, President Bush did not name
the commissioners until almost a year later. Once the Election Assistance
Commission did become genuinely operational, however, it began to
have significant impact. Its four members—two Republicans, two
Democrats—have interacted well, both with each other and with the
states. In addition, the EAC is due to take over the certification process
from the privatized laboratories that have done the certification in the
past. So the wheel is very much in spin at the federal level.

Activity at the State Level

Wider Registration

Nowhere is progress more significant than with felony disenfranchisement laws. Denying voting rights to felons who have "paid their debt to society" is a gross violation of democratic rights, yet reform historically has been difficult due to the racial and political consequences. Also, over the last twenty years, no one wanted to be accused of being "soft on crime," and "allowing criminals to vote" had just such a ring.

Nevertheless, several states have changed their laws after the 2000 Florida debacle. In Connecticut, the legislature passed a law in 2001 that allowed people on probation to register and vote, and a Republican governor signed it into law. More recently, Nebraska enacted a law ending the lifetime prohibition on voting for ex-felons, though in this case it was done by overriding a gubernatorial veto.

The issue has had surprising resonance with some Republicans as well, with the theme of "redemption" being the key. Former congressman Jack Kemp recently told Congress that he strongly supported the restoration of voting rights to people who had completed their sentences. When asked to comment on his supporting testimony to Congress on the extension of the 1965 Voting Rights Act, Kemp said, "Voting in America is the quintessential part of our democracy, and once a felon has paid his or her time and is no longer under any charges, in my opinion, should be given the incentive for civilized behavior by restoring the right to vote...And let's face it. Voting registration in the past was used by some to deny African Americans their right to vote, and this country has an obligation in the twenty-first century to, I think, remove every single impediment to every American having the right to vote and every American having his or her vote count."

A number of states have also lowered their artificial registration deadlines, bringing them closer to, or even to, Election Day. The state of Montana passed legislation in 2005 enacting Election Day registration, making it the seventh state in the country to do so. Massachusetts and Vermont are also poised to pass EDR legislatively as well in 2006. In Connecticut, the registration deadline was pulled closer, to one week before the election. In Illinois, a "grace period" was created that essentially allows people to register up to fourteen days before Election Day; in addition,

Governor Rod Blagojevich signed a 2005 law there in August 2005 to allow registered voters to vote twenty-two days before Election Day.

Easier Voting

Along with making changes to make it easier to register, states have begun to take steps to make it more convenient and accessible to vote as well. Twenty states have initiated early voting, including Arkansas, Colorado, and Georgia, giving voters the option to vote during a specified period prior to Election Day, thus cutting down the congestion and lines on Election Day. Many people feel that one reason the state of Florida did not have as severe voting problems in 2004 as they did in 2000 is because about 20 percent of Florida's voters voted early at voting centers, which meant they were not standing in line on Election Day. In addition to early voting, several states, like North Carolina and Nebraska, have adopted wider options for mail-in balloting, sometimes called "no-excuse absentee ballots." One of the earliest and most prominent versions occurred in Oregon, beginning with local elections in 1981 and culminating with all-mail balloting in the January 1996 special election for the U.S. Senate. The process leads to voting turnout over ten percentage points higher than the national average and it's hugely popular, with 81 percent in a 2003 University of Oregon poll preferring mailing in their ballot to going to a polling place. According to an *American Prospect* article on the innovation:

> At least two weeks before Election Day, every registered Oregon voter gets a ballot courtesy of the U.S. Postal Service. The voter can take the full period, or less, to come to a decision. Then the voter places the ballot into a special envelope and mails it off to one of the thirty-six county tabulation centers. The ballots must be signed and the signature must match one on the registration card, so that theft and fraud are essentially nonexistent...There is no worry of machines breaking down, being in short supply, or hacked; no long lines, no partisan wrangling at polling places; and far less incentive for last-minute smears. And, at a time of electronic horrors, vote by mail is the ultimate paper trail.

Other important reforms have been enacted. The City of San Francisco in 2004 adopted Instant Runoff Voting, which will substantially increase the number of voters participating in the final decision about who will be elected to the mayoralty and the city council. Even comprehensive campaign finance has begun to move. The Connecticut legislature in December of 2005 enacted a comprehensive, full public financing bill, which provides an equal playing field of funding for candidates for governor, Senate, and House by giving funds to the qualifying candidates in amounts that make it possible to run a reasonable campaign without a candidate spending half his or her time raising money. The new law also bans contributions from lobbyists and state contractors in all state races.

To address the remaining problems, Senators Hillary Clinton (D-NY) and John Kerry (D-MA) introduced the "Count Every Vote Act" of 2005. It provides federal guidelines and funds to avoid the long waits at the polls, flawed voter purges, and felon disenfranchisement. The bill also requires paper trails be available from all electronic voting machines, asks for same-day registration to become the norm, and creates a national voting holiday to make voting even easier. Such a "Democracy Day" could be coupled with Veterans Day to give everyone the opportunity to participate in elections. HAVA combined with Count Every Vote could make sure that millions of voters will no longer be limited to one potentially rainy Tuesday in November and help assure the world that we practice at home what we preach abroad.

WHAT RULE OF LAW?
I: TAKING LIBERTIES

"When the president does it, that means it is not illegal."
—President Richard Nixon, 1973

"A state of war is not a blank check for the president."
—Justice Sandra Day O'Connor, 2004

"The greatest dangers to liberty lurk in insidious encroachment by men of zeal, well-meaning, but without understanding."
—Justice Louis B. Brandeis

At first and second glance, the rule of law would appear to be both a bedrock principle of democracy and a cornerstone of conservative thought.

For the law truly *conserves*. A society could be governed instead by the law of the jungle, where lions will eat lambs according to a might-makes-right principle. Thomas Hobbes famously wrote in *Leviathan* in 1651 that life in a state of nature, without government and law, would be "solitary, poor, nasty, brutish, and short." But what happens if numerous lambs organize to attack a lion? There's a reason why business owners should love the law that protects their property from more numerous citizens. Hence we have eight hundred years of Common Law and Constitutional Law which both inhibit and protect all of us from arbitrary rulers or neighbors.

Apparently, however, when he was informed as president-elect that it was his constitutional duty "to faithfully *execute* the laws," George W. Bush took it literally. Other than perhaps Nixon, no president has been so contemptuous of the rule of law.

The origins of his disdain are difficult to pinpoint. As a young man, without seeking his father's advice or help, he applied to the University of Texas Law School—and was rejected. Scorned by this legal institution, he turned to a career in business and would regularly articulate a standard business hostility to federal regulations and lawsuits.

As president, he chose for the position of attorney general not an experienced lawyer or scholar but an ideological soul mate, John Ashcroft. When asked a question at a presidential press conference about the lawfulness of invading Iraq, Bush's tone turned sarcastic. "Is it legal? Oh my, I'd better call my lawyer." When questioned by *FOX News*'s Brit Hume about Tom DeLay's indictment in December 2005, he initially replied that he didn't want to politicize or prejudge the case. Yet when then asked, "Do you believe he's innocent?" Bush plunged in. "Do I? Yes, I do." And when his top political aide Karl Rove spoke about the "war on terrorism" to New York conservatives in 2005, he mocked how "liberals believed it was time to submit a petition...and wanted to prepare indictments" after 9/11—such girly men!—while the right wing prepared for war. (Of course, Bush's Justice Department also tried to "prepare indictments"—that is, prosecute—terrorists, but other than its troubled Padilla case, they have largely failed to do so.)

While hard to locate the origin of Bush's antipathies to law and lawyers, it's not hard to document them. In the Republican world of ends justifying means, the president again and again seems to regard the law as largely a political impediment, to be ignored as one would a heckling questioner. For example:

◆ The Supreme Court, with seven of nine justices being Republican appointees, concluded that a) the rules of incarceration at Guantánamo Bay were an unconstitutional denial of due process of law and b) the refusal of Bush's Justice Department to allow Oregon's "Death with Dignity Act" to take effect was unlawful.

◆ A Court of Appeals in March 2006 unanimously ruled that Bush's Environmental Protection Agency had violated the "plain language" of the Clean Air Act when it allowed many power plants, refineries, and factories to avoid installing new pollution control equipment.

◆ The Bush administration has repeatedly and unilaterally snubbed internationally binding commitments, such as the Chemical and Biological Weapons Convention, the Anti-Ballistic Missile Treaty, the

International Criminal Court, and the Geneva Conventions—and done everything to throttle agreements to limit small arms sales, global warming, and nuclear proliferation.

✦ The Government Accountability Office, an independent, nonpartisan arm of Congress, concluded that the Bush administration had illegally disseminated "covert propaganda" when it gave hundreds of thousands of federal dollars to conservative columnists to write articles supportive of administration policies.

✦ Investigators at the Corporation for Public Broadcasting said that its chairman, Bush appointee Kenneth Y. Tomlinson, had often violated federal law by his partisan and political interference in programming decisions.

✦ White House memoranda condoned torture—and then widespread torture occurred in U.S.-run prisons abroad.

✦ Bush repeatedly ignored the requirement for obtaining a court warrant for domestic spying under the 1978 Foreign Intelligence Surveillance Act.

✦ For the first time in 160 years, a top White House aide has been criminally indicted, actually two White House aides—Procurement Chief David Safavian and Vice Presidential Aide I. Lewis "Scooter" Libby.

✦ As best summarized by Charlie Savage in the *Boston Globe* in May 2006, President Bush has asserted his power to ignore 750 laws enacted by Congress (since he took office)—all signed by him after congressional passage—because of his belief that these laws were unconstitutional. So a couple hundred years after *Marbury v. Madison* established the precedent of judicial review—i.e., as the ultimate decider, courts would judge whether a law was constitutional or not—George W. Bush's theory of the "unitary executive" means he can unilaterally and selectively overrule Congress and courts. Thus does our forty-third president take on the second president, John Adams, who concluded that "the executive shall never exercise the legislative and judicial powers, or either of them, to the end that it may be a government of laws and not men."*

---

*The White House's belief in a "unitary executive," a phrase Bush has mentioned ninety-five times in signing statements and executive orders, is a theory woven out of whole cloth with no serious basis in law. The Supreme Court has repeatedly ruled— in *Ex Parte Mulligan* against Lincoln's suspension of habeas corpus, in *Youngtown Sheet and Tube* opposing Truman's seizure of U.S. Steel companies, and most recently in opposing Bush's illegal confinement of detainees in Guantánamo without hearings—that the president too must obey the laws, even those he doesn't like.

WINKING AT TORTURE

From Washington to Geneva to Gonzales

In a kind of etiquette for killing, armed conflict has always had rules and laws. And since the Revolutionary War, Americans have prided themselves on their treatment of prisoners of war—from refusing to throw captured redcoats into filthy prison ships as the British did to our militiamen; to the execution of Confederate officers for murdering Union prisoners at Andersonville; to the court-martialing of soldiers during World War I for the abuse of captured enemies.

This was the tradition that led to the 1949 Geneva Conventions, and now 192 nations are party to them. They are a series of agreements that together determine how democracies conduct themselves in wartime and treat prisoners of war. While some may regard these extensive policies as roadblocks to victory, the president of the Israeli Supreme Court, Ahron Barak, noted that "sometimes, a democracy must fight with one hand tied behind its back. Nonetheless, it has the upper hand. Preserving the rule of law and recognition of individual liberties constitute an important component of [a democracy's] understanding of security."

The conventions include clear directives regulating detention, even stipulating the number of cigarettes required each day per prisoner. But mostly they concern themselves with preventing abusive interrogation techniques, such as forced nudity, feigned executions, and, in fact, any kind of physical coercion. The reasoning is twofold: first, torture is inhumane; second, if we do it to our enemies, what's to stop them from doing it to us? It was two centuries of American policy against torture that the Bush administration was seeking to undo in the infamous "torture memos" of 2002 that discussed suspending legal protections for captured al-Qaeda members. Written by the White House counsel Alberto Gonzales and law professor John Yoo, these memoranda declared that outright torture by the CIA "may be justified" and that torture in a post-9/11 world is a "necessity" and "self-defense could provide justifications that would eliminate any criminal liability."

Gonzales and Yoo helped build the shaky legal platform for what the federal and military intelligence agencies had long wanted to do: untie both hands and fight dirty. Arguing that interrogation is torture only if it results in "organ failure" or death also seriously damaged our reputation internationally. The most visible example of this legal gray area is the five hundred classified detainees being held by "secret" evidence in Guantánamo Bay, Cuba (Gitmo). Set up shortly after the tragedy of September 11 and the invasion of Afghanistan to hold alleged "terrorists," both domestic and foreign born, this facility has been the laboratory for these new legal theories, just as Iraq has been the testing ground for Secretary Rumsfeld's smaller, quicker, more technology-reliant army.

State Department officials initially disputed the White House's facile dispensing with *habeas corpus* and other protections of terror-suspects, calling the new approach "untenable," "incorrect," and "confused." The State Department also cast doubt upon Yoo's assertion that Afghanistan was a "failed state" and therefore not covered by the Geneva Conventions, including the provisions regarding physical coercion in intelligence gathering. The Gonzales-Yoo approach meant that methods brushing right up against torture would become accepted interrogation techniques because we weren't dealing with "real" soldiers. Now, instead of POWs with clearly defined rights, there were the nebulous "illegal enemy combatants"—a category so vague that it even included American citizens.

The war president suddenly had the ability to erase the legal identity of whomever he wished, tossing them into detainee camps with practically no charges, no lawyers, no legal recourse, and for an unlimited duration. According to the activists in the president's, and especially the vice president's, offices, the October 2001 invasion of Afghanistan could in fact proceed in whatever manner it desired because the Taliban were merely a band of murderers. Together, Gonzales and Yoo were in the process of successfully recasting the commander in chief as an omnipotent emperor.

The Supreme Court, however, disagreed, and in 2005 finally granted the military lawyers representing Gitmo prisoners the right to challenge the secret extra-legal proceedings against their clients. Unfortunately, to forestall this judicial reckoning day, Congress scrambled to pass the Defense Authorization Bill in 2005 that Lindsay Graham (R-SC) said would help "eliminate *habeas corpus* rights for detainees captured during the terrorism fight, to halt 'the never-ending litigation that is coming from Guantánamo.'" In other words, when the Supreme Court ruled against the Bush administration's policies, their party members in the House moved to *change the law* and create another obstacle for those still seeking a modicum of justice.

But ignoring *habeas corpus* and the Geneva Conventions is strategically perilous. To do so strips American troops of standard protections and legal shields should they be captured anywhere by anyone. A war without Geneva is a horror-house mirror that would flip our own crimes back upon us, rendering our troops into "enemy combatants" in the international eye—illegally armed torturers due neither the process nor the writ we have denied the detainees in our prisons. Either everyone is party to the conventions, or no one is.

It is this danger that explains why so many men and women in uniform have come out against any winking at or systematization of abuse. Essential to the success of reconstruction in postwar Japan and Germany—two efforts to which the current imbroglio in Iraq is often compared by the Bush administration—was the fact that the liberating Americans showed unequivocally that they would not torture POWs (as the Japanese did) or physically mistreat "liberated" civilians and civilian officials (as the Red Army did).

When America Tortures: Gitmo and Ghraib

The American public became aware of what these newly sanctioned interrogation tactics looked like only in late 2002, when newspapers revealed that U.S. security agents at Gitmo were regularly implementing "stress and duress" positions during interrogation of prisoners who had been captured over the course of the invasion of Afghanistan. These positions were outlined in a seventy-two point "matrix" and included stripping detainees, depriving them of sleep, subjecting them to bright lights or blaring noise, hooding, exposing them to extremes of heat and cold, and binding them in awkward and stressful positions—all of which would have been considered illegal and abusive in the past. National security officials interviewed at the time answered that the use of violence against captives was "just and necessary." In fact, Donald Rumsfeld himself jotted down his thoughts on the matter of stress positions in the margins of an internal memo: "Why is standing limited to four hours?...I stand for eight hours a day." The message was clear to those who were listening: as one official who worked with the detainees put it, "If you don't violate someone's human rights some of the time, you probably aren't doing your job."

Alberto J. Mora, former general counsel of the navy, which has jurisdiction over Guantánamo Bay, notes that at the time it was felt that "the gloves had to come off. The U.S. had to get tougher" to prevent another attack on American soil. But like the lawyers of the State Department, Mora and his staff were horrified by the sanctioned increase in physical coercion tactics. As one staffer put it, Mora "quickly grasped the fact that these techniques in the hands of people with this little training spelled disaster," and daily interrogation becomes routine abuse.

To justify such harsh treatment, the president has asserted that "these are people picked up off the battlefield in Afghanistan," while "trying to kill American forces," as then press secretary Scott McClellan added. However, it's been shown that of the five hundred detainees currently in Gitmo, fewer than twenty have been al-Qaeda members, many were never Taliban soldiers, and the majority were not captured by Americans but were simply handed over by Pakistani bounty hunters and Afghan warlords looking to cash in a reward from U.S. forces. In fact, some men were detained in Karachi, Sarajevo, and Gambia—not exactly Afghanistan, and certainly not the battlefields implied by the president's descriptions.

Though Gitmo exists in a legal twilight, the practice of "extraordinary rendition" allows crafty intelligence officials to send even innocent prisoners to countries outside of American jurisdiction where they will most certainly be abused. Yet Bush continues to deny the well-documented practice of rendition, asserting that "torture is never acceptable, nor do we hand over people to countries that do torture." So far though, at least sixty-five detainees have been transferred from Guantánamo to places like Pakistan, Eastern Europe, Morocco, and Saudi Arabia—all of which are condemned by the State Department for performing torture. Our Soviet-style authoritarian "ally" Islom Karimov in Uzbekistan, known for throwing his enemies—or any dissidents—alive into boiling water, has opened up his detention and interrogation centers for American intelligence-gathering purposes. "We don't kick the shit out of them," says one official, who participated in rendering captives, "We send them to other countries so *they* can kick the shit out of them."

There is no rule of law beyond that border, because law is about public reckoning—an impossibility when Bush & Co. prefer secret torture chambers in central Asia to the open courts of the United States. Apparently, they do not trust our own institutions to get them the results they desire. As the British ambassador to Uzbekistan, Charles Murray, recalled at one particularly egregious Uzbek "trial":

> An old man came in and he was charged, he had signed a statement saying that two of the accused who were nephews of his were associates of Osama bin Laden, had been to Afghanistan, and met bin Laden on a regular basis. He was standing there, and he was an old gentleman, frail and bowed...and he was standing there while his sentence was given out, mumbling his answers and suddenly he pulled himself erect looked at the judge in the eye and he said, "It's not true—they tortured my children in front of me until I signed this. We are poor farmers, what do we know of Osama bin Laden? What have I to do with bin Laden?" He was quickly hustled out by the military. It felt to me that what he was saying was the truth.

When Murray demanded a U.S. liaison explain the situation, he was told that this was a normal way for the American intelligence community to get information to send back home.

Perhaps that's why the administration has continually blocked efforts by Congress to increase CIA accountability, for to rein them in is to acknowledge that part of the reason we are in the morass of Iraq is because of bad "intel" obtained by illegal torture. As Jane Mayer revealed in her comprehensive *New Yorker* exposé on the "outsourcing" of torture, when American troops captured their first high-ranking al-Qaeda figure, Ibn al-Sheikh al-Libi, in Afghanistan in 2002, he was swiftly rendered to Egypt for interrogation. In this way, al-Libi became the source of one of the biggest myths that helped pave the way to Iraq. It was al-Libi who described Saddam Hussein's offers to al-Qaeda of "chemical or biological weapons" and arms training—the same tall tales that found their way into Colin Powell's infamous 2003 address to the UN.

Dan Coleman, an ex-F.B.I. agent, was disgusted when he heard about al-Libi's false confession. "It was ridiculous for interrogators to think al-Libi would have known anything about Iraq," he said. "I could have told them that. He ran a training camp. He wouldn't have had anything to do with Iraq. Administration officials were always pushing us to come up with links, but there weren't any. The reason they got bad information is that they beat it out of him. You never get good information from someone that way."

While al-Libi was an active member of al-Qaeda, other detainees rendered to Egyptian authorities—like Australian citizen Mamdouh Habib, picked up as he was touring religious schools in Pakistan—have dubious links to any terrorist organizations. In fact, after an embarrassing *Washington Post* article was published in early 2005 about Habib detailing his allegations of torture, the Pentagon released him without explanation back to his home country. Habib described months of being chained in various cells: "One room was filled with water up to his chin, requiring him to stand on tiptoe for hours; another chamber, filled with water up to his knees, had a ceiling so low that he was forced into a prolonged, painful stoop; in the third, he stood in water up to his ankles, and within sight of an electric switch and a generator, which his jailers said would be used to electrocute him if he didn't confess." These "interrogations" were supplemented by regular beatings with a cattle prod; and when Habib was not being as forthcoming as his captors wanted, they threatened that he would be anally raped by specially trained German Shepherds (a claim made by other prisoners). Of course Habib complied and confessed to whatever his interrogators demanded—confessions which clearly were so baseless that the Pentagon had no reservations about his later release.

But as we now know, not all abuse is outsourced to keep American hands clean. A 2005 *New York Times* series uncovered the killing of two Afghan prisoners at the U.S.-run Bagram prison camp in Afghanistan, one of them an innocent taxi driver who was "tormented to death" by American soldiers. A two-thousand-page confidential Army file provided by an anonymous source also described the death by torture of, in the *Times*'s words, "a slight, shy, illiterate young Afghan villager who was shackled by the wrists to the ceiling of his cell for days, struck more than a hundred times in one day for the amusement of captors who found his screams of 'Allah!' funny, and beaten on the legs until the tissue, in a coroner's words, 'had basically been pulpified.' By the time he died, most of his interrogators had concluded that he was guiltless." Investigations into the deaths at Bagram showed that the mistreatment of prisoners was routine: shackling them to the ceilings of their cells, depriving them of sleep, kicking and hitting them, sexually humiliating them and threatening them with guard dogs—the very same behavior that had occurred in Egypt.

Yet President Bush continues to assert that "we do not torture."

British citizen and Muslim convert Richard Belmar also spent six months in Bagram. Like Habib, Belmar had been studying at a religious school when the United States overthrew the Taliban in 2001, trapping him in Central Asia. Belmar was not allowed to brush his teeth or shower during his first two months at the prison, and he was hung "strappado" from the bars of his basement cage when he broke the rule against talking. He still suffers from headaches and sports a noticeable dent in his skull from when he received "this huge blow to the back of my head. I think it was a rifle butt." Moreover, he states, "My memory seems permanently impaired. It's like I'm going senile—but I'm only twenty-five." Another time, he described how a handgun was shoved into his mouth. "It tasted cold, bitter. I thought, 'Yeah, this is getting serious, there's a good chance they will pull the trigger.'"

But the worst were the forced "anal searches" performed in front of an audience of guards, including a female jailor who fondled his genitals. "I told her she was ugly, cheap, and I spat in her face. There were two guys in the room and I was shackled. They got me on the floor and started kicking me up, in the back, in the stomach, they gave me a real beating." Like Habib, Belmar admitted to almost anything his interrogators accused him of, such as going to an al-Qaeda training camp in 1998. Except that Belmar only converted to Islam in 1999. Another time, he was accused of attending a speech made by Osama bin Laden. But, Belmar says, "How could I have done that? I didn't know a word of Arabic."

Such pointless abuses came into starker contrast after the United States invaded Iraq in March of 2003. Hardly a year had passed before Seymour M. Hersh exposed and wrote about the iconic Abu Ghraib photos of hooded or naked men—piled on top of each other or menaced by dogs—in April 2004. Standard denials from administration officials like Secretary of State Condoleezza Rice promising that the U.S. "did not torture" were contradicted by pictures seen worldwide. But the aggressive actions that constitute abuse were both documented across the front pages of newspapers everywhere and, it seems, regularly encouraged by presiding officers on the ground. As Megan Ambuhl, one of the first military police soldiers prosecuted by the Pentagon for her role at Abu Ghraib, explained, "I thought if [military intelligence officers] were doing it, it must be all right for them to be doing it."

No one at the top was directing soldiers in what *not* to do, what the laws were, what the name of the game was thousands of miles from home in hostile, foreign territory. The Pentagon's own investigation into Abu Ghraib revealed "a lack of doctrine [and] systemic failures" as the root cause of the torture-acts depicted in the horrifying photos. In this way, the Pentagon unwittingly admitted that Abu Ghraib was not "a few bad apples" as Rush Limbaugh might have us believe, but a series of failures beginning at the top.

Human Rights Watch issued a report stating that, in 2005, "It became disturbingly clear that abuse of detainees had become a deliberate, central part of the Bush administration's strategy of [interrogation]"—the only country in the world where torture is the *official* policy. At least forty-four prisoners have died in American military camps so far. Later investigations have shown these detainees died under suspicious conditions that imply steady abuse was the main cause of death, including, as the reports say, "strangulation," "asphyxiation," and "blunt force injuries." The leading cause of "natural" death was listed as "arteriosclerotic Cardiovascular disease"—otherwise known as a sudden heart attack.

However, these murdered detainees are not the uniform "terrorists" torture-apologists imagine them to be, nor are those who decry torture, "terrorist-coddlers." Like Habib and Belmar, many of these detainees have no substantive links to any terrorist organization. The need for information to bring home to Washington puts undue pressure on agents in the field to let slide what few rules there still are, while the administration's justifications for these crimes reveal a top-down pressure to torture—not a slip up by subordinates.

Why Torture Is Never Right—and Doesn't Work

Typically, administration officials condemned the release of evidence that American forces have tortured detainees, blaming it for the United States' unpopularity in the Muslim world. And they may have a point. Before Abu Ghraib became the byword for torture, Coalition Provisional Authority polls pegged Iraqi support for the American occupation at 63 percent. Yet only a month after the photos of Abu Ghraib were published, the number had crashed to 9 percent, helping to fuel the murderous insurgency "nobody anticipated." It seems torture got us into Iraq, and torture is what keeps us from winning popular support, which in turn keeps us from leaving. Importantly, "61 percent of Iraqis polled believed that no one would be punished for the torture at Abu Ghraib. Of the 29 percent who said they believed someone would be punished, 52 percent said that such punishment would extend only to 'the little people.'"

In fact, to return to Bush's favorite analogous conflict, it was during the postwar Nuremburg trials that "the principle of command responsibility for abuse" was really established. There, prosecutions were handed down to Nazi officials who had written the legal briefings that advised overriding the conventional protections for POWs and other detainees. In Andrew Sullivan's rebuke in *The New Republic* of the pro-torture advocates defending the Bush administration, "What was supposed to be safe, sanctioned, and rare became endemic, disorganized, and brutal."

Vietnam War veteran Senator John McCain (R-AZ), arguably the most visible opponent of the Bush doctrine on torture, has been unyielding in his push to force this administration to backtrack and honor the Geneva Conventions. "They may be al-Qaeda, they may be Taliban, they may be the worst people in the world, but there are certain rules and international agreements the United States has agreed to." If beating terrorism really is the greatest struggle since the defeat of the Axis, then the documents that grew out of that conflict should never be dismissed as merely "quaint," as our own attorney general Alberto Gonzales put it. Because as important as the notion that torture is inhumane is the undisputable fact that *torture does not work*.

Torturing prisoners to obtain intelligence is totally counterproductive, as Sen. McCain has elaborated: "The abuse of prisoners harms, not helps, our war effort. In my experience, abuse of prisoners often produces bad intelligence because under torture, a person will say anything he thinks his captors want to hear—whether it is true or false—if he believes it will relieve his suffering." When McCain's captors in Vietnam demanded names, he gave them the Green Bay Packers' offensive line.

And it was only after negative reports of their abuses became widespread that the North Vietnamese "decreased their mistreatment" of American prisoners, realizing that souring the world community against their cause was not a smart strategy for victory.

Similarly, abusing members of communities we want to "help"—in a war even Secretary Rumsfeld has admitted is "for hearts and minds"—means that we squander millions of potential allies on the ground. When someone is abused or tortured, particularly if that individual is innocent, their family, their friends, their coworkers lose all sympathy for the torturer's cause. Without that sympathy, the potential for valuable intelligence volunteered by well-wishers is lost—and well-wishers become haters. There is a reason al-Qaeda leadership tells its captured accomplices to claim they have been tortured whether they have been or not: they know that America's reputation in the region is just as important as its military strength.

Yet the Bush administration has been ardently fighting against such an explicit ban on torture—or even legislation filling the legal loopholes enlarged and exploited after September 11. When the Republican Congress finally passed a resolution in late 2005 banning torture, Bush issued a "signing statement" allowing him to ignore the new provisions if he so choose.

Defenders of torture often put forth the "ticking time bomb" scenario as a way to silence critics. The nightmare of a ticking time bomb whose whereabouts can only be obtained through torture is a seductive justification for legalized abuse. However, the ticking time bomb scenario is, when thought out, more the absurd fantasy of a Hollywood screenwriter than a likelihood demanding a rewrite of the criminal code. Has it ever really happened? On the other hand, every damaging revelation of torture has enormous consequences for America's need for allies and friends to disclose information and collaborate with us. And in the million-to-one chance that such a "ticking time bomb" terrorist is ever actually apprehended, wouldn't the agent who tortures him in order to save thousands of lives be more likely to get a presidential pardon than be thrown in jail?

As former vice president Al Gore put it in a January 2006 speech:

> Is our Congress today in more danger than were
> their predecessors when the British army was marching

on the Capitol? Is the world more dangerous than when we faced an ideological enemy with tens of thousands of missiles poised to be launched against us and annihilate our country at a moment's notice? Is America in more danger now than when we faced worldwide fascism on the march—when our fathers fought and won two world wars simultaneously?

It is simply an insult to those who came before us and sacrificed so much on our behalf to imply that we have more to be fearful of than they. Yet they faithfully protected our freedoms and now it is up to us to do the same.

(Un)Patriotic Acts

Since its hurried enactment in the aftermath of September 11, the Patriot Act has become a touchstone for a broad range of Americans who question whether the best way to fight terror abroad is to cut back on freedoms at home. From progressive activists and immigrants to conservative Libertarians, from civil rights lawyers to Midwestern librarians, a growing number of Americans have come to regard the Patriot Act as, at least in part, unpatriotic.

It starts with the fact that the law was not so much debated as stamped through the Congress. The bill emerged from the Justice Department fully formed and was rammed through the legislature a mere forty-five days after the tragedies of 9/11. Many of the new provisions were really conservative holdovers, unpassable until finally stuffed into a bill that was certain to be approved. Few, if any, members of the government outside of former attorney general John Ashcroft's office ever read hundreds of provisions before they became law.

The Patriot Act still passed the Senate ninety-eight to one, with only Wisconsin's Democratic senator Russ Feingold opposing it as a "naked power grab by the government itself." The only acknowledgement that this process was hasty and misguided was that many of the more controversial clauses were "sunsetted"—that is, they expired after several years to allow for a review of what had helped and what had hurt in the war on terror.

To be sure, in the panic following the destruction of the World Trade Center, most Americans wanted a substantial response to the "new" threats posed by Islamist extremists, and their representatives acted accordingly. Even Feingold agreed that changes were needed, recalling the adage that "while the Constitution protects against invasions of individual rights, it is not a suicide pact." Undeniably, many of the Patriot Act's modifications have been very positive, such as streamlining how intelligence agencies like the FBI and the CIA track down terrorists. Both the FBI and the CIA were criticized after 9/11 for their failure to communicate effectively with each other. The Patriot Act broke down some of these bureaucratic walls—while extending statutes of limitation on terrorist-related activities and creating lower thresholds for issuing warrants to investigate the shadowy underworld of terrorism. Prosecution was made easier for abetting terrorists through monetary or organizational aid.

But the Patriot Act also vastly increases the authority of intelligence officials and local investigators both to detain and to punish—with or without solid proof. With the Patriot Act, guilt by association—however tenuous that association may be to designated terrorists—has become the new gold standard. All that is needed is for the attorney general to decide that you are a "threat to national security." He does not need evidence of a crime, of criminal intent, or a solid link to terrorism.

And under something called "expatriating acts," the government has created a new right to strip you of your citizenship should it decide you are unworthy of a civilian criminal trial. This could occur if you somehow provide support to, as the ACLU put it, an "unpopular organization labeled as terrorist...even if [you] support only the lawful activities of such organizations." The consequence is indefinite imprisonment in your own nation as an undocumented alien. Now you can be stopped at Grand Central Station in Manhattan on your way home from work and wake up in Guantánamo Bay, Cuba, without your family ever getting a phone call.

As noted Libertarian and former *New York Times* columnist William Safire protested in the weeks after the Patriot Act's enactment in October 2001, "Misadvised by a frustrated and panic-stricken attorney general, a president of the United States has just assumed what amounts to dictatorial power to jail or execute aliens. Intimidated by terrorists and inflamed by a passion for rough justice, we are letting George W. Bush get away with the replacement of the American rule of law with military kangaroo courts." What most incensed Safire was how the Patriot Act removed judicial oversight from any government actions related to "national security."

The problem is that, while making it easier for government agencies to gather and share information, the Patriot Act never requires these agencies to distinguish between legitimate sources of intelligence and the petty investigations that waste resources and squander public good will. Look at what has come to be known as the "sneak and peak" provision. Sneak and peak allows field agents, without any notification before, during, or after, to enter someone's home, car, or office and poke around. Unlike the standard searches depicted nightly on television's *Law and Order*—which require a judicially sanctioned warrant outlining a location and the specific articles to be sought by law-enforcers—sneak and peak erases the need for oversight of any kind.

Previously, if your home had been searched while you were absent, the government had to notify you within a short amount of time (typically a week) and also provide "probable cause" that a crime had been committed as required by the Fourth Amendment. Previously, judges issued warrants based on a demonstrated need for a search. Now, though, courts cannot question the intelligence agencies' allegations: if the request is part of an ongoing "national security" investigation, it automatically becomes valid. In this way, judges—and by extension the public—have lost their authority to review these agency claims, and a warrant sought is a warrant granted.

The Patriot Act also extends sneak and peak to public records of all kinds—which has led to the infamous "angry librarian" clause. This section of the Patriot Act allows for federal agencies to demand library patrons' records, including the books they've checked out and what websites they've visited on library computers. Now an agent can obtain the roster of anyone who has checked out a book on Osama bin Laden—as was the case in one disturbing instance where someone had scribbled a quotation from the al-Qaeda leader in the margins of a book about terrorism. "A fishing expedition like this just seems so un-American to me," said Joan Airoldi, who runs the library in rural Washington state where this incident occurred. "The question is, how many basic liberties are we willing to give up in the war on terrorism, and who are the real victims?" Reading lists that were previously secure and private are now open, creating the perfect environment for self-censorship: however curious you might be, nobody wants to risk a late-night visit from the feds over their choice of Sunday afternoon reading.

Under a "gag rule," any invocation of the Patriot Act becomes classified information. If the government is looking into your activities, you not only no longer have the right to know but are also prevented from discussing it with anyone should you happen to find out. Moreover, the Justice Department has retained the right to introduce "secret evidence" to defend its actions—evidence that judges receive behind closed doors without your lawyers present (should you have one). For instance, several Muslim charities have had their assets frozen by the Treasury Department. They protested that they were legitimate aide groups and while it's possible that they could have ties to terrorists, the public will never know either way because the government's conduct has been shielded by the Patriot Act's multiple gag orders.

These new powers are not just limited to the upper echelons of terror-fighting. The Patriot Act has given many people in the government, including low-level district intelligence officials, the power to write "national security" letters—a kind of "administrative subpoena" that can pull in all manner of private information. National security letters—now numbering thirty thousand a year—also preclude judicial oversight or judicial recourse for those who don't want to release confidential information. Previously, these letters were not regularly issued against American citizens, and the authority to write one fell to only the most senior officials. But the new standards are considerably less secure, and these letters may be used against anyone, "even if they, themselves, are not suspected of espionage or criminal activity," says Supreme Court expert and law journalist Dahlia Lithwick. The only standard seems to be the vague "relevance" to an ongoing investigation.

Those investigations, of course, include people who are not terrorists themselves. Or who know terrorists, necessarily. The Patriot Act's major changes to American law have less to do with "shoring up" the bureaucratic problems that paved the way to 9/11 than changing the age-old burden of proof from "probable cause" to mere hearsay. Look at the Patriot Act's eased use of roving wiretaps which hook into *any* phone or computer a suspect could use. This means that every computer in an office or a school could be tapped, and any user's activities would be intercepted over the course of the investigation to create a vast archive of private information unrelated to terrorism. This erodes the Fourth Amendment's requisite "particularity" for a valid search, and its inherent randomness cannot possibly be a good use of agents' limited time and energy. That is why constitutional protections requiring a legitimate target of surveillance, supervised by a judge, are important. Not only do they protect the innocent, but they also force the government to do its job well and not rely on such lazy (and previously illegal) "fishing" or "data mining" expeditions into personal emails, travel manifests, and credit card purchases.

The obvious result is that the government's expanded authority will be used to investigate domestic crimes and gather evidence that is totally unrelated to the war on terror. Nadine Strossen, president of the ACLU and a professor of law at New York University, has described how previous reforms to antiterrorist surveillance laws in the 1990s were ultimately used "for drug enforcement, gambling, and prostitution." Combined with the Patriot Act's new allowances, Strossen argues, "again, we're going to have the CIA in the business of spying on Americans—something that certainly hasn't gone on since the 1970s," when such domestic surveillance drew the ire of the public.

Domestic surveillance results in domestic intelligence information vacuumed into a government database containing all of your most personal records—medical, financial, educational, criminal—available for easy perusal by federal agents. This ability goes far beyond the government's existing data collection efforts, like Social Security and the IRS, to everything from video rentals to mosque and church attendance. All records can be combed without telling you, as long as the government does so "to protect against terrorism." As explained by Joshua L. Dratel, an attorney who has filed legal briefs opposing government anti-terrorism policies, "By eliminating any distinction between criminal and intelligence classifications, it reduces the respect for the ordinary constitutional protections that people have."

Just as there was no effort to distinguish between legitimate "persons of interest" and innocent civilians in the post-9/11 immigrant sweeps (see next section on "Domestic Suppression"), there is no safeguard to distinguish between legitimate threats and retributive or wasteful investigations. We do know that it has been possible for police officers to screen their dates and track down estranged wives, as well as to keep files on thousands of people, including anti-police-brutality activists.

The Patriot Act also created a category called "domestic terrorism" to penalize activities involving "acts dangerous to human life that are a violation of the criminal laws of the United States" if the actor's intent is to "influence the policy of a government by intimidation or coercion." Nobody wants another Michigan Militia detonating bombs in the heartland. But neither should we allow local police authorities to spy indiscriminately on innocent citizens who were active in community, political, or religious organizations, all of which could potentially fall under such a vague rubric. For instance, in Denver, Colorado, the police department had kept thousands of files on such "criminal extremist" groups (as they were labeled) as Amnesty International and the Nobel Peace Prize-winning American Friends Service Committee. Yet this surveillance occurred *prior* to September 11, 2001. It had nothing to do with protecting Americans from the kind of terrorism the Patriot Act is meant to avert, and it certainly doesn't now. It was a waste of resources then, and it's a waste of resources today.

That's because these sources of intelligence—roving wiretaps, private records, "national security letters," etc.—have opened up an information black hole, a garbage dump of petty intelligence with no value to the real field work guidelines that were already in place before 9/11. Remember the August 6 memo, "Bin Laden Determined to Strike in U.S."? Remember how intelligence agents in Minnesota had their eyes on the actual perpetrators of al-Qaeda's dirty work, netting "twentieth hijacker" Zacarias Moussaoui? The FBI failed to get proper search warrants only because of "roadblocks" that undermined their "desperate efforts" to obtain one. Those roadblocks were bureaucratic in nature, more infighting and ineptitude, *not* on the intelligence gathering side of things. And the Patriot Act did help remedy this problem, but now by making it *too* easy to obtain a warrant.

Recognizing that the Patriot Act is not a cure-all explains why, over the course of the past few years, a wide array of constituent voices have joined together to express their concern about its potential for abuse. Merchants, librarians, seven state governments, and over four hundred communities have signed onto a resolution demanding the Patriot Act be amended—from small towns to major cities, from liberal Berkeley to conservative Alaska.

Summing up these sentiments during the hearings to renew the Patriot Act in early 2006, Senator Feingold implored his colleagues to remember: "Trust of government cannot be demanded, or asserted, or assumed; it must be earned. And this administration has not earned our trust. It has fought reasonable safeguards for constitutional freedoms every step of the way. It has resisted congressional oversight and often misled the public about its use of the Patriot Act."

Yet for all these misgivings, in March of 2006, the Patriot Act was reenacted in the Senate by a vote of eighty-nine to ten, with several provisions made permanent. Calling it "a piece of legislation that's vital to win the war on terror and to protect the American people," when signing it into law, Bush later issued an executive "signing statement" clarifying his real position: "The executive branch shall construe the provisions that call for furnishing information in a manner consistent with the president's constitutional authority to withhold information." In other words, what little oversight Congress demanded was once again wiped out with one stroke of W.'s pen. Only the gag rule was slightly tempered (now you can challenge your gag order in court, if not the actual charges)—for what could be called another victory for the fear of fear itself.

DOMESTIC SUPPRESSION

Those who ardently supported the renewal of the Patriot Act often did so out of a belief that curbing civil liberties in the short run would help defeat terrorist threats in the long run. But Burt Neuborne, a founder of the Brennan Center for Legal Justice, explains that because the "war on terror" has no discernible end, has abstract ideological enemies, and has few distinct goals—at this point it has lasted longer than the entire American involvement in World War II—"unlike past incidents, if we do damage to our constitutional heritage now, it isn't temporary."

That's one reason the post-9/11 round-up of Muslims for interrogation and incarceration was so troubling. Combined with the Patriot Act's dismantling of many legal protections for American citizens, the arrest of thousands of (ultimately innocent) immigrants set a new precedent on who can be detained, for what, and for how long.

Immediately after the attacks on the World Trade Center, ethnic profiling by the Justice Department netted five thousand foreign nationals—some simply because suddenly suspicious neighbors reported them to local authorities. It turns out that *none* of the detainees were ever charged with terrorist activities and immigration violations were the only crimes any were guilty of. Hundreds were deported despite having absolutely no criminal or terrorist ties. This includes a Nepalese tourist who was held for three months in a tiny cell after he inadvertently included an FBI building in a videotape of New York made for his friends and family at home. More than a third of the people living in Brooklyn's Little Pakistan were either deported or left voluntarily after 9/11, "decimating the neighborhood." As Anthony Romero, executive director of the ACLU, concluded, "The war on terror quickly turned into a war on immigrants."

The Justice Department's own internal audit of the sting described how detainees were given the names of lawyers to call but were provided with inaccurate phone numbers ending in busy signals or a wrong number. Some numbers connected to lawyers who had no intention of providing counsel. It also turns out that those who managed to find legal representation often had their confidential lawyer-client conversations illegally recorded. The inspector general, Glenn A. Fine, found that such abuses were "rooted in part in an unstated policy that allowed the FBI to keep the suspects in detention unless it was established that they were not tied to terrorism."

But whether these ties existed or not made little difference either. Yasser Ibrahim and his brother Hany were quickly cleared of any terrorist connections after they were picked up in Brooklyn on charges that they overstayed their tourist visas. But rather than seek immediate deportation or allow them to return to their apartment, authorities kept them in jail for eight months, during which they suffered the daily verbal and physical abuse described by many of their fellow prisoners. They were slammed against walls during routine transfers between cells, or were tripped repeatedly while their legs were shackled until their ankles were bloody. The inspector general's report found a "pattern" of abuse, from beatings to sexual humiliations, some of it even caught on video surveillance tapes.

The brothers recall that in the days following 9/11, their family begged them to return to Egypt. But "we assured them," said Yasser, "this is the United States. They don't arrest people for no charges. We didn't do anything, so nothing's going to happen to us." That's why they are bringing a lawsuit charging that they were denied due process because of their religion or national origin which resulted in the abuse. "I'm seeking justice," said Yasser. "It's from the same system that did us injustice before. But I have faith in this system. I know what happened before was a mistake."

Along with the immigrant round-ups, September 11, 2001, precipitated an extraordinary push by the attorney general to keep closer tabs on Americans' everyday activities. These intelligence programs received the Big Brother monikers Operation TIPS (Terrorism Information and Prevention System) and TIA (Total/Terrorism Information Awareness). Heading these programs was John Poindexter, a man convicted on five counts of lying before Congress, destroying evidence, and obstructing inquiries into the Iran-Contra mess of the Reagan administration (and released later on a technicality). The programs proposed for the first time a systematization of small-scale snitching, enlisting as many as one million truck drivers, letter carriers, utility workers, train conductors, ship captains, and other "well-positioned" private citizens to report any suspicious activities encountered on their rounds. Said civil liberties lawyer Rachel King, "The administration apparently wants to implement a program that will turn local cable or gas or electrical technicians into government-sanctioned peeping toms."

However, when the extent of these the privacy-corroding initiatives became known, the uproar came from all over the country and TIPS and TIA were swiftly cancelled. At least, Americans were told that the programs had been cancelled. But in reality, their budgets were simply shuffled around and their projects renamed. None of the contracts needed to develop their massive surveillance technologies were actually terminated. "Research under TIA—which developed technologies to predict terrorist attacks by mining government databases and the personal records of people in the United States—was moved from the Pentagon's research-and-development agency to another group, which builds technologies primarily for the National Security Agency," reported *National Journal* writer Shane Harris.

Along with violating the privacy and confidentiality of innocent civilians, these programs seemed strange because Americans have always had the right to report suspicious activity to police or federal authorities. What was so unusual about TIPS and TIA was the total lack of any clear accountability or guidelines about how that information would be used. "The notion that you would actually encourage people, who are not empowered or trained to do so, to snoop on their fellow citizens and report [on] them is particularly spooky," said Joan Bertin, executive director of the National Coalition Against Censorship. Like the federal authorities who mistreated Yasser and Hany Ibrahim in Brooklyn, with TIA and TIPS, Bertin continued, "There seems to be no limits, no controls, no guidelines, no rules, no nothing."

The potential for abuse is obvious. Journalist Alisa Solomon notes that, with this type of government program in place, the Bush administration "has fashioned a domestic arm of its new doctrine of preemption." Now, all previously confidential records will be searched, cross-indexed, and fully "data-mined" (presumably using the technology from the "cancelled" programs) for any information the government sees fit, with no one overseeing abuses or mistakes.

Look at what happened to Muslim convert Brandon Mayfield, an attorney in Oregon who was the victim of just such a mistake. After the FBI's Automated Fingerprint Identification System falsely linked him to the March 2004 Madrid bombings, Mayfield was arrested and sent to prison at an undisclosed location, while his wife and children were left to frantically worry about what had happened to him. He was eventually released after Spanish authorities complained to American agents that those fingerprints belonged to an Algerian—a fact the FBI had known from the beginning and chose to ignore. "That Mayfield was a Muslim highlights how the combination of old-fashioned prejudices and newfangled technology can lead to poor police work," concluded Matthew Brzezinski, author of *Fortress America: An Inside Look at the Coming Surveillance State*.

This kind of crude police work has given rise to many similar problems. Muhammad Ali is a New York-born Muslim American who happens to have one of the most common names among Arabs. In 2003, Ali went to a Western Union in Brooklyn to wire $80 for schoolbooks to a friend in Connecticut. Less than an hour after sending the money, Ali got a phone call from Western Union's Missouri offices informing him his order had been blocked because his name popped up as a variation of one on a government list of known terrorists. He protested, of course, but there was nothing he could do about it. "They told me I couldn't even get a refund until they got a valid photo ID and proof of my country of birth," Ali recalled angrily.

The records made newly available to intelligence agencies include both Social Security and IRS files, which contain a substantial amount of private medical and financial data normally kept under tight wraps. However, in the wake of 9/11, senior officials at the Social Security agency agreed to an "ad hoc" policy. They authorized the release of information to the FBI under the pretense of "investigations related to terrorism" because officials deemed it a "life-threatening emergency." As former secretary of health Tommy Thompson's spokesman put it, "You never did have federal privacy rights" to begin with.

But the government doesn't just rely on its own formal data collection for this kind of personal information. Because of certain clauses in Bush's No Child Left Behind education bill, student records have suddenly come under the purview of any interested intelligence agent. And now, with the Supreme Court's ruling in favor of military recruitment on campuses receiving federal dollars (which would basically include any accredited research institution), colleges could become new targets of information sweeps.

But why should this be limited to public institutions? Corporations interested in currying favor and trading valuable data with the current administration have a stake in violating civil liberties, too. To again quote William Safire, there has been a serious blurring between law enforcement and market research record keeping so that "almost overnight, the law's suspect list married the corporations' prospect list." So corporations can send reams of private information into the waiting hands of intelligence officers. While it's known that these federal agencies rely on personal information purchased from private companies, what's less discussed is the fact that corporate executives have helped write what little legislation governs the data collection industry, including privacy laws.

These corporate records can include airline flight manifests, credit card purchases, and credit rating information. For example, consider what happened in late 2005 to retired Texas schoolteacher Walter Soehnge and his wife Deana when they decided to do the responsible thing and pay off their $6,522 JCPenney Platinum MasterCard. After sending off the money, the Soehnges checked to see if their line of credit was adjusted. But the balance on their account hadn't been changed. It took a few phone calls to find out why. Apparently, when a higher than normal payment arrives, Homeland Security has to be notified, and the money is not allowed to move until the alert status is lifted. Upon hearing this, an infuriated Soehnge was "madder than a panther with kerosene on his tail" and proceeded to alert not just the ACLU, but local TV stations and newspapers, rallying publicity until his money was released.

CHILLING FREE SPEECH

But what about those who don't feel comfortable raising a media storm like the Soehnges? In the post-9/11 and post-Iraq invasion era, the Bush administration has created a hostile environment in which to criticize the government. There is a spirit of intolerance emanating from the White House, from the swift-boating of Kerry to the outing of Plame to the firing of General Shinseki and John DiIulio to the disparagement of Max Cleland's war wounds. So White House press secretary Ari Fleischer told us early in the war on terror that Americans have to "watch what they say." And while "loose lips sink ships," it became apparent just how far Bush & Co. wanted to go in censoring public policy critics when former attorney general John Ashcroft warned: "To those who scare peace-loving people with phantoms of lost liberty, my message is this: Your tactics only aid terrorists."

This is in stark contrast to previous wartime administrations and executives. In 1918, during the hyper-nationalist frenzy of the First World War, Theodore Roosevelt declared, "To announce that there must be no criticism of the president, or that we are to stand by the president right or wrong, is not only unpatriotic and servile, but is morally treasonable to the American public." And during the Second World War, FDR's administration gave special attention to the promotion and exercise of the right to free expression as a way to broadcast "the key differences between American liberty and Nazi tyranny." This included the Justice Department helping to overturn the conviction of Jehovah's Witnesses who refused to salute the American Flag in West Virginia. Hard to imagine that today in a country where "freedom fries" were served in the Capitol building cafeteria and arch-conservative talking head Ann Coulter says things like, "Even Islamic terrorists don't hate

America like liberals do," in her bestsellers accusing Democrats of *Treason* and *Slander* (the titles of her books) for their disagreement with Bush's Iraq fiasco.

From former ambassador Joseph Wilson and his wife Valerie Plame to grieving mother Cindy Sheehan, the Republicans have been more interested in silencing than answering critics. Dissent is not tolerated, and questioning the motives or actions of government leaders is sometimes all but impossible. When Senator Dick Durbin (D-IL) announced his horror about the torture of detainees at Guantánamo Bay, he compared the grotesque sights to what had been done "by Nazis, Soviets in their Gulags, or some mad regime...that had no concern for human beings." His words were strong. But rather than comment on the accusations of torture and mistreatment, his colleagues across the aisle shouted him down and went on television to denounce and bully him into offering an apology. In the end, Durbin was excoriated for his analogy rather than his analysis, since he pointed out something that should have been obvious to everyone: the poor treatment of prisoners at Gitmo was making America look barbarous in the eyes of the world.

In response to Durbin's comments, for example, Senate Majority Leader Bill Frist (R-TN) proposed a statute that would have revoked the national security clearance of any government official who "makes a statement [which is subsequently] used as propaganda by terrorist organizations." Ironically, if it had passed, the bill would have given terrorists the ability to decide whose security credentials they would like to see revoked: all they would have to do is mention that official in a video leaked to Al Jazeera.

Questioning the conduct of the war on terror or the war in Iraq implicitly is now regarded as treason. Aboard *Air Force One* in 2005, a White House spokesman named Trent Duffy commented to reporters that "President Bush believes that those who want the U.S. to begin to change course in Iraq do not want America to win the overall 'war on terror.'" Duffy went on to say that Bush "can understand that people don't share his view that we must win the war on terror, but he just has a different view." Thus did the Bush White House twist criticisms so that dissent became seditious support of terrorists.

According to this reasoning, we are having difficulty in Iraq because the troops' morale is hurt by slights against the commander in chief and not because of incompetent leadership and poor planning. "This administration has tried to tell people that if they are speaking against the war they are speaking against the troops," said Nancy Lessin of Military Families Speak Out, an organization of over twenty-five hundred families with members in the military who do not support the war in Iraq. "Our organization has tried to uncouple those." John Passacantando, executive director of the environmentalist organization Greenpeace, which has protested both Bush's environmental record and the Iraq war, also felt threatened by the growing surveillance of dissident and activist groups. "If the FBI has taken the time to gather twenty-four hundred pages of information on an organization that has a perfect record of peaceful activity for thirty-four years, it suggests they're just attempting to stifle the voices of their critics."

This stifling doesn't have to look like J. Edgar Hoover's infiltration and sabotage of protest groups during the 1960s. The seemingly isolated stories—like a man being arrested in an upstate New York mall for wearing a "Peace on Earth" T-shirt, or the aggressive seizures by New York City Police of anti-Republican protestors during the 2004 convention—point to a larger repression of legitimate dissent across the nation. The G-8 summit in coastal Georgia during 2004 fostered the creation of "free speech zones" for protestors miles from the actual event location, and then only for certain hours of the day. The use of city parks and other public spaces for those seeking to freely express themselves would now be subject to the same fees as a company picnic or carnival, forcing protestors into the "protest pens" far from those who were intended to hear their message.

In 2005, during one of Bush's famously stage-managed speaking events in Colorado, three locals were threatened and then escorted out by a person they thought was a secret service agent. Karen Bauer, one of the "Denver Three," describes how a man "in a suit wearing an earpiece and a lapel pin" told them that they "had been ID'd" and that if they "had any ill intentions [they] would be arrested and jailed." It turns out they had been confronted at the taxpayer-financed event because of a "No More Blood for Oil" bumper sticker on one of their cars. For this minor expression of dissatisfaction with the government, they lost the right to hear their chief executive give a speech. Moreover, it turns out the man who told them to leave was in fact a member of the White

House host committee, not secret service. Impersonating a law enforcer is illegal, but the agency has refused to disclose this man's identity.

At least the "Denver Three" weren't arrested and their vehicle impounded. Which is what basically happened to various groups headed to a large weekend protest in St. Louis, Missouri, in 2003. Sarah Bantz and a bunch of her fellow activists from the Missouri Resistance Against Genetic Engineering must have felt pretty good after giving their speech on how biotech was hurting local farmers. The group had just left the Regional Chamber and Growth Association, climbed into Bantz's van, and driven a little way down the road when "all of a sudden there was one police car and then another, and I was pulled over." Bantz described how "one officer came around and asked me to get out of the vehicle, which I did. The cop started to look through the van without permission. I had some Vitamin C pills sitting out, so they decided that was a drug and they were going to arrest me. They put me in cuffs and put me in the back of the car. They really had no grounds for arresting me, but I spent ten hours in jail." She was ultimately released without charges.

What points to a coordinated effort in Missouri to sabotage the protestors was that the very same day, members of the Flying Rutabaga Bicycle Circus also encountered police difficulties. "We set off on our bicycles for our first performance, a small skit, to let the protesters know about our Caravan Across the Corn Belt tour," says Erik Gillard, one of the Flying Rutabagas, who was riding with eight others. "We were following traffic rules when a big police wagon pulled up with its light on. Gradually, more police officers arrived, and they told us we had to leave our bicycles. We were all arrested for operating our bicycles without a license."

It turns out, however, that no such law exists. After a few hours spent in lock up, the police changed the charge to "impeding the flow of traffic on a bicycle." Gillard says the ticket "was written up for some intersection ten blocks from where we were all picked up." He also tells how, while he and his group were detained, "all of our journals that contained phone directories or email lists or information about where we were going to stay were taken and never returned."

Perhaps these zealous police officers were only trying to avoid the chaos brought on in the 1990s by the World Trade Organization's meetings in

Seattle. But this kind of preemptive action has a more subtle effect than preventing a demonstration from taking place. "If you're involved in a street demonstration, you don't have any expectation that you are going to be part of a government file," says John Raucci, a sixteen-year FBI veteran who runs a Joint Terrorism task force. Even the mere threat of such a file, he notes, can put a chill on political dissent: government workers, people who might want security clearances, or whose background might be investigated for a future job, or those who simply want to remain anonymous while participating in protests, all have reason to fear the inclusion of their name in a police file—especially since such files are increasingly being shared among government agencies. Raucci explains how such monitoring has increased under the Bush administration: "We've doubled, even tripled here since 9/11," he says.

Yet as the emotional heat of 9/11 begins to fade and the daily indignities of civil liberties depredations begin to sink in, Americans are having a change of heart. The percentage of people who say the First Amendment "goes too far in the rights it guarantees" has fallen dramatically. In 2002, the year after the terrorist attacks, almost 50 percent of those polled said the amendment went too far. In 2005, just 23 percent felt that way.

One of the 9/11 Commission's recommendations was the creation of a civil liberties oversight board to ensure that the rapidly expanding powers of the federal bureaucracy did not erode civil liberties. Yet, like most of the 9/11 Commission's proposals, the formation of the oversight board has been incomplete. Or rather, never even started. When questioned why it was taking so long to set up the board, Connecticut Republican representative Christopher Shays responded, "It's not a priority for the administration."

To comply with the intelligence reform laws, the board was technically "funded," but with only a few hundred thousand dollars—in other words, nothing when compared to the millions needed to oversee the entire workings of a national government. Thomas Kean, who chaired the 9/11 Commission, called the delay and the measly budget "outrageous, considering how long it's been since the bill [creating the board] was passed." What's more outrageous is that the chair of the recently sworn-in board is Carol Dinkins, current attorney general Alberto Gonzales's former law partner. Dinkins saw no conflict of interest in the fact that Gonzales will be a prime target of the board's investigations. However, it remains doubtful that any laws or basic democratic rights will be protected by a neglected board staffed by cronies.

Best framing this issue is Ahron Barak, the president of the Israeli Supreme Court and a judge respected around the world for his experience in dealing with terrorist threats in a modern democracy: "Terrorism does not justify the neglect of accepted legal norms. This is how we distinguish ourselves from the terrorists themselves. They act against the law, by violating and trampling it, while in its war against terrorism, a democratic state acts within the framework of the law and according to the law. It is, therefore, not merely a war of the state against its enemies; it is also a war of the law against its enemies."

Spying on Americans

In the closing weeks of 2005, the *New York Times* revealed that, with the personal approval of President Bush, the National Security Agency (NSA) had been wiretapping American citizens without obtaining a warrant as required by the Foreign Intelligence Surveillance Act (FISA) of 1978. And violation of the law was a felony.

FISA originated after revelations about President Nixon's extensive domestic surveillance of American protest groups and reporters became known in the mid-1970s. Nixon had argued that, in a time of war, a president assumes the power to gather whatever intelligence he needs. But according to former congresswoman Elizabeth Holtzman, who sat on Nixon's impeachment hearings in 1973–74, "Although Nixon claimed the wiretaps were done for national security purposes, they were undertaken for political purposes and were illegal. Just as Bush's warrantless wiretaps grew out of the 9/11 attacks, Nixon's illegal wiretaps grew out of the Vietnam War and the opposition to it."

Most Americans recognized that there had to be a balance between privacy and security—hence the enactment of FISA. The rules were clear: in order for domestic surveillance to take place, intelligence agencies must obtain a warrant from the FISA court seventy-two hours after first tapping into private phone or email conversations. Of course, all of this can be done in secret, and the FISA court is extremely lenient in granting these warrants: of the approximately nineteen thousand requests since 1978, only five have been rejected. There is even a provision for wartime emergencies that grants an extended fifteen day period after Congress authorizes military action for federal agents to spy on whomever they need to before seeking a warrant. Legally defined as "the exclusive means" of obtaining permission for domestic surveillance, the FISA court asks only for probable cause that the target is an "agent of a foreign power" before issuing a warrant.

Yet George W. Bush found these accommodating conditions too constricting. And so, with the help of then White House counsel and current attorney general Alberto Gonzales, the Bush administration decided to secretly authorize a new program of wiretapping—one that no longer required a warrant and allowed the NSA, the largest intelligence agency in the government (bigger than both the FBI and the CIA), to intercept domestic phone calls and email exchanges between American citizens.

After the *Times* disclosure, Gonzales was called before a Senate panel to explain the administration's actions. He asserted that warrantless wiretapping by the NSA was 100 percent legal because when Congress passed the Authorization of Use of Military Force (AUMF) against Iraq in October of 2002, they implicitly gave permission to Bush, as commander in chief, unlimited power to do whatever he needed to do to catch terrorists. As explained by administration legal counsel David Addington, "In light of the president's complete authority over the conduct of war...criminal statutes are not read as infringing on the president's ultimate authority in these areas."

There are three problems with this assertion. First, since the president acknowledges that terrorism is a scourge that will likely continue for generations, his claim of extraordinary authority—unlike Lincoln's during the Civil War—is one that is not temporary by any definition of the word. And a permanent state of emergency is not what the Founding Fathers had in mind when they crafted the Bill of Rights.

Second, Bush is commander in chief of the armed forces—*not* the country. Otherwise a president could claim inherent authority to do anything to anyone. The "inherent" line of thinking was too much for Bruce Fein, a prominent conservative lawyer who served in President Reagan's Justice Department: "This is a defining moment in the constitutional history of the United States. The theory used by the administration...could equally justify mail openings, burglary, torture, or interment camps, all in the name of gathering foreign intelligence. Unless rebuked, it will lie around like a loaded weapon ready to be used by any incumbent who claims an urgent need." Fein continued that "Bush's defenders are embracing...a view that would cause the Founding Fathers to weep."

Third, if the president had inherent authority as commander in chief under the AUMF resolution authorizing war against Iraq, then why did his White House seek a provision in the resolution specifically allowing warrantless wiretapping? When told it would be "difficult if not impossible" to obtain permission to eavesdrop on American citizens without a warrant, the administration dropped the request. Former senator Tom Daschle, who was minority leader of the Democrats when voting on the AUMF occurred, says that "the Bush administration now argues those powers were implicitly contained in the resolution adopted by Congress—but at the time, the administration clearly felt they weren't or it wouldn't have tried to insert the additional language."

It's also ironic that an administration full of "strict constructionists" would find so many unstated meanings in both the Constitution and the Military Authorization bill. This sentiment was echoed by Senate Judiciary Chairman Arlen Specter (R-PA), who said that it "just defies logic and plain English," and by Senator Lindsay Graham (R-SC), a politician as conservative as they come, who commented, "I'll be the first to say, when I voted for it, I never envisioned that I was giving to this president or any other president the ability to go around FISA carte blanche." In other words, Congress would not have granted Bush permission to do something that, according to the president, it had already granted him permission to do.

Since a president cannot admit to a crime, Bush tried to explain away the obvious. "Wait a minute...it's like saying 'you're breaking the law.' I'm not," protested Bush at a White House press conference. The act creating FISA "was written in 1978" and now "it's a different world." His statements imply that warrantless wiretapping is legal, but that it doesn't really matter either way because FISA is so outdated and ineffective against terrorists that the government has to take these actions to protect Americans. "This is a different era, a different war," he said. "People are changing phone numbers and phone calls, and they're moving quick. And we've got to be able to detect and prevent."

But judging by how permissive FISA has been in the past, the argument that it is too cumbersome in the face of rapidly evolving threats makes no sense. The FISA court is very flexible in terms of its timing requirements—not to mention that all of its judges were appointed by late Supreme Court Chief Justice William Rehnquist. This suggests that a Republican president would have little trouble obtaining the warrants he desired. Unless, of course, those warrants had no basis in probable cause, violating the Fourth Amendment's protections against "unreasonable searches and seizures." Judge Harold A. Baker, who sat on the intelligence court until last year, said that the president was bound by the law "like everyone else...the president ignores it at the president's peril." As for the 1978 FISA being outdated, what does the president then think about ratification of the U.S. Constitution in 1787? Once again, this argument begs the question of what ever happened to "original intent."

There's a legal expression about "arguing the alternative"—i.e., the lawyer who denies that his client stole a black pot because "it wasn't black, it wasn't a pot, and in any event he didn't steal it." Once warrantless wiretapping was exposed and early arguments proved unpersuasive, others were trotted out. So the administration then claimed that it had, in fact, consulted with Congress about its domestic surveillance program. But this was not substantially true either. These consultations in reality consisted of a single cursory classified briefing of a handful of congressional representatives who were then barred from discussing any of the perfunctory details they learned.

Indeed, if Congress had been consulted as the administration said, then why did Alberto Gonzales refuse to answer so many of the senators' questions when he gave his testimony? Wouldn't the senators already have been familiar with the details Gonzales declined to provide? Gonzales also refused to testify under oath or reveal how many wiretaps had been conducted without warrants since Bush authorized the program in 2002, and he would not even say why he was withholding the information or whether Bush understood that it is illegal to spy on Americans without a warrant within the United States.

The Bush administration also maintained that public scrutiny of the NSA wiretapping would "give the enemy a heads-up on what we're doing" because, said Gonzales, "if they're not reminded about it all the time in the newspapers and in stories, they sometimes forget"—a comment that was greeted by actual laughter at the Senate hearings. But the attorney general is making a dangerous argument—one taken up by the right wing as a way to excuse Bush's law breaking in the first place: that revelations about warrantless wiretapping hurt our efforts to defeat terrorism. Bush's press secretary Scott McClellan inflated this line of reasoning into a partisan attack, going so far at one press briefing as to say, "I think it does raise the question, how do you fight and win the war on terrorism? If Democrats want to argue that we shouldn't be listening to al-Qaeda communications, it's their right." But no Democrat has ever said anything of the sort, and insinuating that Democrats are akin to the "party of treason" is just updated McCarthyism.

Vice President Cheney claimed that if Bush had given the NSA permission to spy on citizens before the attacks on the WTC, "we might have been able to pick up on the two hijackers who were...in touch overseas with al-Qaeda. It's not an accident that we haven't been hit in four years." This is a dangerous exaggeration. Because these men were *not* citizens of the United States, their communication was consequently not protected in the same way as that of Americans. Additionally, if these hijackers had been in the crosshairs of federal agents, why would FISA have rejected a warrant? Presumably the evidence that had led the government to the suspects would have satisfied a warrant's need for probable cause.

Perhaps it's because the NSA spying has been conducted *without* evidence.*

Not only has the wiretapping been more extensive than indicated, as Gonzales acknowledged after his public testimony, it has also been profoundly ineffective. The program is not catching terrorists. Gonzales has said warrantless wiretapping helped identify "would-be terrorists here in the United States." But when Senator Joe Biden (D-DE) asked, "Have

---

*Indeed, despite President Bush's claim in December that such spying only aimed "to intercept the international communications of people with known links to al-Qaeda and related terrorist organizations," the spying turns out to include collecting the phone-call records of tens of millions of Americans speaking to other Americans domestically. When *USA Today* disclosed this fact in May 2006, the president again simply asserted that "we're not mining or trolling through the personal lives of millions of innocent Americans. Our efforts are focused on links to al-Qaeda and their known affiliates." Tens of millions of Americans have possible links to al-Qaeda?

we arrested those people? Have we arrested the people we've identified as terrorists in the United States?" the attorney general replied evasively, "When we can use our law enforcement tools to go after the bad guys, we do that," and left it at that. A frustrated Biden finally declared, "Well, I hope we arrested them—if you identified them. I mean, it kind of worries me because you all talk about how you identify these people, and I've not heard anything about anybody being arrested." That's because nearly all of the Americans wiretapped by intelligence officers have been dismissed as potential suspects, according to accounts from current and former government officials.

Having been caught red-handed committing a crime, the administration's explanations for spying on thousands of citizens appear to be a frantic effort to spin their way out of trouble. Bush was aware of the problem early on when, according to a *New York Times* revelatory account, Gonzales and White House chief of staff Andrew Card went to former attorney general John Ashcroft's hospital bedside to seek his approval for renewing aspects of the secret spying program. James Comey—acting head of the Justice Department during Ashcroft's illness—was unwilling to sign off and "some agency officials wanted nothing to do with the program, apparently fearful of participating in an illegal operation." Despite Gonzales's and Card's cajoling, it is unclear whether Ashcroft, who was initially reluctant to give his consent, ever gave in to the administration's demands or if the White House simply carried on without him.

The real issue in this controversy goes to the rule of law, which all officials—from councilperson to chief executive—must uphold. Not even a president can pick and choose which laws to comply with and which to ignore or reinterpret simply because they have become inconvenient. That is the attitude toward authority advanced by kings. Bush's claims in "signing statements" that he can ignore laws he considers unconstitutional while simultaneously disregarding any limitations on his powers as commander in chief during an unending war on terror amounts to near-dictatorial power. As Louis XIV put it, *"L'état, c'est moi."* From one King George to another?

Even the conservative American Bar Association—four hundred thousand lawyers strong—overwhelmingly approved a task force report concluding that the president was violating both the Constitution and statutory law when he authorized the program. "Nobody wants to hamstring the president," said task force head Neal Sonnett, "But we cannot allow the U.S. Constitution and our rights to become a victim of terrorism." The Congressional Research Service—a nonpartisan government agency—also issued a report rebutting the arguments that the president had authority to order the NSA's secret wiretapping. "It appears unlikely that a court would hold that Congress has expressly or impliedly authorized the NSA electronic surveillance operations here."

So a war launched to export democratic values abroad was now in turn being used to undermine democratic values—one being the rule of law—here at home, an irony probably lost on the Bush team. But the issue of warrantless wiretapping is not about balancing civil liberties and national security. As George Washington Law School professor Jonathon Turley commented, the issue is that the Bush administration is treating the Constitution "as some legal technicality instead of the thing were trying to fight to protect." The Bush White House could better understand America and the Constitution if it looked more closely at Benjamin Franklin's famous aphorism that "they who would give up an essential liberty for temporary security, deserve neither."

WHAT RULE OF LAW?
II: WITH JUSTICE FOR SOME

"Those less favored in life should be more favored in law."
—Professor Thomas Reed Powell

"To my enemies, the law. To my friends, facilities."
—Brazilian Saying

Why Break Laws When You Can Ignore Them?

There is a concept in law enforcement called "prosecutorial discretion." Since there are millions of crimes committed annually and only a few thousand prosecutors in local, state, and federal offices, every prosecutor is necessarily allowed to decide who to investigate and indict—and who to leave alone.

An administration that is indifferent or hostile to white-collar law enforcement need not affirmatively violate laws to help their favored constituencies. Engaging in torture, illegal wiretapping, or pundit payola can result in identifiable victims and culprits. A less risky way to avoid or evade the law is to do...nothing. Here, conservatives borrow two slogans from other venues—"Just say no" and "Don't just do something, stand there!"

At the Justice Department's Civil Right's Division, for example, they haven't been doing a whole lot. This unit of seven hundred, among other obligations, enforces the 1965 Voting Rights Act. Section 5 requires that an affected jurisdiction get "preclearance" for any election law changes that might diminish minority voting participation, something that the division has done tens of thousands of times in the past forty years. The division has had a glorious history and tradition of public service, from prosecuting those who conspired to kill freedom riders Michael Schwerner, Andrew Goodman, and James Cheney in 1965 to bringing to justice police officers who beat Rodney King.

Through Republican and Democratic presidencies alike, from Reagan to Clinton, career attorneys have made legal judgments without interference from political appointees. Until Bush. Several recent situations have shown the same pattern of career staff recommending action only to be squelched by superiors.

In a highly reported incident (see "Legislative Tyranny"), then majority leader Tom DeLay forced Texas state legislators to redistrict congressional lines in 2003 in order to create opportunities for Republicans to win five new seats. While gerrymandering is not unusual, mid-census gerrymandering was something new. Opponents complained to the Civil Rights Division that DeLay's gambit violated the Voting Rights Act because it broke up a cohesive "majority-minority" Dallas-Fort Worth district. All five Civil Rights staff reviewing the facts agreed that the redistricting plan was illegal. In a seventy-three page memorandum discussing the case—and later disclosed by the *Washington Post*—the lawyers concluded that "the State of Texas has not met its burden showing that the proposed congressional redistricting plan does not have a discriminatory effect."

Despite this unanimous recommendation to reverse DeLay's changes, only seven days later the Justice Department approved his redistricting. Mark Posner, who had supervised Section 5 reviews at the Civil Rights Division from the mid-'80s to the mid-'90s, was shocked. "In preclearing Tom DeLay's redistricting plan, the Justice Department significantly and substantially deviated from the decisional practice which, for four decades, has served the department well in enforcing Section 5 in a fair and nonpartisan manner. Of course, we do not know what the Department of Justice's political appointees said to each other, or perhaps to the career staff, before preclearing the plan. But the evidence points to a single conclusion: the Justice Department did not serve the interests of minority citizens in this case but instead served the political interests of the Republican Party."

The Civil Rights Division in 2005 also rejected Georgia's law requiring that voters obtain one of six forms of photo identification. Because a picture ID can cost $20—and could be acquired in only 59 of the state's 159 counties—staff lawyers concluded that the requirement was a kind of Jim Crow poll tax designed to reduce turnout among poor minorities. Yet one day after this recommendation against preclearance, the Justice Department approved the Georgia law, falsely implying that the decision was made with the concurrence of the career staff. The law was later struck down in federal court.

Indeed, prosecution of Civil Division discrimination cases fell by 40 percent in the Bush administration's first five years. Lawyers were involuntarily assigned instead to deportation and other immigration matters. According to the *Washington Post's* Dan Eggen, only three cases were filed under the section prohibiting discrimination against minority voters, none actually involving black voters! The first case accused a majority-black county in Mississippi of discriminating against white voters. So it was not surprising that as cases ceased to be prosecuted and morale fell, career lawyers began to jump ship, with 20 percent leaving the division in 2005 alone.

The pattern of non-enforcement could be seen throughout an administration far more enamored with business tax cuts than prosecution of corporations. Before the Sago mine collapse in 2005, personnel at the Mine Safety and Health Administration fell by 10 percent; correspondingly, penalties leveled against mine owners plunged from 2001–2005— and less than half the fines imposed were actually paid.

At the Environmental Protection Agency, the administration was reducing not pollution but enforcement. In Bush's first three years in office, environmental penalties fell 50 percent, the number of pounds of pollution cleaned up decreased 20 percent, and the agency was conducting three thousand fewer inspections annually. EPA-filed lawsuits filed by the Clinton administration in 1999 and 2000 against nine major power companies and dozens of individual power plants were largely dropped by the Bush administration in favor of its far more lenient "*New* New Resource Review Standards"—which were struck down in early 2006 as violating the clear intent of the Clean Air Act. Again, as at the Civil Rights Division, many senior officials left in protest due to the administration's unwillingness to enforce environmental laws.

Prosecutorial discretion morphed into something akin to prosecutorial desertion when it came to tobacco litigation. With the 1964 surgeon general's report confirming that smoking causes cancer, the industry found itself under assault from public health advocates. In 1995, a global settlement involving $280 billion in restitution resolved a massive lawsuit by *states* seeking restitution for medical costs caused by tobacco firms hiding the dangers of its product. Then in 1999, the Clinton Justice Department filed one of the largest *federal* lawsuits in history, accusing tobacco companies in effect of racketeering, fraud, deceptive advertising, and dangerous marketing practices.

But the new attorney general John Ashcroft, who as a senator had opposed the lawsuit, called the case weak and sought to reduce funding for it. President Bush, in an interview with *FOX News* in early 2001, said, "I worry about a litigious society. At some point you know, enough is enough." Then the tobacco industry, too shrewd to bribe a judge, instead donated $2.7 million to Bush and his party for the 2004 elections. Lo and behold, after five years of litigation, at the eleventh hour, the Justice Department lawyers told a federal judge in June 2005 that they wanted to reduce the damages they were seeking from $130 billion to $10 billion, a 92 percent reduction. (The government's own witness had estimated that a good smoking-cessation program nationally—which would be an ideal remedy—would cost $5.2 billion a year or $130 billion over twenty-five years.)

Judge Gladys Kessler was not pleased, commenting in court that the abrupt shift "suggests that additional influences have been brought to bear on what the government's case is." Then the apparent became confirmed when Eric Lichtblau of the *New York Times* reported that senior department officials had overruled the career lawyers running the case to order the reduced penalties. "We do not want politics to be perceived as the underlying motivation, and that is certainly a risk if we make adjustments in our remedies presentation that are not based on evidence," wrote the two top lawyers for the trial team, Sharon Y. Eubanks and Stephen D. Brody, in a May 30 memorandum to Associate Attorney General Robert D. McCallum. The two lawyers complained that the lower penalty recommendations ordered by Mr. McCallum—whose Atlanta law firm had done extensive legal work for R.J. Reynolds—"create an incentive for defendants to engage in future misconduct by making the misconduct profitable." Six months later, Eubanks—a twenty-two year Justice Department veteran—quit her job. "I didn't feel like I had the support of the political team," she said.

DISCRIMINATION AND DEMOCRACY

Of course, all of us discriminate in our daily lives, inevitably so. Most Americans make distinctions about who are our spouses, friends, and neighbors—which are entirely legal, so long as they're not reinforced by any state action. So if an old private club or new gated community is racially homogenous because of personal preferences and market forces, it may not be the rainbow vision we learned about in civics class but it's probably not against the law. It can actually even be lawful to discriminate against an entire class of people, as when no one under twenty-five has a right to rent a five thousand-pound car from a private company that knows that this age group is far more likely to get into accidents. That's not considered an outright civil rights violation because being under twenty-five is a situation *all* of us can grow out of.

But we can't grow out of inherited traits like sexual orientation and skin color—notwithstanding the cruel tacks of fundamentalist reparative schools and skin bleaching. Conservatives who exploit discrimination to win elections and keep entire groups in the background of the political picture are guilty of violating the values of the American flag far more than those few fools who burn it.

Race in America: I'm OK, You're Not

At the 2005 Milwaukee NAACP convention, Republican National Committee chair Ken Mehlman did something that Bushies never do and Republicans never openly discuss—he not only talked about race but actually apologized for the historically divisive use of racial politicking in the South to win votes. "Some Republicans gave up on winning the African American vote, looking the other way or trying to benefit politically from racial polarization. I am here today as the Republican chairman to tell you we were wrong." The audience dutifully clapped, but was not at all fooled. For Mehlman's act of contrition was less about bridging rifts between the right wing and racial minorities (there are zero black Republicans in the House) than an attempt to moderate his party's image in the view of swing suburban Republicans, most of whom condemn racist posturing. The audience was just part of someone else's larger electoral ploy.

Around the same time Mehlman apologized, NAACP chairman Julian Bond received notice of an upcoming IRS investigation of the tax-exempt status of his organization, which had been harshly critical of Republican failures to engage blacks. And, of course, it took Hurricane Katrina to compel George W. Bush—for the first time in his presidency, if not his life—to acknowledge publicly the enduring reality of race-based poverty in America. Indeed, the percentage of African Americans living in poverty fell from 33 percent to 23 percent during Clinton's administration, yet has been *rising* again under Bush.

Although Republican mediameisters stock their convention podiums with black faces and gospel choirs, it was impossible for a Republican president to explain away the photos of bloated black bodies rotting for days in the submerged Ninth Ward of New Orleans—or images of African Americans going days without food and water at the Superdome and Convention Center. At one point after Katrina, Bush's approval rating among African Americans reportedly crashed to 2 percent. Compared to Hurricanes Charley and Frances in Florida in 2004, when FEMA was praised for its efficiency and Bush visited areas four times in six weeks and personally handed out relief checks to victims, his reluctance to visit the destroyed city center was not just astounding, but insulting. Consider too the blatant bias of newsroom photos of desperate blacks captioned as "looters" and whites labeled merely as "finders" of the food and drink their government neglected to provide during the emergency.

The problems, of course, are deeper than trying to figure out what the photo editors at the AP were thinking. Forty years ago, in his Letter from a Birmingham Jail, Martin Luther King Jr. explained the issue best. "Law and order exist for the purpose of establishing justice and when they fail in this purpose they become the dangerously structured dams that block the flow of social progress." While *Brown v. Board of Education* and the 1965 Voting Rights Act began to redeem the promise of the Constitution's Civil War amendments, "the flow of social progress" is still dammed up in three significant ways—persistent *legal, political,* and *economic biases* continue to imperil a functioning democracy.

When it comes to legal justice and racial prejudice, the imbalance in drug laws and criminal sentencing is revealing. Government studies have consistently shown that whites make up the vast majority of people who consume and sell drugs, yet about 94 percent the New York State prison population incarcerated for a drug offense are African American or

Latino. "There is as much cocaine in the stock exchange as there is in the black community" said Commander Charles Ramsey, one-time head of the Chicago Police Department's narcotics division. Yet the Department of Justice issues alarming estimates that one black man in three will go to jail at some point during his life—more than five times the rate for white men. This stems in part from the fact that blacks are more likely to be stopped and searched for drugs, due sometimes to illegal racial profiling. But Bush's Justice Department tried to suppress reports that reveal how traffic cops treat African American and Hispanic drivers more "aggressively" than whites when stopped. The administration went so far as to demote one department official for attempting to publicize the reports. "It is totally unacceptable for the Justice Department to politicize statistical releases and demote individuals merely because they were seeking to provide accurate summaries" regarding racial profiling, said Rep. John Conyers Jr. (D-MI), a nineteen-term congressman and cofounder of the Congressional Black Caucus.

These disparities also exist in sentencing, like New York's oppressive Rockefeller drug laws, which deal harsher punishments for the crack found in poorer communities than the powder cocaine of richer ones. Different drugs carry different mandatory minimum sentences, guidelines that play well with anxious white voters during election season but which have actually been a primary factor in the breakdown of minority communities.

Racial disparities appear everywhere in our justice system: when far more frequently the death penalty is sought and administered against minority defendants in capital cases; when blacks are sentenced to six times as much prison time as whites convicted of the same crime; and when prosecutors still engage in illegal "jury shuffling" to move large numbers of black jurors to the "back" of the selection panel.

In 1986, the Supreme Court ruled that the Constitution's equal protection clause prohibits using these types of peremptory challenges to eliminate potential jurors based on their race. But that decision did not stop the Texas prosecution team from doing just that during the trial of Thomas Miller-El for a murder during a botched robbery at a Holiday Inn. Though each side was permitted to remove jurors without explanation, illegal discrimination clearly occurred in the Miller-El case when from a jury pool of blacks and whites—who had expressed similar opinions on the death penalty during questioning—only the whites were retained. On overturning the Miller-El conviction in early 2005, Justice Stephen Breyer noted sadly that despite years of work attempting to stamp out bias from jury selection, "the use of race- and gender-based stereotypes in the jury-selection process seems better organized and more systematized than ever before."

Barriers to voting are at least as steep as barriers to courtroom justice. As discussed previously in chapter 1, we all remember the shady felon purges from Florida's voter rolls in 2000, when thousands of eligible voters in heavily black, and thus Democratic-trending, districts were turned away from the polls. Yet the problem is bigger than Broward County: nationally, African Americans account for 40 percent of the disenfranchisement cases and only 12 percent of the population, as noted in "Voter Suppression."

When you make it harder for entire communities of Americans to either vote regularly or obtain impartial justice, it's inevitable that such sanctioned discrimination results in economic and social hardships—the kind that made Katrina all the more devastating. Fifty-two percent of the nation's uninsured are African American or Hispanic, despite being only 29 percent of the population. This lack of access to the infrastructure of equal opportunity is compounded by the fact that less than a third of black students today find themselves in racially integrated schools. Crumbling and underfunded urban schools are a legacy of the white flight of the 1960s and '70s, with the result that the following generation of minority students were more likely to end up in prison than in college.

A front page *New York Times* article in March 2006 showed how the overall situation of young black men has only gotten worse, even as their economic peers have moved up. "We're pumping out boys with no honest alternative" to crime, said Gary Orfield, an education expert at Harvard and editor of *Dropouts in America*. Fifty percent of black men in their twenties who lack a college degree are jobless, as are 72 percent of high school dropouts. Alarmingly, among black men in their twenties who have dropped out of high school, more are in prison on any given day (34 percent) than are working (30 percent).

Even those who manage to graduate from failing schools face dim prospects. According to a recent study by Princeton University, law-abiding black men fare no better than whites released from prison when it comes to interviewing for jobs in New York City. In the study, white candidates who offered resumes mentioning phony criminal backgrounds got called back 16 percent of the time—the same rate as black men with identical credentials and clean backgrounds. Men with criminal records tend to be rejected by potential employers, and black men with crime-free backgrounds "suffer by association" as studies have found.

African Americans and Hispanics are also far more likely to be victims of predatory-lending than whites or Asians. Compared to only 8.7 percent of white and 5.9 percent of Asian American borrowers, 32.7 percent of African American and 20.3 percent of Hispanic borrowers had higher-cost, "sub-prime" mortgages. This mysterious gap can be attributed to the same forces that make employers choose a white ex-con as often as a black man—discrimination.

A *BusinessWeek* article described how Jeweline Simmons went to Shelter Mortgage in East St. Louis, Illinois, for a home-improvement loan in 1999 looking for the lowest interest rate available. It turns out Simmons was qualified for a 9.8 percent rate, but her broker "steered" her to a 10.7 percent loan. For doing so, Shelter received a $600 payment from lender EquiCredit Corporation. "I was rushed through some paperwork without knowing what was going on," Simmons declared. Because of the costlier rate she fell behind on repayments. It was only after she contacted a lawyer that Simmons found out she had been overpaying all along. She subsequently sued Shelter and EquiCredit and settled with them out of court.

But it's not just that minorities aren't getting good loans—they often are squeezed into buying or living in marginal, polluted neighborhoods. A government study concluded that blacks are 79 percent more likely than whites to live in neighborhoods where industrial pollution poses dangerous health risks—this includes housing projects built on cheap land close to factories. These studies showed that blacks were far more likely to reside near "hazardous waste disposal sites, polluting power plants, or industrial parks." The researchers blamed these unfortunate statistics on the fact that minorities had far less "political clout" to "influence land use decisions" in their neighborhoods.

Living so closely to this kind of air pollution "works with many other factors, genetics, and environment, to heighten one's risk of developing asthma and chronic lung disease, and if you have it, it will make it worse," said Dr. John Brofman, director of respiratory intensive care at MacNeal Hospital near Chicago. "Evidence suggests that not only do people get hospitalized but they die at higher rates in areas with significant air pollution."

Responding to charges of "environmental racism" leveled after the studies were published in 1993, President Clinton produced an "environmental justice" order. Clinton called for federal agencies to make sure that minorities are not exposed to any more pollution or environmental hazards than other Americans. However, in 2005 the Government Accountability Office reported that the Environmental Protection Agency had spent little time on "environmental equality" during Bush's first term when it was supposed to be developing methods to implement the revised Clean Air Act. "There is no level playing field," said Robert Bullard, director of the Environmental Justice Resource Center at Clark Atlanta University. "Any time our society says that a powerful chemical company has the same right as a low income family that's living next door, that playing field is not level, is not fair."

When W. E. B. DuBois predicted in 1903 that the "the problem of the twentieth century is the problem of the color-line," it's likely he'd be disappointed, but not surprised, that the color line tests us still in the twenty-first. Leveling racial discrimination is not the work of years, but of generations, perhaps of several more to come. Racial resolutions are especially difficult because the conservative movement still condemns many reforms as "reverse discrimination against whites," when they were not critical of the original discriminatory acts now supposedly being "reversed." Centuries of hateful, occasionally murderous racial discrimination against minorities didn't upset the ideological forefathers of Bush and Frist, but any disadvantage now marginally affecting whites sets them off.

It's doubtful the Republican Party really learned much from former Senate majority leader Trent Lott's ignorant birthday tribute to South Carolina senator Strom Thurmond, saying in 2002 that America would have avoided "all these problems" if Thurmond had won his 1948 segregationist race for president. Lott was rightly excoriated by his colleagues, the media, and the American public, and pressured to step down from his leadership post. But that seemed more a cosmetic gesture than an act of soul-searching by the GOP, which feared a fall in the polls. It's hard to take any apology from the right wing seriously when the Republican Senate leadership refused repeated requests in 2004 for a "roll call" vote that would have put senators on record as expressing regret for the failure in earlier decades to pass antilynching laws (which went unsupported by fifteen Republicans, not all of whom were from the Deep South courting Confederate heritage voters).

Still, while glacial, there has been great progress on "the color line" in past decades, from an explosion of blacks elected in the South following enactment of the 1965 Voting Rights Act, to the emergence of a solid black middle-class in America. Today, 50 percent of all African Americans have what could be described as "white-collar, middle-class" jobs. Additionally, census data reveals that one million blacks have advanced degrees and that more black people are now in college than at any point in the last thirty years. A key moment continuing this progress was the Supreme Court ruling upholding the use of race as a factor in university admissions (over the opposition of the Bush Justice Department), at last giving clear constitutional approval of affirmative action programs.

Grutter v. Bollinger, the deciding case, was a lawsuit brought against the University of Michigan Law School by a white woman who claimed that "her" spot in the incoming class had been taken by a less qualified minority applicant. In her majority opinion, Justice Sandra Day O'Connor noted that "race unfortunately still matters" in many walks of life. She went on to defend the university's recognition of race and ethnic background as compelling factors in building a beneficial "critical mass" to combat racial discrimination.

At times citing the amicus briefs filed by large corporations like 3M and General Motors, O'Connor continued that "these benefits are not theoretical but real, as major American businesses have made clear that the skills needed in today's increasingly global marketplace can only be developed through exposure to widely diverse people, cultures, ideas, and viewpoints." So to undo centuries of past *de jure* discrimination and to create a pool of talented workers in the private and public sectors, O'Connor, speaking for the five to four majority, concluded that affirmative action was constitutional. In essence, the court agreed more with President Clinton's famous "mend it, don't end it" conclusion rather than the hollow rallying cry of "reverse discrimination" coming from the other side.

Indeed, the best evidence indicates that it has been affirmative action—a policy begun by President Nixon in the early 1970s—that has helped to build interracial teams within schools, businesses, and the government. These organizations worried that they might fail—losing clients, customers, students, and researchers—if large numbers of talented Americans were excluded from their ranks merely because of skin color. The same could be said for our democracy.

Gay Baiting and Bashing: The New Southern Strategy

As the 2004 presidential campaign clarified—and W.'s proposed 2006 constitutional amendment indicated—the right wing can't resist resorting to homophobic rhetoric for electoral success. Antigay marriage amendments in eleven swing states were partially credited with an increased conservative voter turnout that favored Republican "morals" candidates over the godless and the gays. It's an ugly strategy—one with more than a whiff of the stale race-baiting policies of the Republican "southern strategy," playing on lies and fears about one of the last minorities who can still be openly discriminated against.

Yet despite reports of Alabama libraries banning "gay" literature (including Shakespeare) or a California private school expelling a cheerleader for having two moms, the issue of gay and lesbian civil rights is not as high voltage as we are led to believe by do-anything-to-win politicos. Contrary to conservative dogma, most Americans don't actually want to discriminate against gays and lesbians. By and large, they support civil unions of some kind (just don't say "marriage" yet), they think gays can be fine teachers, and they oppose firing someone or refusing someone housing merely because he or she is gay.

So why are antigay appeals still such a useful weapon in the political arena? Tactically, even if there's a trend toward tolerance among the *general* population, any election hobgoblin that can motivate a *particular* base to vote in higher numbers can be irresistible to campaigners. And the problem is that some of the Far Right ignorantly believe that gayness is something you learn rather than are born with—that is, more nurture than nature. Almost 70 percent of the population currently do not see homosexuality as an inborn trait, like race, like gender, like ethnicity, which translates into tens of millions of people voting against a "lifestyle choice" without feeling like bigots.

This confusion owes in part to lies promoted by gay-bashing religious leaders and conservative direct-mail fundraisers who, to earn their status and keep, have peddled myths about the gay "lifestyle" (drug-addled, disease-riddled pedophiles) ever since Anita Bryant's 1977 shrill "Save the Children" campaign proved to be such a money-maker. This remains the case in spite of the fact that the American Medical Association removed homosexuality from its list of mental disorders more than thirty years ago *and* that responsible psychologists vehemently disavow the ex-gay movement's practice of "reparative therapy" (usually a fundamentalist boot camp), employed coercively to "cure" homosexuals through religious browbeating.

Robert Rigby Jr., a special education teacher at Falls Church High School in Virginia, went through seventeen years in reparative ministries trying to become straight. While there, Rigby said that "my life was an ongoing disaster." Rather than change his attraction to men, the "therapy" left him increasingly depressed and suicidal. It's clear that the Religious Right's continued labeling of homosexuality as a chosen lifestyle or mental disorder should be taken about as seriously as Senator Bill Frist's medical diagnosis of Terri Schiavo via videotape.

Many leading evangelical groups claim "defending the family" is their primary goal. But how is it a victory for American families when parents feel they have to kick their gay kids out? Indeed, 42 percent of homeless youth identify as lesbian, gay, bisexual, or transgender, and the high rates of gay teen suicide from harassment and rejection are extraordinarily well documented. How is it a victory when Florida's prohibition on gays becoming foster parents means that the backlog of three thousand unhoused, uncared-for children grows longer by the day? What about the archaic sodomy laws that allow a Mississippi court to refuse a boy's request to live with his gay father, even though his mother had remarried a man with a history of substance abuse and violence and who repeatedly beat her in front of the boy? These "victories" are what happens when "pro-family" fanatics without a shred of hard evidence are allowed to dictate public policy for the whole country.

Political homophobia is also fueled by the reactionary framing of the debate. Conservative pundits talk about gays wanting "special rights" above and beyond other citizens—a notion that, while ludicrously untrue, is nonetheless resented by voters who see this as un-American preferential treatment for a "lifestyle choice." The result is that most hate crimes legislation doesn't reference sexual orientation as a protected category. Bills that do try to protect gays' civil liberties simply languish in Congress, such as the Employment Non-Discrimination Act (ENDA) barring workplace discrimination. The right wing stamps these civil rights ordinances "antireligious" First Amendment violations because "under such legislation, preaching against homosexuality could be construed as hate speech," according to Leah Farish, a lawyer who writes for Dobson's website. Farish and others like her repeatedly make these absurd claims even though the ENDA uniformly exempts religious organizations, despite the obvious truth, as any lawyer should know, that hate crimes involve *actions* that injure victims, not just *words,* however ugly they may be.

Perhaps the leading example that ours was a democracy for some occurred with the *Bowers v. Hardwick* decision in 1986, as the Supreme Court ruled against the repeal of state sodomy laws—effectively branding all gays and lesbians criminals in intent, if not practice, for engaging in private, consensual sex. In Oregon six years later, the Christian Coalition-backed Measure 9, which sought to constitutionally designate homosexuality as "abnormal, wrong, unnatural, and perverse," was only narrowly defeated. Mind you, this language originated in 1992 in a West Coast state—not in a theocratic Puritan colony. During the battle over Measure 9, several churches which condemned the measure were torched, numerous instances of gay-bashing were reported, and one opponent was even murdered before the measure failed at the polls.

This was followed by the 1996 passage of Colorado's noxious Amendment 2, a ballot initiative intended again to constitutionally bar gays from being granted their civil rights (those so-called "special rights"). The purpose of this amendment was to prohibit government action "designed to protect the status of persons based on their homosexual, lesbian, or bisexual orientation." Gayle Norton, then-attorney general of Colorado and later the anti-environment Bush secretary of the interior, struggled to come up with expert witnesses to defend the amendment. The Right could not find a single professional, credible expert witness to take its side. Indeed, even the conservative-dominated Supreme Court recognized Colorado's Amendment 2 for what it was: an unconstitutional attempt to designate gays and lesbians as a class unto themselves, a clear deprivation of access to blind justice at the heart of American law.

In the 1997 majority decision striking down the initiative, Justice Anthony Kennedy wrote, "We find nothing special in the protections Amendment 2 withholds [from lesbians, gay men, and bisexuals]. These are protections taken for granted by most people either because they already have them or do not need them; these are protections against exclusion from almost limitless number of transactions and endeavors that constitute ordinary civil life in a free society." Yet the scoring of easy political points by gay-bashing conservatives with misinformed devotees didn't stop with that majority decision.

Despite Bill Clinton's humanistic political impulses, his campaign pledge to end antigay discrimination in the military crashed into a wall of opposition. The military claims that because it is not a force for social change, it cannot "move ahead of society." "Never mind that it did just that," said gay historian John D'Emilio, "when it integrated its ranks in the 1940s," allowing highly competent African Americans to climb the ranks, and that it went further when the service academies were opened to women in the 1970s.

Clinton's eventual compromise, his "don't ask-don't tell" policy, is a monumental, multidimensional failure that has satisfied no one. Every year, this policy proves to be an obvious waste of money—at least $27 million annually in the training costs of lost soldiers. But far worse, it squanders talented recruits, with ten thousand service members having been discharged since 1992 under the provision. Even worse occurs when the armed forces seek tuition restitution from defenseless gay ROTC students, who are essentially being asked to pay the cost of their discrimination.

In one stance, the navy tried to recoup $25,600 from Peter Laska, who was forced by systemic harassment to drop out of NROTC at the University of Pennsylvania. The Navy then placed a lien on the midshipman's family home. This was how his parents found out their son was gay.

In its zeal to pursue don't ask-don't tell, the military has habitually gone so far as to fake evidence, force confessions, bug telephones, open mail, bust into private homes, and ignore open platoon violence—all in the name of boosting "morale" by viciously excluding hardworking, patriotic gays, whatever the costs. These totalitarian tactics are deployed against young, often blue-collar American citizens who, despite choosing military service, have little or no legal recourse because of their "lifestyle choice."

Even Dick Cheney, at the time secretary of defense under Bush 41, reported to Congress in July 1991 that "I think there have been times in the past when [hostility to gays in the military] has been generated on the notion that somehow there was a security risk involved, although I must say I think that is a bit of an old chestnut."

The Bush 43 White House and the Pentagon describe our present allies in Iraq as tough and critical to our effort there. Yet these allies— like the UK, Denmark, and Australia—all allow homosexuals to serve openly in their armed forces, a fact which seems to deflate Top Brass claims that gays and lesbians undermine "unit cohesion" and threaten a functional military. Moreover, in the face of a serious shortage of linguists in government agencies dealing with terrorism, the military has, since 2001, fired twenty Arabic and six Farsi speakers as well as several Korean language speakers for being gay. In an administration constantly talking about a global war on terror, it's irrational that effective, well-trained, and scarce interpreters and combatants would be dismissed when they are, in fact, direly needed.

These include soldiers like Ian Finkenbinder, an Arabic-speaking cryptologic linguist, who acted as a vital interface between the military and Iraqi civilians. Finkenbinder had already served a successful tour of duty (no complaints from his unit), yet was discharged under don't ask-don't tell just before his infantry division's redeployment to Iraq. All of this occurred against the wishes of his commanding officers, who saw how such discrimination put their troops in even greater danger. Speaking for the Servicemembers Legal Defense Network, Steve Ralls concluded that "the military is placing homophobia well ahead of national security." Especially so since a recent survey indicates six in ten Americans favor allowing gays to serve openly in the armed forces.

Just as the military suffers from discriminating against gays and businesses suffer for keeping out racial minorities, schools also lose out when they bar gay people from fully engaging in the academic community. Look at Tim Smith, a Harvard Business School graduate kicked off of Baylor University's Hankamer School of Business Advisory Board.

Baylor is a religious Baptist school in Waco, Texas, whose message of intolerance meant that it was recently ranked third on a list of top twenty "Colleges with Low Acceptance of Gays" by the Princeton Review. Baylor also made headlines in 2003 when former Baylor student Matt Bass was stripped of his seminary scholarship after school officials discovered he was gay.

"I have varied emotions," Smith told the *Houston Voice*. "I'm very sad that my money and time has been good enough for twenty years and now since they found out I'm gay it's not." Smith said the school's dean wanted him to continue as a guest lecturer, an offer he declined. "You might as well tell Rosa Parks that she's welcome to ride the bus as long as she sits in the back," he said. "In my case, it seems like you're saying it's OK for me to serve Hankamer—as long as I stay in my place—in the classroom but not on the board. Any kind of limitation, which puts people 'in their place,' on some basis other than merit is not just bad business, it is wrong."

Yet the easy scapegoating of a minority with little political capital outside of a few big cities became much more difficult with the reversal of *Bowers* in 2003. *Lawrence v. Texas* was a stunning victory that finally ended the notion that America could discriminate freely against gays and still call itself a democracy. In this landmark decision, the moderately conservative Justice Kennedy again wrote the most eloquent entreaty for gay rights. He declared that "the state cannot demean their existence or control their destiny by making their private sexual conduct a crime...It is a promise of the Constitution that there is a realm of personal liberty which the government may not enter." This language transcends even the legal theories of equal protection that the gay movement had depended on, instead establishing (for *everyone*) the fundamental freedom to engage in private consensual relations.

You would think conservatives would be happy with this decision since they usually are for promoting freedom and keeping government out of our private lives. But despite the overwhelming statistical and anecdotal evidence to the contrary, Justice Antonin Scalia still scoffed in his minority opinion in *Lawrence* that mainstream Americans "do not want persons who openly engage in homosexual conduct as partners in their business, scoutmasters for their children, as teachers...or as boarders in their home." The personal liberty described in Kennedy's majority opinion is, in Scalia's view, the equivalent of "prostitution" and the "recreational use of heroin."

Scalia and fellow conservative justice Clarence Thomas—and Bush—are on the wrong side of history here, akin to Strom Thurmond and George Wallace, who only won elections in the 1940s and 1950s by advocating racial segregation. For while 70 percent of Americans over the age of seventy oppose same-sex marriage, only 30 percent of Americans under thirty do so. The fault line over gays in public and private has become a trend line, a democratic trajectory toward eventual equality under the law.

ACCESS TO JUSTICE

With corporations gaining ever more power in the executive and congressional branches, it's essential that victims be able to vindicate their rights in the third branch of government—the judiciary. When the Ford Motor Company decided not to install an $8 plastic shield around gasoline tanks in the 1970s—because it would be cheaper to be occasionally sued later by the families of those who died in survivable collisions and explosions—it was a lawsuit which revealed this calculus of death and which produced a recall and large punitive damages for victims. And it is the plaintiff's bar, not the government, that has won protections and relief for eleven million workers exposed to cancer-causing asbestos, ten thousand thalidomide-affected children, six million Phen-Fen users suffering from heart damage, thousands of women infected by the Dalkon shield, and millions more individual victims of dangerous products and criminally negligent doctors. Indeed, with the federal government becoming ever more lax in its corporate oversight responsibilities, lawyers representing individuals can enforce pollution standards, workers rights, antidiscrimination law, product safety standards, malpractice, and other important human rights.

Which gives Bush & Co. agita. In his 1978, 1994, 1998, 2000, and 2004 campaigns—for Congress, governor, and president—Bush often attacked lawyers and lawsuits for the high cost of medicine. "Tort reform" was his mantra. (The word "tort" comes from the French word meaning "wrong." So tort law is about suing to correct wrongs, as when the victim of an auto defect sues the manufacturer; to Bush, the wrong is the lawsuit against a company, not the personal injury resulting from the product's defect.)

But in fact, throughout this quarter century, the number of lawsuits and the size of judgments overall recently has gone *down,* not up. The National Center for State Courts reports that tort case filings have declined by 8 percent since 1975 when adjustments are made for population growth. As for those "runaway juries," in 2001 the median damages in state courts were $37,000, down from $65,000 a decade earlier, and Bureau of Justice statistics reveal that juries decide against plaintiffs in medical malpractice cases about 75 percent of the time. In the same year, punitive damages were awarded in only 6 percent of all cases—but even then, they are rarely paid because plaintiffs usually settle for much less rather than face teams of corporate lawyers in rounds of expensive appeals. And keep in mind, fewer than 4 percent of all tort actions are ever even decided by a jury, and then only a tiny fraction of those include punitive damages.

Like other Bush administration policies, "tort reform" hurts the poor, women, minorities, and the elderly disproportionately. While there *is* a health care crisis, it's unrelated to the less than 2 percent of all health care costs due to medical malpractice insurance premiums. Making it harder for consumers and shareholders to sue effectively shuts the doors to justice in the face of those without political or market power. What's left of the First Amendment's right "to petition the government for a redress of grievances" if ordinary Americans either can't afford lawyers or can't have their cases heard, or both?

But that's what is happening in Washington, as the Senate in 2004 passed a class-action Catch-22 bill: large class actions will be moved from state to federal courts, where busy federal judges are likely to dismiss them as "unmanageable" (there is one federal court judge for about every fourteen state judges). The result: rights without remedies. Peel back the rhetoric and it becomes clear that tort reform is little more than an attempt to undo democratic judicial checks on corporate power to please Republican corporate donors while defunding their foes on the other side of the aisle.

This dismantling of our civil justice rights is more than just a minor issue for legal policy wonks to wrangle over—it's an attack on democracy itself. The right to a day in court before a jury of peers is a fundamental tenet of democracy promised in the U.S. Constitution. Beyond the First Amendment guarantee noted above, the right to a civil jury trial is further bolstered by the Seventh Amendment, which states, "the right of trial by jury shall be preserved, and no fact tried by a jury, shall be otherwise reexamined in any court of the United States, than according to the rules of the common law."

Gideon v. Wainwright finally affirmed all Americans' right to counsel in criminal cases in 1963, but no such right exists in the civil justice system, which leaves those without means to fend for themselves. Some civil law assistance for America's poor was made available beginning with Lyndon Johnson's Great Society and institutionalized by Nixon's signing of the Legal Services Corporation Act in 1974. However, many of these provisions have been subsequently weakened by Republican Congresses restricting lawsuits and shrinking budgets. It's inconceivable that American citizens who make less than $50,000 a year would be denied the ability to vote, but that's precisely what is happening in our civil justice system.

The Tort Reform Story

At the heart of the "tort reform" movement is the distrust of a basic democratic institution—the jury. The American civil jury is a unique body, unparalleled in the world in giving citizens the power of oversight over egregious corporate misconduct—and for this reason it has long been under attack by big business.

In the 1950s plaintiffs' lawyers started winning battles that made juries more diverse and representative of the American public. At the same time, technological advances led to products with increasingly more dangerous consequences. The explosion of automobile injuries and fatalities, for example, led to a wave of court cases to determine liability for the growing danger of death and disfigurement.

As more of these cases were decided by juries, the insurance industry launched ad campaigns in places like *Life Magazine* and the *Saturday Evening Post* warning potential jurors that they would "pay for liability and damage suit verdicts whether you are insured or not." These ads introduced tort reformers' claims that jurors were "ruled by emotion rather than facts," and that they "arrive at unfounded or excessive awards—verdicts occasionally even higher than requested!" One ad pictured a bailiff guarding a jury room with the phrase "YOUR insurance premium is being determined now." These blame-the-jury scare tactics were the main tool of proto-tort reformers for many years—until they learned the more sophisticated tactic of blaming the victims and their lawyers.

In the 1960s and '70s, as a generation of public-interest lawyers for consumer and civil rights causes won hard-fought battles to improve product safety and curb discrimination in the workplace, corporate leaders grew ever more fearful of potential litigation. The insurance industry added fictional TV programs and paid articles, disguised as hard news, to their arsenal of smear weapons against their enemies in the courtroom, before coming up with their winning formula, the "tort tale." These fictional or barely factual anecdotes were designed to "prove" the supposed litigation crisis in lieu of factual evidence. Consider a 1977 insurance company ad which claimed that a man who was injured misusing a lawnmower as a hedge clipper was awarded $500,000 by an out-of-control jury. The insurance firm that sponsored the ad, Crum and Forester, later admitted they made it all up, but the useful fiction was widely reported and still makes the rounds among tort reformers (sometimes with the plaintiff cutting his hair instead of his hedges, as Dan Quayle twisted the yarn), along with many other grossly false or misrepresented anecdotes of greedy litigants.

The strategy to sway potential jurors was moderately successful. According to a 1979 study published in the *American Bar Association Journal,* jurors who had seen just one ad were prone to back significantly smaller awards for pain and suffering. And studies show that juries today are remarkably skeptical of personal injury and product liability cases.

In addition to creating skeptical juries, the movement won a major legislative victory when California enacted a law in 1976 to cap noneconomic awards (for "pain and suffering") in medical malpractice cases at $250,000—precisely the amount tort reformers want to cap federal malpractice cases at today. Back in the seventies, California insurers claimed that the "lawsuit crisis" of that decade had forced them to raise malpractice insurance 300 percent. When malpractice rates remained high after the legislation was enacted, the state's doctors ended up hiring a trial lawyer themselves to sue the insurance company for price-gouging in the name of an invented crisis. The doctors won a $50 million refund and the state passed reforms to regulate insurance rates.

Yet California's insurance rates these days are *higher* than many states that *do not* have caps. "I don't like to hear insurance company executives say it's the tort system—it's self-inflicted," said Donald J. Zuk, a leading malpractice insurance executive himself, in 2002. Other states that have enacted these caps have also seen little or no impact on insurance rates. In the nineteen states that had them between 1991 and 2002, doctors paid an extra 48 percent in premiums. But the jump was 12 percent lower in the thirty-two states without rate caps, according to a white paper by Weiss Ratings, an independent industry observer.

After its modest successes of the 1970s, the tort reform movement became more organized in the 1980s and '90s. Far Right sponsors established research centers, such as Manhattan Institute's Project on Civil Justice Reform, along with lobby groups like the American Tort Reform Association (ATRA) and the localized Citizen's Against Lawsuit Abuse (CALA). These organizations proceeded to publish misleading "litigation horror stories" to create a scarecrow called the "litigation crisis." In all, there are over one hundred such groups supporting the cause of "tort deform," and by now most states have some limits on tort litigation.

As a result of the 1998 settlement with tobacco companies, we know that in 1995 ATRA got half of its budget from tobacco companies—an industry that was caught lying about its product's deadly addictiveness. In a single year, $5.5 million was funneled from cigarette coffers through law firms to ATRA and on down to the local "grassroots" organizations. Also contributing were insurance companies and corporations with high liability, such as Halliburton and Dow Chemical.

What this movement lacks in substance it makes up in style (and funding). The talented misinformers have no trouble hawking their propaganda to the press. And with the American Trial Lawyers Association (ATLA) focusing on behind-the-scenes lobbying and court appeals, and the underfunded public interest groups unable to match the deformers' media efforts, business interests often have little public competition in the debate. In February 2005, the author was on CNN to respond to President Bush's speech in Milwaukee highlighting the "litigation crisis." When the anchor, Miles O'Brien, asked, "Wouldn't you agree the system is broken?" my one word answer, "No," left him stammering in disbelief as I went on to explain that Bush's description of a litigation crisis was about as real as WMD in Iraq.

A 1992 internal memo from the Manhattan Institute president, William Hammett, describes the movement's strategy:

Journalists need copy, and it's an established fact that over time they'll bend in the direction in which it flows. For that reason, it is imperative that a steady stream of understandable research, analysis, and commentary supporting the need for liability reform be produced. If sometime during the present decade, a consensus emerges in favor of serious judicial reform, it will be because millions of minds have been changed, and only one institution is powerful enough to bring that about: the combined force of the nation's print and broadcast media, the most potent instrument for public education—or miseducation—in existence.

And bend the press to their cause they did. The Manhattan Institute cultivated and marketed anti-tort authors like Peter Huber (*Liability: The Legal Revolution and Its Consequences*) and Walter K. Olson (*The Litigation Explosion*). They publicized their cause with eye-catching inventions like the "tort tax," Huber's estimate of what excessive litigation may cost the economy as a whole. The "tax's hidden impact on the way we live and do business may amount to a $300 billion dollar [sic] annual levy on the American economy," Huber wrote in 1988. The "tort tax" captured the imagination of "tort reformers" and journalists alike—Dan Quayle included the figure in his speeches when the first Bush administration made so-called tort reform a pet cause. But as the *Economist* reported in 1992, "The $300 billion figure has no discernable connection to reality."

These groups also created slogans that have made their way into the vernacular: "jackpot juries," "litigation lottery," "judicial hellhole," "junk science," "loony lawsuits." All are devices designed to undermine our democratic jury system.

The result, according to the Rand Corporation's Institute for Civil Justice, is "very stark": the news media covered 41 percent of verdicts for plaintiffs, according to a survey from 1999, but only 3 percent of verdicts for the defense. And remember, juries find for the defense far more often than the plaintiff. In addition, newspapers are quick to splash big jury awards across their front pages, but few of them actually follow up when those awards are reduced or overturned. When cigarette companies were hit with $144.8 billion in damages by a Florida jury, ten of the biggest newspapers in the country gave it front-page play. When the decision was overturned, only two of them printed a front-page follow up.

Since the 1980s, hundreds of tort tales have been told and retold in the pages and on the TV screens of the American media that are either grossly false, or so distorted as to give a false impression. There is Merv Gravinski who sued Winnebago after he abandoned his driver's seat to grab a coffee from the back of his RV. When the vehicle inevitably crashed, he cashed in for $1.75 million. There's also Amber Carson who sued a restaurant for $113,500 after breaking her tailbone while slipping on a drink that she had thrown in anger at her boyfriend. And don't forget Kara Walton, who fell through the window of a nightclub she was sneaking into and was promptly awarded $12,000, plus dental bills. These stories have two things in common: 1) they never happened; 2) they were reported as fact in media outlets including CNN, *U.S.News & World Report*, *The American Spectator*, the *Oakland Tribune*, the *Ft. Worth Star-Telegram*, Salt Lake City's *Desert News*, the *Akron Beacon-Journal*, the *News and Record* in Greensboro, North Carolina, and the *Chronicle* of Augusta, Georgia.

But far and away, the most retold and referenced tort tale of all is the McDonald's coffee case. In 1994, the "tort deform" movement found its unwitting mascot when Stella Liebeck won a lawsuit against McDonald's for third degree burns from a spilled cup of coffee. From magazines and newspapers to late-night TV and politician's speeches, everyone has been exposed to this "absurd" tale: Woman spills hot cup of coffee on her lap, sues McDonald's, and wins $3 million from a runaway jury. What people don't often hear are the facts of the case because they reveal how deformers distort the reality in order to distort the law.

In February 1992, Stella Liebeck sat in the passenger seat of a Ford Probe as her grandson pulled over so she could add cream and sugar to the coffee purchased a few minutes before from the McDonald's drive-through. Holding the cup between her legs, the seventy-nine-year-old woman pulled up on the lid and spilled the scalding contents in her lap. When her adult grandson realized she was in shock and seriously injured, he helped her out of her hot-coffee-soaked sweatpants and drove her to the hospital. There doctors found serious third degree burns covering 6 percent of her body, including her thighs, buttocks, genitals, and groin, and 16 percent covered in burns bad enough to cause permanent scarring. Liebeck remained in the hospital for a week and underwent agonizing skin grafts to repair the damage. With hospital bills adding up, she left the hospital early and was cared for by her daughter who had to take time off work. In all, Liebeck was partially disabled for about two years.

The long-time Republican did not immediately seek legal help. She sent a letter to the corporation saying that she had "no intention of suing or asking for unreasonable recompense." She simply asked McDonald's to recoup her costs that were not covered by Medicare. In the end, her medical costs came to $20,000; McDonald's offered $800. So Liebeck hired a law firm, which in turn sought a lawyer who had settled a similar case against McDonald's. The judge ordered mediation between the parties where a trained mediator recommended a settlement of $225,000. McDonald's flatly refused.

During the trial, jurors learned that McDonald's coffee was served far hotter than other restaurants or home machines. At 180 to 190 degrees, even the company's quality assurance supervisor acknowledged that he knew the coffee could cause serious burning just from drinking it, but they had no plans to lower the temperature. The jurors were also aware that the company had over seven hundred complaints about the dangerously hot coffee in the previous decade, and had paid roughly $750,000 to settle similar claims. Nor did jurors ever hear Liebeck say that the spill was McDonald's fault, as the anti-access-to-court advocates now like to claim. The plaintiff's case was simply that the coffee was hotter and more dangerous than could reasonably be expected.

"The real question," asked defense attorney Tracy McGee, "is how far you want our society to go to restrict what most of us enjoy and accept?" He further alienated the jury by belittling the previous victims of the company's hot coffee. To try to keep evidence of previous burnings out of court, McGee declared, "First person accounts of sundry women whose nether regions have been scorched by McDonald's coffee might well be worthy of Oprah.... But they have no place in a court of law."

The jury—many of whom later said they had at first been skeptical of Liebeck's claim—initially awarded compensatory damages of $160,000 and punitive damages of $2.7 million. This punitive portion of the award was to punish McDonald's for its egregious behavior and lack of concern for its injured customers. While the company's lawyers argued that seven hundred burned customers over a decade was statistically insignificant, the jurors decided to tell McDonald's, "Hey, open your eyes. People are getting burned!" according to one of them. But in the end the judge slashed the punitive damages from $2.7 million to $480,000, heeding one of the ceilings promoted by tort reformers themselves of awarding no more than three times the compensatory damages. And the compensatory damages were already lowered 20 percent by the jury to account for Liebeck's own role in the accident. With the fast-food mega-corporation prepared to fight tooth and nail over appeals, Liebeck and her lawyers settled for an undisclosed amount, but certainly a smaller sum than the total $640,000 awarded by the court.

Frank Luntz, a Republican pollster, advised Republicans in the 2004 campaign to link this coffee tale to tort reform. "We've all heard the story of the New Mexico woman who bought a cup of coffee from a New Mexico drive-thru, spilled it in her lap, and then sued the fast-food giant for more than $2 million," says a Luntz penned speech. "For those of you wondering why your coffee is always cold...you can stop wondering." Luntz knows what he's doing when he advises his clients to mislead the public. "It's almost impossible to go too far when it comes to demonizing lawyers," Luntz told Republicans. His strategy book elaborates: "When asked what comes to mind when they hear the word 'personal injury lawyers,' Americans use words like...'creeps,' 'bottom-feeders,' 'overpaid,' and 'evil.' You don't want to use those words yourself—and you don't have to—just call them personal injury lawyers—Americans already know what they think of them."

Bush and Rove Get in on the Act

One person who didn't need to read the Luntz playbook to know how to play the tort reform card was Karl Rove. The man who would become "Bush's brain" discovered how important tort reform could be to Republicans while running Texas Supreme Court candidates in the 1980s. In just a few years, Rove orchestrated a Republican takeover of the Texas high court, long ruled by Democrats, by calling attention to his opponents' donations from trial lawyers, while pushing anti-tort buttons to rack up huge big business donations for his candidates. Rove's cause was buoyed by a 1987 60 *Minutes* report that investigated Democratic judges' donations from lawyers whose cases the judges would rule on. (A decade later, the CBS news magazine would return to report the same story about Republican judges taking contributions from corporations for whom they ruled in favor.)

Rove used tort reform early on as "an organizing principle to bring together swing voters, and more importantly, to consolidate business [and professional communities] together," said Kim Ross, a lobbyist for the Texas Medical Association in an interview with *Frontline*. "And frankly, 'tort reform' has a kinder, gentler face.... It's a way of softening the blunt instrument that tort reform is when you're asking to limit damages or to allow to countersue or limit standards for expert witnesses and all the things that are the esoterica of what, essentially, is saying, 'Plaintiff, you had this right, but we're taking it away because we think you've abused it.' And you do it by putting a lab coat on and arguing about access to care and the cost of medical care, not whether or not Dow Chemical is going to pay this or this and punitive damages on a suit where they might or might not be guilty."

Rove then melded his Machiavellian analysis into the politics of George W. Bush. In 1994, while working as a $3,000 a month consultant for the cigarette manufacturer (and tort reform enthusiast) Phillip Morris, Rove led Bush's first campaign for governor. James Moore and Wayne Slater, in their book *Bush's Brain,* remember Rove taking credit for this plank in Bush's platform, "Later, we added tort reform...I sort of talked him into that one."

Rove was drawn to the tort reform movement because the issue served the dual purpose of bringing in funding from big businesses desperate to shrink the cost of litigation by any means while defunding the trial lawyers who faithfully give to Democrats. "Big business flocked to us," said Rove about that 1994 campaign. Indeed it did: among the Texas donors that flocked to Bush and Rove were Ken Lay, the Enron CEO; Bob Perry, the Swiftboat Vet and Kerry hit man; and Ken Starr, the Phillip Morris tobacco lawyer who helped make tort reform a priority in the first Bush White House before championing one of the most expensive, frivolous legal expeditions in history.

When Bush won the election in 1994, and was reelected in 1998, those businesses were repaid with a massive rewriting of Texas tort system, culminating after Bush left office with a narrowly passed constitutional amendment that capped noneconomic jury awards in Texas civil suits at $250,000.

Bush and Rove continued to hang their hats on so-called tort reform in the 2000 and 2004 campaigns for president. But the issue was given its biggest stage in 2004 when Kerry named a trial lawyer, John Edwards, as his running mate. That year, Rove cultivated tort reform not only to bring in big business donations, but also to deflect attention from the health crisis that hung over the embattled president. In Bush's first term, medical costs skyrocketed while wages stagnated. The result was a record number of Americans without health coverage—one out of four Americans spent at least part of two years without insurance. But instead of countering Kerry's reasonable proposal to increase health coverage to the neediest Americans with his own health plan, Bush simply blamed the trial lawyers for increasing the cost of medical malpractice insurance with "frivolous" lawsuits.

The classic Bush argument was on display at the second presidential debate of that election which took place in St. Louis on October 8, 2004. When Kerry corrected the record by saying that medical malpractice insurance, despite the high rates, represented a tiny fraction of all health care costs, the president defended one untruth with another: "He says that medical liability costs only caused 1 percent increase. That shows a lack of understanding. Doctors practice defensive medicine because of all the frivolous lawsuits that cost our government $28 billion a year." The Bush campaign called it the "largest cost in the health care system." But the widely respected and neutral Congressional Budget Office put the overall cost of malpractice on heath care at less than 2 percent while concluding that the effects of "defensive medicine" were "weak or inconclusive."

Bush's jihad against lawyers and litigation isn't supported by General Accountability Office reports. One from August of 2004 found that access problems "were limited to scattered, often rural, locations and in most cases providers identified long-standing factors in addition to malpractice pressures that affected the availability of services." The GAO also found that the cost of malpractice insurance had little effect on the cost of medicine; that malpractice claims were actually growing slower than the rate of inflation; and that the tort system does not encourage unnecessary defensive medicine. Finally, the GAO debunked the claim by Bush and others that the litigation crisis was driving doctors out of medicine and reducing access to care, and that in many of the locations where these claims were made, the number of gynecologists and other doctors were *increasing*.

But that didn't stop our national misleader from claiming, with typical oratorical clumsiness, that "too many OB/GYNs aren't able to practice their love with women all across this country." Bush made a point of calling attention to doctors who claimed they were being driven out of medicine. Like Dr. Robert Zaleski, who went on strike to protest the medical malpractice insurance crisis and was personally invited to a Bush speech on the subject. Of course, neither he nor Bush ever mentioned that Zaleski's patients filed fourteen malpractice cases against him over a fifteen year period. Of those, he was found liable for a combined total of $1.7 million. He had also admitted, under oath, to an addiction to painkillers while he was a surgeon and wrote prescriptions to other addicts to get drug kickbacks.

In similar fashion, Bush touted a Clinton administration acting solicitor general, Walter E. Dellinger III, at an appearance in February 2004 to support the class action bill. But it forgot to mention that Dellinger's law firm had earned $780,000 to lobby in favor of the law.

And the repeated charges by Republicans and W. that medical malpractice claims force doctors out of work and raise the price of health care are simply not true. Apolitical experts widely agree that the chief reason medical malpractice rates jumped in the early part of the decade was the insurance industry's practice to invest their profits in the stock market. When the stocks fell, they raised their rates to replace the lost capital. Speaking to the *Palm Beach Post* in 2003, the president of the largest insurance provider in Florida, Bob White of First Professional Insurance Company, said, "No responsible insurer can cut its rates after a [medical malpractice] bill passes." Indeed, a 2005 report, commissioned by consumer groups, analyzed the annual statements of the fifteen largest medical malpractice insurers in the country and found that they increased their premiums, on average, 120 percent between 2000 and 2004 while payouts rose just under 6 percent. The author of the study, former Missouri Insurance Commissioner Jay Angoff, reported that the malpractice insurers "have been raising their premiums even though both their actual claims payments and their projected future claims payments have been falling." In just three years, leading malpractice insurers increased their surpluses (the profits held by insurers over those that are expected to be paid out in future claims) by more than a third, as their stocks doubled in an otherwise flat market.

These successes are built on a foundation of falsehoods. Scholars have repeatedly found that tort reformers claims of a litigation crisis are all sound and fury signifying nothing. Bush's arguments had their desired effects: they gave him a political alibi to explain why millions had no health insurance, but the fact is that a successful tort lawsuit is a rare thing.

A 1991 study by the Rand Corporation's Institute for Civil Justice—the largest of its kind—found that 81 percent of those who suffer a disabling injury take no action at all. Of the remaining 19 percent who even *consider* making a claim, 6 percent of them let it drop entirely. Of the remaining 13 percent, 2 percent deal directly with the other party, 4 percent deal with an insurer, and 7 percent consult a lawyer. Of that 7 percent, only 4 percent actually hire a lawyer and just 2 percent of them eventually file a suit. And keep in mind, this sample consists of people who suffer a major injury, a relatively rare event to begin with.

Similarly, a groundbreaking Harvard University study on medical errors concluded that "most American doctors fervently believe that the present-day malpractice litigation is excessive and erratic...[However,] the medical setting has provided the strongest evidence that the real tort crisis may consist in too few claims." This study concluded that, out of every one hundred medical injuries caused by negligent professionals, only about twelve result in any claim at all. Of those who end up with at least partial permanent disabilities as a result of medical error, only about fifteen file claims. Other reports have found that 90 percent of all victims of medical errors will never file suit at all.

Meanwhile, state governments exercise negligible oversight over the industry, and medical associations do little to protect patients from the most error-prone physicians, leaving the majority of error-free doctors to make up the cost of medical mistakes with their premiums. About 5 percent of doctors are responsible for about 50 percent of claims—and the Institute of Medicine has estimated that there are as many as ninety-eight thousand deaths in hospitals, and countless more injuries, each year due to medical mistakes. But do we ever hear news reports of the grievously injured who *don't* see a lawyer and *don't* file a claim and get *no* justice at all?

A leading medical malpractice lawyer in California, Linda Fermoyle Rice, concludes that the state's caps prevent her from taking many worthy cases. "The law has made it impossible for many victims to get access to the courts." She had to turn away the family of a fourteen-year-old boy, for example, who had died in a hospital from what appeared to be medical negligence. In Texas, Yvonne Harrison decided to represent herself when her eighteen-year-old son unexpectedly died of pneumonia in a hospital, and a dozen lawyers turned her down because of the state's award caps.

Far from being "vile opportunists," studies show that plaintiff's attorneys act as gatekeepers of the system "taking only the most meritorious cases deserving the greatest compensation." Because of the cost of personal injury cases, which include highly technical research and costly medical experts—and because of their own rational profit motives—lawyers must be sure they have a chance to win and recover the costs of litigation in an award. For this reason, researchers estimate that around 90 percent of those who seek to take civil action are turned down by trial lawyers.

Those who are most affected by limits on tort claims are poor claimants with suits for sums that, while meaningful to them, aren't enough to recoup the costs and warrant a law firm's attention. And while capping damages and preventing class actions make it harder to find a lawyer to work on contingency, government sponsored legal aid is increasingly hard to come by. Approximately thirty-seven thousand legal services lawyers struggle to help one million of the forty-five million Americans who qualify for aid each year.

These programs often provide the only opportunity that low-income Americans have at getting justice in divorce cases, child custody and support, consumer and banking disputes, landlord/tenant disputes, and domestic violence, to name just a few. Government-funded legal assistance programs have long been a target of corporations and their representatives in Congress. Newt Gingrich's "Contract with America" sought to end that aid entirely. The Clinton administration saved the program, but it suffered 40 percent funding cuts and lawyers were barred from pursuing cases based on underlying causes of poverty. Legal services, for example, can no longer aid prisoners and many immigrants or challenge welfare reform laws, lobby for the poor, or file class actions.

And the budget cuts run deep. A groundbreaking 2005 report showed that no less than 50 percent of those who actually seek help are literally turned away. The Legal Aid Society of Salt Lake City, for instance, provided free care for decades, taking on as many as fourteen hundred cases in a year. In 2004 it took only forty-five cases and now charges on a sliding scale of $200–$600 for divorce or child custody litigation—out of reach for some of its neediest clients. Sarah Campbell, director of Kisatchie Legal Services Corporation in Louisiana, describes having to "pick the women who seemed to be in the most immediate danger" for the scarce legal aid. "If they'd had a gun to their heads, or they'd been severely beaten, we'd squeeze them in no matter what. Or if they had kids, we'd take the case. As awful as it sounds, you'd rationalize that a case where several people were in danger deserved priority over one person who's being beaten up."

Caps on noneconomic damages hurt women, children, and the elderly disproportionately. Children and the retired are less likely to lose income and therefore are not compensated properly for disabilities allowed under economic compensation. Meanwhile, women are more likely to suffer reproductive or sexual injuries that, while life altering, don't carry an economic price tag that fits within compensatory damages.

Nobody likes a lawsuit. For many Americans it's not even an option, and for most Americans it's a last resort that we hope we never have to deal with. But it's a last resort that must be available to preserve the basic fairness promised by democracy—that is, any American can go to court to be compensated for injuries caused by negligence, whether caused by a citizen or a corporation. Dismantling our civil justice system may help shareholders and executives but not consumers—who may also be shareholders and executives—if they were disfigured by an exploding Ford Pinto or died from taking Vioxx. Without punitive and noneconomic damages, class action cases, and other legal tools, wrongdoers will be free to write off the mutilation and loss of life their products cause as a simple business expense, never having to face the moral and economic consequences.

Saving Civil Justice

While Republicans have taken the lead on pushing "tort reform," it's not just one party that allows it to happen. The Orwellian-named Class Action Fairness Act, which will keep most classes of victims from receiving fairness in a court, was approved by a seventy-two to twenty-six Senate majority—eighteen Democrats joined in passing a bill that undermines state consumer protections and sends cases to crowded federal courts to get dismissed.

Finally, preserving an effective civil justice system will not matter much to those who can't afford to hire a lawyer. There are over a million lawyers in this country, and growing, and yet an American Bar Association survey from 2002 found that 71 percent of Americans had "some occasion during the past year that might have led them to hire a lawyer," but just half of them said they would hire one—high costs prohibited most. President Jimmy Carter observed in 1978 that "90 percent of our lawyers serve 10 percent of our people. We are overlawyered and underrepresented." Little has changed since then.

Deborah Rhode, a law professor at Stanford University, has argued that bringing more democracy to America by tripling the federal budget for legal aid would come to less than a billion dollars, a trifle when compared to the hundreds of billions we've spent trying to bring democracy to Iraq. Moreover, says Rhode, simply expanding surcharges on lawyer's revenues and court filing fees for those who can afford it "would be a relatively painless and progressive way to expand access to justice."

The "tort reformers" bogus attacks on lawyers and frivolous lawsuits are actually an attack on the victims and on democracy itself. But that doesn't mean there are no bad lawyers—the profession's terrible reputation is precisely why the movement's misinformation has such resonance. The few lawyers that chase ambulances or innocent people into courtrooms only add ammunition to those who seek to limit liability for corporations. So the legal profession needs to address its poor record on discipline—just as the medical profession should better discipline the few doctors that cause the most malpractice claims. The American Bar Association reported that of the 121,000 complaints filed against lawyers in 2002, only 3.5 percent led to formal discipline.

Ordinary citizens suffer twice when "tort reform" is implemented to punish lawyers. Those who have been prey to a predatory lawyer get no compensation when other victims are denied their day in court. Reasonable checks on lawyers should be expanded to protect consumers, but throwing the baby out with the bathwater and playing on hatred of lawyers to cripple consumer access to courts will only hurt average American citizens, and ultimately democracy, more.

INFORMATION MANIPULATION I: HOW DECEPTION POLLUTES THE WELL OF DEMOCRACY

"Someone running for the highest office in the land should stick to the facts."
—GEORGE W. BUSH, October, 2000

"Political language...is designed to make lies sound truthful and murder respectable, and to give an appearance of solidity to pure wind."
—GEORGE ORWELL in "Politics and the English Language"

Remember the early aphorism of the computer age, GIGO—"Garbage In, Garbage Out"? Now imagine a computer program fed false data or a stock trader basing decisions on rigged balance sheets or a tennis player wearing blinders. Just as machines and markets and sports would fail if they relied on corrupted information, a democracy too will fail if important decisions are based on bad data.

In America today, a form of political GIGO exists with falsehoods routinely flowing from the very top of our federal government. While other White Houses surely spun, exaggerated, deceived, misled, or even lied, the Bush administration appears to be the most dishonest. Ever. By a lot. When it comes to simply withholding essential information, Senator Pat Leahy (D-VT) says that "of the six administrations I've worked with, this is the most secretive." When it comes to a government that elevates ideology and theology over science, Bush & Co. are a pin-striped version of the Tennessee School Board in the 1925 *Scopes* trial. And when it comes to a White House being a primary source of information for Americans, in the words of Abraham Lincoln describing a political rival, George W. Bush "has such a high regard for the truth that he uses it sparingly."

TRUTH AND CONSEQUENCES

President Bush would not be the first president to mislead, fudge, or fib in a pinch, citing national security needs to be sure. Dwight Eisenhower thought it necessary to deny that the U.S. was conducting U-2 flights over the Soviet Union. So when a Soviet missile shot down CIA pilot Frances Gary Powers on a spying mission in 1960, "it set a shocking new standard for deceit at the time and left many Americans wondering whether they could trust their leaders," according to Philip Taubman, a *New York Times* reporter, in his book *Secret Empire.* (After leaving office, Ike was asked about his "greatest regret," and he replied, "The lie we told [about the U-2]. I didn't realize how high a price we were going to have to pay for that lie.") And as Robert Dallek detailed in his 2003 bestseller, *An Unfinished Life,* John F. Kennedy deceived the public about his debilitating Addison's disease in 1960.

Lyndon Johnson repeatedly misled the public (and probably himself) in describing developments in the escalating Vietnam War, especially when it came to inflating the Gulf of Tonkin incident into a *causus belli*—hence his "credibility gap." Richard Nixon's lies about Watergate require no further elaboration here, although the moniker "Tricky Dick" predated that colossal presidential deception. Ronald Reagan dissembled his way through the Iran-Contra affair, as he just kept denying what Oliver North was admitting—that he had approved selling arms to the Nicaraguan Contras in order to free hostages in Iran. And Bill Clinton's deceptions about Monica Lewinsky led to an impeachment trial and temporary disbarment.

President Bush is a person who seems to adopt wholesale the views of Mitchell and Machiavelli: it was John Mitchell, President Nixon's attorney general, who told disgruntled conservative supporters in the 1970s to "watch what we do, not what we say"—and it was Machiavelli who, among other enduring observations, concluded that "the great majority of mankind is satisfied with appearances, as though they were realities."

After matching his assertions with the facts, his words with his deeds, it's clear that George W. Bush is a profoundly untruthful president—not necessarily in terms of any one Vietnam-level or Watergate-style lie but in terms of being a serial dissembler day in and day out, on matters small and large. And when a president in a democracy gets his facts so frequently wrong, wrong policies are the inevitable result.

This was a decidedly minority view in 2002 when the author began writing a book (with Eric Alterman)—*The Book on Bush: How George W. (Mis)leads America*—based on this premise. But by late 2005, a large and increasing number of Americans agreed with this conclusion—in a *Washington Post* poll, 58 percent doubted Bush's honesty; 43 percent said the level of ethics and honesty in the federal government has fallen during Bush's presidency, while 17 percent believed that it rose. More ominously, in a *Time* poll from around the same time, 48 percent agreed that the president "deliberately misled Americans to build his case for war" (versus 45 percent who thought him truthful).

Reflecting the athletic axiom that the best defense is a good offense, in late 2005 Bush and Cheney launched a furious assault on critics who said they had misled America into war. "Bush Accuses Foes of Rewriting History," read one *Washington Post* headline. And Cheney, whose speaking schedule makes him appear to be the vice president of military bases and conservative think tanks, told the group Frontiers of Freedom, "The suggestion that's been made by some U.S. senators that the president of the United States or any member of this administration purposely misled the American people on prewar intelligence is one of the most dishonest and reprehensible charges ever aired in this city."

The Bush White House understands well their advantage of using the presidential bully pulpit to keep repeating that falsehoods are facts in the hope that newspapers will write he said/she said headlines and a confused public will dismiss it all as partisan sniping. They understand how hard it is for the media, even the so-called liberal media, to keep rebutting lies or deceptions—because while a politician who repeats talking points can be effective, a newspaper or network that repeats a story is not reporting the "news." The press secretary of President George Herbert Walker Bush (41) laughed off misstatements made during the 1988 presidential debates because "if reporters document that a candidate spoke untruthfully, so what? Maybe two hundred people read it."

Like Jack Grubman's and Henry Bloget's internal emails on Wall Street showing they understood that smart investors wouldn't listen to "buy" recommendations of stocks they knew to be dogs, White House misstatements are meant for the credulous many, not the sophisticated few. This is what playwright Arthur Miller once called Bush's "power of audacity"—just repeatedly and intensely refuse to recognize reality and assume that critics will tire and relent. There are good cinematic examples of this technique: in *Young Frankenstein,* when Frankenstein commiserates with Igor about the foot-high hump on his back, Igor replies, "What hump?"; and when Roxie Hart in *Chicago* catches her husband in bed with another woman, he coolly denies it, saying, "You going to believe what you see or what I tell you?"

However, Bush & Co. are not fictional characters but leaders who run the country. So though tedious and perhaps familiar, the only serious option for an author is to repeat the evidence that they deny. The next sixteen pages then are a brief chronicle of a couple dozen representative exaggerations, disinformation, false analogies, half-truths, or lies, out of hundreds of examples—with Iraq references clustered together, followed by general ones:

✦ President Bush said, preinvasion, that Iraq had "stockpiles" of biological weapons and then, post-invasion, "We have found the weapons of mass destruction." Vice President Cheney declared, "There is no doubt that Saddam Hussein now has weapons of mass destruction and there is no doubt that he is amassing them to use against our friends, against our allies, and against us." Eleven days after the invasion, Secretary Donald Rumsfeld told ABC's George Stephanopoulos, "We know where they are. They're in the area around Tikrit and Baghdad and east, west, south, and north somewhat."*

Actually, as the world now knows, there is "no doubt" that Cheney's lack of doubt was wrong, that Bush erred in saying there were "stockpiles" of biological weapons, and that if Rumsfeld knew where they were, he never told UN inspectors in Iraq. Although the National

---

*When Rumsfeld was questioned about his "we know where they are" assertion three years later in a public forum by ex-CIA veteran Ray McGovern, the secretary denied ever saying it. When his exact words were read back to him, he stammered, "My words—my words were that—no, no wait a minute, wait a minute."

Intelligence Estimate on Iraq in October 2002 did (incorrectly) maintain that Iraq had a biological research and development program, Bush transformed this into "stockpiles"—an example of what Mark Twain would call a "stretcher"; however, at the same time, the State Department concluded there was no evidence that Saddam had nuclear weapons. The International Atomic Energy Agency, headed by (future) Nobel Peace Prize winner Dr. Mohamed ElBaradei, concluded before the war began that there was no evidence of such weapons—as UN inspector Hans Blix and U.S. inspector David Kaye would subsequently agree. Incessant references to Saddam's use of WMD "on his own people" was politically effective and technically true, but that event occurred a decade before, which of course didn't prove that he still had them in 2002.

Moreover, as the *Washington Post* reported on April 12, 2006, the widely touted claim that weapons had been found in trailers and that the invasion was therefore justified, turned out to be completely false. As reporter Joby Warrick wrote, "even as Bush spoke, U.S. intelligence officials possessed powerful evidence that it was not true:"

> A secret fact-finding mission to Iraq—not made public until 2006—had already concluded that the trailers had nothing to do with biological weapons. Leaders of the Pentagon-sponsored mission transmitted their unanimous findings to Washington in a field report on May 27, 2003, two days before the president's statement [about having found weapons].
>
> The three-page field report and a 122-page final report three weeks later were stamped "secret" and shelved. Meanwhile, for nearly a year, administration and intelligence officials continued to publicly assert that the trailers were weapons factories.

Yet in his next State of the Union address in 2004, President Bush talked not about weapons or stockpiles or programs, but about Saddam Hussein's "weapons of mass destruction related program activities."

✦ Bush said in his 2005 Veterans Day speech that "some Democrats and antiwar critics are now claiming we manipulated the intelligence and misled the American people about why we went to war [even though] a bipartisan Senate investigation found no evidence of political pressure to change the intelligence community judgments related to Iraq's weapon's programs."

Actually, the Senate panel said no such thing, as Republican cochair Laurence Silberman explained: "Our executive order did not direct us to deal with the issue of intelligence by policy-makers and all of us agreed that was not part of our inquiry." But numerous independent analyses and investigations have concluded that pro-invasion warriors invariably emphasized worst-case scenarios (see "imminent threat" following) and skipped over any qualifying comments. According to a CIA independent review on prewar intelligence, led by former CIA deputy director Richard Kerr, "Requests for reporting and analysis of [Iraq's links to al-Qaeda] were steady and heavy in the period leading up to the war, creating significant pressure on the Intelligence Community to find evidence that supported a connection. There was a lot of pressure, no question. The White House, State, Defense were raising questions, heavily on WMD and the issue of terrorism."

Here are two examples of W.'s neocons "cherry-picking" intelligence or allowing conclusions to lead to facts. First, the *New York Times* in November 2005 reported that as early as February 2002, a classified Pentagon report exposed a top al-Qaeda member as a liar who became the key source for claims that Iraq trained al-Qaeda members in using chemical and biological weapons. Despite a Defense Intelligence Agency report that "it is more likely this individual is intentionally misleading the debriefers," the administration used this "evidence" for two more years, including in Colin Powell's infamous and now recanted UN speech.

Second, senior German officials responsible for the interrogation of a source code named "Curveball" were astonished when the White House relied on this confirmed drunk's accounts of Iraq's WMD program in their public statements. "*Mein Gott!* We had always told them it was not proven. It was not hard evidence." Yet Bush based his State of the Union's assertions about Iraq's "mobile biological weapons labs" on Curveball's fabrications.

◆ President Bush repeatedly said from mid-2002 to the invasion in March 2003 that he preferred diplomacy and hadn't made the decision to go to war. At a press conference with Prime Minister Tony Blair in July 2005, Bush said, "Look, both of us didn't want to use our military. Nobody wants to commit military into combat. It's the last option."

Actually, there's a Niagara of evidence that he *did* want to go to war as an early option. Former treasury secretary Paul O'Neill describes how Bush discussed regime change in Iraq at his first cabinet meeting in February 2001. Former White House terrorism advisor Richard Clarke, in his book *Against All Enemies,* tells how Bush kept urging him to find the facts to make a case against Saddam right after the 9/11 attacks— and how Clarke had to keep reminding his boss that we'd been attacked by al-Qaeda, not Saddam. Paul R. Pillar, a CIA veteran who oversaw intelligence estimates about the Middle East in 2000–2005, wrote in a 2006 article in *Foreign Affairs* that the Bush White House distorted intelligence about Iraq's unconventional weapons in order to make its case for war.

The distortion began the afternoon of September 11, 2001, as recently released memos from Secretary Rumsfeld's office reveal. "Judge whether good enough hit S.H. [Saddam Hussein] @ same time—not only UBL (Osama bin Laden)," read one aide's note. "Hard to get a good case...sweep it all up. Things related and not."

The so-called Downing Street memo of July 23, 2002, records the minutes of a meeting with Tony Blair's senior foreign policy and security officials eight months before the invasion. At the same time that Bush was saying that he "hoped force would not be necessary," here's what this official document revealed:

> C reported on his recent talks in Washington. There was a perceptible shift in attitude. Military action was now seen as inevitable. Bush wanted to remove Saddam, through military action, justified by the conjunction of terrorism and WMD [which in fact did become the war's rationale when it was launched]. But the intelligence and facts were being fixed around the policy. The NSC had no patience with the UN route, and no enthusiasm for publishing material on the Iraqi regime's record. There was little discussion in Washington of the aftermath after military action.

Also, a confidential British intelligence memorandum summarizing a January 31, 2003, meeting between Tony Blair and George Bush revealed that the president was determined to invade Iraq regardless of whether the United Nations gave their approval or if unconventional weapons were found. "The start date for the military campaign was now penciled in for 10 March," said the memo, which was written five days *before* Colin Powell's crucial presentation at the UN. And the initial attack occurred on March 19.

✦ Bush often reiterates that America has to "stay the course" to stop Iraq from becoming a magnet for terrorists and that "we must fight them there so we don't have to fight them here." The State Department in early 2004 proudly announced that terrorist attacks worldwide had fallen since the invasion of Iraq.

Actually, Brent Scowcroft, Bush 41's national security advisor, told the *New Yorker* that this invasion "was said to be part of the war on terror, but Iraq feeds terrorism." (This view is consistent with his argument at the end of the first Gulf War against occupying Iraq. "We'd be an occupier in a hostile land. Our forces would be sniped at by guerrillas, and, once we were there, how would we get out?") While al-Qaeda and Islamo-fascism hadn't existed in Iraq before the March 2003 invasion, post-invasion Iraq was serving as "a training ground, a recruitment ground as hundreds of foreign terrorists flooded into Iraq across its unguarded border," concluded the National Intelligence Council, an in-house CIA think tank. There is a serious risk that Iraq is now "creating newly radicalized and experienced jihadists who return home to cause trouble in Saudi Arabia, Egypt, and elsewhere." And, the thesis that the war in Iraq reduced terrorism suffered a blow when the State Department had to revise its 2004 estimate—it seems that the number of terror incidents worldwide didn't fall but rather *tripled,* from 175 in 2003 to 655 in 2004. As for fighting them "there" not "here," "coalition partners" like Spain and Great Britain saw terrorist attacks in Madrid and London in 2004 and 2005. If, God forbid, there's another attack in the U.S., does anyone believe that Bush would then admit that this rationale was wrong?

✦ Bush said on September 25, 2002, that "you can't distinguish between al-Qaeda and Saddam when you talk about the war on terror." Several dozen times he would link Saddam and al-Qaeda, saying that we went to war with Iraq "because we were attacked on September 11."

Actually, although Bush's repeated linkage misled a majority of Americans to believe that Saddam was behind the attack on the World Trade Center, the 9/11 Commission officially concluded that there was no such link. Mel Goodman, a twenty-year CIA veteran, put it clearly: "Saddam Hussein and bin Laden were enemies. Bin Laden considered and said that Saddam was the socialist infidel. These were very different kinds of individuals competing for power in their own way and Saddam Hussein made very sure that al-Qaeda couldn't function in Iraq."

Eventually, even President Bush was forced to admit in September 2003 that "we've had no evidence that Saddam Hussein was involved with the September 11 [attacks]." Yet his own admission didn't stop his penchant for repeating his early falsehoods, as when he said two years later in June 2005, "We went to war because we were attacked." In his 2006 State of the Union address, he dramatically observed, "On September 11, 2001, we found that problems originating in a failed and oppressive state seven thousand miles away could bring murder and destruction to our shores." Was he referring to Saudi Arabia, since fifteen of the nineteen hijackers originated there?

✦ Secretary of State Condoleezza Rice said in mid-2005 that it was unfair to criticize Bush's "staying the course" in Iraq because "the administration, I think, has said to the American people that it is a generational commitment to Iraq."

Actually, the administration predicted the war would be short and sweet and affordable. Does Rice not recall Cheney saying three days before the invasion in March 2003 that "we will, in fact, be greeted as liberators...I think it will go relatively quickly." Secretary Rumsfeld also concluded the week before the invasion that "it is unknowable how long that conflict will last. It could last six days, six weeks. I doubt six months." Deputy Defense Secretary Paul Wolfowitz predicted that Iraq's reconstruction could come out of its own oil revenues. And when White House economist Larry Lindsay in 2003 predicted the war's cost at $200 billion, which would be dead-on accurate within two years, he was fired. A "relatively quick" or "six-months" conflict is now approaching the length of World War II.

✦ President Bush in his 2003 State of the Union address said that "the British government has learned that Saddam Hussein recently bought significant quantities of uranium from Africa" in order to make a nuclear bomb.

Actually, as is now well-known, his claim was based on forged documents, according to Ambassador Joe Wilson who had been sent by the CIA to Niger to investigate. Because the agency had gotten this false claim from a draft of a presidential speech in October, Director George Tenet was shocked when he heard the president repeat it in his State of the Union as a cornerstone in the case for war. Then-national security advisor Condoleezza Rice and Tenet both publicly apologized for use of this unsubstantiated and false statement.

✦ White House press secretary Scott McClellan told the press corps on September 29, 2003, that "the president knows that Karl Rove wasn't involved" in outing CIA operate Valerie Plame, Joe Wilson's wife, adding on October 10 that Rove "assured me he wasn't involved in this."

Actually, Rove was involved. In testimony given under oath, *Time* magazine's Matthew Cooper confirmed that Rove told him Plame was in the CIA.

✦ President Bush repeatedly said that he wanted to find out who leaked classified information related to the Valerie Plame case. "If there's a leak out of my administration, I want to know who it is," Bush told reporters in Chicago in 2004. "If the person has violated law, that person will be taken care of."

Actually, it was the president who did it himself. According to a thirty-nine page document from special prosecutor Patrick Fitzgerald in April of 2006, Scooter Libby divulged that President Bush authorized him to disclose portions of the previously classified October 2002 National Intelligence Estimate (NIE) to rebut criticisms leveled by Joe Wilson. The White House defended its actions by noting that the president can declassify intelligence when he regards it in the public interest. However, there is a standard bureaucratic procedure to declassify such material, and it wasn't observed in this case. Instead, the president did it unilaterally and selectively. He released only material from the NIE that bolstered his preconceived positions on Iraq, including claims that had already been disproved, while leaving out information that weakened his positions; and he agreed that it be covertly shown to only one reporter, rather than to any and all interested parties, as a real declassification demands.

✦ In early September 2005, Bush denounced the "immediate withdrawal of our troops in Iraq or the broader Middle East" as a move that "would only embolden the terrorists."

Actually, at the same time, the *Financial Times* was reporting details of Pentagon plans "to pull significant numbers of troops out of Iraq in the next twelve months." Like Nixon in Vietnam, a conservative president appeared to be feeding red-meat rhetoric to his base while pursuing a realistic course of strategic withdrawal or redeployment in America's larger interests. Also, of course, a very strong case can be made that what is emboldening terrorists now—a case made by Brent Scowcroft and Rep. John Murtha—is not a phased withdrawal but rather our first-time ever occupation of a Muslim country.

✦ After the collapse of all his early rationales for invading Iraq—WMD, Saddam and 9/11, links to al-Qaeda—the president resorted to an analogy: a *Washington Post* headline on August 31, 2005, read, "Bush Calls Iraq War Moral Equivalent of Allies' WWII Fight Against the Axis."

Actually, Saddam and bin Laden cannot seriously be compared to Hitler, because a) the Führer had the capacity to conduct a civilizational world war killing millions, b) Americans mobilized to fight fascism in 1941, while in 2003 they enjoyed tax cuts and no draft, and c) W. is no FDR.

✦ Bush and Cheney belittled Democrats for originally supporting the invasion and then switching to opposition, especially since they had "access to the same intelligence."

Actually, when half of Senate Democrats voted for the war resolution in October 2002—John Kerry, Hillary Clinton, John Edwards, Joe Biden, Jay Rockefeller, among others—they were assured by President Bush that Saddam had WMD and that this authority would help avoid the need for war by forcing Hussein to allow intrusive inspections to go forward. But in a classic bait-and-switch, Bush got this approval for diplomacy and then, not waiting for the completion of inspections that would have exposed all the flawed intelligence, rushed to war. Nor was Congress given all the intelligence provided to the president. While he's briefed daily by the CIA director and reads his PDB (President's Daily Brief), members of the House and Senate are not briefed or informed in a remotely comparable way. And we now know that State Department and Defense Intelligence Agency doubts about WMD and the reliability of key informants were withheld from Congress.

✦ Secretary Rumsfeld told reporters in June 2005, "I guess the reason I don't use the term guerrilla war is that it isn't anything like a guerrilla war or an organized resistance." The opposition, he continued, was comprised of "looters, criminals, remnants of the Baathist regime" and a few foreign fighters.

Actually, the CIA told Bush in a briefing two weeks earlier that he was facing "a classic insurgency" in Iraq. And two weeks after Rumsfeld's disclaimer, Centcom commander John P. Abizaid said that the U.S. did indeed confront "a classic guerrilla-type campaign" there.

✦ Secretary Rumsfeld told European journalists in October 2005 that "I never said [that Saddam was] an imminent threat."

Actually, Rumsfeld told the House Armed Services Committee on September 18, 2002, "Some have argued that the nuclear threat from Iraq is not imminent—that Saddam is at least five to seven years away from having nuclear weapons. I would not be so certain." The next May, White House press secretary Ari Fleischer was asked if we went to war "because we said WMD were a direct and imminent threat to the United States," and Fleischer responded, "Absolutely." In the Rose Garden on October 2, 2002, just before the congressional vote authorizing the war, President Bush said the Iraq regime "is a threat of unique urgency." Again and again, in speech after speech, Bush said that Iraq was "a real and dangerous threat" and a "unique and urgent threat." Indeed, what else could Bush and Rice have meant when they said, separately, that the U.S. couldn't wait for the final proof—"the smoking gun that would come in the form of a mushroom cloud"?

Senator Edward Kennedy (D-MA), who witnessed a real imminent threat of a mushroom cloud during the Cuban Missile Crisis of 1962, responded to all this Chicken Little talk: "Nuclear weapons. Mushroom cloud. Unique and urgent threat. Real and dangerous threat. Grave threat. These words were the administration's rallying cry for war. But they were not the words of the intelligence community, which never suggested that the threat form Saddam was imminent or immediate or urgent."

✦ The Pentagon a) denied American forces had used incendiary white phosphorus as an antipersonnel weapon in the 2005 battle in Fallujah, b) claimed that over 171,000 Iraqi security forces had been "trained and equipped" by the summer of 2005, and c) for months publicized that former NFL star Pat Tillman had died gloriously in combat in Afghanistan.

Actually, all these statements were false. The Pentagon subsequently acknowledged using phosphorus as a weapon, even though the 1980 Convention on Conventional Weapons forbids use of such incendiaries (which "cause burns, skin irritation, and damage to organs or bones") against military targets amid concentrations of civilians. It turned out that not 171,000 Iraqis but only 3 of 107 Iraqi battalions—or some 750 soldiers—were able to fight the insurgency without the aid of U.S. troops, "which is what you'd be forgiven for thinking 'trained and equipped' means" wrote *The New Republic,* an early supporter of the conflict.

And after allowing Tillman to become a PR poster boy for fighting terrorists, the Pentagon admitted that he had tragically been killed by friendly fire—and his mother revealed that he had opposed Bush and had said, "This war is so fucking illegal."

✦ President Bush asserts that "we do not torture," adding "nor do we hand over people to countries that do torture."

Actually, as shown in "Winking at Torture" previously, we do both.

✦ President Bush in June 2005, claimed that federal terrorism investigations resulted in charges against over four hundred suspects and that "more than half" had been convicted. Then in December, he told the nation that the U.S. government had foiled ten terrorist plots in this country.

Actually, a *Washington Post* investigation showed that only thirty-nine of those four hundred suspects were related to national security concerns (most had been charged with immigration violations). And at least six of the ten supposed terrorist plots, according to *USA Today,* "involved preliminary ideas about potential attacks, not terrorist operations that were about to be carried out."

✦ In 2004, President Bush said, "Now, by the way, any time you hear the United States government talking about wiretap, it requires—a wiretap requires a court order. Nothing has changed, by the way. When we're talking about chasing down terrorists, we're talking about getting a court order before we do so. It's important for our fellow citizens to understand, when you think Patriot Act, constitutional guarantees are in place when it comes to doing what is necessary to protect our homeland, because we value the Constitution."

Actually, at the very time he was giving a civics lesion about how "a wiretap requires a court order," Bush was secretly authorizing the National Security Agency (NSA) to wiretap American citizens *without getting a court order.* While nearly all legal scholars believed his actions to be illegal when disclosed in late 2005, Attorney General Alberto Gonzales argued that the president had the implicit power in the 2002 congressional resolution authorizing an invasion of Iraq to conduct these warrantless wiretaps. But Senator Arlen Specter (R-PA), chairman of the Senate Judiciary Committee, said that such spying had never been discussed or implied during the debate over the resolution.

When Gonzales had previously testified at his confirmation hearings and was asked by Senator Russ Feingold about warrantless wiretapping of Americans in the war on terror, he answered that such a question was "hypothetical," even though he had approved exactly this type of wiretap previously as Bush's White House counsel.

There's more. When Bush was caught wiretapping without a court order, he stressed that any eavesdropping involved foreigners with known links to al-Qaeda. Actually, spin #167 was false as well when it was revealed half a year later that tens of millions of Americans speaking only to other Americans domestically were having their calls logged.

✦ Vice President Cheney said on CNN on June 21, 2005, that "I think they're in the last throes, if you will, of the insurgency."

Actually, that same week General Richard Myers, chairman of the U.S. Joint Chiefs of Staff, said that "this is a thinking and adapting adversary" and that insurgencies average nine years. Secretary Rumsfeld then said that insurgency could last up to twelve years, which would make for a very long "last throes"—not to mention that the scale of violence has been increasing as attacks on U.S. and Iraqi forces have more than doubled since the Iraqi elections in 2004, and deaths of U.S. troops due to "improvised explosive devices" (IEDs—roadside bombs) has increased 107 percent.

✦ Vice President Cheney said that a) Hussein had reconstituted nuclear weapons, b) "it was pretty well confirmed" that Iraqi agents met with 9/11 mastermind Mohammed Atta in Prague, c) he'd never seen Senator John Edwards before their 2004 vice presidential debate, d) the 2005 energy bill didn't contain subsidies for energy firms, and e) he had no idea who sent Joe Wilson to Niger.

Actually, it's "pretty well confirmed" that Dick Cheney is an incorrigible liar. What other conclusion can a fair-minded observer arrive at? He recanted his national TV claim about "reconstituted nuclear weapons." Although he denied to journalist Gloria Berger ever confirming the Atta-Iraqi meeting once this rumor was debunked by the 9/11 Commission, a gleeful Jon Stewart combined video clips of Cheney's denials with Cheney saying exactly that on *Meet the Press.* Videotapes also showed Cheney and Edwards meeting each other several times before their debate. The 2005 Energy Bill had some $11 billion in subsidies for oil and gas firms. Last, the vice president told Tim Russert: "I don't know Joe Wilson...I don't know who sent Joe Wilson"—*three months after* receiving a briefing about Wilson's trip to Niger from CIA director Tenet and then telling Scooter Libby that Valerie Plame may have helped arrange her husband's trip to Niger.

✦ Asked "of all the people in the United States you had to choose from, is Harriet Miers the most qualified to serve on the Supreme Court?" President Bush answered yes.

Actually, George Will, William Kristol, Charles Krauthammer, David Frum, and Trent Lott—all devout and devoted conservatives—said his answer was self-evidently absurd.

✦ Asked about the 2001 EPA's 268-page report on global warming in 2001, Bush said, "I read the report put out by the bureaucracy."

Actually, explained press secretary Ari Fleischer later, "Whenever presidents say they read it, you can read that to be he was briefed."

✦ As a presidential candidate in 2000, Governor Bush mocked President Clinton's supposed obsession with fund-raising and polling. "I believe they've moved that sign, 'The buck stops here,'" said Bush, "from the Oval Office desk to the Lincoln bedroom and that's not good for the country."

Actually, as Texas governor, he had 203 guests stay overnight at the governor's mansion in 1995, with over half contributing a total of $2.2 million; while Clinton raised $38.7 million in his first eighteen months as president, Bush raised $142 million. And although the Bush-Cheney ticket condemned Clinton-Gore for fund-raising in the White House, within four months of the inauguration Cheney held a reception at his vice-presidential residence for four hundred top Republican donors who had given or pledged at least $100,000 each. The Bush administration "[does] as much polling as the Clinton administration," said former Republican senator Alan Simpson of Wyoming. "I used to think they didn't but they do."

✦ Republicans in Washington are seeking to abolish the "death tax" because it hits small businesses and family farms so hard.

Actually, there is no such thing. No one is taxed when they die (as discussed more extensively in chapter 4). However, an estate tax—beginning with Abraham Lincoln to help pay for the Union side in the Civil War—is imposed on about 1 percent of American couples whose estates are worth over $3 million (which will rise to $6 million in 2009). As pointed out by the Center for American Progress, Americans are four times as likely to be hit by lightning than pay estate taxes on small businesses or family farms. The money collected by the IRS in estate taxes goes to pay for, among other expenses, a) bullets in Iraq, b) drilling subsidies for energy companies, and c) the salaries of Lynn Cheney's staff. To be fair, therefore, when President Bush and Speaker Hastert denounce the "death tax," it's a 99 percent falsehood, not a total lie.

✦ Bush told the Detroit Economic Club on February 8, 2005, that "my budget reduces spending...It keeps us on track to cut the deficit in half by 2009."

Actually, spending under Bush has gone up 23.7 percent and he has raised the federal "debt ceiling" four times to $9 *trillion*—and as of early 2006, he's never vetoed a spending bill. He has accumulated more deficits per year than any of his forty-two predecessors—and his '06 budget does not include the next year's estimated $81.9 billion cost of the wars in Afghanistan and Iraq, nor any upfront transition costs for restructuring Social Security, which he's proposed. In 2001, the Congressional Budget Office projected that total federal surpluses would accumulate to $5.6 trillion over 2002 to 2011; by 2005, this turned into approximately $4 trillion projected deficit—for a swing of $9 trillion plus in just five years (or a loss of $4.6 billion *a day*).

✦ Presidential candidate George W. Bush in 1999 predicted that "the Bush tax cuts benefit all Americans but reserve the greatest percentage for the lowest income families." The Republican National Committee website, controlled by the White House, said that Bush's 2003 fiscal package helps "especially middle-income Americans."

Actually, this is very fuzzy math: as discussed in "A New Aristocracy of Wealth" in chapter 5, Bush's tax cuts are heavily tilted to the rich, befitting a pro-big-business supply-sider like W. Since half of all dividends are earned by those making over $200,000—and half of capital gains are earned by those making over $1 million annually—tax reductions on dividends and capital gains obviously help Donald Trump more than the apprentices he fires. Stating the obvious fell to Senator John McCain, who said on *The Today Show* that the bulk of the tax cuts "goes to wealthier Americans. I would like to see some of that redistributed more heavily to middle-income and low-income Americans."

✦ At the top of Bush's second term agenda was Social Security reform. The president pushed hard, and unsuccessfully, for diverting some part of Social Security payments to private accounts in order to save the program, in his view, from bankruptcy and to provide retirees with a second income stream.

Actually, economists have shown it would do neither. The Social Security Trust Fund will be solvent at least until 2054—and then would be as "bankrupt" as the federal government is now since it too spends more than it takes in. Nor was the White House ever able to explain how shifting from guaranteed Social Security payments to problematic private accounts based on a fluctuating stock market—with a price-tag of $2 trillion in transaction costs and fees—would increase net wealth. Economist and columnist Paul Krugman was withering on this point, again and again exposing W.'s odd calculations that 1–1 = 3. The public agreed, preferring the current system of setting aside a portion of wages for retirement at a very small operating cost, spreading risk among all and guaranteeing benefits. There *is* a long-term demographic and fiscal problem for all entitlement programs that Bush inherited, one that his major tax cuts, major spending increases, and major deficits only worsen.

One more thing. We did have a system of private accounts from 1789 to 1936, before the Social Security system began in 1937. It didn't work well then because three-fourths of all seniors ended up in poverty; now only a tenth do.

✦ In his 2006 State of the Union Address (SOTU), President Bush declared that "America is addicted to oil" and that his "great goal" was "to replace more than 75 percent of our oil imports from the Middle East by 2025."

Actually, he didn't mean it. The very next day, Energy Secretary Samuel Bodman said that Bush "didn't mean it literally" about the 75 percent reduction and that it "was purely an example." And not a very impressive one in any event since Middle East oil represents 17 percent of our total imports or 11 percent of oil consumption—so that 75 percent of 11 percent meant only an 8.25 percent reduction over nineteen years. Within seven days of saying in his SOTU that the "best way to break this addiction is through technology," thirty-two experts at the National Renewable Energy Laboratory were fired because of a $28 million budget cut to this program (money that was quickly restored a day before Bush was scheduled to visit the labs and speak about renewable energy). His $150 million proposal to make biofuels more competitive turned out to be $50 million *less* than the amount already authorized in the prior energy bill—there also wasn't any mention of how to increase auto fuel efficiency or reduce global warming. Nor any mention of how one reason for our "addiction" was an energy policy secretly drafted by oil firms in Vice President Cheney's office in 2001.

✦ After Hurricane Katrina struck the Gulf Coast, the president told ABC's Diane Sawyer that "I don't think anyone anticipated the breach of the levees" and answered critics of his administration's performance by asking, "What went wrong?"

Actually, in 2001 FEMA predicted that a hurricane hitting New Orleans was one of the three most likely disasters that could strike the U.S. (the other two being a terrorist attack in New York City and an earthquake in San Francisco)—and numerous articles in New Orleans newspapers had warned about the catastrophic costs if Lake Pontchartrain overwhelmed the levees protecting a city mostly below sea level. In 2004, FEMA conducted a simulation of a Category 3 hurricane hitting southeast Louisiana and predicted that floodwaters would overwhelm the levees leading to numerous casualties, a mass evacuation, and a half-million homeless. Then the Bush administration cut flood control funding for New Orleans by 44 percent to help pay for the Iraq war. As is now widely accepted, the incompetent crony who ran FEMA—Michael Brown, a college buddy of Bush's campaign chairman in 2000—repeatedly failed to respond adequately before, during, or after the hurricane struck (other than taking a long dinner he wouldn't allow to be interrupted and sending an email to an aide about how he was a "fashion god"). Bush was so thoroughly detached from the situation that aides had to compile video clips from TV to persuade him to interrupt the conclusion of his August holiday.

For good measure, an obviously defensive president also told Sawyer that he hoped "people don't play politics during this period of time." Frank Rich in the *New York Times* was scornful:

> Presumably that means that the photos of him wistfully surveying the Katrina damage from *Air Force One* won't be sold to campaign donors as the equivalent 9/11 photos were...But a president who flew from Crawford to Washington in a heartbeat to intervene in the medical case of a single patient, Terri Schiavo, has no business lecturing anyone about playing politics with tragedy.

Six months later, an eleven member all-Republican congressional panel scathingly contradicted and criticized the George Bush-Michael

Chertoff version that they had learned the levees had been breached on Monday, August 29, when a FEMA official on site had told both the White House and Chertoff of the catastrophe the Monday evening that Katrina hit.

When you add up all these documented "*actuallys,*" one wonders why any reasonable person would believe a word that Bush and Cheney say. Yet while proven frauds like Dr. Hwang Woo Suk and James Frey are defrocked and shunned—for faking tests cloning a human cell and for fabricating parts of an autobiographical bestseller—our president and vice president keep on dissembling and keep on being treated as credible by many journalists and citizens. Based on the evidence, it's hard to see why.

Prominent conservative commentators such as *New York Times* columnist David Brooks, *Washington Post* columnist Charles Krauthammer, and FOX cable news anchor Sean Hannity dismiss criticisms of Bush's honesty as merely the rantings of "Bush-bashers"—or, to quote Brooks, Democrats who believe "the only problem is that the country doesn't hate George Bush enough." But this is largely a debater's trick to avoid engaging the merits of the critique, namely that critics hate not Bush but deceptions that cost lives and treasure. If they and other defenders doubt the conclusion that the Bush administration is the most dishonest in American history, they should try to develop a comparable list—or book—of deception and disinformation about say, JFK or LBJ or Bill Clinton or even Richard Nixon. Can they come up with as many examples of the gap between assertion and reality?

Why this penchant for untruths? And what are its consequences?

When you study Bush's pattern of deceptions, a thread reappears again and again. Even before facts are weighed, he invariably arrives at predictably conservative conclusions. Political but empirical presidents such as Kennedy, Nixon, or Clinton, would usually weigh facts to arrive at conclusions; Bush instead employs a reverse-thinking that arrives at conclusions which in turn lead to "facts." His analysis is more catechistic than logical, as information becomes merely a prop supporting his prefabricated opinions. One senior Bush aide told author Ron Suskind that he was part of "what we call the reality-based community [who] believe that solutions emerge from your judicious study of discernable reality. That's not the way the world works anymore. We're an empire now, and when we act we create our own reality."

Other presidents were also different because they often had a depth of experience or analysis that would enable them to weigh the facts, puzzle through options, and arrive at plausible conclusions, which would then be submitted to the verdict of history. Eisenhower's international sophistication enabled him to swat aside those radicals who urged a preemptive strike against Soviet ballistic missiles when we had a big nuclear advantage. Kennedy probably saved us from nuclear attack the week he refused the advice of his hawks to bomb Soviet missiles in Cuba in 1962 and then balanced enough tough talk and shrewd maneuvering to defuse the crisis. Nixon could jettison his famous antipathy to communism by using China to stalemate the USSR. Clinton, despite a campaign pledge to cut taxes on the middle class, instead began an effort to shrink the size of the federal deficit and federal bureaucracy—his political base protested, but interest rates fell and the economy boomed.

Lacking Ike's experience or the intellectual depth of JFK, Nixon, or Clinton, Bush is prone to grab onto a useful intellectual framework like a life preserver and then not let go—whether it's Myron Magnet's dour interpretation of the '60s in *The Dream and the Nightmare* or Marvin Olansky's exuberant view on government faith-based programs in *The Tragedy of American Compassion* or Paul Wolfowitz's muscular analysis that preventive wars were winnable and essential—starting with Iraq.

So if Bush is guided not by facts but first principles, where do these first principles come from? Basically, Bush invariably does what his base wants, which means the Far Right and big donors. George W. Bush is a naturally conservative man from a very conservative area. In his article, *Made in Texas: George W. Bush and the Southern Takeover of American Politics,* Michael Lind concludes that "the Texas conservatism of George W. Bush combines seventeenth-century religion, eighteenth-century economics, and nineteenth-century imperialism."

The religious reference is especially telling, since, for Bush, the Religious Right is the spine of the hard Right. Bush's own religiosity is sincere and well-known. So when in 2000 Bush was asked who was the most important political philosopher in his life, it was not very surprising when he answered "Jesus Christ." Now, fifteen years after his turn to religion, Bush understands that 85 percent of Americans tell pollsters they identify with some religious faith, that twice as many Americans believe in the devil as in evolution, and that the percentages who believe the world will end in a coming battle of Armageddon—followed by Christ's return to inaugurate a thousand year reign of peace called the Millennium—are 40 percent of the country, 48 percent of Christians and 71 percent of Evangelicals.

Chapter 3 described Bush's close ties to the Far Religious Right and chapters 4 and 5 his close ties to big business. Indeed, until he became governor and president, his entire career had been in the business sector. When one looks for examples of W. opposing big business, it's hard to come up with even one. This the public understands. Even at the height of his popularity in mid-2002, a poll found that by 58 percent to 23 percent the public thought that "big business has too much influence" with Bush.

When a politician views the world through a lens constructed by the hard Right and big business, one is reminded of the adage, "To the jaundiced eye, all looks yellow." When a president's voter and donor base in the twenty-first century requires him to question evolution, stem cell research, and global warming, while supporting the elimination of estate taxes, dividend taxes, ergonomic standards, and affirmative action, the public costs and consequences are very high.

Conservatives have long been powerful proponents of "cost-benefit" analysis whenever an economic regulation is proposed—yes, a safer car is nice, but at what cost? But when it came to a judgment about war—yes, getting rid of Saddam Hussein is a good thing, but at what cost?—the Bush team wouldn't even consider looking at the overall costs and consequences of an invasion and occupation.

Here's the unmentioned debit side of the ledger that conservatives blithely ignore: some twenty-five hundred dead American soldiers and probably some thirty thousand casualties (if one includes accidents, which used to be the case), as well as an estimated thirty thousand Iraqi civilians; the precipitous decline of America's standing throughout the world and—especially after Abu Ghraib—its collapse in the Muslim world; a weakening of alliances needed to fight terrorism collaboratively; misdirecting our energies away from Tora Bora allowing bin Laden to escape from Afghanistan—not to mention a loss of focus on real nuclear threats such as North Korea and Iran; the probability of inspiring more young jihadists to engage in terrorism; and the lessened ability to rally the UN or a global alliance should a real WMD crisis occur.

Yale economist William Nordhaus did a cost-benefit analysis in 2002 and predicted a cost of as high as $1.9 trillion if things didn't work out well. In 2006, economists Joseph Stiglitz, a Nobel Prize laureate at Columbia University, and Linda Bilmes at the Kennedy School of Government, pegged it at $1.3 trillion (counting lives lost, likely future spending, disability payments to veterans, interest on debt, etc.). So is getting rid of Saddam and "liberating Iraq" worth seven to nine times more than the $200 billion Marshall Plan? The latter expenditure, in the view of writer Richard Joffe, "unified Europe for the first time in history, created a market for America's exports, and stopped the spread of Communism to Western Europe—all this without causing a death of a single American soldier or European civilian."

No wonder Bush and Cheney speak only about one side of the Iraqi equation. After American public opinion had soured on Iraq by late 2005, John Mueller, an authority on wars and public opinion, concluded that "people are willing to pay a certain price...but for many people, [the Iraq war] is too rich for their blood."

Sissella Bok, in her 1986 book *Lying: Moral Choices in Public and Private Life*, framed the problem of deception in a democracy:

> Imagine a society, no matter how ideal in other respects, where word and gesture could never be counted upon. Questions asked, answers given, information exchanged—all would be worthless. A warning that a well was poisoned or a plea for help in an accident would come to be ignored unless independent confirmation could be found...Trust is a social good just as much as the air we breathe or the water we drink.

There is an alternative to a presidential dissembler polluting the well of democracy. After a string of misstatements, a frustrated Bush aide told the media in July 2001 that "the president of the United States is not a fact-checker." The FDR White House had a decidedly different approach. FDR's speechwriter Robert Sherwood wrote in his book *Roosevelt and Hopkins*:

The *New York Times* can make mistakes—the *World Almanac* can make mistakes—but the president of the United States must not make mistakes. This constant thought imposed a harrowing responsibility. After 1940, the White House had its resident statistician, Isador Lubin, the Commissioner of Labor Statistics, who was constantly available and incalculably valuable to Roosevelt and to Hopkins in checking every decimal point.

INFORMATION MANIPULATION II: PRO-SECRECY AND ANTI-SCIENCE

"Secrecy—the first refuge of incompetents—must be at a bare minimum in a democratic society, for a fully informed public is the basis of self-government. Those elected or appointed to positions of executive authority must recognize that government, in a democracy, cannot be wiser than the people."
—1960 report from the House Committee on Government Operations

SECRET'S OUT

Secrecy—about evidence for global warming or intelligence or the costs of war—is, and always has been, the enemy of democracy. Without truly informed consent, the integrity and effectiveness of a self-governing republic will evaporate faster than the national budget surplus. "A popular government, without popular information, or the means of acquiring it, is but a prologue to a farce or a tragedy; or, perhaps both," wrote James Madison in 1832. Bush is most definitely both. This White House has done more to shirk public accountability by hiding its fraudulent, wasteful, and incompetent actions than any administration in history.

Of course, certain facts must be shielded from the general population, such as information regarding troop movements, undercover CIA agents, and ongoing criminal investigations. Nobody would insist that the Manhattan Project publish daily progress reports during wartime, nor require Centcom to announce when U.S. troops are going back into Fallujah. And private entities such as corporations have the right to keep their "industry secrets" secret—Coca-Cola does not have to reveal every ingredient of its special formula, nor does KFC have to name its eleven herbs and spices. In order to win wars, protect the innocent in legal proceedings, and encourage innovation, carefully defining what constitutes "privileged information" *can* protect legitimate state and private interests.

But to ensure a healthy democracy with plenty of well-reasoned debate, keeping secrets should be kept to a minimum. This has not always been the norm. During the "hot and cold wars of the twentieth century," concluded the late Senator Daniel Patrick Moynihan, a "culture of secrecy" took root in Washington that has lasted long past the fall of the Berlin Wall. Presidencies prior to Bush's were plenty secretive—at times excessively so—as any student of the paranoid Nixon administration knows. Yet the Bush government has skillfully capitalized on the calamity of 9/11 by using the tragedy as the perfect cover over and over again to concentrate more authority in their "war president."

In the name of fighting terrorists, or protecting the homeland, or whatever pretext the Bush-who-cried-wolf can muster, the current administration has turned the meaning of "national security" squarely on its head. National security is no longer a wartime label but a year-in and year-out strategy allowing Vice President Dick Cheney to negotiate clandestine tax bargains with energy corporations, or hand out no-bid federal contracts to Halliburton. "National Security" keeps Congress in the dark about war expenditures and allows military caskets to be snuck back to the States in accordance with an out-of-sight, out-of-mind strategy.

The following is a partial catalog of the abuses of executive secrecy perpetrated by Bush & Co. in three areas: domestic secrecy, "Foil-ed" documents, and Iraq.

Domestic Shushing

Any kind of inexcusable delay in releasing a government report is functionally equivalent to keeping secrets—more so since all the data collected by the government is paid for by tax revenues, and hence belongs to the taxpayers.

A modest example of this kind of strategic delay occurred during the passage of the pork-laden energy bill in 2005. In the months leading up to the bill's approval, Republicans in power postponed the release of a government report showing that loopholes in federal gas mileage regulations have allowed automakers to manufacture cars and trucks that are *less* fuel-efficient than they were even in the late 1980s. "Something's fishy when the Bush administration delays a report showing no improvement in fuel economy until after passage of their energy bill, which fails to improve fuel economy," said Daniel Becker, the Sierra Club's chief global warming strategist. This is especially true when questions about "energy security" dominate the debates on drilling in the Arctic, the damaging impact of Gulf Coast oil and gas extraction, and deeper motives for the war in Iraq. Critical headlines about the fuel economy report could have jeopardized enactment of a law ardently supported by oil and gas firms—the corporate cornerstones of Bush's base.

Withholding bad news has become habitual in this White House, especially embarrassing news that runs counter to the usual cheery message coming from the presidential podium. So it was no surprise that in the fall of 2003, the administration hid the true cost of its huge Medicare prescription drug legislation until after it was strong-armed through Congress. The bill, now widely regarded as an expensive giveaway to pharmaceutical and insurance companies, will wind up costing taxpayers $1.2 trillion over the coming decade, an astounding increase from the advertised estimate of $400 billion. Richard Foster, Medicare's chief actuary, also admitted that at the time he was warned by his superior, Tom Scully, to "keep the information secret from Democratic lawmakers" in order to prevent political ammunition from falling into the hands of opponents, an action later deemed illegal by the Government Accountability Office. Shortly after the passage of the disastrous legislation, Scully moved on to work for the pharmaceutical industry, just as it began to reap major profits from the new laws—laws that, for instance, needlessly forbid the government from bargaining for lower prescription drug prices.

Another example occurred on Christmas Eve of 2002, when the Bureau of Labor Statistics ended its Mass Layoff Tracking Study, just as jobs began disappearing at a galloping pace. Even though Congressional Democrats harangued their Republican colleagues into restoring funding for the study in February of 2003, the loss of 614,167 jobs in those two months went unannounced to a country still giving the president high post-9/11 approval ratings.

Worse than hushing up the politically uncomfortable news that over half a million Americans lost their jobs just as holiday bills arrived is withholding information that has possibly cost people their very lives. Immediately after the tragedy of September 11, 2001, there was much discussion in both the media and the general public about whether Lower Manhattan was safe and habitable, since the collapse of the Twin Towers had spewed millions of tons of toxic debris in a bull's eye of dust and noxious vapors. A distinct odor clung to New York for miles around Ground Zero, and rumors of strange illnesses in residents and workers persisted in the media despite strong EPA assurances that the air was totally safe to breathe. Those rumors, however, turned out to be true. In 2003, the EPA's own inspector general revealed that the agency "did not have sufficient data and analyses to make such a blanket state-ment" about air safety and that, more seriously, the White House Council on Environmental Quality had pressured EPA officials to "add reassuring statements and delete cautionary ones" from any publicity about the area's air quality. The report cited White House concerns about "reopening Wall Street" and "national security" as reasons for misleading people into returning prematurely to a hazardous area.

On top of this, OSHA was reduced from a safety regulation enforcer on the site to an "advisor," preventing agents from making sure that the men and women cleaning up the witch's brew of asbestos, lead, glass fibers, concrete dust, and other poisonous contaminants wore proper respirators or used various protective gear that was widely available—resulting in some nasty exposures for the sake of keeping up a good appearance.

Subsequently, in 2004 the *New York Daily News* reported that more than seventeen hundred police officers, emergency responders, and fire-fighters had filed lawsuits claiming they were sickened by working both at the World Trade Center site and at the Fresh Kills landfill where the rubble from Ground Zero was removed. Hundreds of respiratory-disability leaves of absence have been taken, up from thirty in the year before 9/11, and fears of cancer clusters linger among those suffering from new cases of debilitating asthma and mouth sores.

Detective John Walcott, like many other cops, filed a notice of claim requesting compensation after he was diagnosed with cancer in May of 2003. Wolcott was told that he had acute myelogenous leukemia (AML), a deadly cancer his doctors think was caused by his constant and unprotected exposure to the various carcinogens he breathed in while sifting through the debris at Ground Zero. AML can be traced to contact with toxic chemicals or radiation, but Walcott, who lives in upstate New York away from the daily dose of pollution most city-dwellers endure, was never a smoker, not much of a drinker, and was in good shape, also moonlighting as a hockey coach. "I've never been sick a day in my life, except for a sore throat or a common cold," he said. Undergoing painful bone marrow transplants, a failed stem cell treatment, and the usual rounds of chemotherapy, Wolcott's afflictions also include often waking up in the middle of the night with blood streaming out of his eyes. "I've had friends of mine who were stationed with me visit me in the hospital and panic, asking me, 'Am I next?'"

A similar indifference to Americans' health and welfare can be seen in the aftermath of Hurricane Katrina in the summer of 2005. Like at the WTC, in the eventual cleanup of New Orleans an illness has emerged nicknamed the "Katrina Cough." Widespread among those returning to and clearing up the city are symptoms that include coughs, sore throats, runny noses, and respiratory ailments blamed on the mold and toxic dirt distributed by Katrina's floodwaters and churned up during the cleaning and salvaging efforts.

Once again, the EPA failed to publicize the risks residents and workers would face—this time from petroleum products, arsenic, lead, mercury, bacteria, and a poisonous mold covering much of the city. Contractors signed by the government to begin recovery and demolition efforts are known to have hired mostly Latino immigrants—many of them illegal and with little recourse should something go wrong—from both nearby communities and Mexico and Central America. The Bush administration briefly suspended federal regulations regarding workplace conditions in an (ultimately illegal) attempt to "speed up" the reconstruction of New Orleans, and many of these workers were hired without getting the proper equipment to protect their health.

The result has been a second tragedy for the already devastated area. In a letter sent to Congress by the New York Committee for Occupational Safety and Health, Juan Alvarez wrote, "I know men who have gotten so sick with diarrhea, skin inflammations, and breathing problems they can't work...[But] the contractors just hire more." With no oversight and little information, the government can paint whatever picture it wishes—even if the EPA's predictions about the economically depressed Ninth Ward's overall habitability won't be as rosy as for Lower Manhattan.

What really set the tone for Bush's executive evasions occurred back on November 1, 2001, when he signed Executive Order 13233, which stipulates that a former president's private papers can be released only with the approval of both that former president (or his family) *and* the presiding one. Prior to Bush's fiat, the National Archives had managed the release of documents under the Presidential Records Act of 1978, a sunshine policy requiring that all papers (except those validly concerning ongoing national security interests) had to be made accessible to the public twelve years after an executive left office. The effect of Bush's new order was an immediate shuttering of Americans' ability to scrutinize the day-to-day motives and performance of their former commanders in chief.

The sealing off of all presidential papers makes sense, though, when you see that one of Bush's first acts as president was to shunt all his gubernatorial records into his father's presidential library at Texas A&M— already credited as the most secretive of all presidential libraries. Combined with Executive Order 13233, the public suddenly lost much of its power to evaluate the past of their new president. As Woodrow Wilson had long ago noted noted, "Everybody knows that corruption thrives in secret places, and avoids public places, and we believe it a fair presumption that secrecy means impropriety." Bush's unprecedented actions to cut off inquiry into his past beg the question about what exactly needed to be hidden away—could it be the War on Terror?—conditions that don't exactly apply to Texas state government offices in 1999.

The squirreling away of those records is a clear example of what low regard the Bush administration has for the American democratic values of clear-headed analysis and debate. Another example is a provision signed by Bush in early 2003 granting the vice president the unheard of right to classify information—power usually reserved for the president. This was a disturbing amount of authority to suddenly put in the hands of Dick Cheney, a man who has shown a continuing "indifference to the public's right to know." When Cheney accidentally shot GOP donor Harry Whittington while hunting on a Texas ranch in February of 2006, the information didn't become public until eighteen hours later—and the VP wouldn't comment until days afterward. News that the vice president of the United States almost killed someone should immediately have been released, but apparently Bush himself remained unaware until an hour after the fact and even then he wasn't told that Cheney was the shooter. It's bad enough that they're keeping secrets from the public, but from *each other?*

One of the most infamous and drawn-out examples of Cheney's allergy to sunshine was his secret National Energy Policy Task Force that gathered in May 2001. As a rule, any committee formed to advise the government on policy matters that includes people who do not work for the government is required to conduct open meetings with a balanced makeup. Yet Vice President Cheney has refused to make the events of his meetings public, even though some White House documents finally obtained by a lawsuit in 2005 show that executives from big energy companies made up most of the attendees. Environmental groups had long suspected this was the case and filed several unsuccessful lawsuits demanding that the information from these pre-9/11 meetings be released.

It's just convenient that the pollution/extraction industries pay ever lower taxes to the federal government, yet keep gaining private audiences with the uppermost members of the executive branch. Even after the multiple lawsuits revealed his activities, Cheney still repeatedly denied that oil executives had made up his task force, standing by his falsehood even as these executives were caught lying to a congressional hearing in late 2005 about their attendance. Senator Frank Lautenberg (D-NJ) was driven in frustration to declare his willingness to involve the Justice Department in the matter, saying, "The White House went to great lengths to keep these meetings secret, and now oil executives may be lying to Congress about their role in the Cheney task force."

But corporate executives are not the only ones with their pants on fire. Even before the events of September 11 gave them better shelter from scrutiny, the Bush administration had been pushing past the accepted limits of what "executive privilege" entails. This is especially ironic because many conservatives—who regularly rejected privilege claims during the Whitewater and Lewinsky investigations of Clinton's presidency—now denounce those calling for disclosures of the Libby-Cheney-Bush links to the outing of CIA operative Valerie Plame as "criminalizing" politics. Corporations favored by this White House, as described in more detail in chapter 4, are especially aggressive in assuming that the government should keep its activism hidden. Sections of the Homeland Security Act (HSA)—ostensibly a piece of legislation meant to maintain American liberty—instead permit corporations to dump incriminating documents into government vaults, citing them as "confidential" infrastructure details imperative to, of course, *national security*, even though most of this information would never otherwise be classified. The HSA legislation prevents consumer advocates from obtaining the data they need to hold government regulators accountable for abusive corporations.

Keeping such secrets can be dangerous. Look at the fate of the database containing "early warning reports" of hazardous defects in motor vehicles. Registered by both manufacturers and customers, the database has been maintained since 2000 by regulators at the National Highway Traffic Safety Administration and was built in response to the faulty Firestone tires and Ford Explorers that killed hundreds of people and resulted in numerous lawsuits. Yet the NHTSA office of chief council has continually refused public access to the database—one of its original purposes. Businesses can now submit their incriminating data, safely knowing that it will never see the light of day or harm their profit margins, while consumers have no way to connect the dots between their own bad experiences and those of others.

FOIA Foiled

Normally, these consumers could rely on the Freedom of Information Act (FOIA) to sue for this data. FOIA has become one of the most important tools for Americans to fix flaws in their democracy. By allowing the average person access to almost any government document or report, minutes from meetings or congressional briefings, FOIA requests guarantee that oversight is ultimately the domain—and responsibility—of the people, and that no government official can ever act with impunity. Initiated by members of the press and aided by sympathetic congressional Democrats, the fight for a more open and accessible government began in the mid-fifties. The demands for FOI laws originated as a reaction to conservative legislators and a Republican administration that fired alleged communists in the federal bureaucracy without sharing the details about who and why—a McCarthyite breach of the public trust that currently echoes the Bush team's secret detentions and illegal wiretap surveillance of "suspicious" Americans. It took several years of heavy lobbying—and a reversal of party control of the White House—for FOIA to become the keystone of modern political life that it is.

When President Lyndon Baines Johnson signed FOIA into law, he described it as legislation that "springs from one of our more essential principles: a democracy works best when the people have all the information." Last year, however, for each $1 spent declassifying old secrets, federal agencies spent $148 creating and storing new secrets. In addition, the pace of classification has jumped by 75 percent since Bush took over in 2001, reversing the Clinton administration's desire for openness as the official presidential policy. An internal memo from October 2001 circulated by then attorney general John Ashcroft spells out that the new stance regarding FOIA requests will be to look for any reason to deny these requests or to defer to administration allies in the Department of Justice. The note implicitly encourages interminable delays in processing those same requests, lowering the chances for any timely or effective oversight action.

In one swoop, W. and Ashcroft reversed a decade-long trend in how our government interacts with the governed: instead of automatically granting FOIA requests *unless* there was a clear exemption under the law, this dynamic duo decided to deny every request *unless* legal action was threatened against them. Charges for processing these requests also jumped considerably. When People For the American Way tried to obtain papers about the detainees rounded up after September 11—who as we know were being prosecuted in secret and denied due process and *habeas corpus*—the Justice Department demanded the non-profit organization pay $373,000 in "search fees" before they would even begin looking. "It's become much, much harder to get responses to FOIA requests, and it's taking much, much longer," said David Schulz, an attorney who helps the Associated Press make FOIA requests. "Agencies seem to view their role as coming up with techniques to keep information secret rather than the other way around."

But this suffocating restriction on government acts and records is now extending even to unclassified documents in national archives and databases. Previously available information is disappearing, leaving only the legally murky label such as "for official use only." Anna

Nelson, a historian at American University, described how on a research trip to the National Archives, she "found four boxes of Nixon documents full of nothing but withdrawal cards," meaning that administrators had officially removed them from public scrutiny. And elsewhere, Nelson recounted how in an area containing records of President Johnson's 1965 invasion of the Dominican Republic, "I found a box of fifty-five withdrawal cards."

This overclassification goes hand in hand with removal of previously unclassified documents from Pentagon websites, similar to what occurred in the National Archives, even though much of this information is still available elsewhere on the Internet or has nothing to do with national security, fighting terrorism, or covert spying. For instance, the Bush administration still refuses to release the results of a study done to calculate how many people were missed in the 2000 census, even though it's *Congress* that requested the information. By hiding everything they can, they are hoping to exhaust their critics and political rivals and stymie future investigations into their possible misconduct.

In 2004, the air force and the army joined NASA and the National Geospatial-Intelligence Agency by taking down formerly public websites and removing data to "restricted portals," requiring preapproved access codes. A U.S. Air Force official portrayed the shift as a kind of user-friendly service, claiming that "by removing redundant, confusing, or inappropriate information available to the public, the [air force] will deliver a more consistent and coherent message to the public." That is to say, the Bush White House can deceive the public by hiding whatever facts contradict its story and then claim it did so in the interests of staying on message!

"He who controls the archives, controls history," says Rick Shenkman, editor of the History News Network Website, which follows the goings-on of historians and archivists around the country. Records are meant to be uniformly declassified after twenty-five years, but now it is lucky to even receive a copy of the 1963 budget for the CIA (the Federation of American Scientists' Project on Government Secrecy sued for the release of spending reports in 2005, and received only this stale record). This is surprising because budgets are one of the only types of government information to which the public is expressly guaranteed access by the Constitution. But intelligence agencies and the Pentagon are notorious for thwarting Congress's requests for information. It has only gotten worse since it has become clear just how ginned up the Iraq *casus belli* were, putting pressure on other branches of the government to look sharp in the face of accusations of distorted intelligence and incompetent management. The more they screw up, the deeper into hiding they go—since when is that how a democracy works?

Iraq and Terrorism

The Pentagon has been shuffling around internal audits that reveal hundreds of millions of dollars in fraud and overbilling in Iraq from private contractors paid to do work previously handled by the federal government. One stunning example is the Halliburton Corporation, which was at one time presided over by Vice President Cheney and received golden handshake no-bid contracts for supplying troops in Iraq. Currently, the Department of Justice is looking into allegations that Halliburton extorted around $61 million for gasoline; also the Pentagon's Defense Contract Audit Agency (DCAA) reviewed Halliburton's billing system for meals served to troops, finding that they charged taxpayers for 36 percent *more* meals than were actually provided. The auditors also found that Halliburton could not defend $1.8 billion of $4.3 billion (43 percent) of the bills submitted by the company for one particular contract.

In May 2004, the DCAA recommended that the Pentagon refuse to pay Halliburton for the overcharges—but not to drop the contracts. Cheney has continued to deny that he receives money from his former employer, saying in 2003, "I have no financial interest in Halliburton of any kind." But extensive records show just the opposite is true. Why is Vice President Cheney still on the payroll—to the tune of $100,000 a year (as well as hundreds of thousands of unexercised stock options)—from a likely war-profiteer?

Fortunately, Bunnatine H. Greenhouse, a civilian working for the Army Corps of Engineers, blew the whistle on the corrupt practices of Kellogg, Brown & Root (KBR), a subsidiary of Halliburton. She cited outrageous overcharges of $45 for each case of soda, $100 per fifteen-pound bag of laundry, and in one instance, the torching of new $85,000 trucks because of easily reparable defects, such as flat tires and clogged fuel pumps, with the intention of placing orders for brand new ones. These practices would have remained "privileged information" in the name of "national security" if the Pentagon had had its way (presumably to prevent KBR from having to refund some of its millions in defrauded profit—something Halliburton has been forced to do for work it did in the Balkans in the 1990s when Cheney was still CEO).

A corporation bilking the government out of taxpayer money is nothing new, but forcing the army to cover up the tracks of war-profiteers is. Concealing Halliburton's misdeeds brings to mind the observation of the late Supreme Court Justice Byron White that "the label of 'national security' may cover a multitude of sins." What else could be behind the military's blocking of officers and enlisted soldiers from providing testimony at congressional hearings about intelligence agency failures, and the failure to share data about terrorist ringleaders prior to 9/11?

Military officials are understandably defensive about their actions, having drawn much fire over secret prisoners at Guantánamo Bay and other "black site" military prisons around the world that are vacuums of information and due process. There are only two members of Congress, both now sworn to secrecy, who have received briefings on these extra-judicial, out-of-sight facilities. The rest of Congress, the media, and the average citizen who might object to the trashing of democratic processes have little ability to determine whether these illegal programs are indeed effective tools in protecting the country.

The Pentagon has also blocked several military officers and intelligence analysts from testifying at an open congressional hearing about an intelligence program that identified a ringleader of the September 11 attacks as a potential terrorist a year before the actual event. Senator Arlen Specter (R-PA), chairman of the hearing on pre-9/11 intelligence, said he was surprised by the Pentagon's decision because "so much of this has already been in the public domain, and I think that the American people need to know what happened here."

The officer in question, Lt. Col. Anthony Shaffer, said military lawyers prevented his group from speaking before the congressional panels or the intelligence agencies. "It was because of the chain of command saying we're not going to pass on information—if something goes wrong, we'll get blamed." Like nearly every Bush administration scandal, from Enron to Abu Ghraib to Valerie Plame, the grunts are held responsible while the execs go blameless.

Yet these policies affect the daily lives of American citizens, too, not just "enemy combatants." The watch-list of terror suspects handed out to airlines by the U.S. government has ballooned from 16 names before September 11, to as many as 325,000. Because the list was created in secret without a public vetting process to ensure no unwarranted names appear, just how exactly one becomes a suspected "terrorist" remains a mystery—especially as several babes-in-arms, and even Senator Ted Kennedy (D-MA), have found themselves barred from flights. Secrecy makes for pretty flawed security.

As one young congressman from Illinois said in 1966, an open government "will make it considerably more difficult for secrecy-minded bureaucrats to decide arbitrarily that the people should be denied access to information on the conduct of government...Public records [are] public property." Those idealistic words were spoken by Donald Rumsfeld, who, of course, grew up to be W.'s secretary of defense famed for his expansive ability to obfuscate, fudge, fib, and fatally bungle the Iraq war. Despite requests from Congress for progress reports on the Iraq conflict and the status of the reconstruction effort, Rumsfeld has managed to never quite finish the assignment. The scant information in the twenty-three page document released in the summer of 2005—several weeks late and after a special reprimand from the Senate—at one point simply shrugs, "The extent of insurgent infiltration [into Iraqi forces] is unknown." Someone never did their homework—or rather, doesn't want to tell what he (hasn't) found out.

Sen. Byron Dorgan, a North Dakota Democrat, said the Pentagon's failure to do anything that Congress had asked "means that the American people continue to lack essential information about operations in Iraq, and Congress is prevented from having an informed debate on the matter." As Colin Powell's former chief of staff, Lawrence Wilkerson, angrily added, "A cabal between the vice president of the United States, Richard Cheney, and the secretary of defense, Donald Rumsfeld...made decisions that the bureaucracy did not know were being made."

Despite such vocal qualms about the secrecy surrounding the (mis)management of the war, Congress keeps passing ever more appropriations bills to fund action in Iraq. In 2003, Bush sought (and obtained) an additional $600 million to continue the search for weapons of mass destruction, although none had been found and most evidence pointed to Saddam Hussein's regime having ended its illegal "weapons of mass destruction related program activities" before the American invasion. The inability to find the WMD and the need to spend nearly $1 *billion* on the failed hunt were perhaps so humiliating to the administration, which had spent a year hyping these weapons as fact, that the request for the funds was buried in a classified supplemental appropriations packet.

What's especially revealing about these covert moves is that the publication of intelligence agency and defense budgets was one of the recommendations proposed by the 9/11 Commission as a means of combating the excessive secrecy undermining the government's performance. We all know the Bush administration fought energetically to prevent the establishment of the commission. Yet the White House has also continually refused to release some sixty-nine documents from the Clinton era that included references to al-Qaeda, Osama bin Laden, and other matters related to the commission's work—documents that pointed to a growing awareness that "Bin Laden Determined to Strike in U.S.," as the fateful August 6, 2001, Presidential Daily Briefing put it.

But because so many CIA reports have been kept under wraps, intelligence officials and their president cannot be held accountable for any of their failures leading up to the tragedy of September 11. Perhaps this is why Bush and Cheney only consented to testify before the panel if they could do so in secret closed hearings. It all adds up to why, in December 2005, the 9/11 Commission issued the government failing grades, despite the White House's best efforts to shirk accountability by keeping the commission's accountants in the dark.

Add up all these policies aimed at suppressing information from average Americans and you understand the conclusion of Steven Aftergood, director of the FAS Project on Government Secrecy: "You have to elect leaders that value openness and public access to information. It's not a problem that can be solved by rewording a policy or a statute here or there—you need to have people in high office who are committed to democracy in a robust sense. Right now we have people who are committed to democracy in the sense that they have elections every few years and that the role of the public is to send them money."

Today, the Bush administration has used the very real threat of al-Qaeda to justify the sort of excessive government secrecy that has served the country so poorly in the past. And it has achieved the same unfortunate results—disastrous policy choices, cronyism, and a further decline in public trust. We know Bush's was supposed to be the "faith-based" presidency, and that's exactly what it's become: with fewer ways to confirm the truth of the administration's claims about keeping Americans safe and secure, we are merely taking things on faith.

SCIENCE *FICTION*

Democracy is about openness, about a commitment to the facts, and about the search for the best solutions. It is not an unyielding ideology that collapses, like the USSR did, under the oppressive weight of its own delusions. Which is what makes the rising assaults on science so alarming—by none other than the government of the United States.

In 2004, a group of twenty Nobel laureates from around the world warned that "the scope and scale of the manipulation, suppression, and misrepresentation of science by the Bush administration is unprecedented." Because we live in an information age—when the government and the economy both rely on the best current information—the undermining of scientific inquiry by political interests has more long-term consequences than missing out on the next *Sputnik*. Just as the manipulation of critical intelligence allowed Americans to stumble into the tragic quagmire of Iraq, the contempt for science allows Republican officials both to reward its corporate backers and to pander to Luddite impulses of its Far Right religious base. But step back a moment and appreciate why there are so many laws in our society for protecting whistleblowers and punishing perjurers—the damage done to a democracy when truth becomes immaterial is as fatal as any roadside bomb in Baghdad.

The OTA Gets Thrown Away

Science is now coming under the myopic scrutiny of a conservative Congress for whom disdaining the research of "liberal" academics is a common way to grandstand in the House. As a result, the government has had a surprisingly easy time closing its eyes and plugging its ears to the most pressing scientific issues of this generation, including stem cell research, reproductive rights, global warming, and, as previously discussed in "Religious Tyranny," evolution.

During the Republican takeover of Congress in the mid-nineties, one of their first belt-tightening budget cuts was to abolish the Office of

Technology Assessment, the nonpartisan agency that authoritatively and objectively distilled complicated scientific issues to aid in the legislative process. Because the OTA's objectivity could put a damper on so many ideological Republican fantasies—most significantly Star Wars—it had long been in the conservative crosshairs. Thus, the OTA became a victim of its own success, getting the axe from newly appointed Speaker Newt Gingrich in 1995, in spite of its miniscule budget (about $22 million) and reputation for integrity. Insiders called the shuttering of the OTA "Reagan's revenge." Roger Herdman, an MD and a Republican who was the last director of the OTA, commented that "the Speaker didn't want an internal congressional voice that had views on science and technology that might differ from his." In its stead, right wing lawmakers began to rely on sympathetic outside sources for their policy inputs, especially cash-happy conservative think tanks such as the American Enterprise, Hoover, and Manhattan Institutes, as well as the Heritage Foundation, all of which grew to national prominence in the 1980s and '90s.

This notion echoes the unintentionally revealing remarks of David Stockman, Reagan's former budget director: "We know what we want to do, and [the OTA will] only give us contrary advice." What they wanted to do, it's become clear, is muddy the waters with "contrarian" science funded by corporations and socially conservative foundations, blurring the carefully built consensus that usually exists in academic scientific communities by introducing "skeptic" researchers to the mix. It's akin to declaring that the loser of an election—the candidate who got *fewer* votes—was actually a winner!

After the demise of the OTA, extremist scientists were at times given the same amount of time in congressional inquiries as their consensus and peer-reviewed—hence *credible*—counterparts, fomenting a "debate" that existed only in the Capitol and newspaper headlines but not in the lab. Phillip Johnson, a professor of law at the University of California, Berkeley, sums up these practices when he describes how fringe scientists "[scavenge] the scientific literature," and then will "take claims out of context and pretend that everything...is controversial. But it's all a big con." They drum up fake controversy so that lawmakers can cherry-pick whatever evidence they need to support their pet positions—from denying the reality of climate change to championing the benefits of abstinence-only education.

This lack of objectivity has been a major problem in the Bush administration. Start with the fact that there's simply a general lack of academic experience—or interest—in the current government. For example, two years into his first term, Clinton had twice as many PhDs in his cabinet as Bush now does—and the Democrat also put scientific advancement at the top of his agenda. Yet while we all know what a "green" Al Gore was, Bush & Co. provided legislative support to their friends and donors in the fossil fuel industry. Moreover, the Bush team spent between one and two years choosing directors for the Food and Drug Administration and the National Institutes of Health—two of the most important government science-based oversight agencies.

On top of this, Bush downgraded the cabinet science-advisory positions elevated under Clinton, moving the directors out of the White House and cutting their staff. According to Nicholas Thompson, a fellow at the nonpartisan public policy group New America Foundation, "geography and staff equal clout in Washington, and unarguably signal how much the people in power care about what you do." When he moves scientists to the back alley, the message comes through loud and clear: George Bush doesn't care about science.

This contempt manifests itself in other insidious ways, including the unprecedented partisan scrutiny nominees to these regulatory scientific panels and agencies now routinely undergo. The Republicans are staffing technical government positions with conservative pod people, turning previously neutral jobs into nakedly political ones. "Not only does the Bush administration scorn science, it is subjecting appointments to scientific advisory committees and even study sections to political tests," says Donald Kennedy, editor in chief of *Science*, a leading publication in the science world. The administration hypocritically argues against "litmus tests" for its judicial nominees, but strictly vets scientific candidates with questions about their positions on such controversial issues as abortion and capital punishment, and—illegally—whether or not they voted for Bush. This is precisely what was asked of William R. Miller, a well-regarded professor of psychology at the University of New Mexico, who was vying for a job at the National Institute of Drug Abuse in early 2002. When he responded no to the Bush question, the interviewer hesitated, hung up, and never called back. Presumably, somebody with the *right* credentials was selected instead of Miller.

Stem Cells—Bush's Pro-Parkinson's Policy

Bad science is certainly evident in the "controversy" over stem cells. Here is a course of research that has the potential to change all future medicine, to cure debilitating diseases, to open up new branches of biology and biotechnology. Stem cells represent a kind of biological blank slate: they are the undifferentiated units that can give rise to over two hundred kinds of specialized cells throughout the body.

There are several sources of stem cells, from umbilical-cord blood to adult bone marrow—yet the single most versatile are embryonic stem cells taken from unimplanted fertilized eggs created in vitro at fertility clinics. These extra "embryos" are actually a jumble of 50 to 150 cells called blastocysts with no chance of surviving outside the laboratory and with none of the defining characteristics we think of as human. Often, they are simply donated to scientific research by the couples who had sought fertility treatment, which itself was initially vilified by the Right as tampering with God's work. Learning how to apply these potent cells to spinal injuries or such degenerative diseases as leukemia, juvenile diabetes, Parkinson's, and, of course, Alzheimer's, intriguingly promises cures or therapies unimagined even a decade ago.

Yet President Bush threw a monkey wrench at stem cell research as one of his first orders of business, even though only 22 percent of Americans think the use of embryonic stem cells is "unethical." Citing his unease about the fact that "extracting the stem cell destroys the embryo, and thus destroys its potential for life," Bush went on television in August of 2001 to explain his decision to cut off federal funding for most stem cell research. In language coded to his Far Right base, he emotionally hinted at a tiny baby being sacrificed to uncaring scientists: "Like a snowflake, each of these embryos is unique, with the unique genetic potential of an individual human being." Co-opting this phrase, religious conservatives running "embryo adoption" programs now call the babies born of these "rescued" cells "snowflakes."

Yet as anybody familiar with the issue could tell you, Bush's characterization of these microscopic blastocysts as tiny humans frozen in a laboratory waiting to be born is ludicrous. So while Bush's decision may have sounded reasonable at the time to over three-quarters of Americans, it was, in fact, quite extreme.

Nancy Reagan, perhaps the most important conservative voice to come out against Bush's resolution, said in a 2004 speech that "I just don't see how we can turn our backs on [stem cell research]...We have lost so much time already. I just really can't bear to lose any more." Naturally, some ideologues turned on her, with at least one Republican legislator contending that real conservatives believe Ronald Reagan would *never* have permitted embryonic stem cell research to proceed. To these scolds, a longtime Reagan adviser and confidant Michael Deaver retorted, "Ronald Reagan didn't have to take care of Ronald Reagan for the last ten years."

Whatever his embrace of the unborn, Bush exhibited a lack of sympathy for the born when he allowed federal research to continue on existing lines of stem cells but not new ones. To make his decision appear like a compromise to the vast majority of this country, which widely supports stem cell research, the president willfully misstated the number of existing stem cell lines he was leaving open for further federally funded investigation. It turns out there weren't sixty "diverse" lines available to study, as Bush contended, rather only about ten—a fact which was widely verified at the time—and so the stem cell "compromise" was fatally compromised from the get-go. According to Evan Snyder, director of the stem-cell program at the Burnham Institute in La Jolla, California, "I don't think science entered into Bush's decision at all."

Frustrating stem cell research was Bush's way of handing a "victory" to fundamentalists in his conservative base, who regard the loss of an embryo as akin to the murder of a fully grown human being. Social conservatives in the Missouri legislature have gone so far as to oppose *all* stem cell research, with some lawmakers taking the position that programs that use stem cells are so immoral they should be a crime. Former Missouri senator John Danforth, who holds degrees in religion from Princeton and law and divinity from Yale, disagrees with other Republicans, especially as his own brother died from Lou Gehrig's disease, which stem cell therapy may help. "What is the thinking behind saying that we should criminalize research? We should criminalize research because we want to save cells in a petri dish that will never be implanted in a uterus and never become people?"

A response from the other side came from Pam Fichter, president of Missouri Right to Life and a supporter of the legislation outlawing stem cell science: "We oppose embryonic stem cell research because it destroys the embryo." Fichter continued, "They're trying to define human life by its geography. It doesn't make any difference if it's in a petri dish, implanted in the womb, or in a nursery. A human life is a human life. Are we going to say a four-year-old is more human than a two-year-old?"

It's hard to seriously debate this kind of hysteria, which is why objective analysis from a nonpartisan authority is so critical if the "debate" about an ethical approach to stem cells is to advance toward a smart result. According to Harold Varmus, the former National Institutes of Health director, "This is the first time that the [federal] government has ever tried to criminalize science." And with no OTA and only three biologists in either house of Congress, a serious stem cell conversation by lawmakers has been stymied.

AIDS and Abstinence

During the height of the AIDS crisis in 1989, even C. Everett Koop was driven to declare, "I am the nation's surgeon general, not the nation's chaplain." He recognized his duty was to prevent the spread of a lethal plague and inform the American public about its infectiousness—not mince words about homosexuals, sex, and condoms to protect the vulnerable minds and delicate ears of the nation's women and children. If Koop felt the need to speak out against the influence of the morals police on science and health policy under President Reagan, with whom nitty-gritty numbers had famously little purchase, then where does that leave us today with an administration ever-more steeped in fire and brimstone rather than facts and figures? Apparently, these American mullahs prefer infected teens to "immoral" ones.

A quarter of a century since the AIDS epidemic exploded around the globe, the promotion of condoms—the absolute most basic, cheap, and effective mode of prevention—is apparently still up for debate by the government courting the approval of the Buckle on the Bible Belt, which rejects the reality of sex outside of marriage. This willful denial of adolescent urges goes hand in hand with the replacement of actual sexual education in the schoolroom by the pseudoscience of abstinence-only education, both here and abroad.

In his first term Bush imposed the "global gag rule" on charitable Non-Governmental Organizations (NGOs) on the forefront of the AIDS crisis, preventing any discussion of abortion and in some cases the use of contraceptives. USAid-backed groups that hand out condoms in developing countries—even if they also preach abstinence—suffer intimidation and slashed funding. And they come under fire by the likes of conservative Oklahoma senator Tom Coburn, himself a former general practitioner, who once notoriously warned of "rampant lesbianism" in our nation's public schools. Richard Marlink, scientific director of the Elizabeth Glazer Pediatric AIDS Foundation, has expressed concern that "for some time the requirement to spend 33 percent of [HIV and AIDS] prevention funds on abstinence programs is limiting the ability of their most pressing needs—including the prevention of mother-to-child transmission of HIV."

"Marriage, not condoms, will protect you emotionally and physically," chides one abstinence-only program. Others deceitfully compare the size of sperm and the AIDS virus to suggest that the virus can squeeze through "holes" that sperm can't, or that HIV can be transmitted via sweat and tears. On this last point, Republican Senate leader Bill Frist, a man who makes so much of being a heart surgeon, refused during a television interview with ABC's George Stephanopoulos to admit that this is an utter and complete lie. Squirming in his seat, Frist was finally forced by the interviewer to acknowledge the statement's inaccuracy—and by extension impugn government-backed abstinence programs across the country that traffic in such nonsense.

But a single live confession of bad information does not change the fact that conservatives are also peddling total falsehoods that link (perfectly legal) abortions with sterility, dementia, depression, and, perhaps most distressingly, breast cancer. Despite a huge Danish study covering 1.5 million women that conclusively dismissed this link, a few lone partisan "scientists" and their pro-life allies have helped to force legislation through state assemblies—including Texas, Kansas, and Minnesota—that requires health-care providers to inform women about supposed cancer risks before performing an abortion.

More than one-quarter of organizations receiving federal abstinence-only money are explicitly antichoice in a faith-based context. Some programs even go so far as to advocate prayer as a way of staving off teenagers' raging hormones. Indeed, Louisiana's abstinence-only curriculum was harshly criticized for its religious content, and it took a lawsuit in 2002 by the ACLU for a court to rule that the program violated the separation of church and state. But since 1996, government spending on abstinence-only education has exploded from a scant $4 million to more than $700 million, heaping cash onto programs that discourage even the mere discussion of premarital sex. It's become quite the movement now that there's money to be made. "All of a sudden, abstinence is business," says Leslee Unruh, founder of the National Abstinence Clearinghouse in Sioux Falls, South Dakota. An entire "industry" of brochures, media campaigns, speakers and "novelty items" to support abstinence programs has sprouted to soak up these millions in federal grants, and Unruh estimates that close to nine hundred new organizations have appeared in the last decade.

Yet it's an industry selling a faulty product. Abstinence-only education does not significantly lower the transmission of sexually transmitted diseases or stop unwanted pregnancies, or even really delay sex until marriage. The programs are designed around lies about condoms and abortion; falsified links between premarital sex, substance abuse, and prostitution; and a reliance on fear, shame, and religious beliefs to browbeat kids into not asking questions that could potentially save their lives. How could these methods possibly be expected to work?

According to SIECUS, the Sexuality Information and Education Council of the United States, teens who promise to stay virgins as advocated by abstinence-only do in fact postpone sex—by an average of only eighteen months. But they are ultimately less likely to use contraception when they do become sexually active. "Virginity pledgers" also have almost the same rates of sexually transmitted diseases as the rest of teens—6.4 percent versus 6.9 percent—despite being "abstinent." Indeed, these programs don't really do what they promise, and in fact leave impressionable young people even worse equipped to deal with the real world.

Now "principals are afraid, teachers are nervous," said Elizabeth Schroeder, a sex-ed trainer and consultant, in an interview with *The Nation* magazine. "We walk around on eggshells when we're offering life-saving, life-enhancing information." SIECUS and Advocates for Youth— another program that promotes open discussion about sex—initiated an online campaign against federal funding of abstinence-only education during Bush's first term. After doing so, both groups were subjected to *three* federal audits each. Eva Goldfarb is assistant professor in health professions at Montclair State University in New Jersey and coauthor of the sexuality curriculum, *Our Whole Lives*. She concludes that objections come not just from fundamentalists. "The difference now is the assault is top down. It's sanctioned at the highest levels."

Plan B

Another example of top-down suppression of science is the political mess surrounding the morning-after pill, Plan B. Taken up to seventy-two hours after intercourse, it prevents a fertilized egg from implanting in the uterus, and can even inhibit fertilization to begin with. Thus by scientific definition Plan B is a contraceptive, not an "abortion pill" as critics argue. It is a safe and effective way to avoid unwanted pregnancies, and so was submitted to the government for study and approval. The FDA, along with normal safety tests, also commissioned *six* independent studies between 2002–2005 confirming that over-the-counter access to such emergency contraception would in no way increase sexual activity among teenagers, an expressed concern of conservatives. Each time, the studies were dismissed by critics as inconclusive for having too small a sample of fourteen- to sixteen-year-olds.

Six consistent, consecutive studies, however, are an unusually large number, not to mention that the underrepresentation of young teens had never before posed a problem for the FDA. The multi-year studies represent a kind of strategic "paralysis by analysis" to prevent approval, a strategy unheard of for even the most toxic of medications. The perpetual study of the drug means Plan B won't reach the hands of Americans who most need it and when they need it. According to Planned Parenthood, access to Plan B has the potential to avoid an estimated eight hundred thousand abortions a year—a fact that's hard to square with the presumably antiabortion opposition to prescription-free Plan B.

Despite the near unanimous recommendation of a panel of experts, the request to sell Plan B without a prescription was eventually rejected by the FDA. David Hager—the lone dissenter and apparently the real "winner" of the dispute—happens to be a conservative evangelical who advises prayer to reduce the symptoms of PMS in his book on Christian women's health. Dr. Hager's written "minority opinion" (which previous employees of the FDA say is never solicited for final reports) stated that Plan B could potentially promote teen sex, in spite of what the studies determined. This unusual—and unscientific—opinion was selected by the agency's former commissioner, Dr. Mark B. McClellan, as the clinching rationale for rejecting Plan B.

Thankfully, the Government Accountability Office, a nonpartisan investigative arm of Congress, was dubious. Its report, issued in November of 2005, revealed that top-down pressure had in fact played a significant role in the eventual rejection of Plan B as an over-the-counter emergency contraceptive. Indeed, the decision to deny this status to Plan B was made *before* the commissioning of the studies, and Dr. McClellan was found to have deleted or "thrown out" all of his email messages and written correspondence on the topic—in clear violation of federal records laws.

As a result of the fiasco, the panel's director, assistant FDA Commissioner Dr. Susan F. Wood, quit in disgust in 2005, saying, "I feel very strongly that this shouldn't be about abortion politics...[Plan B] is a way to prevent unwanted pregnancy and thereby prevent abortion. This should be something that we should all agree on." In a letter sent out to the staff during her departure, Dr. Wood wrote that she could not work at the FDA "when scientific and clinical evidence, fully evaluated and recommended for approval by the professional staff here, has been overruled."

Maybe those officials who want to make Plan B hard to get should talk to the twenty-six-year-old woman who in September of 2005 presented a prescription for emergency contraception at a Target in Fenton, Missouri. She was told by a moralizing pharmacist that "I won't fill it. It's my right not to fill it." The woman later said about her experience that "it seems unbelievable to me that a medical professional could [and] would deny access to a federally approved drug and impose their personal beliefs...I don't know how it would be if I had just been raped or if the condom broke and I was feeling confusion and panic anyway—and then was denied access."

Yet a month later, this is precisely what happened to a twenty-year-old college student from Tucson, Arizona, who, after a sexual assault, was denied emergency contraception by pharmacists claiming that their religious and moral objections to those "abortion pills" precluded the filling of her prescription. Compounding her surprise was the reality that she would have to call nearly fifty drugstores in her area before finding one that dispensed Plan B—only to be told the pharmacist on duty would not fill it for religious and moral reasons. "I was so shocked," said the woman. "I did not understand how they could legally refuse to do this."

There is now a growing movement to institutionalize protections for pharmacists who refuse to fill prescriptions that they have personal objections to. Permitting individual pharmacists to reject legal prescriptions subverts the democratic and lawful will of the majority to have safe and easy access to legal products. As a matter of conscience, people certainly do not have to believe in a particular drug or product. But then they should not become pharmacists who deny someone else *their* conscientious choice. This is not an issue of free speech or free exercise of religious beliefs. It makes no sense that these objecting pharmacists didn't know what they were going to be doing when they were trained—they had to take the class on the pill when they were in school like everybody else. Yet now they are "harming" rape victims and women whose lives are endangered by pregnancies, all while asking for state-sponsored shield laws to keep them from getting fired for *not doing their job*. To make sure that these zealots can't censor medicine, Illinois governor Rod Blagojevich has taken the initiative to institute a state-wide rule that every pharmacy must fill prescriptions, "No delays. No hassles. No lectures."

Lectures are actually another way of wearing down reproductive rights. Since they can't pass an outright ban on abortion or condoms, some conservatives instead focus on changing the way they are discussed—from parental notification laws to mandatory fetal pain advisories in waiting rooms. The Unborn Child Pain Awareness Act, introduced in the Senate by Republican Sam Brownback of Kansas in 2005, demands that doctors read a grotesque statement describing painful fetal dismemberment to their patients before performing the abortion—with the hope of discouraging the procedure altogether.

Yet doctors agree that it is physically impossible for a fetus to feel pain as we know it until twenty-nine or thirty weeks of gestation—at which point few women seek abortions anyhow. Moreover, the conclusion that fetuses experience pain has been determined by several members of Congress, not research doctors or obstetricians, based on their view that fetuses sometimes move when poked. Like those senators who said brain-dead Terri Schiavo responded with smiles to her mother's words of love—despite being in a complete vegetative state with half of her brain atrophied—science is not on these politicians' side.

Nor is their view supported when the abstinence-pushers and right-to-lifers denounce a new vaccine that protects against the virus that causes 70 percent of cervical cancer and that has been linked to oral cancer in both sexes. In effect, they oppose "curing" cancer because they think that inoculated teen girls might interpret their resistance to the cancer-causing human papilloma virus (HPV) as encouraging sexual activity—the same reason they reject making Plan B over-the-counter. "I've talked to some who have said, 'This is going to sabotage our abstinence message,'" declared Gene Rudd, associate director of the Christian Medical and Dental Association. "Parents should have the choice. There are those who would say, 'We can provide better, healthier alternatives than the vaccine, and that is to teach abstinence.'"

Denying the physical integrity of condoms is one thing. But denying women access to a life-saving drug for over-hyped fears of "promiscuity" is as preposterous as it is sexist. It exposes as hypocrites those claiming that they only want to save lives, that the "culture of life" is paramount to scientific evidence or privacy or personal choice. One health advocate likens the HPV vaccine to wearing a seat belt: "Just because you wear a seat belt doesn't mean you're seeking out an accident."

The Sky Is Falling

Disregard for the threat of sexually transmitted diseases (STDs) and teen sexual health stems mostly from religious activism. But the conservatives running the United States government have a vested interest in keeping the public ill-informed for financial reasons as well. In a recent survey, half of Fish and Wildlife Service scientists said they were aware of cases in which "commercial interests have inappropriately induced the reversal or withdrawal of scientific conclusions or decisions through political intervention." While the easing of standards for mercury in water, allowing snowmobiles, logging, and mining in national parks, and weakening of the Environmental Protection Agency indicate the influence of business on government, there's no more glaring example of sacrificing science for profits than in the controversy surrounding climate change caused by global warming.

The years 1998, 2002, 2003, 2004, and 2005 were the warmest on record, with each becoming the warmest since experts began keeping track. It was also a year of record Asian monsoons, lethal summer temperatures, and a seemingly apocalyptic hurricane season. "The so-called once-in-a-lifetime storm isn't even once in a season anymore," says climatologist Judy Curry, chair of the School of Earth and Atmospheric Sciences at the Georgia Institute of Technology. The heat is growing on the Bush administration to do something other than press for drilling in the Arctic National Wildlife Refuge to solve every environmental and energy crisis.

We all knew that Bush and Cheney and much of their inner circle were oilmen when they first came to office—even though they display a flash of diversity since the two top men came from entirely *different* energy firms. So it was little surprise that in March of 2001 the White House reversed its predecessor's support for the Kyoto Protocol on climate change, which called for a 7 percent reduction in heat-trapping greenhouse gas emissions to help slow the rise in global temperatures. Bush followed this with another reversal, this time on his campaign pledge to strictly limit carbon dioxide emissions, by demanding only "voluntary" (read: nugatory) cutbacks.

In dismissing the Kyoto Protocol and ending the previous decade's push for tighter environmental standards, Bush took the same stance as the Reagan administration did on acid rain in the 1980s. He demanded more research and claimed any adjustment would be too costly to the economy. Just as acid rain became a byword for the link between industrial pollution and environmental degradation—nobody would deny it now—it's clear that climate change is set to be the next textbook example of a wasted opportunity to prevent a foreseeable tragedy.

The ever-increasing effects of global warming are no longer played out far away, but in backyards from Louisiana to Indiana as devastating storms linked to increased ocean temperatures grow ever more vicious. Every day articles appear reporting on the lack of Arctic ice cover imperiling wildlife, the swift melting of Andean glaciers leading to potential water shortages in South America, the severe tornadoes, wildfires, and droughts plaguing large swaths of America, and the floods and droughts of Europe and Africa. An article in *Science* reviewed 928 papers on climate change in peer-reviewed scientific publications—and none disagreed with the consensus position.

Bush now calls for "balance" in the "debate" about global warming. But this idea is laughable given the scientific consensus and given that lobbyists for oil, gas, coal, logging, and other extraction industries bounce in and out of administrative positions—writing the mundane reports and policies on the transactions that affect their ex-employers' bottom lines. In fact, Big Oil has essentially written domestic energy and environmental policy since Bush came to power. Paula Dobriansky, the Under Secretary of State for Global Affairs, was given briefing papers where the administration thanked Exxon executives for their "active involvement" in dictating the U.S. stance on climate change. The papers also show the administration openly soliciting Exxon for the environmental policies it would find most "acceptable."

For another example, Philip A. Cooney, a former oil lobbyist with no scientific training, had led the energy industry's fight against limits on greenhouse gases before joining the Bush White House Council on Environmental Quality. There, he was found to have tampered with the language on a major government report on climate change, downplaying the urgency of the findings and the links between carbon emissions and global warming. And though he resigned in the summer of 2005 amid the uproar surrounding his "balancing act," Cooney wasn't exactly chased out of town for his diddling—having worked previously for the American Petroleum Institute, he quickly found a job with Exxon-Mobil. The only real question is whether he had been working for them, in effect, the whole time.

Rick S. Piltz resigned in March 2005 as a senior associate in the office that coordinates government climate research. Piltz says even though "each administration has a policy position on climate change," he has never before seen "a situation like the one that has developed under this administration during the past four years in which politicization by the White House has fed back directly into the science program in such a way as to undermine the credibility and integrity of the program." But this blatant politicization of policy isn't so much about winning votes as it is rewarding corporate and conservative friends—it's about the fundamental price we pay as a nation for ignoring the planet's social, economic, and democratic well-being.

The credibility of the current administration on climate change plummeted in the last year as Hurricanes Katrina, Rita, Wilma, and the quadruplets (Charley, Frances, Ivan, and Jeanne) of 2004 swept across the Gulf Coast. The Bush administration will undoubtedly continue to reject the reality of global warming—touting their fringe scientists funded by companies with a financial interest in discrediting climate change as proof enough. However, Katrina may end up being the 9/11 of climate change. "Sea-level rise and increased storm intensity are no longer abstract, long-term issues but are associated with horrific pictures seen on television every evening," says Christopher Flavin, president of the Worldwatch Institute, a thirty-year-old environmental and social justice research organization.

The Bush fib about responsible environmental stewardship being too expensive is proving as transparent as his fudging on Iraq WMDs. Slowing climate change isn't going to be too costly, as any resident of New Orleans' Ninth Ward would tell you—it's sitting back and not doing anything that is going to cost us in the end. The huge gap between what the public is clamoring for and what the administration does on climate change is yet another barometer of the decline of democracy in this country. The question of whether Big Oil or a big majority control energy policy has an obvious answer.

Even NASA, long a pillar of strong science and an agency seemingly removed from the Foggy Bottom fray, has come under the purview of an administration for whom *everything* is politics. In early 2006, the *New York Times* exposed how George Deutsch, a twenty-four-year-old Bush appointee, was given a position at NASA overseeing scientists with decades of experience. Deutsch's previous job was as an intern in the "war room" of the 2004 Bush-Cheney re-election campaign, and he was forced to resign from NASA when it was revealed that he lied on his resume about graduating from Texas A&M. Whatever happened to security clearances and background checks? Working on a Republican campaign is all the credentials you need to be a science expert in Bush's Washington.

But the real scandal resulted from an email exchange between Deutsch and Flint Wild, a NASA contractor creating Internet presentations about Einstein for middle-schoolers. Deutsch stated that the word "theory" was to be inserted after every mention of the Big Bang, because the Big Bang "is not proven fact; it is opinion." Deutsch continued, "It is not NASA's place, nor should it be, to make a declaration such as this about the existence of the universe that discounts intelligent design by a creator." Bear in mind that since early 2004, NASA scientists and administrators have been under pressure from the White House to keep all projects and news releases within the context of Bush's "vision statement." So Deutsch was merely doing his job when he told Flint that "this is more than a science issue, it is a religious issue. And I would hate to think that young people would only be getting one-half of this debate from NASA. That would mean we had failed to properly educate the very people who rely on us for factual information the most."

A Sense of Consequence

When the church threatened Galileo with being burned at the stake over whether or not the Earth went around the Sun, billions of lives were not in the balance—astronomy just got a little duller for a while. Yet when tobacco firms paid for "scientific" studies in the '50s and '60s to cast doubt on the dangers of smoking, or when current zealots have public misgivings about the truth behind AIDs or climate change—the consequence for this kind of ignorance climbs higher and higher.

The Union of Concerned Scientists issued a report in February of 2004 accusing the Bush White House of politically corrupting "the traditionally objective, nonpartisan mechanisms through which the government uses scientific knowledge in forming and implementing public policy." But no matter how fervently administration officials look to a holy authority or stick their heads in the sand, they and we cannot ignore the reality of hurricanes wracking the Gulf Coast every year—"*Now* are you paying attention?" read the cover of a 2005 *American Prospect* piece on the link between these Category 4s and 5s and climate change. We cannot ignore rising sea levels submerging major cities, with Americans paying the price in dollars and lives. We all lose out when this occurs—economically, when technology companies and research moves abroad and jobs disappear; diplomatically, when a little more of what international prestige we have left is eye-rolled away by the global community; and democratically, by allowing a system of governance that favors dangerous fairy tales over stone-cold facts.

We've all seen what happens when ideology trumps science. Seventy years ago, the USSR biologist Trofim Lysenko argued that learned traits could be genetically inherited, a conclusion that helped Stalin propagandize for Soviet domination and that retarded his country's scientific progress for generations. Two years ago the secretive Chinese Communist Party refused to admit the reality of several dozen SARS (sudden acute respiratory syndrome) deaths. It took four long months of public protests and an Internet campaign—and the brink of a pandemic—before the government reversed course and informed citizens about the problem and its solution. SARS was contained. And when the first three deaths from bird flu in people occurred in late 2005, Chinese authorities immediately moved to confirm them. Eventually, science conquered secrecy even in Communist China because the stakes were too high.

Reaction to the antiscience bias of the Religious Far Right is not at all about bashing people of faith or implementing liberal-mandated "secular elitism." For science doesn't care if you are Catholic or Jew, Muslim, Hindu, or mainline Protestant; whether you believe the world was created in a smattering of days six thousand years ago; if the universe rides on the back of a great divine turtle or was baked up in a big bang. Science is usually the one thing we're all supposed to be able to agree about. Without science, we lose our grasp on a shared reality and a common language. And because science continually expands, refines, self-corrects, and adjusts to new information—while remaining true to its original mission—it is analogous in this way to the best aspects of American democracy.

WHERE ARE THE MEDIA?

"Democracy cannot exist without an informed public."
—BILL MOYERS

The media are good at covering a revolution with its bang-bang and body bags but not an evolution with its slow, incremental changes. So it is hardly surprising that the decline of our democracy has not played out on the front pages of our newspapers or at the top of our newscasts. Instead, any coverage has been relegated to opinion journals, academic outlets, and op-ed pages. Given the preceding chapters that expose the clear and present dangers to our American democracy, we have to ask: Where are the mainstream media? Why have our newspapers, broadcast networks, cable news channels, and Internet news services failed to connect the dots that show this anti-democracy pattern?

From its birth, America has robustly debated national priorities. *The Federalist Papers,* published serially in New York newspapers in 1787, laid out the case for ratifying the U.S. Constitution. In 1847, escaped slave Frederick Douglass established the widely circulated abolitionist *North Star* paper. And in 1953, Edward R. Murrow famously used his television program, *See It Now,* to expose Senator Joe McCarthy's witch hunt for Communists. With just these few examples, the ideal relationship between the disinfecting sunshine of a free press and a vibrant democracy is clear. But that interdependency suffers when the main channels of public discussion are muddied by ideological or corporate agendas. The push-and-pull of public debate can be lost when a few conglomerates, journalists, and politicians have control over not only their industries, but also democracy itself.

THE NEXT CORPORATE SCANDAL

After the corporate scandals of Enron, WorldCom, Tyco, and their ilk, 61 percent of Americans believe that CEO malfeasance is "a widespread problem" not limited to the news-making individuals of the day. But the connotation of the term "corporate scandal" needs to be expanded from accounting errors and insider trading to include media monopoly and consolidation—two problems that affect business *and* democracy. In his recent collection of essays on contemporary journalism, Bill Moyers wrote:

> What's the role of journalism in [democracy]? The founders of our nation were explicit on this point. The First Amendment is the first for a reason: to hold our representatives accountable and to arm the powerless with the information they need to protect themselves against the tyranny of the privileged elite, whether political or economic. The Founders, however, didn't count on the rise of megamedia. They didn't count on huge private corporations that would own not only the means of journalism but also vast swaths of the terrain that journalism should be covering.

In a time when the best channel of communication included Paul Revere and his trusty steed, our Founders could not have anticipated a press that includes thousands of newspapers, magazines, and broadcast stations, let alone the instantaneous reporting power of the Internet. Nor could they anticipate the problems of ownership and consolidation that occurs when megamedia corporations buy up those channels of information in large quantities.

The Nation, America's oldest journal of opinion, brags that "nobody owns *The Nation.* Not GE. Not Disney. Not Murdoch or Time Warner. We are a wholly owned subsidiary of our own conscience." This feisty slogan emerges from the vision of what a free press should look like; every reporter and editor—whether for an opinion journal or a mainstream outlet—should be independent of the agendas and influences of his or her parent-organization's purse strings. Yet serious problems arise when huge corporations own powerful media entities—as General

Electric owns NBC; Viacom, CBS; Disney, ABC; TimeWarner, CNN; and Murdoch, FOX and Sky TV. It is Economics 101: when these large and diversified companies own major network news outlets, the priorities of the free press can be secondary to the company's bottom line. In addition to owning NBC, GE produces nuclear power, household appliances, financial services, and health care; Disney owns ABC and produces movies, children's books, and vacation resorts. These multibillion-dollar corporations buy network or cable stations as investments, which are expected to pay dividends just like other subsidiaries. This means that, according to James T. Hamilton of Duke University, "News is a commodity, not a mirror image of reality."

When Ted Koppel signed off in 2005, after more than a quarter-century at the anchor desk of ABC's late-night news program *Nightline,* the *San Diego Union-Tribune* hailed him: "Democracy defined as responsible self-government can never be stronger than a properly informed citizenry. Kudos to Ted Koppel and the program he built into a hallmark of distinguished broadcast journalism for serving that worthy end." Born out of Koppel's coverage of the Iran hostage crisis, *Nightline* exhaustively covered the most important stories of the day. *Vanity Fair* once called it a "guerrilla public-affairs program." Yet Koppel's important work was not always valued so highly, at least not among the top brass at Disney-ABC. Despite polling data that showed that people young and old wanted to have Koppel as an option at 11:35 p.m., Disney-ABC tried to woo CBS funnyman David Letterman and his *Late Show* into Koppel's slot. Suddenly, the intrinsic value of *Nightline* was reduced to dollars and cents and the news program financially came in second place to Letterman.

Defending *Nightline*'s commercial and substantive success, Koppel wrote in a *New York Times* op-ed, "Over the past twenty-two years we have been, and continue to be, a consistent, competitive second. In times of crisis, we often have the largest late-night audience in broadcasting. I like to believe that this is because we provide a genuine public service." But Tucker Carlson, then of CNN's *Crossfire,* handily summed up the position of Disney-ABC:

> In this case, it's all about money, is it not? I mean, just take a look at these numbers. I think they tell the whole story. On *Nightline,* a thirty-second spot commands

$30,000. On *The Late Show,* it's $40,000. Bottom line, [annual] profits: *Nightline,* $13 million; *Late Show,* $25 million. Now if you're a shareholder in one of the companies that owns these two...you're interested, legitimately, in having a more profitable show on. So why is it illegitimate for the network executives to say put the moneymaker on?

As it turned out, Carlson's question was easy to answer: these companies may have shareholders but they ultimately answer to the public. The airwaves Disney-ABC uses are public property and are licensed by the government. That ownership—along with Americans' power to vote with their remote controls—demands a certain level of responsibility and decency from broadcasting companies. Circuses *and* bread. This time, coming in second place in the money race was not reason enough for Disney-ABC to replace *Nightline* with a talk show. As negotiations between Letterman and Disney-ABC continued, press coverage continued to worsen for the company. Even Letterman, who ultimately resigned with CBS, admonished Disney-ABC for its treatment of Koppel, explaining that "what [Koppel] has done and his contributions to American culture speak for themselves. He is one of a very small group of men and women who represent the absolute highest echelon of broadcast achievement." Funny that Disney-ABC did not take a page from one of its own warm, animated classics: Cinderella's wicked stepsisters did not win Prince Charming's heart with strategies and poaching—Cinderella won him with substance.

This episode played out in the country's most-read newspapers and entertainment magazines, but the local effects of corporate ownership have been under the radar and undermining news stations for years. With the rise of new media outlets like the Internet, fewer Americans sit down to watch the news each night and advertising rates have fallen accordingly. Yet the costs of producing quality local news segments have risen and corporate owners have continued to demand the same profit margins. Station managers have learned to cover such financial shortfalls by slashing local news budgets. According to a 2005 survey by the Project for Excellence in Journalism, a full 71 percent of stations had budget cuts when they actually needed more resources to produce better or even more programming. Local producers, stretched thin, have fallen back to filling time with increasing amounts of "feed" material (news segments produced by outside sources, such as the government). Currently, almost a full quarter of local stories include material not produced by reporters, and only 43 percent of stories actually feature a local reporter.

The reality of these statistics is that local news broadcasts are growing more "vapid and banal," according to the Newsbreakers, an activist group from Rochester, New York. By interrupting the live broadcasts of local reporters with characters like the "Cheese Ninja," "Invisible Suit Guy," and the "Rev. Utah Snakewater" who exorcizes viewers, the Newsbreakers are producing instantaneous satire, skewering the weakness of local news. This group may not be offering a nuanced critique, but the point is clear: regional news, on the whole, is often a farce. And with this devolution of the quality and substance of the thousands of local outlets, the free press has lost one of its catalysts for cogency and debate.

Corporate media owners are following an economic model that says that good journalism is too expensive to produce and that it is acceptable to replace real reporting with feed material and talking heads, thus the rise of the punditocracy. The problem is not that corporations are trying to make a profit overall; the problem is that they are doing it in the wrong industry. The tools of quality reporting—foreign bureaus, local reporters, and fact-checkers—are expensive to maintain when compared to the pundits of infotainment.

But the latter are not an equal substitute for the former and the result is that our media is filled with tragic but overexposed media stories like the Runaway Bride, Natalee Holloway's disappearance, and Michael Jackson's sex scandals. Just think of the costs of covering, for example, the American economy—keeping experts on staff, numerous lengthy interviews, several on-location visits, constant polling, and research—as compared with the costs of covering the Michael Jackson trial, which means sending a reporter and a camera man to one location to sit outside the courthouse.

As former vice president Al Gore lamented, "I thought the exhaustive, nonstop coverage of the O.J. Simpson trail was just an unfortunate excess that marked an unwelcome departure from the normal good sense and judgment of our television news media. But now we know that it was merely an example of a new pattern of serial obses-sions that periodically take over the airwaves for weeks at a time." The issue is less that Americans are obsessed with these human interest sto-ries and more that executives are naturally obsessed with the low cost of producing them. According to author Arianna Huffington: "The mainstream media regularly confuse the interesting with the important. What's more, they don't even do the former very well, and they largely ignore the latter."

At the same time that media firms are concerned about what pro-gramming will bring in the highest ad rates and what programming is the cheapest to produce, advertisers are concerned about the program-ming or news coverage with which their ads appear. Big corporations spending millions on advertising campaigns spanning all types of media want assurance that their products appear in a favorable envi-ronment—not juxtaposed to coverage or programming that dissuades prospective consumers from consuming their product. In April 2005, General Motors suddenly pulled millions of dollars in ads out of the *Los Angeles Times* the day after a Pulitzer-prize winning automotive journalist called for "impeachment proceedings" at the Big Three company.

GM is free to take their business elsewhere, but the newspaper indus-try has long been suffering falling circulation and, accordingly, needs advertising revenue more than ever. This grim diagnosis leaves papers more susceptible to advertiser censorship: GM only returned to the *Times'* pages after vague "productive conversations." While there is no easy resolution to this situation, it is clear that the real loser will be the ideal of a free press if major advertisers are allowed to bully the news.

Consolidation: The Terrible Power of One

Profit-driven news content is not the only consequence of corporate media ownership: years of "deregulation" have created a consolidated media that lacks diversity and accuracy. Beyond the fact that the economic priorities of big corporations are antithetical to the pro-democracy aspi-rations of a free press, the trouble is that large corporations own nearly the entire media landscape. Today, almost every print, radio, and televi-sion outlet is owned by one of ten major corporations. Consider only some of News Corporation's holdings:

+ Thirty-five FOX television stations in major cities like New York, Los Angeles, Chicago, Detroit, Dallas, Philadelphia, Boston, Phoenix, Denver, and more;

+ Thirteen cable channels including FX and the National Geographic Channel;

+ 20th Century Fox, Fox Searchlight Pictures, and Fox Television Productions;

+ *The New York Post* as well as twenty-five newspapers abroad;

+ Satellite television companies DirecTV, BskyB, and more; and

+ HarperCollins, ReganBooks, and Zondervan publishing.

Given how many media pies this one corporation has its fingers in, Americans must work hard to seek out media that is not owned by one of the megacorporations. And even then they probably cannot avoid the influence wielded by these companies, which often serve as arbiters of news and celebrity for entire industries.

This is especially true in American radio where just two corporations own 40 percent of the market. This consolidation of the radio industry occurred quickly after the passage of the 1996 Telecommunications Act that removed limits on radio ownership under the guise of "deregulation." Until 1996, companies could not own more than forty stations nationally and no more than two in any given market. Today, the largest radio company is Clear Channel, which boasts twelve hundred stations, more than half of all pop-music stations, and, until December 2005, boasted the largest concert-promotion operation in the country. This eight hundred-pound gorilla molds the music tastes of the American public to its own artists and pushes out competitors.

In 2001, the aptly named promotional company Nobody in Particular Presents (NiPP) decided to fight back as Clear Channel took control of the Denver concert market. Filing an antitrust law suit, NiPP accused Clear Channel, which owned eight local stations, of using its control over radio playlists to coerce performing artists to sign with the company's concert promotion arm over independent local companies like NiPP. In short, the message was: "Sign with Clear Channel for your concert PR or we will not play your music on our stations." Since most bands earn their money through concerts—not CD sales—the prospect of being held off the radio is a powerful deterrent from signing with the NiPPs of the music industry. While Clear Channel eventually settled out of court for an undisclosed amount of cash in 2004, this anti-competition case hinted at the pay-to-play underbelly of the radio and music industry. Talent and creativity are diminished when a few powerful gatekeepers—not American listeners—define the range of new music and play lists.

Radio consolidation can have more immediate and harmful effects than the slow loss music variety in localities. Industry experts have estimated that Clear Channel is made up of what were once seventy companies, making it a significant contributor to the ten thousand radio jobs lost due to the Telecom Act. When efficiencies of scale meant Clear Channel began favoring automated stations over having producers and disc jockeys, airwaves may have been filled, but the halls of stations went silent. Suddenly, stations that were run by people were being run by remote computers. Then, in Miniot, South Dakota, where Clear Channel owns all six of the commercial radio stations, a train carrying five cars of anhydrous ammonia fertilizer jumped the tracks in the early morning hours in January 2002. As a poisonous cloud spread over the city of thirty-seven thousand, there was no radio coverage for more than an hour. With the phones out, one resident searched the stations for any news about what happened but gave up at the hour mark. "The only thing on the radio was music—no one telling us what happened or what to do," said Jennifer Johnson in the *Bismark Tribune*.

With Clear Channel piping in material from outside the community (automated material accounts for as much as 70 percent of Clear Channel's broadcasting), the designated emergency announcement station had only one employee on duty that night. When the Emergency Alert System failed to work and authorities could not reach the lone employee who was besieged with listener calls, authorities had to use the Yellow Pages to find other station employees who could broadcast an alert. It was not until nearly an hour and a half after the derailment that an alert went on the air. The "accident ought to persuade us to be very concerned about absentee ownership [and] concentration of ownership," said North Dakota senator Byron Dorgan. He also said that, "the public airwaves are extraordinarily valuable and we have licensed them to be used by companies and over time the usage has changed very substantially and I think the public is not getting the kind of benefit from it that they used to get."

Yet the situation is not hopeless. Take what happened when, despite the deterioration of the radio industry under the Telecom Act, the Chairman of the Federal Communications Commission (FCC), Michael Powell, tried to do the same thing for the rest of the traditional media outlets. Using the positive connotation of "deregulation" as a code word for "consolidation," Powell pursued an increase in the cap on local market ownership from 35 percent to 45 percent nationally. His new rules would have expanded the number of outlets one company could own in a local market to three television stations, eight radio stations, and the leading newspaper. In many cities, this would constitute the entire media market. Imagine one Rupert Murdoch owning all media outlets in one community.

Americans across the political spectrum recognized the danger of these proposed rule changes. Over 750,000 letters and emails—mostly of protest—were sent to the FCC. "Why do we have more channels but fewer real choices today?" asked William Safire in one of a series of *New York Times* columns he dedicated to attacking Powell's rules. "Because the ownership of our means of communication is shrinking. Moguls glory in amalgamation, but more individuals than they realize resent the loss of local control and community identity." Yet, in June 2003, the commission voted along party lines, three Republicans to two Democrats, to approve the looser ownership rules.

Fortunately, the U.S. Court of Appeals, persuaded by the public outcry, ultimately overturned the rules—citing the "magnitude of the issue and the public's interest in reaching the proper resolution." The final ruling rejected the FCC's argument that ownership limits should be lifted unless evidence showed they were still necessary. Instead, the court said the FCC fell "short of its obligation to justify its decision to retain, repeal, or modify its media ownership regulations with reasoned analysis." Simply, the court said that Powell's rules were too threatening to media diversity and democracy.

The problem, as explained by William Greider, author of *Who Will Tell the People:* "The corporate concentration of media ownership has put a deadening blanket over the usual cacophony of democracy, with dissenting voices screened for acceptability by young and often witless TV producers. Corporate owners have a strong stake in what gets said on their stations." The narrow range of ownership means that fewer people are defining the parameters of public debate. Those CEOs and executives are similarly situated individuals who have other business ventures and bottom lines to protect. They share a collective but limited perspective that shapes the news programming policies on television, in print, and on the radio.

Corporations: Content to Be Conservative?

When the percentage of Americans who regularly watched the FOX News Channel rose by half from 2000 to 2004, competitors, anxious to get in on the ratings and advertising dollars, began to mimic FOX's infotainment lineup of conservative pundits and flag-themed graphics. FOX branded itself with the taglines "Fair and Balanced" and "We Report, You Decide" even though its viewing audience held the most misperceptions of any major outlet. In 2003, a study by the University of Maryland found that 80 percent of Americans who use FOX as their main news source had at least one of three major Iraq War-related misperceptions: that Iraq and al-Qaeda are connected, that WMDs were found in Iraq, or that world public polling showed overall support for going to war in Iraq. Meanwhile, only 47 percent of people who use print media as their main news source had one of those misconceptions and less than 25 percent of those who use NPR and PBS did. This brings new meaning to comedian and pseudo-pundit Stephen Colbert's crack that "reality has a well-known liberal bias."

Even so, the FOX model spread beyond *The O'Reilly Factor* and *Hannity & Colmes* to the other prominent cable news channels like MSNBC and has come to represent a bigger trend in the megamedia corporations: the tendency to embrace and project a conservative agenda. In 2002, the Microsoft and NBC venture hired talk show pioneer and veteran Phil Donahue to host a new prime-time show, airing against O'Reilly and CNN's then-forthcoming show with Connie Chung. Counting on a "grudge match" between a conservative, a liberal, and another media celebrity, MSNBC hoped Donahue's fame—the show was simply called *Donahue*—and natural style would help the struggling cable news channel move up in the ratings.

But executives made two mistakes: first, they thought they could get ratings on Donahue's reputation alone, even if they prevented him from asking the hard-nosed questions that earned him that reputation. For six months, Donahue tried to produce substantive shows—like one with Molly Ivins, Ralph Nader, and former Enron employees or his interviews with Pat Buchanan and Desmond Tutu—but producers required that he dilute this substance by interviewing government apologists and lightweight celebrities.

Despite these restrictions, ratings were slowly rising. *Donahue* surpassed *Hardball with Chris Matthews* as the channel's most-watched program. Yet MSNBC was about to make its second mistake: they caved to industry pressure to be more conservative even though *Donahue* was gaining ground. In an interview on FOX News's *Hannity & Colmes*, Donahue explained that MSNBC had required them "to have two conservatives on for every liberal. I was counted as two liberals." Then a leaked internal memo asserted that Donahue presented "a difficult face for NBC in a time of war." They needed to appear more "patriotic"—code word for "conservative." So, MSNBC quickly shuffled its programming, adding the conservative Tucker Carlson to a lineup that already included former Republican congressman Joe Scarborough. Donahue knew that MSNBC had tried to "out-FOX FOX" and that he was the casualty. MSNBC did not think that American viewers were smart enough to 1) appreciate the division between Donahue's perspective and his excellent reporting, 2) recognize when a host has been muzzled, making him just another talking head, and 3) recognize that dissent and debate are patriotic.

The effects of political ideology on media corporations have reached beyond cable talk shows to entertainment programming. In the fall of 2003, there was a conservative outcry against CBS's biopic on late president Ronald Reagan and his wife, Nancy. Even before the *The Reagans* aired, conservatives condemned the film for its cast—Democrats James Brolin and Judy Davis starred as the First Couple—and for portions of the script that portrayed the president in an unfavorable light. The biopic did cover some controversial moments of Reagan's presidency—for example, his oft-noted disinterest in addressing the HIV/AIDS epidemic—but producers were not any more malicious or sensational than is common among such TV docu-dramas. And the film gave Reagan considerable credit for ending the Cold War and accepted that Reagan knew nothing of funds from weapons sales to Iran being transferred to the Nicaraguan Contras. Interestingly, there were level-headed observers who thought that the film was biased but still defended it in the interest of free speech. *Boston Globe* reviewer Matthew Gilbert thought the film heavy-handed but pointed out that "as a rule, biopic makers exaggerate dramatic moments and exploit myths to fashion a piece of entertainment, moving from iconic moment to iconic moment with cartoonish overtones."

Yet when forty thousand conservatives visited a website calling for a boycott, CBS caved and pulled the film. This was likely the first time any broadcast network had pulled a completed piece due to political influence. What makes it all the more surprising was the network's careful research for and production of the film from start to finish. "This was very important for me, to document everything and give a very fair point of view," CBS head Leslie Moonves had told the *New York Times*.

While MSNBC and CBS may have bowed to outside political pressure, this troubling pattern of conservative media control has, at times, come from within. Take the work of Sinclair Broadcasting, the nation's largest television conglomerate, which reaches 24 percent of American television viewers. During the 2004 campaign, the company announced that it would run a documentary, called *Stolen Honor: Wounds That Never Heal,* accusing Democratic presidential nominee John Kerry of betraying prisoners of war in Vietnam, on all sixty-two of its television outlets. It was produced not by an independent source or one of the networks, but by Carlton Sherwood, a journalist-turned-Republican activist who had worked for the Bush and Reagan administrations. And when it was learned that Sinclair's owners, the Smith brothers, had given over $100,000 to the Republican Party in the five years prior, the assertion that Sinclair was acting in the public's best interest rang hollow.

Federal Communications Commissioner Michael J. Copps, known for his pro-democracy advocacy, called the documentary "an abuse of the public trust. And it is proof positive of media consolidation run amok when one owner can use the public airwaves to blanket the country with its political ideology—whether liberal or conservative." With public outrage backing Copps's sentiments, the company was forced by falling stock prices and an advertiser boycott to cancel the documentary.

This episode was part of a conservative trend at Sinclair. Only months before the proposed airing of *Stolen Honor,* Sinclair Broadcasting pulled an episode of *Nightline* from its ABC affiliates. Sinclair executives felt that it was "contrary to the public interest" for Ted Koppel to read the names of the U.S. soldiers killed in Iraq to that date. The Smiths argued that there was a liberal political agenda behind Koppel's program. Yet, in a letter to Sinclair CEO David Smith, former POW John McCain wrote: "Your decision to deny your viewers an opportunity to be reminded of war's terrible costs, in all their heartbreaking detail, is a gross disservice to the public, and to the men and women of the United States Armed Forces. It is, in short, sir, unpatriotic. I hope it meets with the public opprobrium it most certainly deserves."

With Republican control of the major institutions in Washington and much of the corporate world and the media, it is time to start pining for the discarded "Fairness Doctrine." Even though it only applied to radio and over-the-air television stations, the doctrine encouraged a spirit of balance across all media. Broadcasters were considered "public trustees" and were required to cover the key controversial issues of the day—with opinions from all sides—and to give political candidates the right to respond to any editorializing against them or for their opponents.

But in 1988, President Ronald Reagan abolished the "Fairness Doctrine," opening programming up to the pressures and biases that tempt broadcasters to try things like pulling *Donahue* and *The Reagans* and pushing *Stolen Honor.* The question of whether the media is liberal can now be laid to rest; the real question is whether it is even fair.

FEAR AND LOATHING AT THE PRESS CLUB

Journalists and editors who ideally should be fighting for transparency, free speech, and a vibrant public dialogue are more fundamentally fighting a war on two other fronts: to accurately report the news and to maintain their ethical independence. If perception is reality—a truth journalists likely understand more than most—then they are losing these battles. According to a 2005 study by the Annenberg Public Policy Center, 48 percent of Americans believe that the press often does not get its facts straight. And Americans consider journalists to be highly ethical at rates similar to lawyers, government officials, and politicians.

With such numbers, it is not a surprise that the call for better journalism is coming from all sides of the political spectrum. Scholar Todd Gitlin writes in *Mother Jones* that "if ever there were a time for unbridled journalism, this would be it: terrorist mayhem, war, corporate scandal, ecological crisis, [and] economic upheaval." On the Right, Karl Rove believes that "the work journalists do at this time is paradoxically more important than ever, so the need to get it right far more often than they get it wrong is absolutely critical to the function of a free society."

Of course, some of the smartest and most influential Americans are journalists pursuing a common good. There are certainly easier ways to make a good living. Reporters have to gather the news each day and then document and describe it on short deadlines—whether for the five o'clock news, a twenty-four-hour news network, or a newspaper. These are the people who withstand the criticism or wooing of editors, corporate owners, pundits, and politicians to hold a mirror up to government and business powers. Many do exceptional, even pioneering work under these cross-pressures, like Paul Krugman on Social Security, Walter Pincus on Iraq, Linda Greenhouse on the Supreme Court, Dana Milbank on White House ethics, Juan Williams on race and American culture, Dana Priest on the intelligence community, and Seymour Hersh on torture, among numerous others.

With important reporters like these, it is no surprise that 90 percent of Americans think it is at least somewhat important to "live in a country where news organizations can report the news without government censorship." What is surprising is the oft-overlooked corollary that journalists and editors can themselves be censors. Every day reporters and editors make choices about holding or running stories; this is a natural aspect of journalism, but there are right reasons (for further reporting or a better lead) and wrong reasons (to stay in good graces with a source) for holding a story. Thus, access can at times be the enemy of accuracy, as 42 percent of reporters believe that self-censorship occurs at least sometimes to protect one's relationship with a source.

It is, after all, part of human nature to want to be "on the inside" or "in the know." Television producers give their broadcasts names like *Inside Politics, The Situation Room,* and *Access Hollywood.* This nod to exclusivity reflects the tenuous relationship that reporters have with their subjects. Though the two groups are dependent upon one another, reporters are by definition reactive and must largely rely on the release of information by those in power. Friendships and understandings develop across the no-man's-land between reporters and their subjects, creating a "courtier press" according to *Harper's* publisher John

MacArthur. "Everyone wants to be at Versailles. Washington is Versailles. [Reporters] want to be close to le roi soleil, they want to be part of the power structure."

Media Self-Censorship: Reporters or Enablers?

In 1972, the late muckraker Hunter Thompson wrote that "the most consistent and ultimately damaging failure of political journalism in America has its roots in the clubby/cocktail personal relationships that inevitably develop between politicians and journalists—in Washington or anywhere else where they meet on a day-to-day basis." Perhaps the most entertaining example of how the media are enablers of elites rather than their critics is the annual dinner of the White House Correspondents Association. Tradition holds that the sitting president is always the keynote speaker and is always expected to be funny, using coverage of his agenda as material. At this televised black-tie event, the chummy characteristics of the relationship between the press corps and the White House are laid out. Jon Stewart lampooned the event on his *Daily Show* by speculating on what conversation must be like between the media and the politicos: "Deep down, we're both entrenched oligarchies with a stake in maintaining the status quo—enjoy your scrod."

The wining-and-dining of the correspondents' dinner makes good C-SPAN programming, but it is one of the more innocuous examples of borderline-problematic friendships between the reporters and the reported. An exemplar of this conundrum is Bob Woodward. An editor-at-large at the *Washington Post,* Woodward is the famed reporter who broke the Watergate story and the Nixon presidency with the information from the FBI's number two, W. Mark Feldt. After Feldt revealed himself as "Deep Throat," Woodward told the tale of their unlikely friendship that formed outside the White House Situation Room and that would later become a covert relationship of source and reporter. Given the way Watergate would ultimately disabuse Americans of idolizing presidents, Woodward's longtime silence on the identity of Deep Throat represents the good that can come from reporters' protecting sources.

But with Watergate, Woodward gained access to high-powered Washington circles and, as the years passed, many suspected that he began to parse the truth to keep that access. His most recent books, *Bush at War* and *Plan of Attack,* were seen as stunningly flattering portrayals when published and then were undermined further by disclosures about Bush's manipulation of intelligence information. Mocking Woodward's status as the "official recipient of the official leak at a very high level," *Harper's* John MacArthur explained that Woodward "made a straight business deal [with the Bush administration], 'You give me the minutes of the National Security Council meetings, and I'll make you look good in the months after 9/11.'" Woodward's fall from high truth-teller was complete when he admitted in 2005 that he had withheld his involvement in Plamegate—in order to avoid a subpoena in an investigation he has repeatedly called "laughable." Woodward conveys, according to journalist Sidney Schanberg, "the attitude of a sometime insider reluctant to offend—and that is hardly a definition of what a serious, independent reporter is supposed to be. It's a far piece from Watergate."

Media critics regularly complain that this proximity to power makes the nation's elite reporters more susceptible to self-censorship, and *New York Times* reporter Elisabeth Bumiller candidly confirmed as much during the lead up to the war:

> I think we were very deferential [to the president] because...it's very intense, it's frightening to stand up there. Think about it, you're standing up on prime-time live TV asking the president of the United States a question when the country's about to go to war. There was a very serious, somber tone that evening, and no one wanted to get into an argument with the president at this very serious time.

Later Bumiller also admitted that, despite the serious subject matter and consequences, it was somehow unacceptable to say the president was wrong or deceptive. After writing one particularly convoluted "upside-down statement" to avoid calling out Bush for not telling the truth, Bumiller recalled that she had received criticism for her purposeful vagueness. A reader emailed to ask her, "What's wrong with you guys? What can't you just say it plainly?" Her telling answer: "You can't just say the president is lying."

From across the "pond" and an ocean of journalistic gumption, Irish reporter Carol Coleman—not part of any implicit Beltway power structure—took a different approach to W.'s manipulation of the truth. She became a minor media celebrity for asking President Bush the difficult questions on many people's minds—and for preventing him from giving his standard answers. As Bush responded to her questions in an early 2004 interview, Coleman thought: "[M]y heart was sinking. He was resorting to the type of meandering stock answer I had heard scores of times…Going back over this old ground could take two or three minutes and allow him to keep talking without dealing with the current state of the war. It was a filibuster of sorts. If I didn't challenge him, the interview would be a wasted opportunity."

So she did challenge him and for her temerity received some of the most revealing thoughts the president had given on the Iraq War. Of course, Coleman was punished for ignoring the entrenched media etiquette surrounding the president; she lost an interview with First Lady Laura Bush for pushing her source—here the president—to answer her questions more fully. In fact, a White House aide called Coleman immediately after the interview to express disappointment at Coleman's handling of the situation: "You were more vicious than any of the White House press corps or even some of them on Capitol Hill…The president leads the interview." Coleman's quick response: "It's the journalist's job to lead the interview."

Perhaps American journalists should take a page from Coleman's notepad: a dedicated reporter cannot pull punches because she wants the approval of the newsmaker. News veteran Dan Rather brings the point home: "There's no joy in saying this, but beginning sometime in the 1980s, the American press by and large somehow began to operate on the theory that the first order of business was to be popular with the person or organization or institution that you cover."

In 2005, there were several instances in which major news outlets chose to hold back extraordinary stories from the public, such as the *Washington Post*'s decision to withhold the locations of the CIA's "secret network of interrogation and detention black sites in Eastern Europe." Coming two years after the revelations of torture at Abu Ghraib and "widespread prisoner abuse" in other military prisons, this new knowledge, that there are an undisclosed number of camps in undisclosed places, left people at home and abroad reeling. The *Post* rationalized its actions by citing officials "familiar with the program" who argued that "disclosure might disrupt counterterrorism efforts in those countries and elsewhere and could make them targets of possible terrorist retaliation." However, given the fact that Vice President Cheney was then pursuing, on behalf of the CIA, an exemption from new legislation prohibiting "cruel and degrading treatment" of prisoners, the *Post*'s decision to withhold information makes them responsible for more than just a choice to censor themselves at the request of sources.

National Security Archive analyst Peter Kornbluh explained: "This is probably the most important newspaper capitulation since the *New York Times* yielded to John F. Kennedy's call for them to not run the full story of planning for the Bay of Pigs. By withholding the country names, the *Post* is directly enabling the rendition, secret detention, and torture of prisoners at these locations to continue. That is a ghastly responsibility."

Of course, the immediate effects of any given reporter's decision to censor parts of his or her own story vary with the circumstances and vary in magnitude. Take the *New York Times'* poor coverage in the lead up to the war in Iraq. The *Times* did not cause the war, but as Daniel Okrent, former public editor of that paper, said, "The general rolling-over on the part of the American press allowed the war, to happen…and I think that the press is extremely chastened by that—that we all know how bad it was." There are significant consequences for society and democracy whether the censorship is Bob Woodward weaving pleasant profiles of our leaders, the *New York Times* pulling punches on questions about WMD in Iraq, or the *Post* withholding the locations of prison camps. Editors and journalists need to take a closer look at who and what they are protecting to make sure history does not repeat itself.

Standing Up to the Rising Tide
In an essay for the *New York Review of Books,* Joan Didion recalled:

> I once heard a group of reporters agree that there were at most twenty people who run any story. What they meant by "running the story" was setting the terms, setting the pace, deciding the agenda, determining when and where the story exists, and shaping what

the story will be. There were certain people who ran the
story in Vietnam, there were certain people in Central
America, there were certain people in Washington.

One of the consequences of the phenomenon so richly described here
is that the culture of reporting has grown lazier, allowing copycat articles
and news segments to cement a narrative no matter how erroneous it
may be. Because the first-pass framing of an item is often the only perspective the American public will see, healthy debate can be stymied.
Take, for example, one obvious question begged by Didion's recollection:
who ran the story on WMDs in Iraq?

Even after the *Commission on the Intelligence Capabilities of the
United States Regarding Weapons of Mass Destruction* showed that the
intelligence behind then-secretary of state Colin Powell's speech to the
United Nations was faulty, few took the Iraq policymakers or the media
to task for their roles in this debacle. Wrote columnist Eric Alterman:
"One aspect of this shameful episode went by largely forgotten: the
media's willingness to publicize, vouch for, and frequently hype the dishonest case the administration put forth." The media allowed the White
House—not the report's findings—to frame this news item. Instead of
continually hitting the president with questions about his rationale for
going to war, on television, radio, the Internet, and in newspapers, the
press repeated Bush's new rationale—that rescuing the Iraqi people from
Saddam Hussein's violent regime and bringing democracy to the Middle
East were moral imperatives regardless of WMDs. The press repeated
this again and again—thus lending it validity. In the end, the report that
officially outlined how the administration took the U.S. to war on faulty
evidence caused only a blip on the news radar.

The disparate coverage of two grim milestones in Iraq is another
interesting demonstration of the bandwagon press. The one thousandth American soldier's death and the two thousandth were covered
differently from each other but similarly among news sources. The one
thousandth mark came in September 2004 just before the Republican
National Convention; the two thousandth death came a little over a
year later in October of 2005. The first milestone was marked by very
little press coverage—the president did not speak of it, his then-opponent
Senator John Kerry spoke of it only briefly. Newspapers carried small

headlines for the first thousand because, according to Robert Thompson, a Syracuse University media professor, "A lot of journalists were very worried that if they were critical, they would be accused of something tantamount to treason, as *Nightline* had been."

Yet when the second milestone came around, it seemed journalists got together and said, "Okay, this time we're interested." The story was splashed across headlines and newscasts. Some analysts suggested the heightened coverage was the result of the high disapproval rates of the war among Americans. Or perhaps it was the result of a collective guilty conscience: Americans had begun to tune out the daily reports of death in Iraq and were jerked awake when the number of dead hit a haunting number. Regardless, at both milestones, media outlets should have considered what the story should be, independent of the framing by a so-called small group of "story-runners" creates.

Sometimes the media just misses a story completely. Blogger Josh Marshall observed that "news stories have a twenty-four-hour audition on the news stage, and if they don't catch fire in that twenty-four hours, there's no second chance." Marshall wrote this about the previously discussed Downing Street Memo, a story that started out as the rule but became the exception. When the story first broke, the White House quickly belittled its importance, with then-press secretary McClellan claiming that there was "no need" to respond despite the fact that the memo apparently documented Bush's early eagerness for war.

Even though the memo provided the strongest documentary evidence yet that the Bush administration was itching to go to war for whatever reason, the mainstream media bought McClellan's take and the story remained outside the mainstream press for five weeks. "[I]t's shocking when you see how easily they fold in the media today," said Senator Hillary Clinton, specifically of the Downing Street Memo episode. "They don't stand their ground. You know, if they are criticized by the White House, they just fall apart. I mean, come on, toughen up, guys. It's only our Constitution and country at stake. Let's get some spine going here."

Author and blogger Arianna Huffington searched the news transcripts of six major news outlets in the weeks after the story first broke for coverage of the memo in comparison with two serial obsession stories of the time. In the given time period, ABC News had 42 segments mentioning the disappearance of Natalee Holloway, 121 mentioning Michael Jackson, and none mentioning the Downing Street Memo. CBS News also had no segments mentioning the memo but had almost double ABC's numbers mentioning the other two stories. NBC News, CNN, and FOX all had some segments mentioning the memo but those segments were outnumbered at least ten to one with stories on Holloway and at least eighteen to one with stories on Jackson.

If the eventual coverage of the Downing Street Memo was an early indication of growing media backbone, the coverage of Hurricane Katrina was another example of strength. CNN anchor Anderson Cooper's strong questioning of Senator Mary Landrieu—"There was a body on the streets of this town yesterday being eaten by rats because this woman had been laying in the street for forty-eight hours…Do you get the anger that is out here?"—came to represent a possible turning point for a media that was featuring President Bush helping to rebuild a New Orleans home. "After years of credulously reciting administration talking points about WMD and candy-throwing Iraqis, the corpse-lined streets of New Orleans have spurred reporters to finally get feisty with mendacious officials and slippery politicians," wrote *The New Republic*'s Franklin Foer.

As the deaths in Iraq mount and the president's poll numbers fall, the White House press corps has begun asking harder questions and rejecting diversionary tactics. A strong democracy requires strong journalists challenging the powerful at all times, not just in bursts of righteousness that coincide with their subject's political problems.

RIGHTING THE MEDIA

President Ronald Reagan's quip, "I like photographers; you don't ask questions," likely reflects President George W. Bush's view of the media. As demonstrated in the earlier chapter on secrecy, this administration maintains control over as much information as possible. They seem to operate under a sort of a play on the old axiom: "What the public doesn't know can't hurt the administration." As the press is dedicated to the reporting of news and information, it is obviously the democratic institution most directly affected by Bush's news management style. "My biggest frustration is that this White House has chosen an approach with the White House press corps, generally speaking, to engage us as little as possible," complained NBC's correspondent David Gregory.

The democratic value of the fourth estate is rooted in the gathering and mediation of information. But the growing use of executive orders and signing statements is granting the Bush presidency greater powers of secrecy and manipulation than ever before. "[T]his White House just sees the media as another constituency to feed, a special interest group, and doesn't have a lot of respect for it," said Craig Crawford, author of *Attack the Messenger: How Politicians Turn You Against the Media.*

Bush and the Far Right, showing contempt for democracy and journalism, have created a new model for dealing with the press: first, spin the news. If that does not work, then create diversionary news; and if that does not work, then strong-arm reporters and news outlets into your corner.

The Oval Office Is Spinning

"Spin" has become an institutionalized part of our government's day-to-day business. Elected officials hire press experts to frame and explain current events from an expedient perspective. Using spin as the story instead of as the framing often shifts the nation's focus from the big issues to petty mudslinging. *Washington Post* columnist E. J. Dionne observed that "the Bush machine is so skillful at turning little things into big things—always with help from Rush and FOX and the rest of the party-line conservative media eager to read scripts generated by the White House." In fact, when Bush's press coverage was riddled with the difficulties of the Iraq War, NSA spying, and low approval ratings, he hired a FOX veteran as head spinmeister, White House press secretary. As an experienced television pundit, radio host, and columnist, Tony Snow was meant to bring a fresh, polished face to an administration in want of credibility and good news.

Take the scandal dubbed "Memogate" involving Dan Rather, CBS, and the president's Air National Guard records. Two months before the 2004 presidential elections, Dan Rather reported on the preferential treatment President Bush received while in the Texas Air National Guard during the Vietnam War. The evidence on which Rather and his producer at *60 Minutes Wednesday* built the story was a set of documents supposedly from Bush's commanding officer, the late Lieutenant Colonel Jerry Killian. Conservative bloggers began raising questions about the legitimacy of the documents almost immediately, adding another dimension to an already mean-spirited presidential campaign season. Over the course of nearly two weeks, bloggers and the mainstream media debated the ins-and-outs of how CBS verified the documents and whether Dan Rather and his producer had an agenda to attack Bush's campaign in its final weeks. Spun by bloggers and then the White House as a political attack with dubious origins, the accurate revelations of Rather's report—that the president's time in the Air National Guard (ANG) *was* marked by favors and cover-ups—were superseded by the admittedly flawed authentication of the documents.

"Lost in the commotion over the authenticity of the documents is that the underlying facts of Rather's *60 Minutes* reports are substantially true," according to James C. Goodale, the general counsel to the *New York Times,* who represented that paper in the Pentagon Papers case. "Bush did not take the physical exam required of all pilots; his superiors gave him the benefit of any doubt; he did receive special treatment, and Lieutenant Colonel Jerry Killian, Bush's commanding officer, was unhappy with the loss of ANG's investment in him when Bush informed Killian he was leaving for Alabama." Four people, including Dan Rather, stepped down from CBS over this report, but no real discussion ever arose about whether the president abused his much-coveted spot in the Texas Air National Guard.

The successful spinning and quashing of this embarrassing story encouraged the White House to try it again after the shocking accounts and pictures of American soldiers torturing Iraqi prisoners at Abu Ghraib. Public opinion at home and abroad ridiculed the sentencing of two low-level soldiers as just a show trial, in effect letting the military and the administration scapegoat the entire affair.

Cue *Newsweek*'s serious mistake: the news magazine erroneously reported in a small "Periscope" item that interrogators at Guantánamo Bay had flushed a copy of the Koran down a toilet as a means of torturing their Muslim captives. The report sparked fatal anti-American rioting in Afghanistan and other Muslim countries. White House press secretary Scott McClellan then pounced: "This report, which *Newsweek* has now retracted and said was wrong, has had serious consequences. People did lose their lives. The image of the United States abroad has been damaged; there is lasting damage to our image because of this report. And we would encourage *Newsweek* to do all that they can to help repair the damage that has been done, particularly in the region." So, *Newsweek* is to blame for anti-Americanism and riots in the Muslim world but not a president's preemptive war and occupation of a Muslim country? *New York Times* columnist Frank Rich summed up this sadly spun situation:

> The administration's attempt to pass the entire buck to *Newsweek* for our ill odor among Muslims, including those Muslims who abhor jihadists committing murder, is laughable. Yet there's something weirdly self-incriminating about the language it uses to do it. Richard Boucher, the State Department spokesman whose previous boss, Colin Powell, delivered a fictional recitation of Saddam Hussein's weapon capabilities before the United Nations Security Council, said it's "shocking" that *Newsweek* used "facts that have not been substantiated." Bryan Whitman, a Pentagon spokesman, attacked *Newsweek* for hiding "behind anonymous sources," yet it was an anonymous source, an Iraqi defector known as Curveball, who fed the fictions that Mr. Powell spouted to gin up America for war. Psychological displacement of this magnitude might give even Freud pause.

Don't Like the News? Make (Up) Your Own

Naturally, with power centralized in one person, the presidency has a podium of greater media draw than the judicial or legislative branches of government. Add that to the high-stakes games of running for reelection or building legacies and the temptation to make up news for the sake of public image looms large. So administrations supply the press with stories and "facts" that reflect a desired reality, not the real thing. Bush may have told the Irish reporter Carole Coleman, "History will judge what I'm about," but he is doing his best to influence the history books.

Take, for example, President Bush famously donning a flight suit and landing on the USS *Lincoln* in the spring of 2003—only six weeks into Operation Iraqi Freedom—to announce the end of major combat operations in Iraq. The powerful images of Bush walking across the aircraft carrier's deck certainly implied that the war was then essentially over. Similarly, in the summer of 2005, the White House used a bait-and-switch media strategy: the "bait" was a new Supreme Court nominee, and the "switch" was Bush's political point man's involvement in Plamegate. At the time, 60 percent of Americans following the story believed Karl Rove should step down. Republican allies of the White House reported that the president had moved up his plans to announce a nominee in order to take the heat off Rove. It worked—and the leaked nominee shortlist, which included women and Latinos, had the added benefit of insulating the president's ultimate pick of a white male, John Roberts.

Both of those examples typify the rules of Washington media manipulation since the advent of the press secretary some fifty years ago. Yet such diversions are not the most brazen of the administration's tendency to create news. The trophy for undermining media and democracy goes to government attempts to pass propaganda off as news. The White House has shown a preference for buying good coverage at home and abroad instead of earning it, creating obvious credibility and democracy gaps. The first revelations of pundit payola surrounded the Department of Education's payment of $240,000 to syndicated columnist and pundit Armstrong Williams to promote the No Child Left Behind education law. Armstrong feigned ignorance of the standards regarding conflicts of interest that apply to the "media elite," but the Government Accountability Office found that "such a contract with the government is illegal. It is against the law for the federal government to pay commentators covertly to market its policies."

The GAO also condemned the administration's production and distribution of so-called "video news segments" that do not identify the government as the source. In total, twenty executive branch agencies have $250 million at their disposal to create such *Pravda*-like segments, that look just like local news spots with friendly faced, generic reporters and which are broadcast to twenty-two million households. The most prominent examples covered information on drug use by teens and on the benefits of the new Medicare bill for seniors. The GAO did not take issue with the content of the pieces—but that there was no indication the information was government produced. "This is more than a legal issue," argued GAO Comptroller General David Walker. "It's also an ethical issue and involves important, good government principles, namely the need for openness in connection with government activities and expenditures. We should not just be seeking to do what's legal. We should be doing what's right." Even though this argument closely echoed Bush's 2000 campaign promise—"We will ask not only what is legal, but what is right"—the White House rejected the GAO's findings, arguing that the pieces were not propaganda. That was easy to do because the GAO has no enforcement powers.

Administration use of propaganda reaches beyond our borders to the nascent democracy in Iraq where the U.S. military has bribed Iraqi papers to run pro-American articles, again without any indication that the stories were written by American soldiers. "Though the articles are basically factual," reported the *Los Angeles Times,* "they present only one side of events and omit information that might reflect poorly on the U.S. or Iraqi government." A Pentagon contractor, the Lincoln Group, funneled the stories for the U.S., placing them in papers with headlines like "Iraqis Insist on Living Despite Terrorism." One military official said that the U.S. had also secretly purchased an Iraqi newspaper and radio station to promote the American operation without identifying the source.

Strong-Arming the Media

While White House press offices have obviously tried to sway coverage in a daily push-pull with the media, the Bush administration has taken this power into the realm of punishing reporters for even asking probing questions. First, reporters are subject to a tit-for-tat game of favors for access. "I recently did a story on a senior figure in the Bush White House and was told in advance, 'It better be good,'" recalled the late anchor Peter Jennings, who had interviewed every president since Nixon until Bush. "Which I thought was rather naked. It wasn't a threat, but it didn't sound like a joke. There is a feeling among some members of the press corps that you are either favored by the administration or not, and that will have something to do with your access."

During the early "honeymoon" period of Bush's presidency and in the aftermath of September 11 and the two wars that followed, the media were disinclined to ask too many tough questions without an opposition figure to whom they might attach the story. The reporters who did keep asking tough questions or writing critical stories suddenly found themselves sitting in the back row, not called on or not called back. How many journalists are willing to write an article exposing Bush's disinformation knowing that the White House or the Bill O'Reillys would retaliate or call it unpatriotic? Bush's infrequent press conferences hardly invite candid exchanges. It was so obvious at his pre-Iraq invasion press conference that he was calling on preselected reporters that even Bush joked that "this is scripted." Journalist Lawrence McQuillam, a veteran of six White Houses, sat in the front row and quickly understood what was happening. "Eventually futility sinks in," he told the *American Prospect*. "I've just never been to a press conference where the president never looked at the audience to see if anybody was raising a hand to ask a question."

Bush has also tried to use this muscular approach to media control against the Corporation for Public Broadcasting (CPB). When the president proposed his 2007 budget, he tried to gut CPB, the entity established to protect National Public Radio (NPR) and the Public Broadcasting System (PBS) from political pressures. Conservatives have long complained that PBS programming is slanted to the left even though 80 percent of Americans believe PBS is balanced and 90 percent believe it "provides high quality programming." Even so, Bush's proposed cuts of tens of millions of dollars came on the heels of a wide-ranging CPB scandal involving the White House and then-CPB chairman Kenneth Tomlinson. Appointed chairman by the Bush administration, Tomlinson was so focused on turning CPB and ultimately PBS into Republican institutions that he acted in a manner that completely contradicted his mandate to protect public television from Beltway wrangling.

His main target was the highly acclaimed investigative news program, *NOW...With Bill Moyers*. The host had been an aide to President Lyndon Johnson and was present at the birth of public television.

Moyers built his show on two principles: 1) its reporting had to continue the "conversation of democracy" by talking to people across the political spectrum, and 2) the show had to challenge the powerful. Despite its numerous awards and high ratings, Tomlinson went ahead and—without the board's approval—paid a conservative researcher to watch *NOW* with an eye for liberal biases. In the end, this $14,000 report was a joke: it called Republican senator Chuck Hagel a liberal for suggesting that the White House's Iraq policy deserved questioning.

Moyers told the real story at the National Media Reform Conference in 2005:

> Most of those who came [on the show] responded the same way that Ron Paul, the Republican and Libertarian congressman from Texas, did when he wrote me after his appearance, "I have received hundreds of positive emails from your viewers. I appreciate the format of your program, which allows time for a full discussion of ideas.... I'm tired of political shows featuring two guests shouting over each other and offering the same arguments.... *NOW* was truly refreshing.

Moyers went on to explain how Tomlinson and others responded to *NOW*'s hard questions and careful reporting: "This is the point of my story: Ideologues don't want you to go beyond the typical labels of left and right. They embrace a worldview that can't be proven wrong because they will admit no evidence to the contrary. They want your reporting to validate their belief system and when it doesn't, God forbid."

After attacking Moyers, Tomlinson looked to stack the CPB staff with Republicans and consulted with a Bush staffer on what CPB's ombudsperson office should look like. He pushed to hire a former cochairperson of the Republican National Committee as CPB's new president. He worked with Karl Rove to nix a plan that would put people with experience in local broadcasting on the board. Tomlinson even personally shepherded a conservative *Wall Street Journal* program, *The Journal Editorial Report,* into the PBS lineup despite the fact that federal statutes prohibit board members from influencing programming decisions. In the end, a report by CPB inspector general Kenneth A. Konz faulted Tomlinson for these and other efforts that were completed in secret or were in violation of CPB standards. Since carrying the water of an administration ran directly counter to the PBS mission of independence, Tomlinson was forced to resign from the CPB when the board reviewed the results of Konz's report.

WHAT IS THE TRUTH? CALLING A SPADE A SHOVEL

When David Grosh, a minion in Jack Abramoff's lobbying network, testified without a lawyer before a Senate committee, his plain truth-telling made headlines. The *New York Times* ran an amused little piece about Grosh's endearing naiveté and simplicity; the pull-quote read: "The sophisticates of the political class are often charmed by an innocent." The story effectively characterized Grosh's honesty as childlike and inconsequential. This characterization of a person with a clear sense of right and wrong demonstrates what plagues the free press even more than the problems of the megamedia, the access-hungry reporters, and a secretive White House: *just what is the truth?*

Every now and then, a journalist or politician mourns the time when the government was more honest with the American people. Perhaps the turning point will be Eisenhower and the U-2 planes or Nixon and Watergate. We are likely lamenting a golden era of honesty that never really existed, but the constant barrage of news and punditry has made us more discerning and cynical observers. All the spin, press releases, and sound bites are forcing us to face the fact that a media unsure of the truth will create a democratic crisis.

As Americans are force-fed "realities" by our elected and media leaders, we seem further than ever from knowing what our democracy should look like and how the free press should support it. "While some executive was nodding, C-SPAN started showing us Britain's House of Commons during Question Time," opined Gore Vidal. "This is the only glimpse that most Americans will ever get of how democracy is supposed to work. These party leaders are pitted against one another in often savage debate on subjects of war and peace, health, and education. Then some six hundred members of Parliament are allowed to ask questions of their great chieftains." American media, by and large, has traded such revealing debate for a shallower and unexamined version of reality.

Right now, the best questioning seems to be coming from the *Daily Show with Jon Stewart,* which has consistently asked the obvious questions that our mainstream media is somehow missing or avoiding. According to media activist John Nichols, at a colloquium organized by the author called *Saving Our Democracy* in January 2006, this turn to satire is more than just an attempt to find humor in the news. Comparing it to trends in apartheid South Africa and the Soviet Union, he explained that this "is a model that develops when people have completely lost faith in the existing media."

CONCLUSION:
SAVING OUR DEMOCRACY

*"Democracy can come undone. It's not something that's
necessarily going to last forever once it's been established."*
—Sean Wilentz in *The Rise of American Democracy*

*"The idea that anything of great consequence depends on the
condition of America's democracy sounds quaint."*
—George Packer in *The Fight for Democracy*

"We cannot defend freedom abroad by deserting it at home."
—Edward R. Murrow

It is an irony that probably escapes George W. Bush, seemingly secure in "the eternal sunshine of his spotless mind." But just as the last half of the twentieth century saw a quadrupling of the number of democracies—just as, in Professor John Gaddis's view, "the world came closer than ever before to reaching a consensus...that only democracy confers legitimacy"—the greatest democracy ever is becoming less and less democratic. And leading the war on democracy is a president lauding its virtues.

President Bush does not wake up every day wondering how to sabotage democracy. But the issue is not his *intent*—intent being a key element in criminal law—but his *actions*. And connecting the dots of Bush's presidential actions reveals a clear and present danger to our democracy. While we surely haven't *lost* our democracy, we are now only another Bush-like presidency, another couple of John Cornyns or Tom Coburns in the Senate, another couple of Antonin Scalias away from *losing* our democracy. To paraphrase Sinclair Lewis, it can happen here.

That conclusion is not so much alarmist as descriptive.

In the introductory chapter, we saw that a working democracy requires leaders who believe in and govern based on accountability, transparency, the rule of law, and respect for debate and dissent. In each area, our American democracy has recently surrendered ground to a new authoritarianism.

Accountability? Those responsible for proven calamities are either retained, promoted, or awarded the Presidential Medal of Freedom (Rumsfeld, Rice, Wolfowitz, Tenet, Chertoff, those FBI officials who refused to investigate Moussaoui pre-9/11 because it might hurt their careers)—with FEMA's poor Michael Brown being the sole exception. Transparency? If Bush and Cheney were any more secretive, they'd govern from a secure bunker in that Virginia mountain, coming out only for State of the Unions and speeches to AEI.

The rule of law? This government invades a country contrary to the UN charter, condones torture, outs a CIA operative, ignores warrants for wiretaps, selectively leaks classified information for partisan gain, rounds up thousands of American Muslims without evidence, incarcerates hundreds at Guantánamo without charges or lawyers, and asserts the power to ignore duly enacted laws because of an unending war on terror—and then Bush urges the world to follow his devotion to "the rule of law."

Toleration of debate and dissent? Whenever an administration official commits candor, it seems that they're either fired or ridiculed or both. When questioned about whether Secretary Rumsfeld would stay at the Pentagon given the calamities in Iraq, Bush simply asserts, "I am the decider," betraying a temperament inconsistent with the spirit of "government by discussion," Lord Byron's phrase that nicely describes the essence of democracy.

To mask their attacks on democracy, Bush & Co. engage in mendacity and pageantry. Their repeated falsehoods before the Iraqi invasion were simply the most blatant and consequential examples of a pattern of deception as chronicled in chapter 9. And in a tactic Kim Jong Il could admire, the administration hires Hollywood movie set designers to create photo opportunities from the "Mission Accomplished" moment on the USS *Abraham Lincoln* to backdrops to speeches about

Iraq with the word VICTORY repeated in huge letters. In a country where 42 percent believe in demonic possession—and where most are understandably anxious about terrorism after 9/11—the political exploitation of patriotism did manufacture significant support and a reelection win. Few seemed to understand Mark Twain's wise saying that "patriotism is supporting our country all of the time, and your government when it deserves it."

Eventually, however, a government engaging in a kind of Snow White "wishing makes it so" ran into a wall of reality called the failures of Iraq, Katrina, Medicare drug benefits, social security privatization, and more. It was almost painful to watch Attorney General Alberto Gonzales twist himself into a pretzel explaining why illegal wiretaps were legal or Secretary Rumsfeld try to justify post-invasion chaos and looting because "freedom's untidy. And free people are free to...commit crimes and do bad things." Citizens guided by logic and fact can only shake their heads when reading the December 2005 report by Ken Herman of the Cox News Service that "President Bush said Wednesday the invasion of Iraq was the right thing to do even if it was for a reason that turned out to be wrong."

It's one thing for a president to make an occasional or even spectacular misjudgment, like Kennedy about the Bay of Pigs. A policy failure alone does not undermine the democratic process. But when a president combines ignorance with serial deception and messianic certainty on issue after issue, then a democratic model depending on open debate and the scientific method gets short-circuited.

Also troubling for the notion of popular sovereignty is the fact that Washington is now the occupied territory of democracy, a city being run by and for the wealthy, the religious, and the ideological. From K Street lobbyists writing laws for clients, to the Religious Right speed-dialing the White House, to conservative think tanks funded by big business concocting plausible fig leafs for reactionary policies, the Bush administration and Congress are dancing to the tunes of the Jack Abramoffs, James Dobsons, and Grover Norquists. Their purpose is to redistribute wealth to the wealthy, breach the wall of separation between church-and-state to advance religion, and to exploit patriotic fervor for political votes. The kooks urging the government to impeach Chief Justice Earl Warren in the 1950s have *become* the government fifty years later.

When has there been such a radical anti-democracy government in our history? Long-settled issues are being reversed—like policies promoting reproductive choice, environmental safety, access to courts, freedom of information, progressive taxation, social security, and policies against torture, illegal wiretapping, and preemptively invading and occupying another country. All administrations have had some out-of-the-mainstream voices trying to stretch policy. In Bush's administration, radical conservatives are not just proposing but actually making policies so radical as to alarm such mainstream Republicans as Brent Scowcroft, John Danforth, Christine Todd Whitman, Lawrence Wilkerson, General Anthony Zinni, and the list goes on.

This extremism is going unchecked by the checks-and-balances built into our constitutional framework precisely because Washington has become such a one-party town. With Congress completely in Republican hands in 2001–2006—and with "partyology" and business contributions neutering congressional Republican leaders—the Bush team has felt free to run roughshod over rules and laws. In a parliamentary system, such a government would fall. Not in Washington today. When Bush was in effect caught going 95 mph on warrantless wiretapping, congressional cops not only failed to ticket him but obligingly upped the speed limit from 55 to 95 mph.

Extremism posturing as democracy may be shocking, but it's not surprising, not if one thinks about Bush's philosophy, experience, and base. He himself comes out of a hierarchical CEO background where Ayn Rand heroes pronounce policy from Olympus, damn the consequences and shareholders. Half his base are radical Religious Rightists, who are accustomed to demanding fealty to divine or priestly pronouncements, parishioners and the poor be damned. Such business and religious leaders are accustomed to governing by catechism not collaboration, by standards far closer to autocracy than democracy. Author George Packer accurately describes Bush officials as "secretive, hierarchical, unwilling to discuss, contemptuous of compromise, unashamedly cozy with friends, dismissive of doubters, ruthless with opponents. If it wasn't clear during the Florida recount that the Bush team deeply dislikes democracy, it has become clear enough since they began to govern."

One more ingredient added to this stew makes it unusually toxic. Bush uses the catastrophe of 9/11 as a license to engage in all kinds of illegal or unprecedented behavior. But awful as that day was, 9/11 is not more important than the U.S. Constitution and over two hundred years of democratic progress. To think otherwise is to concede to bin Laden a perverse victory.

But doesn't Bush speak often about freedom and democracy? Yes, if you add up all his references, in his inaugural, State of the Union, and pro-war addresses. It's hard, however, to take his rhetoric at face value since he's never advanced any serious pro-democracy policies in his years as governor or president. When has he done anything to enhance the franchise, access to courts, public information, or corporate accountability? Also, nearly all his references appear to be after-the-fact rationalizations for invading Iraq. Democracy in the Middle East *is* a fine ideal, but one that must be more than an afterthought, as elections elevating radical Islamists in Iran and the Palestinian Authority have shown.

Bush's idea of "democracy" is not the one embraced by the rest of the world. Most people have admired America as a "light unto nations" and a political model because democracy means citizen participation, social justice, civil rights, and civil liberties. That is, freedom *to* enjoy certain rights. The Bush contingent, however, believes in freedom *from* restraints, like consumer and environmental regulation. As in so many other areas, radical conservatives have attempted to privatize freedom. According to scholar Orlando Patterson, "Freedom is largely a personal matter having to do with relations with others and success in the world. Freedom, in this conception, means doing what one wants and getting one's way. It is measured in terms of one's independence and autonomy, on the one hand, and one's influence and power, on the other."

Bush's version of freedom and democracy, then, is profoundly hostile to the public sector. Government is seen as a fourth axis of evil bothering businessmen with regulations and taxes and religious leaders with rules against endorsing candidates from pulpits. His blame-government-first followers have no appreciation of how government can in fact *expand* democracy, by protecting speech, encouraging affordable healthcare, improving education, advancing legal and social justice so that more than the top 1 percent can enjoy the blessings of America. His version of democracy is therefore anti-democracy, notwithstanding his rhetoric to the contrary. Bush Republicans may mouth the lyrics, but they don't know the music of democracy.

In other words, Bush's philosophy and style make him a natural exemplar of the new authoritarianism—which combines aspects of a plutocracy transference wealth to his contributors, a theocracy transferring power to religious supporters, an imperial presidency contemptuous of Congress and popular opinion, as well as aspects of a monarchical transferring of power from father to son. Was anyone really surprised to hear his jokes that a "dictatorship would be a heck of a lot easier" than a democracy, or that his political base was "the haves and the have mores"?

In contrast to the Bush "I am the Decider" top-down approach to governing is the Breyer "We the People" approach. Justice Stephen Breyer, in his small but powerful 2005 book *Active Liberty,* proposes that America today embrace the Founders' spirit of "active liberty—the need to make room for democratic decision-making." He approvingly refers to, in philosopher Benjamin Constant's phrase, the peoples' right "to an active and constant participation in collective power." Breyer is arguing not so much for a policy as a process, one that always asks the question of what best promotes democracy. So, for example, when it comes to the issue of campaign finance laws the standard should not be how to expand freedom for a few multimillionaires to spend yet more money but how to increase the voice of the 99 percent who contribute from $200 or under. It comes back to Madison in *Federalist 30*: "Rest all our political experiments on the capacity of mankind for self-government."

Presidents come and go, but the ingrained habits of culture and society endure. So while today's attack on democratic values is real, radical, and consequential, it's far too early to tell whether Bush will permanently diminish our democracy or—according to the law of physics that for every action there's an opposite reaction—helpfully remind Americans of the democratic heritage that Breyer writes about.

One-party rule in the Kremlin from 1917 to 1991 and in Nassau County, New York, in the 1960s–1990s collapsed when a disgusted population said, "*Basta!*" Polling data indicates a public now also souring on Bush's failures and falsehoods. But, ultimately, saving our democracy requires two preconditions—citizens being made participants rather than spectators in our public conversation and leaders laying out a Contract for Democracy to pursue and enact.

A labor organizer once remarked that "American politics is long a contest between organized money and organized people." Indeed, democracy originates from the Greek word *demos* meaning "people." Democracy can't flourish if "organized money"—PACs, lobbyists— dominate the unorganized majority.

If other countries can have pro-democracy movements, so can America. We have in the past. Periodically, "organized people" have led our leaders. From the civil rights movement of the 1950s and 1960s, to Earth Day in 1970, to the woman's movements of the 1920s and 1970s, to the anti-Vietnam activism in the 1960s, to the four hundred communities protesting aspects of the original "Patriot Act," periodically Americans have challenged elites to respond to urgent issues.

Until now, the reality that we're slowly losing our democracy has not been regarded as urgent or newsworthy. For most Americans, this threat remains relatively remote—a concept applicable only to the past or to foreign countries. In essence, it can't happen here. This public placidity assumes that someone is watching out for our best interests. But who? Republicans controlling the bully pulpits and podiums in Washington can hardly be expected to discuss a war where they are the aggressors. President Bush seems to discuss terrorism and taxes 90 percent of the time, with democracy *abroad* filling the remainder. The mainstream American media are largely reactive, responding to what they are told or what they see—whether it's from administration officials issuing terror alerts or dead bodies floating in New Orleans. A Congress could raise questions, but, as explained previously, they have been more comfortable as enablers rather than exposers of the assault on democracy.

So, as with earlier movements, a response to the anti-democracy policies of Bush, the Religious Far Right, and big business must come from the bottom up, not the top down. Around the country, there are thousands of unheralded organizations trying to win our democracy back—from ACORN fighting for a living wage to Demos fighting against felony disenfranchisement laws. They are chronicled in "The Contract for Democracy" (www.newdemocracyproject.org).

Here are a couple dozen proposals that could comprise an initial Democracy Program for candidates and activists in 2006 and 2008:

◆ Voting should occur on a Saturday in early November called "*Democracy Day.*" We can combine a day honoring veterans who died for our democracy with a non-workday where we practice it.

◆ States that have experimented with *mail-in ballots, same-day registration,* and *early balloting* (voting any time over a specific period pre-election day) have seen turnout increase by 10 percentage points and more.

◆ *Electronic voting machines* are the future, but they must have *paper trails* (as ATMs manage to do) to deter or detect fraud.

◆ Since former slave states have *felony disenfranchisement laws* which disproportionately suppress the vote of minorities, all ex-offenders in non-capital cases who have "paid their debt to society" should become full citizens, including the right to vote.

◆ Instead of political gerrymandering rigging "elections" so they destroy electoral competition, a nonpartisan system of *former judges should oversee the drawing of the legislative lines,* as in Iowa.

◆ Congress should enact three campaign reforms—a) *establishing a system of public matching funds* for qualifying candidates so that small donors diminish the sway of big donors; b) providing *guaranteed TV/radio time* for qualifying federal candidates as a condition of holding lucrative Federal Communications Commission licenses; and c) prohibiting lobbyists from *picking up the tab for congressional junkets* and from hosting fundraisers in the Washington, D.C., area.

◆ Either *the Electoral College should be abolished* by Constitutional amendment and replaced by majority rule—or states should pass laws committing to cast their electoral votes for the winner of the national popular vote, which become binding when the states with such attain a majority in the Electoral College.

◆ Congress should *mandate annual oversight hearings* whenever either the chairman, or a third of a committee's members, believe that they're warranted.

◆ Because there's an established federal prosecution agency with a possible bias to allowing security concerns to supplant civil liberties concerns, *Congress should create a bipartisan Civil Liberties Protection Office.* It would watch out for civil liberties violations much like civilian review boards monitor local police departments—by receiving reports from federal agencies, launching investigations, issuing subpoenas, deposing witnesses, proposing laws and regulations, and reporting regularly to Congress.

✦ Votes on federal legislation should *not be held open for more than thirty minutes.*

✦ Federal or state programs that *proselytize for a particular faith* cannot receive public funds.

✦ *Science classes cannot teach religion or religious-based doctrine,* such as creationism or "intelligent design."

✦ The Federal Communications Commission shall *enact cross-media ownership rules* prohibiting one corporate owner from monopolizing print and electronic news in a defined population area.

✦ Early "open access" protections have fostered an Internet that promotes free, democratic discussion. To maintain it, telecommunications and cable companies must recommit to *treating all technologies and content equally to their own* (e.g., if Verizon owns a local cable infrastructure, the company cannot start forcing media outlets to pay for access to the public).

✦ To keep closing the digital divide and making government more accountable, *high-speed wireless Internet access should be treated as a utility,* like phones and electricity.

✦ States shall create a "civil Gideon"—*providing counsel to the indigent in major civil cases* as provided in criminal cases under *Gideon v. Wainwright.*

✦ CEOs should not earn (in pay or benefits) *more than fifty times more* than the lowest paid employee of a company, and the minimum wage—now a third less in real dollars than thirty years ago—should become a real living wage.

✦ Consumers shall *again be allowed to file consumer class actions* in state courts.

✦ A Presidential Executive Order should establish that a federal agency should *presume to release all reasonably requested information under the Freedom of Information Act,* unless it can be affirmatively shown that the information fits into an exempt category—i.e., there's a "right to know," not the requirement of proving a "need to know."

✦ *Presidents should obey the law.*

"Stronger than all the armies," Victor Hugo famously wrote, "is an idea whose time has come." The idea that democracy works and requires participating citizens is an idea that is coming again. It's time to put the self back in self-government.

ACKNOWLEDGMENTS

No book is an island, as John Dunne could have said. *Losing Our Democracy* would not exist without collaborators who helped me in every possible way.

Three experts especially—Miles Rapoport of Demos on "Voter Suppression: After Florida and Ohio," Peter Montgomery on "Religious Tyranny," and Adam Vogt on "Legislative Tyranny"—were brilliant collaborators on those sections. Executive director Lauren Strayer and research director Zac Rose at the New Democracy Project—the public policy organization that produced this volume—worked with great skill for much of 2005–2006 on all aspects of this book, from research to proofing. Kevin McCarthy and Gregory Krakower also lent their time and talent.

And a group of generous contributors enabled us at the New Democracy Project to spend the time necessary both to organize our January 2006 Cooper Union national conference, "Saving Our Democracy," as well as *Losing Our Democracy*. They include: Paul Beirne; Steven Gluckstern; Francis Greenburger and Isabelle Autones; Wade Greene; Jane and Sidney Harman; Anne Hess and Craig Kaplan; Fred Hochberg; Ken Lerer; William Little Jr.; Jeffrey and Tondra Lynford; Paul Newman; George and Dorothy Ring; Jane Rosenthal and Craig Hatkoff; Bernard and Irene Schwartz; David E. Shaw and Beth Kobliner Shaw; Sam Simon; Michael Sonnenfeldt and Katja Goldman; Katrina vanden Heuvel; Hermine Warren and Joseph Warren, The Dorothy Perlow Fund at the New York Community Trust; OPEIU and Michael Goodwin; Retail, Wholesale and Department Store Union and Stuart Appelbaum; SEIU Local 32BJ and Michael Fishman; UNITE HERE! and Bruce Raynor; and the United Federation of Teachers and Randi Weingarten.

Also, *Losing Our Democracy* occasionally relied on material in my prior books when earlier research coincided with an exact point in this volume—including *The Book on Bush: How George W. (Mis)leads America* (with Eric Alterman, Viking 2004) on Bush's misstatements and treatment of the SEC; *Selling Out* (ReganBooks 2002) on campaign finance; and *The Challenge of Hidden Profits* (with John Berry, William Morrow 1985).

The author is especially grateful for the generous institutional and intellectual support provided to the New Democracy Project—again both for the colloquium and this book—by the Nation Institute, Demos, and People For the American Way.

And, as always, I'm amazed at and reliant on the love of Deni, Jenya, and Jonah, who encouraged—and critiqued!—me throughout this journey toward a stronger democracy.

Mark Green
May 1, 2006

Endnotes

INTRODUCTION

3 **John Adams:** Sean Wilentz, *The Rise of American Democracy: Jefferson to Lincoln.* (2005).

4 **African American elected officials:** Rick Lyman, "Extension of Voting Act is Likely Despite Criticism." *New York Times,* March 29, 2006.

4 **William Galston and rules of the road:** William Galston, "Taking Liberties." *Washington Monthly,* April, 2005.

6 **Frank Luntz:** Ryan Lizza, "Write Off." *The New Republic,* March 14, 2005.

8 **Tom Paine:** Harvey J. Kaye, "The Lost Founder." *The American Prospect,* July, 2005.

CHAPTER 1. LEGISLATIVE TYRANNY I

9 **The two of us have been immersed:** Norman Ornstein and Thomas E. Mann, "If You Give a Congressman a Cookie." *New York Times,* January 19, 2006.

10 **Republicans' backing of Bush's agenda:** Peter Slevin and Chris Cillizza, "Cities Show All Politics Is Local by Weighing In on Iraq." *Washington Post,* November 20, 2005.

11 **Cannon and House rules:** Booth Mooney, *Mr. Speaker.* (1964) p. 101–102.

12 **To get along, go along:** Ronald M. Peters Jr., "Part II, Perspectives on the Speakership, Chapter 1, The Speakership in Historical Perspective." The Cannon Centenary Conference, November 12, 2003.

12 **Chameleon-like quality:** Marshall Frady, "The Big Guy." Book Review of *The Years of Lyndon Johnson: Master of the Senate* by Robert A. Caro. *New York Review of Books,* November 7, 2002.

13 **I believe in a division of labor:** David Donnelly, "President-Come-Lately." Tompaine.com, August 30, 2004 (www.tompaine.com/print/presidentcomelately.php).

13 **Tom DeLay's rise in politics:** Lou Dubose & Jan Reid, *The Hammer.* (2004) p. 39–41.

15 **I am the federal government:** Lloyd Grove, "Close, but No Cigar." *Washington Post,* May 15, 2003.

16 **College Republicans' political tactics:** Franklin Foer, "Writers' Bloc." *The New Republic,* May 16, 2005.

16 **The paragraphs on DeLay and the labor policies in the CNMI are largely drawn from:** Garance Franke-Ruta, "Perfectly Legal." *The American Prospect,* June 6, 2005.

16 **Pregnant workers forced to have abortions:** *ABC News,* "Women Forced to Work." 20/20 special investigation (www.globalexchange.org).

16 **The Commonwealth's garment industry produced:** James Brooke and Kate Zernike, "In Pacific Islands, Mixed Feelings About the Work of a Lobbyist." *New York Times,* May 6, 2005.

17 **DeLay's request for Abramoff to raise money:** Philip Shenon, "DeLay Asked Lobbyist to Raise Money Through Charity." *New York Times,* November 4, 2005.

17 **Meeting with Gale Norton:** John Solomon, "DeLay's Staff Tried to Help Abramoff." *Associated Press,* November 3, 2005.

18 **Abramoff on Bush's memory:** David Margolick, "Washington's Invisible Man." *Vanity Fair,* March, 2006.

19 **One of the weakest, most baseless indictments:** Alex Markels, "Tom DeLay: How the 'Hammer' Got Nailed." National Public Radio, December 6, 2005 (www.npr.org).

20 **Boehner distributing checks on the House floor:** Sheryl Gay Stolberg, "Push to Control Lobbying Produces Unexpected Shifts and Alliances." *New York Times,* January 18, 2006.

20 **Boehner parties:** Sam Rosenthal, "Meet the New Boss." *The American Prospect,* March, 2006.

20 **The real problem wasn't DeLay:** David Brooks, "Saving the House." *New York Times,* January 5, 2006.

20 **Partyology:** Miles Benson, "The Deficit Hawk Is Becoming an Endangered Species." *Newhouse News Service,* March 18, 2003.

20 **Earmarking $24 billion for 6,376 projects:** Jeff Jacoby, "The Republican pork barrel." *Boston Globe,* August 4, 2005.

20 **Armey revealed to a reporter:** Joe Conason, "Bush's Crony Capitalism Shows G.O.P.'s True Face." *New York Observer,* September 19, 2005.

22 **Kerry and McCain on fuel efficiency:** Nick Nyhart, "Counting Reasons Congress Hates, Won't Back Fuel Efficiency." *Dodge City Daily Globe,* April 26, 2002.

24 **"The problem with":** Interview with Ellen Miller, April 19, 2002.

25 **Private system of financing:** The author's 1991 study put the cost of federal corporate welfare at $50 billion, a number that would now be far higher given Bush's extensive corporate tax cuts: Public Citizen's Congress Watch and The Democracy Project, *Public Funding vs. Private Funding,* May, 1991.

26 **Taylor and Schlesinger:** See Mark Green, *Selling Out,* (2002) p.285–6.

27 **Business must learn the lesson:** Memo from Lewis Powell to Eugene B. Sydnor Jr., Chairman, Education Committee, U.S. Chamber of Commerce. Media Transparency, August 23, 1971 (www.mediatransparency.org).

28 **Lobbying and the 2003 Medicare law:** Robert Pear, "Medicare Law Prompts a Rush for Lobbyists." *New York Times,* August 23, 2005.

28 **The sum of all lobbies:** Thomas L. Friedman, "Too Much Pork and Too Little Sugar." *New York Times,* August 5, 2005.

29 **Nearly 2,300 energy companies:** "LobbyWatch: Issue—Energy & Nuclear." Center for Public Integrity, August 30, 2005 (www.public-i.org).

29 **Contributed over $180 million:** "Industries: Oil & Gas—Long-Term Contribution Trends." Center for Responsive Politics, August 30, 2005 (http://opensecrets.org/industries).

29 **Lobbyists, 9/11, the Iraq War, and Hurricane Katrina:** John M. Broder, "In Storm's Ruins, a Rush to Rebuild and Reopen for Business." *New York Times,* September 10, 2005.

30 **Rep. Joe Barton and influence of energy companies:** Adam Cohen, "A Lawmaker Works, Oddly Enough, to Keep His Voters' Backyards Dangerous." *New York Times,* May 26, 2005.

30 **Campaign contributions to Rep. Barton:** Center for Responsive Politics data, Chemical & Related Manufacturing industry contributions (http://opensecrets. org/industries).

30 **Oil & gas industry contributions:** Center for Responsive Politics data, Oil & Gas industry contributions (http://opensecrets.org/industries).

30 **The paragraphs on the GOP's financial advantage are drawn from data compiled by the Center for Responsive Politics:** (http://opensecrets.org/industries).

31 **Dachle staffer seeking lobbying job:** Geoff Earle, "Dems fear lobbying blacklist." *The Hill,* November 16, 2004.

31 **Studied insult; ability to work with the House and Senate is greatly reduced:** Elizabeth Drew, "Selling Washington." *New York Review of Books,* June 23, 2005.

32 **The Republican purge of K Stree:** Elizabeth Drew, "Selling Washington." *New York Review of Books,* June 23, 2005.

CHAPTER 2. LEGISLATIVE TYRANNY II

33 **For my purposes, they're irrelevant:** Juliet Eilperin, "House GOP Practices Art of One-Vote Victories." *Washington Post,* October 14, 2003.

33 **When you look at the way the House of Representatives:** "Clinton's 'plantation' remark draws fire." CNN, January 17, 2006 (www.cnn.com).

33 **Democratic Senators and Democratic votes:** Hendrik Hertzberg, "Nuke 'Em." *The New Yorker,* March 14, 2005.

34 **Bush votes and congressional districts:** Steven Hill, "Why the Democrats Will Keep Losing." *Mother Jones,* June 10, 2005.

34 **Bush and Gore split the vote:** Jeffrey Toobin, "The Great Election Grab." *The New Yorker,* December 8, 2003.

34 **The most heavy-handed, arrogant abuse of power:** Edward Epstein, "GOP makes time for Patriot Act vote." *San Francisco Chronicle,* July 9, 2004.

35 **The paragraphs on the House Republicans use of the Rules Committee to influence legislation are drawn from:** "Broken Promises: The Death of Deliberative Democracy." House Rules Committee Minority Office, March 8, 2005 (www.housedemocrats.gov/Docs/BrokenPromises.pdf).

36 **The House has become a place:** Statement of Rep. Jim McGovern (D-Mass.), House Rules Subcommittee on Technology Hearing, June 23, 2003 (http://thomas.loc.gov).

36 **Reagan on conference committees:** Paul C. Light, "Filibusters Are Only Half the Problem." *New York Times,* June 3, 2005.

37 **Rep. Markey excluded from energy bill conference:** Susan Milligan, "Back-room dealing a Capitol trend." *Boston Globe,* October 3, 2004.

37 **Clash between Rep. Thomas and Ways & Means Democrats:** James G. Lakely, "Thomas says he regrets calling Capitol Police." *Washington Times,* July 24, 2003.

39 **Senate Intelligence Committees:** Scott Shane, "Senate Panel's Partisanship Troubles Former Members." *New York Times,* March 12, 2006.

41 **Secret CIA prisons:** Dana Priest, "CIA Holds Terror Suspects in Secret Prisons." *Washington Post,* November 2, 2005.

41 **Hastert/Frist letter to Intelligence Committee chairmen:** Raw Story (http://rawstory.com).

42 **Badgering a lobbying organization over its hiring of a Democrat:** David Stout, "Ethics Panel Gives Rare Rebuke." *New York Times,* May 14, 1999.

42 **Votes postponed on trade measures:** David Plotz, "A Bug's Life." *Slate,* December 5, 1998 (www.slate.com).

44 **Rep. Lamar Smith's contributions to DeLay's defense fund:** Richard Simon, "DeLay Critic Removed from Ethics Committee." *Los Angeles Times,* February 3, 2005.

44 **Rep. Barney Frank discussing ethics committee:** Carl Hulse, "Steps toward standoff on House ethics panel." *New York Times,* April 18, 2005.

45 **Likened the Social Security program to an act of cannibalism:** "Janice Rogers Brown: In Her Own Words." People For the American Way Report (www.pfaw.org).

45 **An unconscionable act of judicial activism:** "The Dissents of Priscilla Owen: A Judicial Nominee Who Would Make the Law, Not Interpret It." People For the American Way Report, July 16, 2002 (www.pfaw.org).

45 **Pocket filibusters:** "The Senate, the Courts and the Blue Slip." People For the American Way Report, (www.pfaw.org).

46 **Sen. Frist and the attempted Paez filibuster:** "Frist's Hypocritical and Dishonest Attack on Democracy." Center for American Progress Report, January 4, 2005 (www.americanprogress.org).

46 **We did business that way for years:** Jeffrey Toobin, "Blowing Up the Senate." *The New Yorker,* March 7, 2005.

47 **Senatorial saucer:** U.S. Senate report, "Senate Legislative Process: Overview: The Legislative Framework in the Senate" (www.senate.gov/legislative/common/briefing/Senate_legislative_process.htm).

48 **Better hope the Democrats never regain:** Charles Babington, "Hey, They're Taking Slash-and-Burn to Extremes!" *Washington Post,* December 21, 2003.

49 **Democrats are certainly not without sin:** Jonathan Weisman, "Democrats Unveil Lobbying Curbs." *Washington Post,* January 19, 2006.

CHAPTER 3. RELIGIOUS TYRANNY

50 **Chellie Pingree on lobbying abuses:** Quoted in Jim Drinkard, "Lobbying Bill Quite Different from First Draft." *USA Today,* April 28, 2006.

51 **Blood-stained banner of the cross of Christ:** Ted Wendling, "Televangelist's Rally Draws 2,000 to State Capitol." *The Plain Dealer,* October 15, 2005.

52 **An agenda commanded by our God:** Mark Niquette, "'Let the Reformation Begin'; A Call for Converts, Voters." *The Columbus Dispatch,* October 15, 2005.

52 **Parsley's institutions and influence:** Sarah Posner, "With God on His Side." *The American Prospect,* November 23, 2005. A significant resource for information on Parsley's organizational muscle and influential role within the Republican Party.

52 **We cannot sit back:** Joe Hallett, "Blackwell Enlists Pastors to Mobilize 'Values Voters' for 2006." *The Columbus Dispatch,* August 26, 2005.

53 **Pastor trusted Bush:** Michelle Goldberg, "We Shall Overcome Liberals." *Salon,* January 9, 2006 (www.salon.com).

53 **Government get out of the way:** See Sarah Posner (above).

54 **Kennedy speech:** Address of Sen. John F. Kennedy to the Greater Houston Ministerial Association, September 12, 1960 (www.jfklibrary.org).

54 **Push the bishops:** John L. Allen, "The Word From Rome." *National Catholic Reporter,* June 11, 2004.

54 **Voting for Kerry would be a sin:** Sidney Blumenthal, "Holy Warriors." *Salon*, April 21, 2005 (www.salon.com).

56 **Ten Commandments:** "High Court Split on 10 Commandments." CNN, June 27, 2005 (www.cnn.com).

57 **Carter on fundamentalism:** Jimmy Carter, *Our Endangered Values*. 2005.

57 **Moral Majority was born:** Adele M. Stan, "The Religious Right of the '60s and '70s." *Mother Jones*, November/December, 2005.

57 **I endorse you:** William Martin, "How Ronald Reagan Wowed Evangelicals." *Christianity Today*, June 22, 2004.

57 **Instructions from God himself:** *Washington Post*, February 15, 1988 (www.mediamatters.org).

58 **Body bag:** Quote and other Christian Coalition history from People For the American Way (www.pfaw.org).

58 **Ralph Reed a candidate:** "You Ain't Seen Nothing Yet." *The Economist*, July 23, 2005.

58 **Pro-family:** Matthew Continetti, "A Decade of Reed." *Weekly Standard*, June 27, 2005.

58 **Tone down their rhetoric:** Carole Shields and Norman Lear, "Changing the Soul of Politics, With Civility." *Los Angeles Times*, June 17, 1996.

59 **Millions of voter guides:** See PFAW website history of Christian Coalition (www.pfaw.org).

59 **Rove would rather risk an international holy war:** Michele Cottle, *The New Republic*, April 21, 2003.

59 **Give up their Bibles:** Kevin Drum, "Bible Banning." *The Washington Monthly*, September 18, 2004.

59 **Pastors Netork:** David Kirkpatrick, "Pastors' Get-Out-the-Vote Training Could Test Tax Rules." *New York Times*, March 21, 2006.

59 **Tax exemption:** "IRS Overreach." *Washington Times* editorial, March 12, 2006.

60 **Death penalty for doctors:** Robert Schlesinger, "Medicine Man." *Salon*, September 13, 2004 (www.salon.com).

60 **Most influential evangelicals:** "The 25 Most Influential Evangelicals in America." *Time*, February 7, 2005.

60 **Own zip code:** Brian MacQuarrie, "Dobson Spiritual Empire Weilds Political Clout." *Boston Globe*, October 9, 2005.

60 **Utter destruction of the family:** "Dobson's Choice: Religious Right Leader Becomes Political Power Broker." People For the American Way Foundation Report, February 24, 2005.

60 **Compared Supreme Court to KKK:** "Dobson dissembled, backed away from earlier comparison of Supreme Court to KKK." Media Matters for America, May 25, 2005 (http://mediamatters.org).

61 **Specter's right-wing challenger:** Gail Russell Chaddock, "Senate Race Highlights GOP Divide." *Christian Science Monitor*, April 26, 2004.

61 **Money paid to Duke:** Max Blumenthal, "Justice Sunday Preachers." *The Nation*, April 26, 2005 (www.thenation.com).

61 **Hostile to Christianity:** Rob Garver, "Justice Sunday." *The American Prospect*, April 13, 2005 (www.prospect.org).

62 **D. James Kennedy:** Information on Kennedy's organizations from People For the American Way online reporting on Kennedy remarks (www.pfaw.org).

62 **Skepticism, atheism, Marxism, humanism, and secularism:** D. James Kennedy and Jerry Newcombe, "One Nation Under God." Coral Ridge Ministries Newsletter, October 2003.

62 **A lie propagated by Thomas Jefferson:** Rob Boston, "D. James Kennedy: Who Is He and What Does He Want?" *Church & State,* Americans United for Separation of Church and State; April 1999.

62 **Reclaim America for Christ:** Rob Boston, "D. James Kennedy: Who Is He and What Does He Want?" *Church & State,* Americans United for Separation of Church and State; April 1999.

62 **Distinguished Christian Statement Award:** People For the American Way (www.pfaw.org).

62 **New breed of leaders:** Jackson and Sheldon quotes from Neela Banerjee, "Black Churches Struggle Over Their Role in Politics." *New York Times,* March 6, 2005.

62 **High Impact Leadership Coalition:** Jackson information from "Background Info: Coalition of African American Pastors and Bill Owens" (www.savethecourt.org).

63 **No man shall be compelled:** Thomas Jefferson Memorial, National Park Service (www.nps.gov/thje).

63 **Dance with the one who brung him:** Carol Eisenberg, "Religious Political Revival." *Newsday,* November 5, 2004.

63 **They despise your Christ:** Errol Louis, "The Scary Right." *New York Daily News,* November 26, 2004.

64 **Arlington Group:** David Kirkpatrick and Sheryl Gay Stolberg, "Backers of Gay Marriage Ban Use Social Security as Cudgel." *New York Times,* January 25, 2005.

64 **McCain and Falwell:** Gal Beckerman, "McCain, Reconsidered." *CJR Daily,* Real-Time Media Criticism from *The Columbia Journalism Review;* April 6, 2006.

64 **McCain to Stewart:** *The Daily Show with Jon Stewart,* posted on Crooks and Liars (www.crooksandliars.com).

65 **Incompatibility between fundamentalism and democracy:** Andrew Sullivan, "Christianists and Islamists." The Daily Dish blog, February 6, 2006 (http://time.blogs.com/daily_dish).

66 **Demands of dogma:** Andrew Sullivan, "Pharmacists and Fundamentalists." The Daily Dish blog, January 30, 2006 (http://time.blogs.com/daily_dish).

67 **War between law and religion:** Chronology of congressional and White House action on Schiavo case taken from Carl Hulse and David Kirkpatrick, "Congress Passes and Bush Signs Legislation on Schiavo Case." *New York Times,* March 21, 2005 and Steven Thomma, "How GOP base flexed its political muscle." *Knight Ridder* Newspapers, March 21, 2005.

67 **They will of course deserve it:** Peggy Noonan, "Don't Kick It." *Wall Street Journal,* March 18, 2005.

67 **Starvation and Dehydration of Persons with Disabilities Prevention Act:** Pete Winn, "Schiavo the Subject of Last-Minute Legislative Flurry." Focus on the Family Citizen Link alert, March 17, 2005.

67 **Political dirty trick:** Mike Allen, "Counsel to GOP Senator Wrote Memo on Schiavo." *Washington Post,* April 7, 2005.

67 **She won't do it:** Sidney Blumenthal, "A Confederacy of Shamans." *Guardian,* March 24, 2005.

68 Absurdity of self-proclaimed defenders: William Saletan, "As She Lay Dying." *New York Times Book Review,* November 6, 2005.

68 Ending life support...for poor patients: E. J. Dionne Jr., "A Thin View of Life." *Washington Post,* March 25, 2005.

68 Not let her go peacefully: "The Nation Reacts." Focus on the Family Citizen Link Alert, March 31, 2005.

68 Judeo-Christian Council for Constitutional Restoration: Conference information from "The Right's Crusade Against the Independent Judiciary." People For the American Way Right-Wing Watch Online, April 2005 (www.pfaw.org).

68 No man, no problem: Dana Milbank, "And the Verdict on Justice Kennedy Is: Guilty." *Washington Post,* April 9, 2005.

69 Political extension of a religious movement: John C. Danforth, "In the Name of Politics." *New York Times,* March 30, 2005.

69 Phillips and *New York Times* poll: Kevin Phillips, "Theoncons and Theocrats." *The Nation,* May 1, 2006.

69 The category of being theocrats: Ryan Lizza, "Beached Party: Republicans Prepare for Life After Bush." *The New Republic,* October 21, 2005.

69 Half of Congress backed by Religious Right: Bill Moyers, "There Is No Tomorrow." *The StarTribune,* January 30, 2005.

70 $25 million Creation Museum: Michael Powell, "In Evolution Debate, Creationists Are Breaking New Ground." *Washington Post,* September 25, 2005.

70 IMAX theaters refusing to book documentaries: Cornelia Dean, "A New Screen Test for Imax: It's the Bible vs. the Volcano." *New York Times,* March 19, 2005.

70 Museum reconsidered: Alan Leshner, CEO of American Association for the Advancement of Science, letter to the Association of Science-Technology Centers, March 28, 2005.

70 Symptoms of rejecting a Supreme Being: "Creationism Show Trial." People For the American Way Right-Wing Watch Online, March 2005 (www.pfaw.org)

71 Dr. Kenneth Miller...reconciles faith in God and faith in science: Liz Marlantes, "The Evolution of a Controversy." *The Christian Science Monitor,* December 23, 1999.

71 Dr. Robert Jones: Robert Jones, Center for American Values in Public Life, People For the American Way Foundation, interview by email.

71 Court rulings on creationism: "The Evolution Controversy: Historical Timeline." American Geophysical Union (www.agu.org).

72 "Both sides ought to be properly taught": Jacob Weisberg, "Evolution vs. Religion." *Slate,* August 10, 2005 (www.slate.com).

72 Watch in a field: Richard Milner & Vittorio Maestro, eds., "Intelligent Design? A Special Report." *Natural History,* April 2002.

72 The science within these papers has been demolished: Jonathan Alter, "Monkey See, Monkey Do." *Newsweek,* August 15, 2005.

72 *National Geographic:* David Quammen, "Was Darwin Wrong?" *National Geographic,* October 2004.

72 American Association for the Advancement of Science resolution: Ben Adler, "Evolutionary War." *The New Republic,* July 7, 2005 (www.tnr.com).

72 Dembski and Baylor University: Laurie Goodstein, "Intelligent Design Might Be Meeting Its Maker." *New York Times,* December 4, 2005.

73 **Santorum and No Child Left Behind:** Glenn Branch, "Farewell to the Santorum Amendment?" National Center for Science Education.

73 **45 percent of Americans believe:** Jacob Weisberg, "Evolution vs. Religion." *Slate*, August 10, 2005 (www.slate.com).

73 **Grand Canyon:** Leon Jaroff, "Faith-Based Parks? Creationists Meet the Grand Canyon." *Time*, November 17, 2004.

73 **Thomas More Law Center:** Laurie Goodstein, "In Intelligent Design Case, a Cause in Search of a Lawsuit." *New York Times*, November 4, 2005.

74 **Dover intelligent design ruling by Judge Jones:** Martha Raffaele, "Judge Bars 'Intelligent Design' From Classrooms." *Associated Press*, December 20, 2005.

74 **Robertson on God and Dover:** Pat Robertson, appearing on *The 700 Club*, November 9, 2005. Robertson said, "I'd like to say to the good citizens of Dover. If there is a disaster in your area, don't turn to God, you just rejected Him from your city. And don't wonder why He hasn't helped you when problems begin, if they begin. I'm not saying they will, but if they do, just remember, you just voted God out of your city. And if that's the case, don't ask for His help because He might not be there."

74 **Scientists named Steve:** Jerry Adler, "Doubting Darwin." *Newsweek*, February 7, 2005.

74 **Wedge strategy:** "The Wedge Strategy," Center for the Renewal of Science and Culture (www.stephenjaygould.org/ctrl/crsc_wedge.html).

75 **Of course my motives were religious:** "Sabotaging Science: Creationist Strategy in the 1990s." People For the American Way Foundation Report, November 1999.

75 **Krauthammer on intelligent design:** Charles Krauthammer, "Let's Have No More Monkey Trials." *Time*, August 8, 2005.

75 **Can you imagine? Four appointments!:** Ron Suskind, "Without a Doubt." *New York Times Magazine*, October 17, 2004.

76 **Tear away at our moral foundation:** "Judicial Tyranny." Center for Moral Clarity (www.centerformoralclarity.net/pdf/CRJudicialTyranny.pdf).

76 **Revolution:** Pat Robertson, *700 Club*, November 8, 1999, People For the American Way press release, "Robertson Urges Revolt, Tells Viewers: Throw Off the Shackles of the Courts."

77 **Herdahl story:** "Lisa Herdahl's Struggle for Religious Liberty in Pontotoc County, Mississippi." People For the American Way Foundation Report.

77 **Rosenauer:** Steven Rosenauer, Testimony Before the U.S. Senate Judiciary Subcommittee on the Constitution, Civil Rights and Property Rights, June 8, 2004, available at People For the American Way Foundation Clients: Profiles in Courage (www.pfaw.org/pfaw).

78 **Bailout and betrayal:** Focus on the Family press release, May 23, 2005.

79 **Anti-Catholic:** Paul Kane, "Second Round of 'Anti-Catholic' Ads Slated." *Roll Call*, August 18, 2003.

79 **Weird social experiments:** "Rick Scarborough Calls on President to Appoint a Constitutionalist to Replace O'Connor." Vision America press release, July 1, 2005.

79 **Thomas does not believe First Amendment applies to the states:** "Courting Disaster 2005." People For the American Way Foundation Report, 2005.

80 **Rob us of our Christian heritage:** Charles Babington, "Frist to Participate in Anti-Filibuster Telecast." *Washington Post*, April 16, 2005.

80 **Choose between his faith in Christ and public service:** Alfred Doblin, "Defend the faith, then define it." *Herald News* (Passaic County, NJ) April 22, 2005.

80 **Second Justice Sunday:** Quotes by Jim Daly and Zell Miller from "Justice Sunday II: A promise to 'bring the rule and reign of the cross.'" People For the American Way (www.pfaw.org).

80 **Overt attack on Christmas:** "The Right Wing's War on 'Happy Holidays.'" People For the American Way (www.pfaw.org).

81 **War on Christmas:** Notes on "War on Christians" conference from People For the American Way Foundation Report (www.pfaw.org).

81 **Harrassed as heathen:** David Van Biema, "Whose God Is Their Co-Pilot?" *Time*, June 27, 2005.

81 **Atmosphere of religious intolerance:** "Air Force Academy Leader Admits Religious Intolerance at School." Associated Press, June 3, 2005.

81 **Denigrating and demonizing Christians:** Mike Allen, "GOP Congressman Calls Democrats Anti-Christian." *Washington Post*, June 21, 2005.

82 **Diana Eck on religious pluralism:** Dr. Diana L. Eck, Keynote Address, MAAS International Conference on Religious Pluralism in Democratic Societies, August 20–21, 2002.

82 **Ash heap of history:** "Low-Lights from the Right." People For the American Way, June 7, 2005.

82 **Executive orders:** Amy Sullivan, "Faith Without Works." *Washington Monthly*, October, 2004.

82 **$204 million to teach abstinence:** Jackie Calmes, "Bush Adds to Various Constituent Programs." *Wall Street Journal*, February 21, 2006.

83 **Operation Blessing:** Bill Sizemore, "Religious charities putting their faith in federal money." *The Virginian-Pilot*, January 28, 2006.

83 **Bush chose rich over poor:** Amy Sullivan, "Faith Without Works." *Washington Monthly*, October, 2004.

83 **Head of the Religious Right:** Dana Milbank, "Religious Right Finds Its Center in Oval Office." *Washington Post*, December 24, 2001.

84 **Bush and God:** Kevin Phillips, "Theocons and Theocrats." *The Nation*, May 1, 2006.

84 **The delusional is no longer marginal:** Bill Moyers, "There is No Tomorrow." *Star-Tribune*, January 30, 2005.

CHAPTER 4. CORPORATE TYRANNY I

86 **Lindblom quotation:** C. Lindblom, *Politics and Markets: The World's Political-Economic Systems.* (1977) p. 356.

88 **Senator Paul Douglas:** Lindblom, p. 31

89 **Caro on LBJ:** *Master of the Senate.* (1902) p. 411–412.

89 **Numbers of Lobbyists:** Jeffery H. Birnbaum, "The Road to Riches Is Called K Street." *Washington Post*, June 22, 2005.

89 **Sidney Blumenthal on lobbying:** "Fall of the Rovian Empire?" *Salon*, October 6, 2005 (www.salon.com).

89 **Allen Cigler comment:** in Jeffrey H. Birnbaum, "The Road to Riches Is Called K Street." *Washington Post*, June 22, 2005.

90 **Michael Kinsley comment:** "Business as Usual: Corrupt." *Washington Post*, December 2, 2005.

90 **Vioxx and FDA panel:** Gardner Hariss and Alex Berenson, "10 Advisors Voting on Pain Pills' Sale Have Industry Ties." *New York Times*, February 25, 2005.

90 **JD Williams comment:** William Greider, *Who Will Tell the People: The Betrayal of American Democracy.* (1992) p. 256.

91 **Hewlett-Packard director comment:** Jeffrey H. Birnbaum, "The Road to Riches Is Called K Street." *Washington Post*, June 22, 2005.

92 **Jim VandeHei analysis:** "Business Sees Gain in GOP Takeover." *Washington Post*, March 27, 2005.

95 **Warren Buffet on "Dead Billionaires Tax":** *Newsday*, May 25, 2003.

96 **Michael Scherer on tax bill and Bush's comments at Wilkes-Barre:** "Make Your Taxes Disappear." *Mother Jones*, March/April, 2005

97 **Antonia Lopez Paz:** Steven Greenhouse, "Union Organizers at Poultry Plants in South Find Newly Sympathetic Ears." *New York Times*, September 6, 2005.

98 **Productivity study:** Mark Green and John F. Berry, *The Challenge of Hidden Profits.* (1985) p. 108, 116.

98 **Taco Bell Boycott:** Katie Renz, "People Power: An Interview with David Solnit." *Mother Jones*, March 22, 2005.

98 **Coalition of Immokalee Workers:** Bill Broadway, "Churches Back Boycott Over Migrant Workers; Labor Unions Decry Treatment by Taco Bell, Mt. Olive Suppliers." *Washington Post*, November 22, 2003 and Bernice Powell Jackson, "Witness to Justice." *Philadelphia Tribune*, March 29, 2005.

98 **Wal-Mart actually increases countywide poverty rates:** Liza Featherstone, "Wal-Mart's P.R. War." *Salon*, August 2, 2005 (www.salon.com).

98 **Health Insurance:** James B. Parks, "Forging a Common Vision." *America@work*, February 2003.

99 **Stats on percentages of organized labor:** "Brothers at arms." *The Economist*, May 12, 2005.

99 **Stuck in bad jobs and Glenn quote:** Joel Millman, "Moving Up: Challenges to the American Dream." *Wall Street Journal*, June 6, 2005.

99 **Bernard quotation:** David Glenn, "Labor's Diversionary Tactics." *Mother Jones*, April 13, 1997.

99 **Manufacturing Job Loss Stats:** James B. Parks, "Forging a Common Vision." *America@work,* February 2003.

99 **Reagan de-funds NLRB:** Eds., "Labor Pains." *The New Republic*, January 17, 2005.

100 **NLRB case statistics:** Ralph Nader, "The Good Fight." (2004) p. 146.

100 **NLRB bias:** Eds. "Labor Pains." *The New Republic*, January 17, 2005.

100 **NLRB rulings and Gross quote:** Steven Greenhouse, "Labor Board's Detractors See Bias Against Workers." *New York Times*, January 2, 2005.

100 **"Loosening" of OSHA:** Stephanie Armour and Michelle Kessler, "Outsourcing, friction with labor to go on." *USA Today*, November 4, 2004 and Asra Q. Nomani, "Businesses find allies to launch attacks on federal job-safety and labor regulations." *Wall Street Journal*, July 20, 1995.

101 **U.S. Trade Deficit Review Commission stats:** Ralph Nader, "The Good Fight." (2004) p. 145.

101 **Titan International:** Russell Mokhiber and Robert Weissman, "Enemies of the future: The ten worst corporations of 2000." *Multinational Monitor*, December, 2000.

101 **America's bad labor laws:** Richard B. Freeman and Joel Rogers, "A Proposal to American Labor." *The Nation*, June 24, 2002.

101 **Property rights:** Kim Phillips-Fein, "A More Perfect Union Buster." *Mother Jones*, September/October, 1998.

102 **Nader on the "right to work":** Ralph Nader, "The Good Fight." (2004) p. 147.

102 **Examples of the government busting its own unions:** Stephen Barr, "New Homeland Security Work Rules Blocked." *Washington Post*, August 15, 2005.

102 **Suspension of guidelines:** John R. Wilkie and Brody Mullins, "After Katrina, Republicans Back a Sea of Conservative Ideas." *Wall Street Journal*, September 15, 2005.

102 **Governors weaken unions:** Joi Preciphs, "Three Republican Governors Hit Unions." *Wall Street Journal*, August 11, 2005.

102 **Permanent leave vs. firing:** Ralph Nader, "The Good Fight." (2004) p. 148.

102 **20,000 workers fired:** JoAnn Wypijewski, "The Days of Bread and Roses." *Mother Jones*, July/August, 2005.

103 **Lobbying figures:** LobbyWatch the Center for Public Integrity and Lou Dobbs, "Lobbying against America." CNN, August 8, 2005 (http://money.cnn.com).

CHAPTER 5. CORPORATE TYRANNY II

105 **Merton observations:** David Callahan, *The Cheating Culture*. (2004).

106 ***Wall Street Journal* on crime:** November 11, 1975, p. 22.

107 **Surveys on business fraud:** This paragraph is drawn from Mark Green, *The Challenge of Hidden Profits: Reducing Corporate Bureaucracy and Waste*. (1985) p. 258.

107 **Business Week poll of CFOs:** Cited in Michael Kramer, "Step One: Limit All Those Options." *New York Daily News*, July 10, 2002.

107 **Ethics Resource Center:** Cited in David Callahan, *The Cheating Culture*. (2004) p. 283.

108 **"Elite group of Wall Street Internet pundits":** Om Malik, "To Be an Internet Analyst." *Forbes*, February 25, 1999 (www.forbes.com).

108 **Blodget & Merrill emails:** "Vested Interest." *NOW*, May 31, 2002. PBS (www.pbs.org/now).

108 **Mollifying investment bankers:** "The Sheriff of Wall Street." *60 Minutes*, May 25, 2003. CBS (www.cbsnews.com).

108 **Merrill Lynch manager:** Testimony of Eliot Spitzer. United States Senate Committee On Commerce, Science and Technology Subcommittee on Consumer Affairs, Foreign Commerce and Tourism. Hearing on Corporate Governance. Washington, D.C., June 26, 2002.

108 **Firing analysts:** "The Sheriff of Wall Street." *60 Minutes*, May 25, 2003. CBS (www.cbsnews.com).

109 **Checks for investors:** Greg Farrell, "Checks for Faulty Research Goes Out." *USA Today*, December 21, 2005 (www.usatoday.com/money).

109 **Discussion of Marsh & McLennan's practices and deceptions:** *People v. Marsh & McLennan*. Complaint, reprinted at www.oag.state.ny.us/press/2004/oct/oct14a_04_attach1.pdf. (Oct. 14, 2004) ("Complaint").

110 **Marsh's victims:** Office of New York Attorney General Eliot Spitzer, "Investigation Reveals Widespread Corruption in Insurance Industry." Press Release, October 14, 2004.

110 **"Crimes against capitalism":** Editorial, "Why Insurance Needs a Cleanup." *Business Week,* November 1, 2004.

110 **Outcome of Marsh's crimes:** Office of New York Attorney General Eliot Spitzer, "Insurance Broker Agrees to Sweeping Reforms." Press Release, January 31, 2005.

110 **FDR and power companies:** Asif M. Ismail, "Enron's Deregulation Fight." The Center for Public Integrity, January 6, 2003.

110 **Enron argues against PUHCA:** Josh Feit, "Zapped." *Willamette Week,* Portland's News Weekly. August 5, 1998.

110 **Enron focuses on deregulation:** Asif M. Ismail, "Enron's Deregulation Fight." The Center for Public Integrity, January 6, 2003.

110 **Enron in California:** Bethany McLean and Peter Elkins, *The Smartest Guys in the Room: The Amazing Rise and Scandalous Fall of Enron.* (2004) p. 265.

110 **The California energy crisis:** Bethany McLean and Peter Elkins, *The Smartest Guys in the Room: The Amazing Rise and Scandalous Fall of Enron.* (2004) p. 267-274.

111 **Enron traders recorded:** Richard A. Oppel Jr., "Word for Word/Energy Hogs; Enron Traders on Grandma Millie and Making Out Like Bandits." *New York Times,* June 13, 2004.

112 **Herbert Edelbertz comment:** *The Nature, Impact and Prosecution of White Collar Crime.* The National Institute of Law Enforcement and Criminal Justice (1970).

112 **Inflates prices by some 25 percent:** Snuth, "Antitrust and the Monopoly Problem: Toward a More Relevant Legal Analysis." *Antitrust Law and Economics Review,* Spring, 1969, p. 79.

112 **Savings from Clean Air Act:** Information can be found on the Sierra Club's website, (www.sierraclub.org/cleanair).

113 **Liberty Mutual Report:** Dar Haddix, "AFL-CIO Marks Workers' Memorial Day." UPI, 2004. This article can be found archived at (www.washingtontimes.com).

114 **John De Lorean comment:** "How Moral Men Make Immoral Decisions—A Look Inside GM." Mark Green and Robert Massie, *The Big Business Reader: Essays on Corporate America.* (1980) p. 43.

114 **Best studies on "waste, fraud and abuse":** See chart in Mark Green and John F. Berry, *The Challenge of Hidden Profits: Reducing Corporate Bureaucracy and Waste.* (1985) p. 386–387.

116 **Christopher Stone comment:** *Where the Law Ends.* (1975) p. 46.

117 **Newsday on Bush's Regent Hotel Speech:** Ellils Henican, "Don't Believe Tough Talk." *Newsday,* July 10, 2002.

118 **Arthur Leavitt comment:** *Take on the Street: What Wall Street and Corporate America Don't Want You to Know.* (2002) p. 119.

118 ***Newsweek* on Pitt:** Jonathan Alter, "Whose Side Is Bush On?" *Newsweek,* July 22, 2002.

118 **Appointing a laissez-faire Republican:** Robert Kottner, "Bubblehead." *The American Prospect,* August 2005.

120 ***Economist* on Sarbanes-Oxley:** "A Price Worth Paying?" *The Economist,* May 21, 2005.

120 **Alan Hevesi comment:** Stephen Labaton, "Four Years Later, Enron's Shadow Lingers as Change Comes Slowly." *New York Times,* January 5, 2006.

121 **Alan Greenspan about income disparity:** David Cay Johnson, "Richest Are Leaving Even the Rich Far Behind." *New York Times,* June 5, 2005.

122 *Crain's* chart: "New York Area's Fortunate 100." *Crain's New York Business*, June 20, 2005.

122 It's interesting to break down this $113.7 million. $42.7 million is a departure bonus based on the company's 2005 pretax profit, although it fell from 2004 to 2005. He's also getting $54.8 million of restricted stock and stock options, plus retirement benefits with a value of $11 million. And there's also "medical benefits, an office, and administrative and secretarial expenses every year for the rest of his life, and, Morgan Stanley will make $250,000 in charitable donations a year in his name." Remember, this was a package for someone *who was fired.*

122 **Purcell and Crawford deals:** Material drawn from Eric Dash, "The Reward for Leaving: $113 million." *New York Times*, July 16, 2005.

123 **Tom Friedman on Mack:** "Learning from Lance." *New York Times*, July 27, 2005.

123 **David Brooks of DHB Industries:** Editorial, "Another Marie Antoinette Moment." *New York Times*, January 2, 2006.

124 **"The showy wealth":** Geraldine Fabrikant, "Old Nantucket Warily Meets the New." *New York Times*, June 5, 2005.

124 **Buffet in 2005 annual report:** Gretchen Morganson, "Consultants' Pay Advice May Not be Independent." *New York Times*, April 10, 2006.

125 **Barney Frank comment:** Joseph Nocera, "Disclosure Won't Tame CEO Pay." *New York Times*, January 14, 2006.

125 **Century Foundation on household income and wealth:** *The New American Economy: A Rising Tide That Lifts Only Yachts.* (2004).

126 **Gene Sperling on pensions and savings:** "Building a Real Investor Class." *Blueprint Magazine*, June 30, 2003.

126 **Spend everything and save nothing:** David K. Shipler, *The Working Poor.* (2005) p. 4.

127 **Philip L. Swagel comment:** "Working Families Win." Project of Americans for Democratic Action Fund, September 2, 2005. See also *New York Times*, August 31, 2005.

129 No-bid contracts for the Katrina cleanup grew so frequent that even the Homeland Security Department's inspector general publicly said, "We are very apprehensive about what we are seeing." He should be. Major beneficiaries include the Shaw Group and Kellogg, Brown & Root, a subsidiary of Halliburton, both previously represented by Joe Allbaugh—who was Bush's 1990 presidential campaign manager, former head of FEMA, and college buddy of Michael "Heckuva job, Brownie" Brown.

Over at the Pentagon, a veteran army contracting officer complained about a Kellogg, Brown & Root oil contract in Iraq—one among many Iraq contracts worth $10 billion to the form—as "the most blatant and improper contract abuse that I have witnessed during the course of my professional career." She added that the defense secretary's office had improperly interfered in the awarding of the contract. In response, the Pentagon demoted her for "poor job performance."

129 **The most blatant and improper conduct:** Erik Eckholm, "Army Contract Official Critical of Halliburton Pact is Demoted." *New York Times*, August 29, 2005.

129 **Kelliher email:** Natural Resources Defense Council press release, April 26, 2002 (www.nrdc.org).

130 **Declining consumer confidence:** Paul Krugman, "Secretary, Protect Yourself." *New York Times,* June 2, 2006.

Chapter 6. Voter Suppression

132 **International Voter Turnout Statistics:** "Voter Turnout Since 1945: A Global Report." *Turnout in the world—country by country performance, Section II* (2002). International Institute for Democracy & Electoral Assistance (IDEA). (www.idea.int/vt/survey/voter_turnout_pop2.cfm).

132 **2000 Demographic Profile:** U.S. Census Bureau. *Census 2000 Demographic Profile Highlights.* (http://factfinder.census.gov).

132 **Global statistics on women's balance in national parliaments:** "Getting the Balance Right In National Parliaments." *Gender & Governance Program, Factsheet 4* (2005) Women's Environment & Development Organization (WEDO). (www.wedo.org/files/5050factsheet4.pdf).

133 **Brazil's Corruption Scandal:** "Holier-than-thou no more." *The Economist,* July 12, 2005.

133 **Carter's rejection to monitor a U.S. election:** Andrew Gumbel, *Steal this Vote: Dirty Elections and the Rotten History of Democracy in America.* (2005) p.1.

133 **Canada's Election Administration:** André Blais, Louis Massicotte, and Antoine Yoshinaka, *Establishing the Rules of the Game: Election Laws in Democracies.* (2004).

134 **International voter registration procedures:** Pennsylvania Election Reform Task Force, *Task (d) Document Library—Voter Participation.* (www.dos.state.pa.us).

134 **Compulsory voting in Australia:** Australian Electoral Commission, *Electoral Backgrounder No. 17: Compulsory Voting.* (www.aec.gov.au).

135 **Elections in Puerto Rico:** Roman, Ivan, "Let Puerto Rico Show You How to Run an Election." *Orlando Sentinel.*

135 **Voting in Puerto Rico:** Anna. Telephone interview, January 27, 2006.

135 **John Pappageorge on voter suppression:** "Locally Speaking." *Detroit Free Press,* July 16, 2004.

136 **Voter suppression:** Jo Becker and David Finkel, "Voting tricks hit new lows." *Houston Chronicle,* November 1, 2004. Jo Becker and David Finkel, "Now they're registered, now they're not." *Washington Post,* October 29, 2004.

138 **Voter Intimidation:** Garance Franke-Ruta and Harold Meyerson, "The GOP Deploys." *The American Prospect,* February, 2004.

139 **Election Day Challengers in Michigan:** David Eggert, "Challengers Challenged on Election Day in Michigan." *Associated Press State & Local Wire,* November 3, 2004; David Eggert, "Michigan GOP files a lawsuit over election challengers." *Associated Press State & Local Wire,* November 2, 2004.

139 **Questionable addresses:** Greg J. Borowski, "GOP demands IDs of 37,000 in City." *Milwaukee Journal Sentinel,* October 30, 2004. Meg Jones, "GOP, city reach deal on voter list." *Milwaukee Journal Sentinel,* October 31, 2004.

139 **Mail-checks:** Andrew Welsh-Huggins, "Ohio GOP loses bid to fight registrations." *Associated Press,* October 29, 2004.

139 **Ohio lawsuits:** Connie Mabin, "Little-used 1953 law in battleground Ohio allows voter challenges." *Associated Press,* October 14, 2004.

139 **Vote challenge disparities:** "Election contests thwarted." *The Enquirer,* October 30, 2004.

140 **Emergency stay:** Melissa Block and Robert Siegel, "Ohio court rules only poll workers can challenge voters' eligibility." *All Things Considered,* National Public

Radio, November 1, 2004; Lisa A. Abraham, "Federal Judges Issue Stay of Two Earlier Rulings." *Akron Beacon Journal*, November 2, 2004.

140 **Minority debarment:** Greg Palast, "The Best Democracy Money Can Buy." Plume: 2003, p. 11–12; Hearing before the United States Commission on Civil Rights on information regarding ChoicePoint's work with the Florida Division of Elections. "Statement of George Bruder, Vice President Public Records Group ChoicePoint Inc." February 16, 2001 (www.choicepoint.net).

141 **State abandons felon list:** Bill Cotterell, "Nelson joins suit to open records." *Tallahassee Democrat*, June 8, 2004; Lesley Clark, "List Abandoned, but Doubts Linger." *Miami Herald*, July 17, 2004; Chris Davis and Matthew Doig, "E-mail on Felon List Contradicts Governor." *Sarasota Herald-Tribune*, October 6, 2004.

141 **80 pound card stock:** Secretary of State J. Kenneth Blackwell, Directive No. 2004–31 September 7, 2004.

141 **Blackwell retracts:** Catherine Candisky, "Secretary of State Lifts Order on Voting Forms." *Columbus Dispatch*, September 30, 2004.

141 **Dismissing registrations:** Jay Weaver, "Judge Takes up Rejected Voting Forms." *Miami Herald*, October 16, 2004.

142 **Judge blames Blackwell:** House Judiciary Committee Democratic Staff, *Preserving Democracy: What Went Wrong in Ohio.* January 5, 2005 (www.nvri.org/about/ohio_conyers_report_010505.pdf).

142 **Short poll workers:** "U.S. short at least 500,000 poll workers." *Associated Press.* October 29, 2005.

142 **Short bilingual poll workers:** "Severe shortage of poll workers." *New York Times*, November 1, 2004.

143 **Polling workforce:** National Conference of State Legislatures, *Voting in America: Final Report of the NCSL Election Reform Task Force, Recommendations on Election Day Workers.* August, 2001 (www.ncsl.org).

143 *Financial Times* **on separate election authorities:** Editorial, "Electronic Voting Switch Threatens Mass Confusion." *Financial Times*, May 1, 2006.

144 **Kenyon College lines:** Ford Fessenden and James Dao, "Ohio Remains A Battleground As Late Voting Delays Count." *New York Times*, November 3, 2004.

144 **Refusal to keep polls open:** "Ohioans Suffer through Long Lines, Leave Lawsuits to Others." *Akron Beacon Journal*, November 3, 2004.

145 **Fewer machines:** "Suburbs were busiest, even with more machines." *Columbus Dispatch*, November 5, 2004.

145 **Losing machines:** Ohio Public hearings on Election Day 2004 irregularities: Cleveland, Ohio Public Hearings. People For the American Way. November 13–15, 2004.

147 Direct Recording Electronic voting machines (DREs) are an electronic implementation of the old mechanical lever systems. Like lever machines, there is no ballot. The possible choices are visible to the voter on the front of the machine and the voter directly enters their choices with the use of a touch-screen push-button. Voter's choices are stored in these machines via a memory cartridge, diskette, or smart-card and added to the choices of all other voters. An Optical Scan System reads and tabulates paper ballots that have been marked by a voter. These paper ballots can be hand-counted if necessary.

147 **Bev Harris observation:** Bev Harris, "Perils to Democracy by Electronic Voting." *A Buzzflash Interview*, December 4, 2003.

148 **Bev Harris warning:** Bev Harris, *Black Box Voting: Ballot Tampering in the 21st Century.* (2004) p. 64.

148 **Why paper trails matter:** "Election Reform Briefing 12: Recounts: From Punch Cards to Paper Trails." Electionline.org. October 2005 (www.electionline.org).

148 **20 States continue to use punch card voting systems:** Election Assistance Committee, *2004 Election Day Survey Results, Chapter 10 Voting Machines* (www.eac.gov).

150 **Personal stories of felony disenfranchisement:** Sasha Abramsky, "Despite New Victories, Disenfranchisement Laws Continue to Erode Democracy in the U.S."*Demos Democracy Dispatches*, December 12, 2005.

150 **Florida House Speaker Feeney on Felony Disenfranchisement:** Sasha Abramsky, *Conned: How Millions Went to Prison, Lost the Vote, and Helped Send George W. Bush to the White House.* (2006), p. 30.

151 **Easy disenfranchisement:** Marc Mauer And Tushar Kansal, "Barred for Life: Voting Rights Restoration in Permanent Disenfranchisement States." The Sentencing Project, February, 2005.

151 **A state-by-state report card of felony disenfranchisement laws:** "Right to Vote, Purged! Will Eligible Voters Be Purged From Election Rolls?" Demos: A Network for Ideas & Action, American Civil Liberties Union. October 27, 2004.

153 **In 2004, 435 House seats were contested:** "2004 Election Results." CNN (www.cnn.com/ELECTION/2004/pages/results/senate/full.list) and www.cnn.com/ELECTION/2004/pages/results/house/full.list); Juliet Eilperin, "You Can't Have a Great Election Without Any Races." *Washington Post*, November 13, 2005; "Race for Congress leaves 90 percent out." *USA Today*, November 7, 2000.

153 **Statistics about incumbents:** "The Shape of Representative Democracy, Report of the Redistricting Reform Conference." The Council for Excellence in Government & The Legal Campaign Center. June 2005 (www.campaignlegalcenter.org/attachments/1460.pdf); "Arnold Schwarzenegger's California," *The Economist*, November 3, 2005.

153 **Proportional representation:** "What is Full Representation?" FairVote: Program for Representative Government (www.fairvote.org).

159 **Jack Kemp on Voting Rights Act:** Jack Kemp, "Felony Disenfranchisement and the Voting Rights Act." *News & Notes with Ed Gordon*, National Public Radio, October 24, 2005 (www.npr.org).

160 **Banning contributions:** Election Assistance Committee, *2004 Election Day Survey Results, Chapter 4 Turnout Source* (www.eac.gov); National Conference of State Legislatures, "Absentee and Early Voting." (www.ncsl.org).

155 **John Fund quotation:** John Fund, "How to Steal an Election." *City Journal*, Fall, 2004.

156 **Real ID Bill:** Commission on Federal Election Reform, *Final Commission Report: Building Confidence in U.S. Elections. Section 2—Voter Registration and Identification.* September 19, 2005.

157 **Bob Holmes quotation:** Errin Haines, "Black lawmakers vow to repeal state's voter ID law." *Associated Press*, December 27, 2005.

157 **Sue Burmeister quotation:** "Voter ID memo stirs tension." *The Atlanta Journal Constitution*, November 18, 2005.

160 **Oregon mail voting:** See the symposium on this subject in the May, 2006, *American Prospect:* Robert Kuttner, "Going Postal"; Phil Keisling, "A Technology Too Far"; Don Hamilton, "The Oregon Voting Revolution"; and Sam Rosenthal, "On the Oregon Trail."

CHAPTER 7. WHAT RULE OF LAW? I

164 **History in Business:** See generally, Bill Minutaglio, *First Son: George W. Bush and the Bush Family Dynasty.* (1999).

164 **Death with Dignity:** Editorial, "The Assisted Suicide Decision." *New York Times*, January 19, 2006.

164 **Court of Appeals on Clean Air Act:** Michael Janofsky, "Judges Overturn Bush Bid to Ease Pollution Rules." *New York Times*, November 16, 2005.

165 **Snubbed international accords:** Eric Alterman and Mark Green, *The Book on Bush: How George W. (Mis)leads America.* (2004); J. Peter Scoblic, "Moral Hazard." *The New Republic,* August 8, 2005.

165 **GAO on "covert propaganda":** Robert Pear, "Buying News by Bush's Aids Is Ruled Illegal." *New York Times*, October 1, 2005.

165 **CPB and Tomlinson:** Stephen Labaton, "Ex-Chairman of Public Broadcasting Violates Laws, Inquiry Suggests." *New York Times*, November 16, 2005.

165 **Savage on Bush:** Charlie Savage, "Bush Challenges Hundreds of Laws." *Boston Globe*, April 30, 2006.

166 **Ahron Barak comments:** Ahron Barak, keynote address to Brandeis University, Class of 2003, delivered May 18, 2003.

167 **State Department doubts Bush advisors:** Jane Mayer, "Outsourcing Torture." *The New Yorker*, February 14, 2005.

167 **Lindsay Graham on eliminating Habeas Corpus:** Corine Hegland, "Guantanamo's Grip." *National Journal*, February 3, 2006.

168 **72 point torture matrix:** Kenneth Roth, "Time to Stop 'Stress and Duress.'" *Washington Post*, May 13, 2004.

168 **National Security Official's defense:** Lisa Hajjar, "In the Penal Colony." *The Nation*, January 7, 2005.

168 **Rumsfeld memo:** Fareed Zakaria, "Pssst...Nobody Loves a Torturer." *Newsweek*, November 14, 2005.

168 **Violating Human Rights:** Dana Priest and Barton Gellman, "Stress and Duress Used on Terrorism Suspects Held in Secret Overseas Facilities." *Washington Post*, December 26, 2002.

169 **Alberto Mora:** Jane Mayer, "The Memo." *The New Yorker*, February 27, 2006.

169 **Not Afghanistan:** Stuart Taylor Jr., "Falsehoods About Guantanamo." *National Journal*, February 6, 2006.

169 **Bush comments:** "Torture by Proxy." *Los Angeles Times*, March 11, 2005.

169 **From Gitmo to Eastern Europe:** Michael Isikoff, "Secret Memo: Send to Be Tortured." *Newsweek*, August 8, 2005.

169 **Kicking shit:** Dana Priest and Barton Gellman, "Stress and Duress Used on Terrorism Suspects Held in Secret Overseas Facilities." *Washington Post*, December 26, 2002.

170 **Uzbek "trial":** Transcript of speech February 24, 2005, at York University by Amb. Craig Murray, "The Uses of Torture." *Scoop* (www.scoop.co.nz).

170 **All of al-Libi's story:** Jane Mayer, "Outsourcing Torture." *The New Yorker*, February 14, 2005.

171 **Habib's story:** Jane Mayer, "Outsourcing Torture." *The New Yorker*, Feb 14, 2005.

172 **Laughing at his screams:** "The Talk of the Town." *The New Yorker*. May 30, 2005.

172 **Bagram looks like Egypt:** "Patterns of Abuse." *New York Times*, May 23, 2005.

172 **Bush quotation:** "Bush: 'We do not torture' terror suspects." *Associated Press*, November 7, 2005.

172 **Belmar's story:** David Rose, "Beatings, sex abuse and torture: how M15 left me to rot in US jail." *The Observer*, February 27, 2005.

173 **Megan Ambuhl's comments:** Josh White, "Former Abu Ghraib Guard Calls Top Brass Culpable for Abuse." *Washington Post*, January 23, 2006.

173 **Pentagon's failures:** Fareed Zakaria, "Pssst... Nobody Loves a Torturer." *News week*, November 14, 2005.

173 **Human Rights Watch:** Barry Schweid, "Rights Group Says Abuse Was U.S. Strategy." *Associated Press*, Jan 18, 2006.

173 **Tortured to death:** Fareed Zakaria, "Pssst... Nobody Loves a Torturer." *Newsweek*, November 14, 2005.

174 **Support crashes for U.S.:** George Packer, *The Assassins' Gate: America in Iraq.* (2005).

174 **Iraqi's don't believe punishment will extend "to the little people":** Fareed Zakaria, "Pssst... Nobody Loves a Torturer." *Newsweek*, November 14, 2005.

174 **Nuremberg trials:** Anthony Lewis, "The Torture Administration." *The Nation*, December 26, 2005.

174 **Sullivan's rebuke:** Andrew Sullivan, "The Abolition of Torture." *The New Republic*, December 19, 2005.

174 **McCain's comments on international agreements:** Errol Louis, "Now, U.S. becomes the enemy." *Daily News*, January 3, 2006.

175 **McCain's comments on his own torture:** Sen. John McCain, "Torture's Terrible Toll." *Newsweek*, November 21, 2005.

175 **Reputation is important:** Andrew Sullivan, "The Abolition of Torture." *The New Republic*, December 19, 2005.

176 **Al Gore's speech:** Al Gore, MLK Day Speech in Washington, DC, January 16, 2006.

176 **Feingold's statements on the Patriot Act:** James Davison, "Feingold visits UW, speaks on Patriot Act." *University of Wisconsin Badger Herald*, April 5, 2004.

177 **Expatriating Acts and security threats:** Timothy, H. Edgar, "Interested Persons Memo: Section-by-Section Analysis of Justice Department draft 'Domestic Security Enhancement Act of 2003' also known as PATRIOT Act II." American Civil Liberties Union, February 14, 2003 (www.aclu.org).

178 **William Safire quotation:** William Safire, "Seizing Dictatorial Power." *New York Times*, November 15, 2001.

178 **No more probable cause:** Dahlia Lithwick and Julia Turner, "A Guide to the Patriot Act, Part 3." *Slate*, September 8, 2003 (www.slate.com).

179 **Charity fund freezes:** David Cole, "The Missing Patriot Debate." *The Nation*, May 30, 2005.

179 **National Security Letters:** Dahlia Lithwick and Julia Turner, "A Guide to the Patriot Act, Part 4." *Slate*, September 8, 2003 (www.slate.com).

180 **Roving wiretaps:** Dahlia Lithwick and Julia Turner, "A Guide to the Patriot Act, Part 3." *Slate*, September 8, 2003 (www.slate.com).

180 **Nadine Strossen quotations:** Kelly Patricia O'Meara, "Police State." *Insight Magazine*, December 3, 2001.

180 **Searching video rentals to protect against terrorism:** Dahlia Lithwick and Julia Turner, "A Guide to the Patriot Act, Part 1." *Slate*, September 8, 2003 (www.slate.com).

180 **Dratel quotation:** Dan Eggen, "FBI Applies New Rules to Surveillance." *Washington Post*, December 13, 2003.

181 **Screening dates, tracking wives:** Matthew Brzezinski, "Watching the Detectives." *Mother Jones*, June 17, 2005 (www.motherjones.com).

181 **Domestic terrorism:** Dahlia Lithwick and Julia Turner, "A Guide to the Patriot Act, Part 4." *Slate*, September 8, 2003 (www.slate.com).

181 **Denver Police Department:** Timothy, H. Edgar, "Interested Persons Memo: Section-by-Section Analysis of Justice Department draft 'Domestic Security Enhancement Act of 2003' also known as 'PATRIOT Act II.'" American Civil Liberties Union, February 14, 2003 (www.aclu.org).

181 **Moussaoui in Minneapolis:** Seth Ackerman, "Who Knew? The Unanswered Questions of 9/11." *In These Times*, September 4, 2003.

182 **Community resolutions against and Senate opposition to the Patriot Act:** John Nichols, "Feingold Beats Bush In Patriot Act Fight." *The Nation*, blog posting December 16, 2005 (www.thenation.com).

182 **Feingold's statements:** Senator Russ Feingold, "I Strongly Oppose Patriot Act Deal." Delivered on the Senate floor, February 15, 2006 (www.truthout.org).

182 **Bush signs renewal of Patriot Act:** Charlie Savage, "Bush shuns Patriot Act requirement." *Boston Globe*, March 24, 2006.

182 **Patriot Act renewed:** Editorial, "Easy win for Patriot Act." *Boston Herald*, March 4, 2006.

182 **Burt Neuborne:** Nat Hentoff, "The War on the Bill of Rights and the Gathering Resistance." (2003) p. 17.

183 **The post-9/11 roundups:** David Cole, "The Missing Patriot Debate." *The Nation*, May 30, 2005.

183 **Nepalese tourist arrested:** Editorial, "Guilty Until Proven Innocent." *New York Times*, April 12, 2005.

183 **Chertoff and the decimation of "Little Pakistan":** Paul Krassner, "Guilty Without Charges." *The Nation*, January 31, 2005.

183 **Lawyer wrong numbers and Romero quotation:** Adam Liptak, "For Jailed Immigrants, A Presumption of Guilt." *New York Times*, June 3, 2003.

183 **Immigration detentions:** Eric Lichtblau, "Ashcroft defends Detentions as Immigrants Recount Toll." *New York Times*, June 5, 2003.

183 **Detainees suing because of treatment:** Nina Bernstein, "Held in 9/11 Net, Muslims Return to Accuse U.S." *New York Times*, January 23, 2006.

184 **Rachel King for the ACLU:** "Safety or Stasi?" *Associated Press*, July 17, 2002.

184 **TIA and TIPS never really ended:** Shane Harris, "TIA Lives On." *National Journal*, February 23, 2006. (http:// nationaljournal.com).

184 **Shane Harris:** Shane Harris, "TIA Lives On." *National Journal*, February 23, 2006. (http://nationaljournal.com).

185 **Bertin statement:** George Sanchez, "The Furor Over TIPS." *Mother Jones*, July 17, 2002 (www.motherjones.com).

185 **Solomon, Fleischer and Ashcroft quotations:** Alisa Solomon, "The Big Chill." *The Nation*, June 2, 2003.

185 **Brandon Mayfield's tale:** Matthew Brzezinski, "Watching the Detectives." *Mother Jones*, June 17, 2005 (www.motherjones.com).

186 **Muhammad Ali:** Michael Scherer, "Business Blacklists." *Mother Jones*, May/June, 2003.

186 **No federal privacy rights:** William Safire, "The Intrusion Explosion." *New York Times*, April 22, 2002.

186 **Law enforcement and corporate record keeping:** William Safire, "Goodbye to Privacy." *New York Times Book Review*, April 10, 2005.

186 **Growing surveillance, from corporations to police:** Matthew Brzezinski, "Watching the Detectives." *Mother Jones*, June 17, 2005 (www.motherjones.com).

187 **Investigating credit cards:** Bob Kerr, "Pay too much and you could raise the alarm." *Providence Journal*, February 26, 2006.

187 **Solomon, Fleischer and Ashcroft quotations:** Alisa Solomon, "The Big Chill." *The Nation*, June 2, 2003.

187 **Roosevelt and the Jehovah's Witnesses:** Eric Foner, "Suspension of Disbelief." *The Nation*, December 6, 2004.

188 **Dick Durbin:** Richard Cohen, "GOP wrong to kill the messenger." *Daily News*, June 21, 2005.

188 **Frist's amendment:** Judd Legum, Faiz Shakir, Nico Pitney, Mipe Okunseinde, and Christy Harvey, "Rove Knew Her Name and Leaked Her Name." *The Progress Report*, July 15, 2005.

188 **Trent Duffy:** Judd Legum, Faiz Shakir, Nico Pitney, Christy Harvey, "Demonizing Dissent." American Progress Action Fund, July-December, 2005 (www.american-progressaction.org).

189 **Nancy Lessin:** Jarrett Murphy, "The New Fight Against the War." *Village Voice*, September 19, 2005.

189 **Peace on Earth:** Alisa Solomon, "The Big Chill." *The Nation*, June 2, 2003.

189 **Karen Bauer:** E.J. Dionne Jr., "Stepford Town Meetings." *Washington Post*, April 1, 2005.

190 **Denver Three:** Elizabeth Bumiller, "Evicted 'Denver Three' Gain Support in Quest." *New York Times*, June 27, 2005.

190 **Sarah Bantz and the Flying Rutabaga Circus:** Matthew Rothschild, "Protest at Your Own Risk." *The Progressive*, January 21, 2004.

191 **John Raucci:** Robert Dreyfuss, "The Watchful & the Wary." *Mother Jones*, July/August, 2003.

191 **First Amendment support:** Mark Memmott, "First Amendment gains support as fears ease." *USA Today*, June 27, 2005.

191 **Civil Liberties oversight board:** Caroline Drees, "Civil Liberties Board struggles into existence." *Reuters*, August 4, 2005.

191 Thomas Kean's outrage: Michael Isakoff, "Watchdog: What Ever Happened to the Civil Liberties Board?" *Newsweek*, March 13, 2006.

192 Ahron Barak quotation: Anthony Lewis, "One Liberty at a Time." *Mother Jones*, November 25, 2003.

192 Holtzman on Nixon: Elizabeth Holtzman, "The Impeachment of George W. Bush." *The Nation*, January 30, 2006.

192 19,000 approvals and 5 rejections: James Gordon Meek, "Inside the secret wiretap court." *Daily News*, December 25, 2005.

193 Unfettered powers: Sidney Blumenthal, "The law is king." *Salon*, December 22, 2005 (www.salon.com).

194 Bruce Fein: Charlie Savage, "Views are mixed on domestic spying." *Boston Globe*, March 1, 2006.

194 Bruce Fein: Charlie Savage, "On Eve of Hearing, Split on Spying." *Boston Globe*, February 5, 2006.

194 "Difficult if not impossible": David Cole, "NSA Spying Myths." *The Nation*, February 20, 2006.

194 Tom Daschle comments: Richard W. Stevenson, "Congress Never Authorized Spying Effort, Daschle Says." *New York Times*, December 23, 2005.

194 Gonzales refuses to answer question and Specter quote: Editorial, "The Art of Saying Nothing." *New York Times*, February 8, 2006.

194 Lindsay Graham, carte blanche: Bob Herbert, "Illegal and Inept." *New York Times*, February 9, 2006.

194 Bush, "it's a different world": Elisabeth Bumiller , "Bush Sees No Need for Law To Approve Eavesdropping." *New York Times*, January 27, 2006.

194 Bush thinks it is a "different era": Peter Baker and Charles Babington, "Bush Addresses Uproar Over Spying." *Washington Post*, December 20, 2005.

195 Judge Harold A. Baker: Eric Lichtblau, "Judges on Secretive Panel Speak Out on Spy Program." *New York Times*, March 29, 2006.

196 Bush and Gonzales, terrorists "forget": E&P Staff, "Attorney General Hits the Press for Reminding Terrorists That, Maybe, the U.S. Might Be Watching Them." *Editor & Publisher*, February 6, 2006.

196 Cheney defends spying: James Gordon Meek, "W spy uproar heats up." *New York Daily News*.

196 Extensive eavesdropping: Eric Lichtblau and James Risen, "Spy Agency Mined Vast Data Trove Officials Report." *New York Times*, December 23, 2005.

196 Tens of millions: Leslie Cavley, "NSA has massive database of Americans' phone calls." *USA Today*, May 11, 2006.

197 Gonzales and Biden: Bob Herbert, "Illegal and Inept." *New York Times*, February 9, 2006.

197 Kate Martin and worried agency officials: Katrina vanden Heuvel, "Spying and Lying." *The Nation*, blog posting, December 18, 2005 (www.thenation.com).

198 ABA condemns spying: Michael Conlon, "Lawyers Group Slams Bush on Eavesdropping." *Reuters*, February 13, 2006.

198 Jonathan Turley: CNN's *Countdown* conversation with Keith Olbermann, March 17, 2006.

CHAPTER 8. WHAT RULE OF LAW? II

200 **Texas redistricting and Civil Rights Division:** Charles Lane, "White House Defends Texas's Remapping Plan to Justices." *Washington Post*, February 2, 2006; Dan Eggen, "Justice Staff Saw Texas Districting as Illegal." *Washington Post*, December 2, 2005; Dan Eggen, "Civil Rights Focus Shift Roils Staff at Justice." November 13, 2005; Mark Posner, "Evidence of Political Manipulation at the Justice Department: How Tom DeLay's Redistricting Plan Avoided Voting Rights Act Disapproval." *FindLaw's Legal Commentary* (www.writ.findlaw.com).

200 Courts rarely overrule such redistricting plans and a federal district—not knowing about the staff's contrary views—upheld the preclearance. But then the United States Supreme Court agreed to hear the case in March of 2006 and may rule by late spring.

201 **Georgia voter ID law:** This story was broken by Dan Eggen, "Criticism of Voting Law Was Overruled." *Washington Post*, November 17, 2005; Editorial, "Fixing the Game." *New York Times*, December 5, 2005.

201 **Personnel and cases at Mine Safety and Health Administration:** Joe Conason, "Will the Media Forget Tragedy in the Mines?" *New York Observer*, January 10, 2006.

201 **EPA non-enforcement:** See generally, Eric Alterman and Mark Green, *The Book on Bush: How George W. (Mis)leads America*, (2004) p. 25–26; Robert F. Kennedy, "We Must Take America Back." speech delivered at the Sierra Summit, September 2005; Paul Krugman, "All the President's Friends." *New York Times*, September 12, 2005.

203 **Mehlman at NAACP:** Mike Allen, "RNC Chief to Say It Was 'Wrong' to Exploit Racial Conflict for Votes." *Washington Post*, July 14, 2005.

204 **NAACP investigated by IRS:** Bob Herbert, "An Empty Apology." *New York Times*, July 18, 2005.

204 **Black poverty increases:** Jacob Weisberg, "An Imperfect Storm." *Slate*, September 7, 2005 (www.slate.com).

204 **Bush at 2 percent with Blacks:** Dan Froomkin, "A Polling Free-Fall Among Blacks." October 13, 2005.

204 **Bush hands out FEMA checks:** Jacob Weisberg, "An Imperfect Storm." *Slate*, September 7, 2005 (www.slate.com).

204 **Looters vs Finders:** Aaron Kinney, "'Looting' or 'Finding?'" *Salon*, September 1, 2005 (www.slate.com).

204 **New York State prison population:** "Stupid Irrational and Barbarous: New York Judges Speak Against the Rockefeller Drug Laws." *A Report of the Public Policy Project of the Correctional Association of New York,* October, 2001.

205 **Charles Ramsey quotation:** Ron Harris, "Blacks Feel Brunt of Drug War." *Los Angeles Times*, April 22, 1990.

205 **Black vs. white jailing rates:** "Free to succeed or fail." *The Economist*, August 6, 2005.

205 **Suppression of racial-profiling data:** Dan Eggen, "Official in Racial Profiling Study Demoted." *The Washington Post*, August 25, 2005.

205 **Sentencing discrepancies:** Ralph Nader, *The Good Fight*. (2004), p. 48.

206 **Miller-El trial:** Editorial, "Prosecutorial Racial Bias in Texas." *New York Times*, June 14, 2005.

206 **Disenfranchisement data:** Editorial, "Disenfranchisement of People with Felonies Rooted in Race." *New York Times*, August 29, 2005.

206 Uninsured information: "A Lack of Access to Quality Healthcare Is One of the Biggest and Most Egregious Civil Rights Issues of Our Times." *Broward Times*, June 17, 2005.

206 Minorities in prison rather than college: George M. Frederickson, "Is There Hope for the South?" *New York Review of Books*, October 21, 2004. And see Pedro Noguera and Robert Cohen, "Beyond Black, White and *Brown*." *The Nation*, May 3, 2004.

206 Young black men: Erick Eckholm, "Plight Deepens for Black Men, Studies Warn." *New York Times*, March 20, 2006.

207 Discrimination in hiring: Rick Harrison, "Study finds clean black man equals white ex-con." *New York Daily News,* 2005; Erick Eckholm, "Plight Deepens for Black Men, Studies Warn." *New York Times*, March 20, 2006.

207 Sub prime loan discrepancies: Jonathan Peterson, "Blacks and Latinos are far more likely than whites to get high-cost mortgages, a study finds." *Los Angeles Times*, September 14, 2005.

207 Jeweline Simmons' story: Justin Hibbard, "The Fed Eyes Subprime Loans." *Businessweek*, April 11, 2005.

207 Minorities living in polluted areas: This was extensively reported and analyzed for the AP by David Pace, "More Blacks Live With Pollution." *Associated Press*, December 13, 2005.

208 Trent Lott's remarks: Thomas B. Edsell, "Lott Decried for Part of Salute to Thurmond." *Washington Post*, December 7, 2002.

209 Roll call vote failure: Scott Shepard, "Anti-Lynching Vote: Critics: Frist vetoed roll call Sponsors dispute claim they asked for voice vote." *Atlanta Journal-Constitution*, June 15, 2005.

209 Black middle class and college degrees: Wendi C. Thomas, "Large black middle class isn't sexy, so it's forgotten." *The Commercial Appeal* (Memphis, TN), July 26, 2005.

210 Affirmative action: Michael Bérubé, "And Justice for All." *The Nation*, January 24, 2005.

210 Antigay action in Alabama and California: "Alabama Bill Targets Gay Authors." *CBS News*, April 27, 2005; "School Expels Girl for Having Gay Parents." *Associated Press*, September 23, 2005.

210 Rising acceptance of gays: Will Lester, "Poll: opposition to gay marriage declining." *Associated Press*, March 23, 2006.

211 American idea that gayness is a "lifestyle choice": The Pew Research Center, "Religious Beliefs Underpin Opposition to Homosexuality." November 18, 2003.

211 Robert Rigby's story: V. Dion Hayes, "Sex-Ed Panel Aims to Sway Lessons on Gays." *Washington Post*, September 26, 2005.

211 Effects of pro-family antigay legislation: "Holidays time of heightened concern for gay runaways in San Francisco." *Associated Press*, November 19, 2000.

212 Leah Farish and the ENDA: Ralph Nader, *The Good Fight*. (2004), p. 55; Leah Farish, "Hate Crime Laws—Some Victims More Equal Than Others." (www.family.org).

212 Oregon's Measure 9: Michelangelo Signorile, *Queer In America*. (1994), p. 331–333.

213 Colorado's Amendment 2: Ed. John D'Emilio, William B. Turner, Urvashi Vaid, "From *Bowers* to *Hardwick*" in *Creating Change: Sexuality, Public Policy, and Civil Rights*. (2002).

213 **Military cannot "Move ahead of society":** John D'Emilio, "All that you can be." *The Nation*, June 7, 1993; Eric Konigsberg, "Gays in Arms." *Washington Monthly*, November, 1992.

213 **Wastefulness of don't ask-don't tell:** Shelley Murphey, "U.S. Seeks to Clamp 'Don't Ask' Court Foes." *Boston Globe*, July 9, 2005.

213 **Peter Laska's story:** David M. Halperin, "ROTC Under Fire." *The Thistle*, Volume 9, Issue 9.14 (http://web.mit.edu).

214 **Dick Cheney quotation:** Eric Konigsberg, "Gays in Arms." *Washington Monthly*, November, 1992.

214 **Dismissal of linguists:** Nathaniel Frank, "Stonewalled." *The New Republic*, January 24, 2005.

214 **Ian Finkenbinder's story:** Nathaniel Frank, "Stonewalled." *The New Republic*, January 24, 2005.

214 **Steve Ralls quotation:** "Report: More gay linguists discharged than first thought." *Associated Press*, January 13, 2005.

214 **Allow gays to serve openly:** Will Lester, "Poll: opposition to gay marriage declining." *Associated Press*, March 23, 2006.

215 **Tim Smith's story:** Eric Ervin, "Baylor removes gay board member." *Houston Voice*, November 18, 2005.

216 **Opposition to same-sex marriage:** The Pew Research Center, "Religious Beliefs Underpin Opposition to Homosexuality." November 18, 2003. (http://pewcenter.org).

216 **Asbestos, thalidomide, and Phen-fen figures:** Dan Zegart, "The Right Wing's Drive for 'Tort Reform.'" *The Nation*, October 25, 2004.

217 **National Center for State Courts and Bureau of Justice statistics on tort cases:** Stephanie Mencimer, "False Alarm." *Washington Monthly*, October, 2004.

217 **Number of tort actions decided by juries:** Dan Zegart, "The Right Wing's Drive for 'Tort Reform.'" *The Nation*, October 25, 2004.

218 **1953 insurance industry jury ad 1:** Stephanie Mencimer, "False Alarm." *Washington Monthly*, October, 2004.

219 **1953 insurance industry jury ad 2:** Stephen Daniels and Joanne Martin, "The Strange Success of Tort Reform." *Emory Law Journal*, Summer, 2004.

219 **Tort tale:** This term is borrowed from William Haltom and Michael McCann's, *Distorting the Law: Politics, Media, and the Litigation Crisis*, an expertly researched scholarly history of tort reform and its social and political impact. William Haltom and Michael McCann, *Distorting the Law*. (2004).

219 **Lawn mower tale:** Jonathan Turley, "Legal Myths: Hardly the Whole Truth." *USA Today*, January 31, 2005.

219 **Elizabeth Loftus study:** Stephanie Mencimer, "False Alarm." *Washington Monthly*, October, 2004.

219 **Studies show that juries today are remarkably skeptical:** For a full discussion of these studies, see William Haltom and Michael McCann, *Distorting the Law*. (2004), p. 297; Stephen Daniels and Joanne Martin, "The Strange Success of Tort Reform." *Emory Law Journal*, Summer, 2004.

219 **California doctors sue insurer:** Fred Payne and Robert Zaleski, "Malpractice Makes Prefect." *Washington Monthly*, October 2003.

220 **Donald J. Zuk:** Rachel Zimmerman and Christopher Oster, "Assigning Liability: Insurers' Missteps Helped Provoke Malpractice 'Crisis.'" *Wall Street Journal,* June 24, 2002.

220 **Weiss Ratings white paper:** Weiss Ratings Inc., "Medical Malpractice Caps Fail to Prevent Premium Increases, According to Weiss Ratings Study." June 2, 2003 (www.weissratings.com).

220 **Big tobacco support for ATRA:** Carl Deal and Joanne Doroshow, *The CALA Files: The Secret Campaign by Big Tobacco and Other Major Industries to Take Away your Rights.* Center for Democracy and Justice, 2003, p.12–24; *See also* William Haltom and Michael McCann, *Distorting the Law.* (2004), p. 46.

221 **William Hammett memo:** Stephanie Mencimer, "False Alarm." *Washington Monthly,* October, 2004.

221 **Tort tax:** Peter Huber, *Liability.* (1988); William Haltom and Michael McCann, *Distorting the Law.* (2004) p. 54.

221 **The $300 billion figure:** "Order in the Tort." *The Economist,* July 18, 1992.

222 **Media coverage of tort cases:** Myron Levin, "Coverage of Big Awards for Plaintiffs Helps Distort View of Legal System." *Los Angeles Times,* August 15, 2005.

222 **Merv Gravinski, Amber Carson and Kara Walton:** Myron Levin, "Legal Urban Legends Hold Sway." *Los Angeles Times,* August 14, 2005.

224 **Stella Liebeck v. McDonald's:** There has, unfortunately, been far too much ink spilled over this case through the years. It is not hard to find the articles from 1992 and after that badly distort or leave out key facts. It is harder to find the corrective pieces that give Ms. Liebeck a fair representation in the court of public opinion. Ralph Nader and Wesley J. Smith helped restore context and dignity to Ms. Liebeck's case in their 1996 book *No Contest.* This retelling relies on the more recent research by William Haltom and Michael McCann, *Distorting the Law.* (2004).

224 **Frank Luntz: "It's almost impossible to go too far":** Stephanie Mencimer, "Trial and Error." *Mother Jones,* October, 2004.

224 **Frank Luntz's playbook:** This book of Republican strategies for framing issues was discovered in 2004 and is available online at http://thinkprogress.org.

225 *60 Miuntes:* Andrew Wheat, "Winning the White House in the 'Lawsuit Lottery': The Bush-Rove Ticket to Power." *Multinational Monitor,* March/April, 2005.

225 **Kim Ross:** *Frontline,* "Karl Rove—the Architect: Tort Reform in Texas: 'Rove's Genius at Work.'" PBS, April 12, 2005 (www.pbs.org).

225 **Karl Rove, consultant to Phillip Morris:** Andrew Wheat, "Winning the White House in the 'Lawsuit Lottery': The Bush-Rove Ticket to Power." *Multinational Monitor,* March/April, 2005.

225 **Bush's Brain:** Dana Milbank, "The Political Mind Behind Tort Reform." *Washington Post,* February 25, 2003.

225 **Karl Rove: "big business flocked to us":** Stephanie Mencimer, "Trial and Error." *Mother Jones,* October, 2004.

225 **Bush's Texas donors:** Andrew Wheat, "Winning the White House in the 'Lawsuit Lottery': The Bush-Rove Ticket to Power." *Multinational Monitor,* March/April, 2005.

226 **Bush/Kerry Debate:** Transcript, "The 2004 Campaign: The 2nd Presidential Debate." *New York Times,* October 9, 2004.

226 **Largest cost in the health care system:** Dan Zegart, "The Right Wing's Drive for 'Tort Reform.'" *The Nation*, October 25, 2004.

226 **CBO study on defensive medicine:** United States Congressional Budget Office, "Economic and Budget Issue Brief: Limiting Tort Liability for Medical Malpractice." January 8, 2004 (www.cbo.gov).

227 **GAO Medical Malpractice Report:** United States General Accounting Office, Report to Congressional Requesters, "Medical Malpractice: Implications of Rising Premiums on Access to Health Care." August 2003 (www.gao.gov).

227 **Dr. Robert Zaleski:** Fred Payne and Robert Zaleski, "Malpractice Makes Prefect." *Washington Monthly*, October, 2003.

227 **Clinton administration solicitor general:** Elisabeth Bumiller and Stephen Labaton, "Bush Holds Event to Back Curbs on Class-Action Lawsuits." *New York Times*, February 9, 2005.

227 **Bob White:** Phil Galewitz, "Underwriter Gives Doctor Dose of Reality." *Palm Beach Post*, January 29, 2003.

227 **Jay Angoff report:** Jay Angoff, "Falling Claims and Rising Premiums in the Medical Malpractice Insurance Industry." July, 2005 (www.centerjd.org/ANGOFFReport.pdf).

228 **Rand Corporation's Institute for Civil Justice 1991 study:** See William Haltom and Michael McCann, *Distorting the Law*. (2004), p. 83.

228 **Harvard University Study:** Lucinda M. Finley, "The Hidden Victoms of Tort Reform: Women, Children, and the Elderly." *Emory Law Journal*, Summer, 2004; See also William Haltom and Michael McCann, *Distorting the Law*. (2004), p. 83.

229 **Linda Fermoyle Rice:** Steve Lohr, "Bush's Next Target: Malpractice Lawyers." *New York Times*, February 27, 2005.

229 **Yvonne Harrison:** Dan Zegart, "The Right Wing's Drive for 'Tort Reform.'" *The Nation*, October 25, 2004.

229 **Taking only the most meritorious cases:** Michael J. Saks, "Do We Really Know Anything About the Behavior of the Tort Litigation System—And Why Not?" *University of Pennsylvania Law Review*, 1992, p. 1192; See also William Haltom and Michael McCann, *Distorting the Law*. (2004), p. 86.

229 **90 percent of those who seek to take civil action:** William Haltom and Michael McCann, *Distorting the Law*. (2004), p. 86.

229 **Legal services unavailable for most who qualify:** American Bar Association, "Agenda for Access: the American People and Civil Justice—Final Report on the Implications of Comprehensive Legal Needs Study." 1996.

230 **50 percent turned away from legal services:** Legal Services Corporation, *Documenting the Justice Gap*, September, 2005 (www.lsc.gov).

230 **Legal Aid Society of Salt Lake City:** Elizabeth Neff, "Legal Aid Shifts From Free to a Fee." *Salt Lake Tribune*, April 10, 2005.

230 **Sarah Campbell:** Brennan Center for Justice, "Struggling to Meet the Need: Communities Confront Gaps in Federal Legal Aid." March, 2003 (www.brennancenter.org).

230 **Caps on noneconomic damages hurt women, children and the elderly:** Lucinda M. Finley, "The Hidden Victims of Tort Reform: Women, Children, and the Elderly." *Emory Law Journal*, Summer, 2004.

231 **71 percent of Americans had "some occasion during the past year that might have led them to hire a lawyer":** Gary M. Stern, "Polishing the Image." *National Law Journal*, September 16, 2002.

231 **Deborah Rhode on legal aid:** Deborah L. Rhode, *Access to Justice.* (2004), p. 188.

231 **Lawyer discipline statistics:** American Bar Association, "Survey on Lawyer Discipline Systems." 2002.

CHAPTER 9. INFORMATION MANIPULATION I

235 **Polls on Bush's honesty:** Richard Morin and Dan Balz, "Bush's Popularity Reaches New Low." *Washington Post,* November, 4 2005; *Time,* December 12, 2005.

237 **National Intelligence Estimate on "stockpiles" of biological weapons:** Elizabeth de la Vega, "The White House Criminal Conspiracy." *The Nation,* November 14, 2005.

238 **Bush on "bi-partisan senate investigation" and Silberman:** discussed in Eric Alterman, "The Lies That Bind." *The Nation,* December 5, 2005.

238 **Kerr on pressure:** Robert Dreyfuss, "The Yes-Man." *The American Prospect,* November, 2005.

238 **Al-Qaeda member as liar:** Douglas Jehl, "Report Warned Bush Team about Intelligence Doubts." *New York Times,* November 6, 2005.

238 **"Mein Gott!" and Curveball:** Bob Drogin and John Groetz, "How U.S. Fell under the Spell of Curveball." *Los Angeles Times,* November 20, 2005.

239 **Pillar on misleading intelligence:** *Foreign Affairs,* March/April, 2006.

239 **Rumsfeld's 9/11 memos:** Paul Krugman, "Osama, Saddam, and The Ports." *New York Times,* February 24, 2006.

239 **Downing Street Memo and early planning information:** Mark Danner, "The Secret Way to War." *New York Review of Books,* June 9, 2005; see also, Robert Dreyfuss and Jason Vest, "The Lie Factory." *Mother Jones,* January/February, 2004.

240 **Penciling in the Iraq war:** Don Van Natta Jr., "Bush Set on Path to War, Memo by British Advisor Says." *New York Times,* March 27, 2006.

240 **Brent Scowcroft on "Iraq feeds terrorism":** Jeffrey Goldberg, "Breaking Ranks." *The New Yorker,* October 31, 2005.

242 **Bush vows to find leaker:** "Bush welcomes probe of CIA leak." CNN, February 11, 2004 (www.cnn.com).

243 **Financial Times on withdrawal:** Cited in Hendrick Hertzberg, "War and Antiwar." *The New Yorker,* September 5, 2005.

244 **Congress same intelligence:** Editorial, "Decoding Mr. Bush's Denials." *New York Times,* November 16, 2005.

244 **Rumsfeld on insurgency:** Joe Klein, "Saddam's Revenge." *Time,* September 26, 2005.

245 **Senator Kennedy on "imminent threat":** Speech delivered November 10, 2005, "Kennedy's Statement on the Administration's Efforts to Exaggerate Threats in Their March to War."

245 **Pentagon and phosphorus:** Editorial, "Shake and Bake." *New York Times,* November 29, 2005; Michael Ratner, letter-to-the-editor, *New York Times,* December 1, 2005.

245 **Only three of 107 Iraqi Battalions:** "Very Reliable Sources." *The New Republic,* August 8, 2005.

245 **Pat Tillman and mother:** David Zirkin, "Pat Tillman, Our Hero." *The Nation,* October 24, 2005.

247 **Doubling of troop deaths:** John Barry, Michael Hastings, and Evan Thomas, "Deadly Puzzle." *Newsweek,* March 27, 2006.

250 **Social Security Data:** Jonathan Chait, "Fact Finders." *The New Republic*, February 28, 2005; see also, David Gross, "Social Security Bashing: A Historical Perspective." *New York Times*, January 16, 2005.

250 **Bush's energy proposals in State of the Union:** See Richard Lowry, "'Oil Addict's Idiocy." *New York Post*, February 4, 2006; Editorial, "The State of Energy." *New York Times*, February 1, 2006; Editorial, "Next Steps on Energy.," *New York Times*, February 6, 2006.

251 **FEMA and New Orleans:** Sidney Blumenthal, "No one can say they didn't see it coming." *Salon*, August 31, 2005 (www.salon.com).

251 **FEMA simulation:** Editorial, "Actually, It Was FEMA's Job." *New York Times*, October 2, 2005.

251 **Bush seeing video clips of New Orleans flooding:** Evan Thomas, "How Bush Blew It." *Newsweek*, September 19, 2005.

252 **Republican Panel:** Eric Lipton, "Republicans' Report on Katrina Assails Administration Response." *New York Times*, February 1, 2006.

252 **Bush Aide to Ron Suskind:** Ron Suskind, "Without a Doubt." *New York Times Magazine*, October 17, 2004.

255 **Cost-benefit estimates of Iraq War:** Louis Uchitelle, "When Talk of Guns and Butter Includes Lives Lost." *New York Times*, January 15, 2006.

255 **Richard Joffe's Marshall Plan comparison:** *New York Times Book Review*, November 6, 2005.

255 **Mueller on paying a price:** Dan Balz, "Bush Faces Dual Challenges on Iraq." *Washington Post*, November 25, 2005.

CHAPTER 10. INFORMATION MANIPULATION II

258 **Moynihan quotation:** Joe Pitts, "President Bush's Penchant for Secrecy Is Moving Us Toward a Closed Society." *The Washington Spectator*, October 1, 2005.

259 **Daniel Becker Quotation:** Danny Hakim, "EPA Holds Back Report on Car Fuel Efficiency." *New York Times*, July 28, 2005

259 **Medicare Bill information:** Joe Conason, "Rx for GOP doom." *Salon*, February 17, 2006 (www.salon.com).

259 **Scully's scuttles:** Bob Guldin, "As Transparent as Crude Oil: Four Years of Bush Secrecy." *Public Citizen News*, September/October, 2004.

259 **Mass Layoffs Tracking Study:** Arlie Hochschild, "Let Them Eat War." *The Nation*, October 8, 2003.

260 **EPA at the WTC:** Amanda Schaffer, "Katrina Cough." *Slate*, November 15, 2005 (www.slate.com).

260 **OSHA fails at the WTC:** Amanda Schaffer, "Katrina Cough." *Slate*, November 15, 2005 (www.slate.com).

261 **WTC workers sue:** Michelle McPhee, "1,700 sue over 9/11 sickness." *New York Daily News*, May 24, 2004.

262 **Terrible conditions in New Orleans:** Amanda Schaffer, "Katrina Cough." *Slate*, November 15, 2005 (www.slate.com).

262 **Executive Order 13233:** Kitty Kelley, "Bush's Veil Over History." *New York Times*, October 10 2005.

262 **Texas A&M:** Eric Alterman, "Bush's War on the Press." *The Nation*, May 9, 2005.

262 Dick's "indifference": Editorial, "Secrecy: The Bush Byword." *New York Times,* March 28, 2003.

263 Cheney shoots man: James Frank, "Slow (White House) Trigger on Cheney." *Chicago Tribune,* February 12, 2006.

163 Secret Energy Task Force Meetings: Dana Milbank and Justin Blum, "Document Says Oil Chiefs Met With Cheney Task Force." *Washington Post,* November 16, 2005.

164 NHTSA's refusing database access: Public Citizen, "Early Warning Database and Confidential Business Information." (www.citizen.org).

165 LBJ quotation about FOIA: Freedom Of Information Act article (www.bushsecrecy.org).

165 Increase in classification: Steven Aftergood, "The Age of Missing Information." *Slate,* March 17, 2005 (www.slate.com).

165 Ashcroft's official secretness policy: Information taken from memo by Attorney General John Ashcroft, October 12, 2001 (www.bushsecrecy.org).

165 David Shulz comment: Eric Alterman, "Bush's War on the Press." *The Nation,* May 9, 2005.

266 Anna Nelson at the National Archives: Steven Aftergood, "The Age of Missing Information." *Slate,* March 17, 2005 (www.slate.com).

266 Classifying the Census: David E. Rosenbaum, "When Government Doesn't Tell." *New York Times,* February 3, 2002.

266 Air Force goes offline: Steven Aftergood, "The Age of Missing Information." *Slate,* March 17, 2005 (www.slate.com).

266 Rick Shenkman quotation: Linton Weeks, "Guarding the Past." *Washington Post,* March 31, 2005.

267 Halliburton Malfeasance: A handy guide is www.halliburtonwatch.org, from which these facts were drawn. They maintain an archive of federal testimony and audit reports. See also "Cheney's Halliburton Ties Remain." *Associated Press,* September 26, 2003; and "Whistleblower's Iraq claims to be investigated." CNN, November 18, 2005 (www.cnn.com).

268 Military blocks officers from testifying: Philip Shenon, "Pentagon Bars Military Officers and Analysts from Testifying." *New York Times,* September 20, 2005.

268 Anthony Shaffer comment: Philip Shenon, "Officer Says Military Blocked Sharing of Files on Terrorism." *New York Times,* August 16, 2005.

269 Terror watch list: Walter Pincus and Dan Eggen, "325,000 Names on Terrorism List." *Washington Post,* February 15, 2006.

269 Byron Dorgan quotation: David S. Broder, "Share the Facts on the War." *Washington Post,* August 4, 2005.

269 Lawrence Wilkerson on the "cabal": Jim Lobe, "Powell Aide Blasts Rice, Cheney-Rumsfeld 'Cabal.'" *Inter Press Service,* October 20, 2005.

270 Hiding funding for WMD searches: James Risen and Judith Miller, "Officials Say Bush Seeks $600 Million to Hunt Iraq Arms." *New York Times,* October 2, 2003.

270 Stephen Aftergood on secrecy: Interview by telephone, October 19, 2005.

271 Nobel Laureates criticize Bush: Tristan Hunt, "For Bush, science is a dirty word." *Guardian,* March 22, 2005.

272 History of the OTA and Stockman quotation: Chris Mooney, *The Republican War on Science.* (2005).

272 **Phillip Johnson and the "con":** William Safire, "On Language: Neo-Creo." *New York Times Magazine,* August 21, 2005.

273 **Nicholas Thompson on "geography and clout":** Nicholas Thompson, "Science Friction." *Washington Monthly,* July/August, 2003.

273 **Donald Kennedy quotation:** Nicholas Thompson, "Science Friction." *Washington Monthly,* July/August, 2003.

273 **William R. Miller story:** Daniel Smith, "Political Science." *New York Times Magazine,* September 4, 2005.

274 **22 percent find stem cells unethical:** Katha Pollitt, "Practice What You Preach." *The Nation,* May 16, 2005.

275 **Nancy Reagan stem cells:** "Nancy Reagan plea on stem cells." BBC (http://news.bbc.co.uk).

275 **Michael Deaver on Ronald Reagan:** Alessandra Stanley, "Nancy Reagan, in a Whisper, Fights Bush Over Stem Cells." *New York Times,* September 29, 2002.

275 **Wrong number of stem cell lines cited:** Michael Kinsley, "Taking Bush Personally." *Slate,* October 23, 2003 (www.slate.com).

275 **John Danforth's comments:** Peter Slevin, "'St. Jack' and the Bullies in the Pulpit." *Washington Post,* February 2, 2006.

276 **Pam Fichter quotation:** Peter Slevin, "In Heartland, Stem Cell Research Meets Fierce Opposition." *Washington Post,* August 10, 2005.

276 **Harold Varmus quotation:** Nicholas Thompson, "Science Friction." *Washington Monthly,* July/August, 2003.

276 **C. Everett Koop quotation:** Chris Mooney, "Blinded by Science." *Columbia Journalism Review,* November/December, 2004.

277 **Tom Coburn's comments:** Ron Jenkins, "GOP Senate candidate in Oklahoma speaks of 'rampant' lesbianism in schools." *Associated Press,* October 11, 2004.

277 **Misleading information in sex-ed classes:** "FDA Consultant Quits Over Contraceptive." *Associated Press,* October 7, 2005.

277 **Abstinence is anti-choice:** Sharon Lerner, "Louisiana Purchase the Feds Recruit Culture War Cadets." *The Nation,* August 29, 2005.

278 **Increased funds for abstinence:** Sharon Lerner, "Louisiana Purchase the Feds Recruit Culture War Cadets." *The Nation,* August 29, 2005.

278 **Leslee Unruh's comments:** Christina Larson, "Pork for prudes." *Washington Monthly,* September, 2002.

278 **Abstinence-only doesn't work:** Sharon Lerner, "Louisiana Purchase the Feds Recruit Culture War Cadets." *The Nation,* August 29, 2005.

279 **Auditing critics:** Lara Riscol, "Sex, Lies and Politics." *The Nation,* August 30, 2004.

279 **FDA studying Plan B:** Gardiner Harris, "Report Details F.D.A. Rejection of Next-Day Pill." *New York Times,* November 15, 2005.

279 **Preventing abortions:** "Political Prescription." *Daily News,* September 1, 2005.

279 **All about David Hager:** Ayelish McGarvey, "Dr. Hager's Family Values." *The Nation,* May 11, 2005.

280 **Dr. McClellan's misconduct:** Gardiner Harris, "Report Details FDA Rejection of Next-Day Pill." *New York Times,* November 15, 2005.

280 **Dr. Wood's email:** Gardiner Harris, "Official Quits on Pill Delay at the F.D.A." *New York Times,* September 1, 2005.

280 **Missouri woman's comments:** "Target Pharmacist Refuses to Fill Emergency Contraception Prescription." Save Roe, October 27, 2005 (www.saveroe.com).

281 **Arizona woman's story:** Carla McClain, "Rape victim: 'Morning after' pill denied." *Arizona Daily Star,* October 23, 2005.

281 **No Fetal Pain:** William Saletan, "I Feel Your Fetus's Pain." *Slate,* August 30, 2005 (www.slate.com).

281 **Poking fetuses:** William Saletan, "I Feel Your Fetus's Pain." *Slate,* August 30, 2005 (www.slate.com).

282 **Gene Rudd's comments:** Rob Stein, "Cervical Cancer Vaccine Gets Injected with a Social Issue." *Washington Post,* October 31, 2005.

282 **Alan Kaye's retort:** Rob Stein, "Cervical Cancer Vaccine Gets Injected with a Social Issue." *Washington Post,* October 31, 2005.

282 **Fish and Wildlife Scientists' comments:** Chris Mooney, "Intelligent Denials." *American Prospect,* February 22, 2005.

283 **Judy Curry quotation:** Jeffrey Kluger, "Global Warming: The Culprit?" *Time,* October 3, 2005.

284 **Active solicitation of Enron:** John Vidal, "Revealed: How Oil Giant Influenced Bush." *Guardian,* June 8, 2005.

284 **Philip Cooney comes and goes:** Roland Watson, "Aide who doctored global warming report joins Exxon." *The Times,* UK, June 16, 2005.

284 **Rick S. Piltz comments:** Andrew C. Revkin, "Official Altered Reports on Links to Global Warming." *New York Times,* June 8, 2005.

285 **Christopher Flavin comments:** Mark Hertsgaard, "Global Storm Warning." *The Nation,* October 17, 2005.

286 **George Deutsch and NASA:** Andrew C. Revkin, "NASA Chief Backs Agency Openness." *New York Times,* February 4, 2006.

286 **Union of Concerned Scientists:** Daniel Smith, "Political Science." *New York Times Magazine,* September 4, 2005.

CHAPTER 11. WHERE ARE THE MEDIA?

289 **Bill Moyers:** Matt Hagengruber, "Moyers: Big Media Threaten Freedom." *Wisconsin State Journal,* November 9, 2003.

290 **CEO malfeasance widespread:** *NBC News/Wall Street Journal* Poll, July 19–21, 2002 (www.pollingreport.com/ business.htm).

290 **What's the role of journalism in [democracy]?:** Bill Moyers, *Moyers on America: A Journalist and His Times.* (2004), p. 104–105.

291 **News is a commodity:** James T. Hamilton, *All the News That's Fit to Sell: How the Market Transforms Information into News.* (2004), p. 7.

292 *Nightline vs. Letterman:* CNN Saturday, CNN, March 9, 2002 (http://transcripts.cnn.com); *Nightline,* Ted Koppel, "Network News Is Still Serious Business." *New York Times,* March 5, 2002; Tucker Carlson, "Is It Time for ABC to Put 'Nightline' to Bed?" *Crossfire,* CNN, March 8, 2002 (http://transcripts.cnn.com); "Letterman Re-ups with CBS, 'Nightline' to Stay Put," CNN, March 27, 2002 (www.cnn.com).

292 **71 percent of stations experienced budget cuts:** Marion Just and Tom Rosenstiel, "All the News That's Fed." *New York Times,* March 26, 2004.

293 **A quarter of local stories are "feed material":** "Local TV, Content Analysis." *The State of the News Media 2006*, Project for Excellence in Journalism, (www.stateofthenewsmedia.org); Marion Just and Tom Rosenstiel, "All the News That's Fed." *New York Times,* March 26, 2004.

293 **Newsbreakers:** Mark Lasswell, "Media Activists Who Smile and Throw Cheese." *New York Times,* June 26, 2005.

294 **Al Gore on "serial obsessions":** "Text of Gore Speech at Media Conference." *Associated Press,* October 6, 2005.

294 **Confuse the interesting with the important:** Arianna Huffington, "Just Say Noruba." *Huffington Post,* June 20, 2005 (www.huffingtonpost.com).

294 **General Motors pulls ads in *Los Angeles Times*:** "GM Pulls Ad from *L.A. Times* Over Coverage." *Reuters,* April 7, 2005; Jon Fine and Jean Halliday, "GM Shoots the Messenger as Woes Mount." *Advertising Age,* April 11, 2005; Randi Schmelzer, "GM Returns Ads to 'L.A. Times.'" *Adweek.com,* August 2, 2005.

294 **Ten corporations own most media:** Mark Crispin Miller, "What's Wrong with This Picture?" *The Nation,* January 27, 2002.

295 **News Corporation holdings:** Compiled from the News Corporation website on March 19, 2005 (www.newscorp.com).

295 **Clear Channel corporate facts:** Eric Boehlert, "One Big Happy Channel?" *Salon,* June 28, 2001 (www.salon.com).

296 **NiPP case against Clear Channel:** Eric Boehlert, "Suit: Clear Channel Is an Illegal Monopoly." *Salon,* August 8, 2001 (www.salon.com); Will Shanley, "Clear Channel Dials Back a Bit." *Denver Post,* May 1, 2005.

296 **Clear Channel made from seventy companies:** Eric Boehlert, "One Big Happy Channel?" *Salon,* June 28, 2001 (www.salon.com).

296 **Jennifer Johnson:** Eric Magnuson, "Anyone Listening?" *The Nation,* May 23, 2005.

296 **Clear Channel's role in fallout from North Dakota train derailment:** Jennifer Lee, "On Minot, N.D., Radio, A Single Corporate Voice.' *New York Times,* March 21, 2003; Eric Magnuson, "Anyone Listening?" *The Nation,* May 23, 2005.

296 **Byron Dorgan:** "Coverage You Can('t) Count On." *On the Media* transcript, NPR, February 7, 2003 (www.onthemedia.org).

297 **FCC pursues looser cross-ownership and consolidation rules:** "Court Rejects FCC Ownership Rules in Historic Victory!" *Free Press* (www.freepress.net); Frank Ahrens, "Court Rejects Rules on Media Ownership." *Washington Post,* June 25, 2004; Frank Ahrens, "FCC Drops Bid to Relax Media Rules." *Washington Post,* January 28, 2005; Gal Beckerman, "Tripping Up Big Media." *Columbia Journalism Review,* Issue 6: November/December, 2003 (www.cjr.org); **750,000 letters and emails:** Neil Hickey, "FCC: Ready, Set, Consolidate." *Columbia Journalism Review,* Issue 4: July/August, 2003 (www.cjr.org).

297 **Why do we have more channels:** William Safire, "The Great Media Gulp." *New York Times,* May 22, 2003.

297 **Corporate concentration of media ownership has put a deadening blanket:** William Greider, "All the King's Media." *The Nation,* November 21, 2005.

298 **FOX News viewership rose from 17 to 25 percent:** "News Audiences Increasingly Politicized." The Pew Reach Center, June 8, 2004 (http://people-press.org); Jim Rutenberg, "Cable's War Coverage Suggests a New 'FOX Effect' on Television Journalism." *New York Times,* April 16, 2003.

298 **80 percent of FOX viewers had at least one misperception:** "Misperceptions, the Media and the Iraq War." The PIPA/Knowledge Networks Poll, October 2, 2003 (http://65.109.167.118/pipa/pdf/oct03/IraqMedia_Oct03_rpt.pdf).

299 **MSNBC caves to political pressure to cancel *Donahue*:** Bill Carter, "MSNBC Plans to Bring Back Phil Donahue." *New York Times*, April 3, 2002; "MSNBC Axes Phil Donahue." *Associated Press*, February 25, 2003; Bill Carter, "MSNBC Cancels the Phil Donahue Talk Show." *New York Times*, February 26, 2003; John Nichols, "Exit Phil Donahue." *The Nation*, February 27, 2003; Monica Collins, "Savage Makeover." *Boston Herald*, March 11, 2003; Phil Donahue, interview, *Hannity & Colmes*, FOX News Channel, October 28, 2004.

300 **CBS and *The Reagans*:** Matthew Gilbert, "Beyond 'Reagans' Hoopla, a Critical, Typical Biopic." *The Boston Globe*, December 1, 2003; Elaine Monaghan, "Thousands Rally Behind Reagans: Website Protesting CBS Miniseries Crashes after 40,000 Log on to Defend Former President." *The Times* (UK), November 3, 2003; Jim Rutenberg, "Grumbling Trickles Down from Reagan Biopic." *New York Times*, October 21, 2003.

300 **Michael Copps:** David Lieberman, "Plan to Air Divisive Film Raises Questions." *USA Today*, October 12, 2004.

300 **Sinclair Broadcasting tries to air *Stolen Honor: Wounds that Never Heal*:** Paul Farhi, "Sinclair Stations to Air Anti-Kerry Documentary." *Washington Post*, October 11, 2004.

301 **John McCain:** Bill Carter, "Debate Over 'Nightline' Tribute to War Dead Grows, as McCain Weighs In." *New York Times*, May 1, 2004.

301 **48 percent believe the press often does not get its facts straight:** Topline Report, "Public and Press Differ about Partisan Bias, Accuracy and Press Freedom, New Annenberg Public Policy Center Survey Shows." Annenberg Public Policy Center, University of Pennsylvania, May 24, 2005 (www.annenbergpublicpolicycenter.org).

302 **If ever there were a time for unbridled journalism:** Todd Gitlin, "The Great Media Breakdown." *Mother Jones*, November/December, 2004.

302 **Karl Rove:** Dana Milbank, "Rove's Reading: Not So Liberal as Leery." *Washington Post*, April 20, 2005.

302 **90 percent of Americans believe it is important that media is free of government censorship:** Topline Report, "Public and Press Differ about Partisan Bias, Accuracy and Press Freedom, New Annenberg Public Policy Center Survey Shows." Annenberg Public Policy Center, University of Pennsylvania, May 24, 2005 (www.annenbergpublicpolicycenter.org).

303 **John MacArthur:** Kristina Borjesson, ed., "Everybody Wants to Be at Versailles." *Feet to the Fire: The Media after 9/11.* (2005) p. 98–99.

303 **White House Correspondents Dinner:** Hunter S. Thompson, *Fear and Loathing: On the Campaign Trail '72.* (1973), p. 18.; Michael Massing, "The Enemy Within." *New York Review of Books*, Volume 52, Number 20, December 15, 2005.

304 **Bob Woodward:** John MacArthur: Kristina Borjesson, ed., "Everybody Wants to Be at Versailles." *Feet to the Fire: The Media after 9/11.* (2005), p. 114; Sydney Schanberg, "Woodward's Dis." *Village Voice*, November 15, 2005; Jim VandeHei and Carol D. Leonnig, "Woodward Was Told of Plame More Than Two Years Ago." *Washington Post*, November 16, 2005. For further discussion of Bob Woodward's recent work, see the March/April, 2006 exchange between Woodward

and *The Nation* reporter David Corn on Corn's blog, *Capital Games*. Woodward responds to questions about his insider status in Corn's original piece, "Woodward and Reality." (www.thenation.com).

304 **Elisabeth Bumiller:** From a panel discussion in Washington, D.C., sponsored by Northwestern's Medill School of Journalism, transcript excerpts printed in *Extra!*, January/February, 2005.

305 **Carol Coleman interviews President Bush:** Carol Coleman, "Coleman: I Wanted to Slap Him." *The Sunday Times*, October 9, 2005.

305 **Dan Rather:** "Rather's Retirement and Liberal Bias." Media Advisory, *Fair.org*, March 2, 2005 (www.fair.org).

306 ***Washington Post* withholds location of CIA "black sites":** Dana Priest, "CIA Holds Terror Suspects in Secret Prisons." *Washington Post*, November 2, 2005.

306 **Peter Kornbluh:** Gal Beckerman, "The *Washington Post* Gets Scooped—On Purpose?" *CJRDaily*, November 3, 2005 (www.cjrdaily.org).

306 **Daniel Okrent:** Bill Densmore, "Blogs will win unless newspapers transfer their brand integrity onto the Internet, says ex-*NYTimes* ombudsman." *Media Giraffe Project*, April 4, 2006 (www.mediagiraffe.org).

307 **At most twenty people run any story:** Joan Didion, "The Deferential Spirit." *New York Review of Books*, September 19, 1996.

307 **One aspect of this shameful episode:** Eric Alterman, "Case Closed." *The Nation*, April 25, 2005.

308 **Robert Thompson:** Katherine Q. Seelye, "Complexity of a Simple Number." *New York Times,* October 31, 2005.

308 **Disparate coverage of 1000th and 2000th deaths in Iraq:** Katherine Q. Seelye, "Complexity of a Simple Number." *New York Times,* October 31, 2005.

308 **Downing Street Memo:** Arianna Huffington, "Just Say Noruba.," *Huffington Post*, June 20, 2005 (www.huffingtonpost.com); Patrick Healy, "Senator Clinton Assails G.O.P. at Fund-Raiser." *New York Times,* June 6, 2005; Paul Krugman, "The War President." *New York Times*, June 24, 2005; Peter Grier, "What the 'Downing Street' Memos Show." *Christian Science Monitor*, June 21, 2005.

309 **Coverage of Downing Street Memo, Natalee Holloway, and Michael Jackson:** Arianna Huffington, "Just Say Noruba." *Huffington Post*, June 20, 2005 (www.huffingtonpost.com).

309 **The was a body on the streets of this town yesterday:** Anderson Cooper, *Anderson Cooper 360.* CNN, September 1, 2005.

309 **Hurricane Katrina makes reporters "get feisty":** Franklin Foer, "The Mole: The Case Against Anderson Cooper." *The New Republic*, September 26, 2005.

310 **This White House has chosen...to engage us as little as possible:** Ken Auletta, "Fortress Bush." *The New Yorker*, January 19, 2004.

310 **Craig Crawford:** *The Saturday Early Show,* CBS, July 30, 2005.

310 **"The Bush machine is so skillful":** E.J. Dionne, "Kerried Away." *Washington Post*, June 10, 2005.

311 **Dan Rather reports on President Bush's Air National Guard record:** James C. Goodale, "The Flawed Report on Dan Rather." *New York Review of Books*, Volume 52, Number 6, April 7, 2005; "CBS ousts 4 for Bush Guard Story." *CBS News*, January 10, 2005 (www.cbsnews.com).

312 **White House response to** *Newsweek's* **erroneous Koran report:** White House Press Briefing by Scott McClellan, May 17, 2006 (www.whitehouse.gov); Frank Rich, "It's All Newsweek's Fault." *New York Times*, May 22, 2005.

312 **History will judge what I'm about:** Carol Coleman, "Coleman: I Wanted to Slap Him." *The Sunday Times*, October 9, 2005.

313 **Bush announces Supreme Court Nomination to deflect press from Plamegate:** Kristin Jensen, "Supreme Court Pick Shifts Attention from Rove, Agent Disclosure." *Bloomberg*, July 21, 2005 (www.bloomberg.com); Howard Kurtz, "Supreme Timing." *Washington Post*, July 20, 2005 (www.washingtonpost.com).

313 **Bush Administration pays Armstrong Williams for Education propaganda:** Howard Jurtz, "Administration Paid Commentator." *Washington Post*, January 8, 2005.

314 **Government propaganda condemned by GAO and David Walker:** Christopher Lee, "Administration Rejects Ruling on PR Videos." *Washington Post*, March 15, 2005; "White House defends Video News Releases." *Associated Press*, March 14, 2005.

314 **Military places propaganda in Iraqi papers:** Mark Mazzetti and Borzou Daragahi, "U.S. Military Covertly Pays to Run Stories in Iraqi Press." *Los Angeles Times*, November 30, 2005; Jeff Gerth and Scott Shane, "U.S. Is Said to Plant Articles in Iraq Papers." *New York Times*, December 1, 2005.

314 **Peter Jennings:** Ken Auletta, "Fortress Bush." *New Yorker*, January 19, 2004.

315 **Lawrence McQuilliam:** Mary Lynn F. Jones, "No News Is Good News." *The American Prospect*, May 2003.

315 **Bush and Tomlinson attack PBS and Bill Moyers:** Paul Farhi, Joe Conason, "Must-Flee TV: The G.O.P. on PBS." *New York Observer*, May 9, 2005; James Poniewozik, "A Man in Sesame Strife." *Time*, July 4, 2005; Stephen Labaton, "Panel Would Cut Public Broadcasting." *New York Times*, June 10, 2005; Stephen Labaton, "Public Broadcasting Monitor Had Worked at Center Founded by Conservatives." *New York Times*, June 21, 2005; "Investigation Faults Ex-Chairman of CPB." *Washington Post*, November 16, 2005; Jennifer Kerr, "Report: Ex-Broadcasting Chairman Broke Law." *Associated Press*, November 15, 2005.

316 **Most guests appreciate** *NOW*: Bill Moyers, "Bill Moyers' speech to the National Conference for Media Reform." *Free Press*, May 15, 2005 (www.freepress.net).

316 **Reaction to David Grosh:** Sheryl Gay Stolberg, "Simplicity Takes a Star Turn in Washington." *New York Times*, June 26, 2005.

317 **Britain's House of Commons:** Gore Vidal, "Something Rotten in Ohio." *The Nation*, June 27, 2005.

318 **Model that develops when people have completely lost faith:** John Nichols, Speech "Saving Our Democracy: A colloquium to rescue our democracy from the far right." New Democracy Project, January 21, 2006.

CONCLUSION

319 **Gaddis on democracy:** Quoted in review by Michael Beschloss of *The Cold War: A New History*, in the *New York Times*, January 12, 2006. *New York Times* columnist Paul Krugman did a good job summing up the problem: "Government is relatively clean when politicians are sufficiently afraid of scandal to resist temptation. But when a political machine controls all branches of government, and these officials charged with oversight are also reliably partisan, politicians feel safe from

investigation. Their inhibitions dissolve, and they take full advantage of their position, until scandals become too big to hide."

322 **Packer on Bush officials:** George Packer, "A Confederacy of Cronies." *Mother Jones*, November/December, 2002.

323 **Orlando Patterson:** Orlando Patterson, "The Speech Misheard Round the World." *New York Times*, January 22, 2005.

325 **"Organized people":** Ernie Cortes quoted in Bill Moyers, *Moyers on America: A Journalist and His Times.* (2004).

INDEX

G